Crime in Developing Countries

CRIME IN DEVELOPING COUNTRIES

A Comparative Perspective

MARSHALL B. CLINARD

and

DANIEL J. ABBOTT

A WILEY-INTERSCIENCE PUBLICATION

JOHN WILEY & SONS, New York · London · Sydney · Toronto

Library of Congress Cataloging in Publication Data:
Clinard, Marshall Barron, 1911-

   Crime in developing countries.

   "A Wiley-Interscience publication."
   Includes bibliographical references.
    1. Underdeveloped areas—Crime and criminals.
  2. Crime and criminals—Uganda.   I. Abbott, Daniel J.,

joint author.   II. Title.
HV6030.C54   364'.9172'2   73-4031

ISBN 0-471-16060-1

Printed in the United States of America

10 9 8 7 6 5 4 3 2

Preface

A comparative sociology and a comparative criminology are both emering slowly. Our study represents a contribution to this growth in the form of a comparison between crime in the developed and the developing countries. Within the framework of a number of theoretical constructs derived from criminological research in the United States and Europe we have brought together most of the existing findings on crime in Africa, Asia, and Latin America, and the results of our own extensive research in Uganda. Throughout this book we have tried to show the similarities and differences between the developed and the less developed countries. In a cross-cultural setting we have discussed the relation to criminal behavior of urbanization, migration, the social organization of slum areas, differential association and peer-group structures, and differential opportunity. It is possible that some of the applied conclusions in the concluding chapter reflect the viewpoint of professional persons such as we from developed countries. In the long run the ultimate decision of the practicality of these conclusions lies with those officials who are facing the real task of framing a more effective crime-control policy in developing countries.

Conditions in the less developed countries have exhibited many similarities to those that suddenly produced extensive crime a century or more ago in Europe. Today the process of development is bringing pronounced changes, and among the more serious is the general increase in crime. In fact, one measure of the effective development of a country probably is its rising crime rate. Despite this increase, almost no reference is made to any less developed country in the standard criminological reference books, and a similar striking omission is almost no mention of crime in works on development or even on urbanization in developing countries. In this book we have discussed in a comparative setting the incidence, types, and forces that produce crime in the Third World.

Both of us have had a long interest in comparative sociology, particularly in the field of comparative criminology. The senior author in 1954–1955 was a Fulbright Research Professor in Criminology in Sweden and spent three years with the Ford Foundation in India as a consultant to the Delphi Pilot Project in social change in Indian slums. In this work he gathered much material on crime. In 1965 in Stockholm and in 1970 in Kyoto he participated as a rapporteur and panel member at the United Nations Congress on the Prevention of Crime and the Treatment of Offenders. Both meetings were chiefly directed at crime in the developing countries, and an opportunity was provided to talk to and gather materials from their delegates. The junior author did development work in Bolivia from 1963 to 1966 and has traveled widely in Latin America. He has also specialized in academic work in the area of socioeconomic change.

In 1968, two years before the military coup of General Amim, the senior author received a teaching and research grant from the Rockefeller Foundation to go to Uganda for a year to help develop a program in deviant behavior and criminology at Makerere University, formerly the University of East Africa, in Kampala. The grant also provided funds for the junior author to help with a research project that would lead to a doctoral dissertation. Both of us taught at Makerere, and additional funds were supplied to employ and train a research staff.

While in Uganda we planned and carried out what is probably the first comprehensive study ever made of crime in a developing country, comparable to any in the developed countries. We gathered trend data on crime in Uganda as a whole and on Kampala, the capital, which has a population of more than 300,000 inhabitants. More than 30,000 cards were prepared on crimes reported to the police and persons arrested in the city during 1968. A series of hypotheses was tested on a large sample of Kampala property offenders and a control group of nonoffenders, both aged 18 to 25. Two Kampala slum areas were selected, one with a high and one with a low crime rate, and interviews were conducted with a total sample of 534 males divided between those between 18 and 25 and those over 25. For both the offender and the slum community studies interview schedules were constructed which took about an hour and a half to administer. All questions were asked in English, the national language of Uganda, and in Luganda or Swahili.

It is not easy to do criminological research in a developing country. Both of us had to spend many hours becoming familiar with many aspects of Uganda. Officials of developing countries are suspicious of research done by outsiders, and permission to gather statistics in the police stations and to carry out interviews in the prisons was delayed for several frustrating months, during which time numerous meetings with government officials were held. Permission to interview in slum areas presented no problem because of our university affiliation also with the Makerere Institute of Social Research. We had at all times, however, to worry about how much cooperation we would receive, and as the research proceeded it was necessary to make various adjustments in terms of the local situation.

We could not have carried out this research without the advice, excellent assistance, and full cooperation of our Uganda research staff. It was composed of 14 university students or graduates who were hired to do this work during the long vacation period—Deo Kajugira, George Bagamuhunda, Sammy Ochiengh, Jane Olwoc, Margaret Bikangaga, Victoria Mugwanya, Sison Sali, Sam Saramba, Edward Esegu, Christopher Lubwama, Emmanuel Serufusa, James Ilemut, and Christopher Kibirige. George Mukulu, who had been associated with a number of research projects carried out by foreign reseachers, was especially helpful in the translations of the interview schedules. All of the interviewers had a two-week training period and were active in the construction and translation of the interview schedules and in the formulation of individual items. The interviewers were asked to make any relevant observations at the end of each interview that would provide a continual source of information on African urban problems and community life.

We should like to acknowledge the excellent cooperation of the United Nations Social Defence Institute in Rome who appointed the senior author a fellow during a brief period in 1969. There much material, published and unpublished, from various United Nations reports and studies, was made available. In particular, Dr. Edward Galway, then the director of the Institute, Professor Franco Ferracuti, Guisseppe Di Gennero, and Badr Kasme, the librarian, were most helpful. William Clifford, Chief, Section of Social Defence, United Nations, made several suggestions, and we have made use of his criminological research in Zambia. Nothing that we have said here should in any way indicate, however, that it is a position of the United Nations staff. The experience and the writings of Manuel López-Rey, who for more than 20 years was the Social Defence Advisor for the United Nations and in this capacity visited a large part of the developing world, are reflected in various parts of this book.

In Uganda the help of many should be acknowledged, including F. S. Okwaare, then director of the prison administration, and the members of his staff, as well as numerous police and other officials at the national and local levels. Eric Kibuka, who has long been active in social defence work in Uganda and who is now lecturer in the School of Social Work, Makerere University, furnished many helpful suggestions. Musa Mushanga, who is now lecturer in criminology at Makerere University, read the manuscript and made a number of suggestions. Helpful suggestions were also made at Makerere by Regina Solzbacher, Stephen Taber, and Professors Joseph Gugler and Peter Rigby.

Besides our appreciation to the Rockefeller Foundation, we should like to acknowledge the additional research funds provided by the University of Wisconsin Research Committee, which enabled us to employ research staff in Uganda and to make our computer analyses, the National Science Foundation which provided a fellowship that made it possible for the junior author to spend a year analyzing the statistical data, and to Professor Henry Hill, formerly Dean of International Studies and Programs, University of Wisconsin, who helped with many of our problems while we were in Africa. S. Kirson Weinberg, who himself has carried out criminological research in Ghana, made several important theoretical suggestions. Much of the typing and editing of this manuscript which required many hours of arduous work both in Uganda and at home was done by Ruth Clinard. She contributed much effort in trying to make this a well-organized, accurate, and readable book.

MARSHALL B. CLINARD
University of Wisconsin, Madison

DANIEL J. ABBOTT
Louisiana State University, New Orleans

January 1973

Contents

Tables

Chapter 1 Comparative Criminology and the Developing Countries

A truly comparative criminology must approach existing data and conduct new research by using theoretical frameworks, propositions, or models that can be tested across various societies. For an adequate comparative criminology it is essential to ascertain whether similar social processes account for crime in technologically developed and less developed societies. For developed societies, such as the United States and the countries of Europe, the most important causal factors have been shown, generally, to be increasing urbanization and the persistence of slum areas. A universal process that crosses cultural lines is the migration of large numbers of rural people into the cities, where the subsequent process of urbanization modifies their behavior. The probabilities are high that many of these migrants and, if they are married, their children, who, if they had remained in their own rural homes, would most likely not have engaged in crime, will become involved in some sort of criminal activities in an urban context. If certain uniform social processes, such as urbanization, contribute to criminal behavior, existing variations can be assumed, conversely, to be related to variations in these processes, including urbanization.

A basic question is whether certain sociological theories of crime apply to the developing countries. They are, first, the theory of differential association, that is, the view that crime is learned in association with others, and, second, differential opportunity, a theory that, although based on the theory of anomie, proposes that differential access to certain goals in a society and to illegitimate means to achieve these goals accounts for crime. It is important to find out whether crime in developing countries is committed primarily by youth and learned from companions, as it appears to be in most developed countries. There is, furthermore, the

1

question whether the types of crime of major concern in the countries of the developing world, including white-collar crime, are similar to those of the developed world. This study attempts to test the applicability of these frames of reference to less developed countries by organizing existing data and the findings of new studies carried out in Africa.

The goal of a comparative criminology should be to develop concepts and generalizations at a level that distinguishes between universals applicable to all societies and unique characteristics representative of one or a small set of societies [1]. To be applicable criminological theories must be tested, modified, retested, and again modified until they can account for exceptions or at least predict exceptions. Durkheim recognized the importance of testing theoretical propositions in a variety of social settings as wide as is available to a scientific investigation.

One cannot explain a social fact of any complexity except by following its complete development through all social species. Comparative sociology is not a particular branch of sociology; it is sociology itself, in so far as it ceases to be purely descriptive and aspires to account for facts [2].

To obtain the objective of comparative criminological theory research should proceed, according to Durkheim's criteria of a comparative sociology, first in a single culture at one point in time, such as the United States, second, in societies generally alike, such as many countries in Europe which have similar cultural, economic, and technological conditions, and third, after proper modification, tested on completely dissimilar societies, yet sharing some common features such as those of many less developed countries. If any theoretical formulation in criminology is to be explained on a universal basis, it should be tested under all three conditions. In such comparisons it is not always necessary to use precisely similar research procedures providing the hypotheses and theoretical framework to be tested are the same. In this study, following Durkheim, we have tried to expand criminological research into the third stage, namely in developing societies that may be considered to be dissimilar to the developed countries of the world, particularly the United States and Europe, but, at the same time, are undergoing many similar processes.

For many decades comparative sociology tended to decline, despite the scientific need for it and the extensive comparative work of such pioneering sociological giants as Durkheim, Marx, and Weber [3]. In the last 20 years, however, there has been a revival of interest and work in this field by an increasing number of sociologists who have devoted themselves to detailed systematic comparisons and the construction of types in such areas, for example, as organizations, social stratification, political and kinship structures, patterns of socially significant behavior, and the analysis of total societies. Among the major factors that have stimulated the more recent interest in comparative sociology are developments outside the discipline in the comparative analysis of institutions by English social anthropologists like Radcliffe-Brown and Evans-Pritchard and the cross-cultural survey work in the United States of Murdock and the "culture and personality" school of anthropology. Other major contributions to a comparative sociology have been the development of area studies, the foundation of the United Nations and UNESCO, and, as Merton has said, "the emergence of new, self-conscious societies, and a growing sense of the interdependence of societies" [4].

Although comparative sociology, as a whole, has been increasing, so far there has been only limited development in the area of criminology. In Marsh's survey of 1146 comparative sociology articles between 1950 and 1963, for example, only 29 dealt with deviance and only a small part of them with criminology [5]. DeFleur has stated that "students of juvenile delinquency have frequently pointed to the urgent need for cross-cultural comparisons of youthful misconduct" [6]. On the whole criminologists have had an ethnocentric tendency to assume or to make claims that findings based on their work in one national culture are applicable to others. This is particularly true of most criminologists in the United States, where criminology is the most highly developed, who assume implicitly that findings from studies of American society and culture constitute generalizations applicable to others. Close examination of most basic books on American criminology reveals that they are based almost entirely on research done in the United States and thus are primarily descriptive of American society. There is an implicit but untested assumption that theories and research findings would generally fit other societies. Some European writers, however, have suggested that many of the American findings in criminal behavior are limited to American society because of the extensiveness of culture conflict, the frequency of horizontal and vertical mobility in the United States, and the fact that extensive immigration has disturbed the social stability of the country. American research findings would still be applicable elsewhere, however, provided that the conditions, factors, or variables discovered were found to apply to other societies.

In the use of cross-cultural criminological studies there have been a few notable exceptions; for example, the Philadelphia studies of Wolfgang on the subculture of violence as an explanation of such crimes as homicide and assault have been extended, with the collaboration of the Italian criminologist Ferracuti, to a comparative study of the subcultural violence in many cultures [7], and both Clinard and Friday have made comparative studies of crime in Sweden in which they have applied theories

of urbanization, differential association, and differential opportunity derived from the United States [8]. In England Downes has tried to repli-
cate Cloward and Ohlin's theory of gang delinquency [9], and several
comparative studies of crime have been made in the Scandinavian countries through the collaborative efforts of Nordic criminologists. Joint
studies of youth crime have also been carried out in Yugoslavia, England,
and Poland, primarily by criminologists at the University of Ljubjana. In
addition the Council of Europe has tried to develop collaborative European studies, particularly in the area of organized crime. Also important
are the works of European criminologists Mannheim, Hurwitz, and
López-Rey, all of whom have surveyed criminology from a comparative
viewpoint but have concentrated heavily on studies from Europe and the
United States [10]. The Social Defence Section of the United Nations has
issued a number of reports on crime in less developed countries, but
although they contain much useful descriptive material only a few of
them attempt to test comparatively some basic propositions about crime.
There have also been a few examples of comparative research: among
the most important are Weinberg's work in testing United States-based
urbanization and differential association theories of crime in Ghana and
DeFleur's tests of North American gang theories in Argentina [11]. All
of this is somewhat similar to the situation of comparative sociology in
general. "Many sociological propositions are, of course, stated as if the
relationships and generalizations hold true for all societies, social systems,
and even social action. However, such propositions have rarely been tested
outside of modern American and Western European societies"[12].

In many ways crime in the less developed countries is currently at a
stage that provides a reflection of England, the United States, and other
developed societies as they were at the time of rapid industrialization,
urbanization, and development in the early nineteenth century [13].
Eventually men and women everywhere will be drawn into the modern
world by urbanization, industrialization, the spread of mass education,
and various mass media. In terms of observing and understanding the
processes that lead to criminal behavior in various social environments,
it is important at this stage of developmental world history to attempt
cross-cultural research studies. Clifford has pointed out the significance
of such research in connection with the rapid changes now taking place
in Africa:

In the years ahead even the imperfect attempts to study crime which we
can make now may not be possible in anything like the same context. For the
time being, we can find peoples in Africa comparatively unaffected by industrialization and economic development and we still have an opportunity to com-

pare *their* standards and *their* methods of dealing with crime with those of larger city groups who are moving ever more rapidly to the urban pattern common to all developed countries. Everything indicates that this is a situation which will not last very long. As the years pass, more and more people in Africa are affected by the spread of education and by industrial change and urbanization. As the economies develop so will a more uniform pattern of living extend throughout these countries. Differences between the various communities will be reduced and information which might be gathered now may just not be available in the future. This, then, is the argument for not letting present opportunities slip by without doing the little we can. We may not have the background we require but even crude or speculative work at this stage may be worth a dozen carefully contrived and methodologically sound investigations later when the chance to compare societies has gone by [14].

The problems in cross-cultural research in the less developed countries are formidable and might well account, in part, for the limited efforts in this field. There is the question whether differences encountered in comparing developing countries with one another or with the industrialized nations are based on unique cultural occurrences or on different levels of development [15]. Some writers feel that the direct transference of many criminological theories developed in the industrialized nations may well be totally inappropriate in a developing country, since initial conditions vary greatly from society to society [16]. Research in such cross-cultural settings may encounter unexpected problems and even resistence at each stage of the process. The overall project may be hindered by restrictions imposed by customs, taboos, and values or by political hierarchies of authority and prestige [17]. Many technical problems such as the inability to administer questionnaires to a largely illiterate population or to contend with local taboos about answering certain questions [18], also exist, of course, in carrying out cross-cultural research, but in spite of the theoretical difficulties raised by the cultural diversity in the world today a basic set of commonalities in culture renders cross-cultural analysis a fruitful task [19].

SOCIAL CHANGE AND DEVELOPING COUNTRIES

An understanding of the major forces and pressures that influence social change in these countries is imperative in any analysis of their crime situations. As the less developed nations attempt, in one or two generations, to bring about transformations that have culminated from several centuries of development for most of the industrialized nations, severe social repercussions are often evident [20] At no other period, perhaps, in the history of the people of developing countries have values and living pat-

terns undergone such extreme alterations over the span of one lifetime
[21]. The magnitude of the social revolutions taking place throughout
the world clearly signifies an intensive period of societal transformation.
The resultant disruptions are greatly intensified when "social change is
disorderly, when the degree of social change is high, and the creation of
new institutions is great" [22]. Among the 123 countries that are members of the United Nations 81 are considered definitely "underdeveloped"
and 20 to 25, borderline. As viewed by the United Nations, "underdeveloped," "less developed," or "developing" refers not to cultural development but rather to the country's failure to "develop" an adequate
standard of living [23]. The concept of "development" encompasses such
a broad spectrum of social, economic, and technological factors that it
defies clear definition. The term is imbued with ideological and value
overtones that alter its interpretation in each economic and political
system.

Merely associating the concept of development with the idea of
"progress" introduces a set of considerations that effectively blocks the
possibility of a consensus. Culbertson refutes this concept of economic
development as a single-track idea of inevitable human progress born, he
says, in the optimism of the 1950s [24]. The critical social phenomena
circumscribed by the concept of development refer to a more limited
sphere of activity than the broad inferences in the term "change."
Human development implies specific categories of change that can be
evaluated as better or worse over time, reflect the quality of the human
condition, and retain their significance in cross-cultural comparisons. Any
enumeration of basic elements associated with the use of the concept development must necessarily reflect, to a certain extent, the assumptions
of its author.

Although food, shelter, and health, and the substructures required to
provide them, must be included in the perspective of human development, any exploration of the enormous societal upheavals which trace
their origins to the transformations that occurred two or three centuries
ago in England and Western Europe must be cognizant of productivity,
human aspirations, and political participation. The unparalleled expansion of technological capacities available to many societies, plus the
continued contrast between the "haves and the have-nots," renders economic change the most prominent, visible, and discussed feature of the
twentieth century. A principal source of thrust in the struggle toward
economic parity is the ground swell in humanity for a better standard of
living and a particle of influence in the decision-making process [25]. The
response to this explosive world awakening reveals enormous inconsisten-
cies in every society. Development may flourish in one sector while sup-

pression or regression is characteristic of another [26]. Nonetheless, the unique combination of technological mastery and the concomitant, to a certain degree resultant, expansion of human horizons marks a period in human development generally termed "modernization."

The growth of industrialization affects the direction and nature of urbanization and both, in turn, affect the growth of modernization. Physical, organizational, and financial facilities required to support an expanding industrial sector become concentrated in cities, and vast population shifts to urban centers occur as a response to the economic and social stimulus [27]. The urban population growth in developing countries has been a continually accelerating process. From 1940 to 1960 the population in urban areas of 20,000 or more in Latin America increased from 19 to 32%, from 7 to 13% in Africa, 8 to 14% in South Asia, and 13 to 20% in East Asia [28]. Latin America's urban population grew from 25.2 million to 67.8, Africa's from 13.8 to 36.4, South Asia's from 50.5 to 116.1, and East Asia's from 81.6 to 160.5. These changes signify a doubling or tripling of the urban sector in a 20-year period, a transformation that is part of a worldwide expansion of the population proportions in urban environments.

In relation to their population proportions, urban areas often achieve much higher levels of influence in developing countries than their counterparts in developed countries. One city, or a few cities at most, becomes dominant socially, economically, and politically and is thus termed the "primate" city in the developing country. Concentrated in this urban sector are the government, commercial centers, transportation and communication facilities, and even the administrative talent crucial to industrial development. Investment funds flow into it, job opportunities are centered there, and it becomes the major target of migrants seeking a better or a different way of life [29]. Since the large city is the ultimate destination for extensive population movements as well as the main contact with the outside world, it serves as primary initiator for an entire country's changing goals, values, and normative patterns. Acting as it does as a focus for world observers, pressures are understandably acute to have the primate city present an appearance of affluence and success. Large sums of money are poured into projects such as impressive national monuments, government buildings, and prestige hotels, and short-term rather than permanent employment positions are created. Resources are diverted from the construction of industries or their supporting infrastructures. At the same time increasing numbers of migrants are drawn to the city because of its growing splendor, modernity, and complexity. Thus the ability of the economy to generate urban employment is reduced, whereas the probability of a greater influx of untrained manpower is enhanced.

Heightened expectations plus inadequate physical, organizational, and financial resources conspire to foment an extensive degree of "over-urbanization" in most of the less developed countries. Both the push of the burgeoning rural population and the pull of the city inundate urban areas with unskilled migrants who cannot be absorbed into the more slowly expanding industrial sector. Subject to continual unemployment or underemployment, destitute migrants gravitate toward the only housing available—the vast tracts of physically depressed living structures. The plight of the urban dweller is in sharp contrast to his mental set which rejects the fatalistic acceptance of a poor environment and demands the means to pursue his own destiny in more human conditions [30].

One immediate result of these industrialization and urbanization trends is a complex division of labor and a growing differentiation among the people. Although the strong push toward industrialization has been accompanied by an equal emphasis on literacy and education in developing countries [31], few newly independent nations have educated and trained their own technical and administrative personnel to build a rapidly expanding industrial economy. Governments have launched comprehensive programs to fill the needs of their own citizens and to remove the stigma of illiteracy. As education becomes the key to wealth and status, there is a strong impetus in the urban environment to pursue these goals with impassioned vigor and high hopes. Only a comparatively small percentage of the population can expect to attend a university and achieve high positions in the economic or political structures, but students with some secondary education often cannot find employment at a level they consider commensurate with the education they have managed to acquire. With even a few years of primary education students may have changed their self-images and their goals to such an extent that they may refuse to farm the land [32]. As a result, large concentrations of partly educated youth in urban areas cannot obtain employment, yet they refuse to leave the city. The emphasis on education, with the relatively few possibilities of success, produces social structural conditions that create deep feelings of alienation in many young.

Communication in developing countries undergoes radical changes with the advance of mass media even to their most remote sections. The expansion of social horizons creates a transformation in the individual, and, according to Lerner, generates the development of "psychic mobility," or empathy, the capacity to see one's self in the other fellow's situation [33]. This empathy does not connote sympathy or concern but is merely the inner mechanism that enables the newly mobile person to operate efficiently in a changing world. As the individual becomes increasingly aware of his total society, he wants greater participation in its affairs. Whether a society chooses the "mobilization" or the "reconciliation" system, as described by Apter, the individual plays a more active role [34]. In the former he is absorbed into a political system in which many qualities similar to a religion demand total allegiance. In the latter he is part of a complex web of groups, each of which freely makes demands on the political system. He is "transformed from being defined as his father's son into a citizen" [35]. Increased responses to the mass media and interest in national affairs serve to augment the material expectations of the people to make them increasingly dissatisfied with their poverty and living conditions, and to incite them to make demands on their governments to provide greater amenities.

Concomitant with the impact of urbanization and industrialization are basic changes in social institutions. The urban environment has a secularizing effect on man's beliefs and relationships as contact with modern science minimizes strict adherence to traditional religious views and practices. Goode has stated that whenever any movement toward industrialization occurs the family moves toward some kind of "conjugal" pattern; that is, few kinship ties are kept with distant relatives and the emphasis is on the nuclear unit of husband, wife, and children [36]. The heterogeneity of the city also brings the people into contact with varied patterns of living. The need for skilled labor and management often decreases the amount of traditional nepotism in business and government. Modernization brings increased concern with health problems. Broad strides have been taken to combat such diseases as malaria, smallpox, and tuberculosis and to reduce infant mortality. Since decreases in infant mortality are not generally accompanied by a declining birth rate in developing countries, sharp increases occur in the growth rate of the population [37].

Modernization also fosters the development of a set of values and attitudes generally associated with modern man. Moore claims that certain value changes are essential to extensive economic transformation, since "economic growth necessitates high individual mobility and a placement system based on merit" [38]. Based on the underlying logic of industrialization and urbanization, attitudes and values which are constant across cultures, supposedly develop [39]. In a cross-cultural study of six developing countries Smith and Inkeles attempted to construct an instrument for rating a degree of modernism that would be valid for all emerging societies. By giving batteries of questions to samples in the respective countries and employing factor analytical and correlational techniques, they isolated a set of items with high cross-cultural reliability [40]. In an extensive attempt to measure these values empirically Kahl found seven factor scales that reflected the value system of modern man [41].

The international effect of the recent push toward modernization has been analyzed by Lagos in a discussion of what he has called "atimia" [42]. This concept refers to inconsistency in the status of nations. Although they are formally equal to developed nations, independent and full voting members of the United Nations, they are not equal in economic power or prestige. The resultant overriding concern with rapid economic development and preoccupation with presenting an acceptable image to the world impinges on the consciousness of political élites and becomes a critical factor in governmental decision making. Developing countries, however, face formidable barriers as they attempt economic modernization. Comparing the preindustrial phase of the developed countries with the presently less developed countries, Kuznets points out that when the developed countries began to industrialize they had a much smaller population and a lower population growth rate [43]. Basic financial and market substructures were already apparent, and political independence was a reality in most of the industrialized nations. In most cases the per capita income was several times higher than the current per capita income of many of the less developed countries. These factors combine seriously to retard governmental efforts to generate the savings necessary for capital investment and to attain a sustained economic growth which surpasses population expansion. Political leaders are driven toward policies of forced saving among people who already live close to subsistence and who have greatly increased their material desires by the dual efforts of aspiring politicians and the deluge of products from industrialized nations.

In summary, the development process includes industrialization, urbanization, and concomitant changes in the values and structures of most social institutions. In the less developed countries serious asymmetries tend to appear as societies seek to propel themselves into the modern world:

1. An imbalance between the concentration of modernization and economic power in urban areas and the backwardness of the rural population.

2. An imbalance between population growth and the ability of the economy to create employment.

3. An imbalance between the demands for talent by the economic system and the development of skills.

4. In urban areas a reduction of the role of the family and elders as the main socializing agents of youth without adequate social control replacement by other institutions, resulting in the development of behavior patterns among youth that differ radically from family expectations.

5. Changes in values that reject a fatalistic acceptance of the relatively impoverished conditions under which people traditionally have lived.

INCREASE OF CRIME IN DEVELOPING COUNTRIES

Despite the variations in the adequacy of statistics and the criticism justly leveled at official crime reports, data concerning the extent and serious nature of the crime problem almost unanimously substantiate the generalization that criminality is rapidly increasing in less developed countries. The president of the Ivory Coast supreme court stated in 1968 that "the more a country develops, the more crime increases. There is a relationship between the economic development of a country and the struggle against crime" [44]. This relationship is a reality that governmental élites cannot ignore. Using a series of social indicators to rank a large number of countries as developed or developing, Wolf, for example, compared their ranks from 1958 to 1962 in crimes reported to Interpol (International Police Organization) [45]. He concluded that crime rates increase with the developmental status of a country, compared with other contemporary nations [46]. This does not imply that increases in the amount of crime are greater in less developed countries but rather that the rate of increase is more acute at this point in their history [47].

In 1970 the United Nations Congress on the Prevention of Crime and the Treatment of Offenders came to the following conclusion:

As any country begins to open up, outgrow its traditionalism and respond to outside influences or new ideas by modernizing, industrializing and concentrating people in certain areas, its people and particularly its younger generation seize the many new opportunities. And in doing so, a small but progressively increasing number of them succumb to temptations and seek illegal satisfaction through crime [48].

Even as far back as 1955 a United Nations report stated, with reference to Africa, Asia, and Latin America:

From observation of experts and from limited statistical data in such areas, it can be said that juvenile delinquency became a problem of concern in those countries when industrialization has increased and where urban centers have been established [49].

Juvenile delinquency was then becoming more pronounced as a social phenomenon, particularly in Latin America. The report went on to point out that there were only a few regions of the world, such as various islands in Polynesia and Melanesia, Brunei, Sarawak, St. Helena, and some limited areas of Africa, in which juvenile delinquency was slight or did not exist at all. In these areas cities either did not exist or they were small, and close family, community, and tribal organizations had not yet been disrupted.

Recent reports collected by the United Nations in countries in Asia, Africa, and Latin America indicate a continued increase in crime rates [50], and current United Nations studies in Chile, India, and Zambia report a progressive growth in both the volume and serious nature of juvenile delinquency [51]. Arrests in Thailand, for example, rose from 146,270 cases to 648,142, or a 350% increase from 1940 to 1964, whereas during this same period the population increased by about 72% [52]. Convictions for serious crimes showed a somewhat similar pattern. This profound change does not appear to be simply a reaction to additional categories of crime or increased ratios of arrests to crimes. In fact, "it is highly probable that because of present conditions there are actually fewer arrests now than at some previous time" [53].

In Venezuela, from 1953 to 1956, reported crimes against property increased from 20,477 to 24,243, or approximately one-fifth [54]. From 1950 to 1965 the city and province of Buenos Aires experienced a rise in juvenile crime rates more serious than those of Argentina as a whole, crimes against property representing a predominant 70% of the total [55]. In Puerto Rico cases of juvenile delinquency increased sevenfold between 1956 and 1964, although the population increased only slightly [56]. A Puerto Rican study has commented as follows on these various changes:

The Commonwealth of Puerto Rico has for many years been experiencing an extremely accelerated rate of social, economic and political change. Indices of these changes are many, including the rate of population growth, the rate and degree of internal and external migration, the change in the economy from agrarian to industrial, the increased urbanization of the island, the changing family roles, the rise in income levels, the change in the occupational structure, the emphasis on material wealth, and the like. Another important indicator of change, however, and one less optimistic, is the increase in various types of individual and social pathology which generally accompany such change and which are often generated by it [57].

Accurate statistics for the Arab countries are not available, but their representatives at various meetings have expressed concern for what appears to be a serious increase in crime. The Second United Nations Seminar for the Arab states on the Prevention of Crime and the Treatment of Offenders, held in 1969, contended that serious increases in juvenile delinquency are a problem of paramount importance in all Arab countries [58]. Algeria has had a steady increase in new cases of crime:

19,049 in 1963, 41,898 in 1966, 62,379 in 1967, and 123,638 in 1969 [59]. Between 1965 and 1970 cases of juvenile delinquency increased 200% in Madagascar, and in Ghana criminal cases reported to the police per 10,000 population rose from 84 in 1959 to 97 in 1964 [60]. A Zambian study of delinquency between 1939 and 1962 showed a great rise in juvenile delinquency (229 offenders in 1939, 441 in 1950, 837 in 1955, and 1979 in 1962), but it did not find a positive correlation between it and an increase in police activity [61]. Although his findings were not conclusive in this respect, Clifford concluded that they did "strengthen the view that juvenile crime is a real social problem which is growing" [62].

Uganda: A Case of Rapid Increase in Crime

This volume reports the results, in appropriate places, of an intensive research study that we carried out with Ugandan research staff members in 1968–1969 of crime in Uganda, particularly in Kampala, the capital [63]. This study included the collection and analysis of detailed criminal statistics, in both Uganda and Kampala, interviews with offenders, and the study of two slum areas in Kampala, one with a high and the other with a low crime rate. Such intensive in-depth research makes it possible to move beyond the uncertainties raised by the use of only official records and the limited studies available from other countries. The study was carried out prior to the seizure of political power by General Amin in 1971.

Uganda provides a rich panoply of social conditions and unique features relevant to a study of criminal behavior in a developing country. It covers 93,981 square miles, of which 16,364 acres are lakes and swamps, and its average elevation is 4000 feet above sea level. Its population numbered 9,500,000 in 1969, and its economy is primarily agricultural, with more than half the gross domestic product in farming. Agriculture provided 85 to 88% of Uganda's export earnings in 1968, and 95% of its labor force is involved in agricultural pursuits. The most important cash crops are coffee, cotton, and tea. Although phosphate, copper, and beryl are mined in commercial quantities, mining represents only a small proportion of the economy. In 1968, however, it was one of the fastest growing industries.

Because of its remote location, being more in Central than in East Africa, and because of the relatively high level of indigenous organization, Uganda did not experience the extensive colonial control that was the lot of its neighbors or the countries in West Africa, in which contact with the colonialists came much earlier. Its fortunate obscurity is reflected in the comparatively late date of its protectorate status (1897) [64]. The prevalence of malaria and the tsetse fly discouraged European settlers, and the national product was based on the crops grown by African farmers on small peasant holdings. The "mailo system" of land tenure forbade the sale of land to foreigners except under special conditions. Buganda, the principal kingdom, through its highly structured system of a king and chiefs, retained administrative control over its land and people during the colonial period—in fact until 1966.

In spite of its limited colonial subjugation, Uganda's economy was still dominated by non-Africans as recently as 1972, when a policy of forced large-scale emigration of Asians was adopted. Asians (Indians and Pakistanis) handled a large portion of the retail trade and shared it and the wholesale trade with Europeans. African cooperatives had made significant progress, however, in capturing a portion of the market. Efforts are being made to correct the inferior economic position of Africans by the development of African-owned businesses.

Uganda occupies a comparatively low position on the scales of economic and social development. In an attempt to construct indices on which to compare countries, Russett ranked all nations (from data available in 1957) on numerous social and economic variables [65]. In 1957 Uganda had a gross national product per capita of 64 dollars, ranking it 107th among 122 countries. This figure had increased to 94 dollars per capita in 1968, but it is doubtful whether Uganda's world position had been altered significantly [66]. The number of students per 100,000 population enrolled in higher education was 14 in 1960, thus placing Uganda 95th in 105 countries, but it had risen to 32 by 1968. Other indicators, such as literacy, also put Uganda in approximately the same position.

Since its independence Uganda has experienced substantial growth in various indicators normally used to measure socioeconomic development: increases in gross domestic product, the percentage of employment in manufacturing, electrical consumption, and numbers of telephones and passenger cars. Increases have also been noted in the number of hospital beds, a measure of health-care improvement. Each index points to a different aspect of the process of modernization, but all constitute a part of the developmental process. In themselves, none of these changes could be considered a cause of the increase in crime, but as a group they are indicators of a process that has a reverberating influence on the entire social structure of the country.

The relative changes in these variables are shown in Figure 1. In the 1963–1968 period, on the basis of an annual growth rate of 2.5%, the

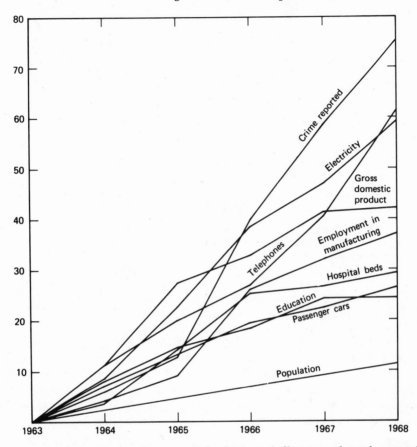

Fig. 1 Cumulative percent increase of development indicators and total reported crime—Uganda—1963–1968.

estimated population increase for all of Uganda was 11.2%. The gross domestic product at factor cost increased 42% from a base of 502 million dollars. The number of passenger cars in use rose from 26,400 to 32,800, a 19% increase, the number of telephones in use, 62%, and the number of hospital beds increased 30%. In 1957 the production and sales of electricity totaled 634,940,000 kilowatt hours; by 1966 this figure had increased 327.0%.

At the same time crimes reported to the police in Uganda have shown a consistent increase. The reported crime rate nearly tripled in the 20-year period (1948–1968) from 309 to 874 per 100,000 population (see Table 1). The crime index rose 78% between 1964 and 1968, from

Table 1   Reported Crime Rate per 100,000 Population,
Uganda, 1948 to 1968

Year	Population	Total Reported Crime	Rate per 100,000
1948	4,942,000	15,115	309
1955	5,950,000	27,376	462
1959	6,513,000	39,760	620
1964	7,367,000	48,830	664
1968	9,248,000	80,866	874

Note. Population for 1964 and 1968 represents estimated projections based on the 1959 and 1969 censuses. Crime data from police reports.

48,830 to 80,866, or a rate of 664 to 874. Two major conclusions can be drawn about crime and development in Uganda:

1. All indicators of development are rising more rapidly than the general population is increasing.

2. The cumulative increase in reported crime is greater than that of any other variable considered. In fact, crime has continued to increase so much that by 1971 the Minister of Internal Affairs of Uganda stated that Uganda's crime rate was among the world's highest [67].

India: A Case of Slow Increase in Crime

Crime has not increased so rapidly in India as it has in other developing countries. For years the rate remained about the same, even declining [68]. Pointing to this slow increase, Bayley stated that up until 1963, "rising crime rates are the rule among nations of the world and an almost static incidence of crime measured in absolute terms is unheard of." Since 1963 there has been an increase in the rate of reported crimes per 100,000 population from 143.5 in 1963 to 164.7 in 1968. The total number of persons arrested, which was under 700,000 in 1965, rose to about a million in 1968. Robbery increased 18.7% over the five-year average; dacoity (gang robbery), 21.1; burglary 3.2; ordinary theft, 6.7; cheating (fraud), 10.3; and counterfeiting 29.1 [69]. During the same period murder increased 13.8% and kidnapping and abduction, 13.8%. In 1969 the prison population was only 192,832 in a country of well over 500 million persons.

Bayley's study of the public's perception of insecurity about crime in the country somewhat confirmed official crime figures [70]. He had the Indian Institute of Public Opinion conduct surveys in 1965 in two large cities, Bangalore and Kanpur, and in a rural district of Mysore. This survey showed that 1 out of 10 urban males had been victims of a crime, although only one in 100 rural males had been. Nine out of 10 people in the samples showed no anxiety about the safety of their neighborhoods, and only 1 in 5 questioned whether it was safe to keep valuables like money and jewelry in the house. Some 21% had doubts about whether it was safe to travel outside the village or the neighborhood, although a much larger percentage felt it was unsafe to travel away from their immediate environments.

TRENDS IN PROPERTY AND PERSONAL CRIMES

Since crimes against property constitute the bulk of all major crimes and increase with the developmental process, they greatly affect the total picture [71]. Studies in Ghana, for example, have noted property offenses as the predominant offense; Tooth has reported that crimes against property between 1937 and 1945 represented 80% of the crimes committed in Ghana [72]. In the Ivory Coast in 1966 69% of 9585 crimes reported to the police involved thefts, and two-thirds of all minors brought before the courts in the Cameroon were prosecuted for property offenses. In Morocco four-fifths of all prosecutions of minors were for property offenses [73]. In comparing reports from Madagascar, Dakar, Guinea, and the Ivory Coast, Mangin calculated that property crimes were seven times greater than personal crimes [74]. A study of 79,377 cases of delinquency in Mexico City, which covered the period between 1927 and 1956, found that 51.1% were crimes against property [75].

These findings are not unique to the developing countries. In England crimes against persons account for less than 5% of all crimes [76]. In the United States the same percentage in 1968 was 13.9 [77]. The Report of the President's Commission on Law Enforcement and Administration of Justice stated that "other studies of crime trends indicate that in most other countries reported rates for property offenses are rising rapidly, as they are in the United States, but there is no definite pattern in the trend of crimes of violence in other countries" [78]. On the whole, development appears to be more directly related to property crime and not to crimes against the person. Homicide, assault, and forcible rape, for example, tend to emanate from an established subculture of violence evident in both developed and developing countries, but this subcultural formation does not appear to be directly linked to the type of social change presently occurring in the less developed countries [79].

In Uganda the proportion of reported property crime is consistently larger than the proportion of reported crimes against the person, although as a percentage it has declined because of the increase in the proportion of other offenses (see Table 2) . The rate of reported property crime, however, increased between 1955 and 1968 from 309 per 100,000 to 485 per 100,000. The rate of reported crime against the person rose from 116 to 276 during the same period, an increase of nearly 250%.

Table 2   Crimes Reported to the Police—Type by Year and Rate per 100,000 Population, Uganda, 1955–1968

	1955		1959		1964		1968	
	No.	Total Reported Crime (%)	No.	Total Reported Crime (%)	No.	Total Reported Crime (%)	No.	Total Reported Crime (%)
Against property	18,431	67.5	25,363	63.8	26,960	55.2	44,892	52.7
Rate/100,000	309		389		366		485	
Against person	6,932	25.3	9,190	23.1	14,100	28.9	25,575	31.5
Rate/100,000	116		141		192		276	
Population[a]	5,950		6,513		7,367		9,248	

[a] Population for 1964 and 1968 represents estimated projections based on the 1959 and 1969 censuses. Crime data from police reports.

This pattern of reported crime may well fit the Ugandan situation. It suggests that although the country remains at a relatively low level of urbanization and industrialization it has moved beyond the early stages of modernization and must now respond to one of the cost factors in the decision to enter the modern world. A report of the Fourth United Nations Congress on the Prevention of Crime and the Treatment of Offenders states that property offenses greatly increase with the process of economic growth and structural changes in any country [80]. This report gives some indication, however, that crimes against the person may at first tend to decline proportionately with urban growth and industrialization but may eventually increase in amount, seemingly reaching a new gravity and significance in some countries as they become the forms of violence associated with robbery, extortion, and other offenses [81]. This conclusion is supported by a study that compared a large number of developed and developing countries and found that the ratio of the number of reported murders per 100,000 population to the number of reported larcenies per 100,000, for the period 1958–1962, decreased with increasing social and economic development [82].

A more detailed analysis of the changes in serious crime between 1955 and 1968 in Uganda reveals that robbery and aggravated assault have experienced the sharpest increase in reported crime. The highest percentage increase was for robbery. The percentage increase in the rate of reported robbery was approximately three times that of burglary, and robbery experienced the sharpest increase of the major crime categories in the 1964–1968 period (Table 3). In Uganda, particularly in urban areas like Kampala and similar to situations in other developing countries, there has been increasing concern about a rapidly growing form of armed robbery called "kondoism," which usually involves severe violence. Gangs of men using knives or guns attack isolated huts, stores, or individuals, stealing whatever there is to be found and often injuring or killing the victims. By 1971 these robberies had increased to such

Table 3   Crimes Reported to Police—Rates per 100,000 Population and Percent Increase in Rate, Uganda 1955–1968

	1955		1959		1964		1968
	Rate	Percent Increase	Rate	Percent Increase	Rate	Percent Increase	Rate
Murder	8.3	51.7	12.6	45.6	18.4	18.5	21.8
Aggravated assault	22.2	51.8	33.7	88.1	63.4	37.2	87.0
Theft	144.0	17.8	234.4	−8.4	215.5	22.6	264.1
Robbery	14.0	42.8	20.2	30.0	26.1	62.5	42.4
Burglary	63.5	56.8	99.6	9.1	107.6	19.5	128.1
Population[a]	5950		6513		7367		9248

[a] Population for 1964 and 1968 represents estimated projections based on the 1959 and 1969 censuses. Crime data from police records.

proportions that large sections of the populace were terrified. In fact, the third in a list of 13 reasons given for the 1971 army coup in Uganda was the uncontrolled spread of robbery and violence in the country, "the frequent loss of life and property arising from almost daily cases of robbery with violence and kondoism without strong measures being taken to stop them. The people feel totally insecure, yet kondoism increases every day" [83]. Newspapers carried such articles as the following in 1968:

Six men armed with pangas and stones broke into the house of Livingstone Kalyana, assaulted him and stole clothing valued at 238/ [84].

Eight men broke into the house of Mr. Mohamed Kato of Buyonvu, Buddu, assaulted him together with his porter, Isa Ndararihige, and stole 1,040/. The victims were admitted to Masaka Hospital [85].

John Yirumba, a fishmonger was taken to Mulago Hospital with head injuries and bruises after having been attacked by three men armed with clubs who robbed him of 56/ and fish [86].

Not only in Uganda but in neighboring Kenya it appears that the physical courage and daring of criminals in connection with robbery increases as development progresses. A 1971 account of Kenyan crime indicates that between 1970 and 1971 there were 23 daylight bank robberies in Nairobi and more than $200,000 was stolen.

Some Nairobi bank robberies have been carried out by gangs armed only with pangas—long-bladed brush machetes—although illicit pistols have become increasingly common. Stringent gun control laws have not helped. A British businessman was recently robbed in daylight on Kampala Road, Uganda's main street, while getting his mail from the main post office. The thieves then took his car as well. The latest gambit in Nairobi is "accident gangs." Men in stolen cars deliberately run into another car at night. When the occupant alights to exchange insurance information, he is robbed. The police have instructed drivers not to stop when involved in such accidents, but to take the car number and race to the nearest police station [87].

Even though this spread of serious violence occupies a prominent position in the Ugandan consciousness, property crime may still be the more prolific facet of development. In the Ugandan study a sample of 534 men in two low-income sections of the capital, Kampala, were asked whether anything had been stolen from them in the last year. Almost a third of the respondents (30%) replied affirmatively: they had been victims of a property crime within the last year. With such a high volume of property loss, the defense of one's belongings undoubtedly reaches the level of a constant preoccupation.

TRENDS IN PUBLIC CONCERN ABOUT CRIME

An alternate method for assessing the crime situation is the public's concern about criminality. News media remain important means of transmitting public anxieties, although public opinion surveys are probably the best measure. Other measures are public pressures for legislation and reform. Although public sentiment, unfortunately, might reflect a sudden expansion of awareness rather than a great increase in crime, consistent complaints by the public and news media about a problem do indicate some basis for a realistic concern.

Newspaper reports in Kenya and Uganda showed increasing public concern about crime from 1959 to 1968. The *East African Standard* was selected for the study primarily because it is the largest newspaper in East Africa; although it is published in Kenya, it contains news from Uganda [88]. Content analysis was used to measure the relative importance that the editors gave the crime situation. By selecting every other issue, one-half of the editions of the *East African Standard* in 1959 and 1968 were analyzed for front-page articles, editorials, and letters to the editor relating to crime. A simple quantitative measure was then constructed. In 1959 only three articles related to crime appeared on the front pages of the *Standard*; no letters to the editor and no editorials about crime were published. In 1968 there were 18 front-page stories on crime, seven letters to the editor, and two editorials. From these data it is apparent that public concern about crime as expressed in the newspapers rose during the 10-year period. Although the magnitude of the concern does not appear to be so acute in Kenya as it is in Uganda, the trend is clear. The concern of the press in Uganda can be similarly demonstrated with a sample of newspaper excerpts. The following examples are only a few of the many editorials and letters to the editor on crime that appeared from 1968–1970.

Spiralling crime figures in Kampala, especially crimes of violence, caused concern and a mounting public concern [89].

Insurance companies around Kampala have expressed their deep concern about the tremendous increase in car thefts in the city, now estimated at 1000 cars valued at 15 million shillings per year: "Though most of the cars have burglar alarms, these thieves have got magic fingers to stop them," said one insurance manager [90].

These days it has become impossible for any passerby to go to the aid of a victim of these gangsters unless he is prepared to risk a bullet. This has happened before and our newspapers have reported incidents involving shooting or panga-slashing of people at random [91].

Robberies of large amounts of money from cooperative ventures all over the country are increasing alarmingly. Since last November more than three-quarters of a million shillings have been reported stolen from various cooperatives in the country. The robbers employ maximum violence in most cases [92].

Similarly, newspaper articles in Caracas in 1968 which reflected great concern about crime could probably be duplicated in most developing countries today:

The crime in the Metropolitan area has become a real public catastrophe which threatens the security of persons and property and detracts from more creative forms of labor [93].

The city exists in a permanent state of insecurity. A major portion of the citizenry refrains from evening strolls after certain hours in many sectors of the capital due to fear of attack from thieves [94].

RELIABILITY OF CRIME STATISTICS IN DEVELOPING COUNTRIES

Official crime statistics in developed countries are being increasingly subjected to critical examination. Some of the more important questions raised are whether official statistics reflect the actual amount of crime, whether changes in law enforcement and methods of recording affect an analysis of crime trends, and whether the characteristics of arrested offenders are really representative of those actually committing crimes. As we shall see, similar reservations should be applied, along with others, to the crime statistics of developing countries.

In all countries "crimes known to the police" is the best available index, since it represents crimes "reported to the police" by citizens or crimes discovered by them and noted in their records. Each alternative measure—arrest, court, or prison statistics—loses reliability as it becomes further removed from the actual offense. Arrest data depend on police efficiency. Further, police hold great discretionary powers to arrest or dismiss a suspect, and their decisions are influenced by such factors as the appearance and the social status of the suspect, the type of crime, and the available institutional facilities. In less developed countries court statistics are heavily influenced by the prosecutor's decision whether to go to trial. Such variable factors as concrete evidence, public pressure, and the seriousness of the crime impinge on the disposition of each case [95]. With arrest, such crimes as murder and forcible rape tend to be prosecuted more often, and the defendant's chances of being found guilty are greater. Prison statistics are totally dependent on the form of punishment decided by the court. The frequent lack of local jails for confinement and the availability of only minimal probation services often limit the range of alternative punishments to fines or prison. Fines are often used by the courts, and the practice further negates the usefulness of prison data as an indicator of the total amount of crime in a society.

Even official crime statistics of known crimes, however, cannot and do not represent an accurate picture of the real amount of criminal behavior in a developing country. The latter is always greater than the amount reported to the police. Their data represent only a sample of delinquency and crime in the total criminality, the remaining unknown crimes being the "dark figures" of criminal statistics [96]. As one example, a survey in India in 1967 revealed a substantial amount of unreported delinquent behavior among lower income groups in the three major cities and the one district reviewed. The district survey, which covered both urban and rural areas, revealed that there were 9162 unreported thefts per 100,000 persons under 21 years of age and 6668 sexual offenses [97]. On this basis it was estimated that out of every 100 important crimes reported in India 45 to 48 remain undetected [98]. Another Indian study showed that about 25% of a sample interviewed failed to report crimes committed against them [99]. About this situation Bayley has written:

Unless a police force is ubiquitous, crime can only be recognized if it is reported by the citizen, whether as victim or witness. There are many reasons why people may be reluctant to do so. The offense may be too trivial; the distance to a police station may be too great; the expectation of productive outcome too meager, as in the case of cycle thefts; reporting may expose the individual to harassment from the criminal or his friends; the individual, family, or group may not welcome the intrusion of outsiders and prefer to handle the matter themselves; the offense may be embarrassing to the victim, as in the case of sex offenses; and, finally, there may be neither victim nor witness who feels that a wrong has been committed, as in narcotics cases, prostitution, gambling, and some kinds of sex deviation. It is probably true that the more serious the offense the less likely it is that it will not be reported [100].

Also, for one reason or other, persons in developing countries often do not report criminal offenses to the police. In more traditional areas crime is often handled informally within groups, without involving law enforcement agencies. Only in the case of serious offenses such as homicide is a crime likely to be reported to the police. In developing countries, furthermore, individuals may be too far from a police station to report an offense and other means of communication are lacking. About Uganda, for example, one researcher states:

The convenience of the police station to the injured party is important and there is a hypothetical ratio between the importance of the crime and the distance to the police station which would show in the police figures. Central Government police stations are concentrated in the principal townships and are situated on the main roads. Large areas are without policing in the sense of permanently resident police and there appears to be little regular patrolling outside towns and industrial areas because of staff shortages and problems of cost. A minor theft ten miles from a police station would not be reported but a similar offense at a distance of two hundred yards would. The Uganda police have stated that the immediate consequence of the erection of a new police station is a substantial increase in reported crime. The physical convenience of reporting is of paramount importance as there are no other means of getting information to the police—in the absence of a rural telephone system they cannot be rung up and information by letter except for very serious offenses will not receive quick attention. If the police are to control crime in the absence of a national home communication network they have to be physically present in detachments which these countries cannot afford and which does not have to be the case with European and North American police forces [101].

Various features of the legal system, as viewed by the victim, may also inhibit the reporting of crimes in developing countries, as in the case of Uganda:

The general public believe that the criminal does get away with far too many offenses through the niceties of courtroom procedure, and also they find that the courts are not apparently sympathetic to their position as aggrieved citizens; there are difficulties over the giving of evidence when the court rules require non-Bantu customary procedure and the frequent use of an alien language in front of an alien magistrate. There are also high costs of attendance at court, when there may be prolonged delays before giving evidence, involving both loss of time which cannot be retrieved by an agriculturalist at planting or harvesting, and money because he may have to pay for accommodation as well as food during the hearing. The more serious the case, the more distant the court of hearing will be from the site of the crime; even though the Judges of the High Court tour to provincial centres where there are also Resident Magistrates with power to try most cases other than those involving capital punishment, the witness in any case of rural crime will have to sleep away from home which is a worrying experience for both farmers and cattlemen. There are also insuperable difficulties over sentences in court in which the compensatory provisions of a customary law sentence are often ignored. The victim often gets nothing out of the fine or imprisonment sentence. [102].

Some people feel that it does little good to report a crime to the police. One-third of 528 low-income residents in Kampala, Uganda, indicated that something had been stolen from them in the last year, and when they were asked whether they had reported the crime to the police 41% admitted they had not. The most frequently given reason for this neglect (42%) was that they attached almost no importance to notifying the authorities. A common reply was: "There was no need to report it." Fear of confrontation with the police may have entered into the decision for some, but no one offered this idea as justification for such inaction. The remaining responses were equally divided between two major categories: (a) little hope of recovering their property and (b) futility, because the victim did not know the identity of the offender. Both responses carry the implication of a distrust of the law enforcement officer's ability to apprehend the criminal or to recover the property. In other cases people may simply not report a crime because of their dislike for the police. If they have been harassed about license or tax regulations, or treated in an overbearing manner, many cases of crime will not be reported at all. In some cases, furthermore, crimes will not be reported if there is possible personal danger involved.

The more police and the technical facilities used by them are available, the more persons arrested and the higher the crime rate, as shown by statistics. Whether an offender in a developing country, as elsewhere, is arrested, prosecuted, convicted, and imprisoned depends, in part, on the available law enforcement personnel. Police departments generally have insufficient manpower, jail facilities are limited, prosecuting authorities and judges are few, and prisons are small in comparison to the total population of offenders. Consequently, some criminal laws can hardly be enforced at all. For infractions of other laws persons have to be picked out for arrest, whereas other suspects are less likely to be apprehended and processed [103]. Moreover, first-hand police knowledge of crime is not only limited by the number of personnel but by the lack of proper training and by the amount of motorized equipment and communication facilities available to them. The efficiency of police departments varies and arrest policies change. In general, a relatively small proportion of crime is cleared by arrest, and when the ratio is high it is often suspected that certain reported crimes have been withheld from the statistics on crimes reported until the arrest had been made.

In the developed countries increasing information is made available on police discretion, that is, who is selected for arrest, whereas little is known about these processes in the developing countries. The criteria, in terms of age, social class, religion, caste, and tribal background, used by the police in the decision to arrest or to release a suspect, are generally unknown in developing countries because studies have not been made. It appears, however, that in less developed countries, as is often the case in the more developed, differential arrest and conviction particularly affect the lower class person and those who live in slums. When social inequalities and power considerations are present, law enforcement is likely to fit the status of the offender. Police are loathe to pursue vigorously a suspect who has money or influential connections. They will, however, carry on their investigation with some degree of seriousness if the suspect is illiterate, poor, and has no friends in high places. When a theft or other crime is committed, rightly or wrongly, the police usually concentrate their search in the slum areas. Once they have apprehended the suspect and he is found to have "no status, no money" they often manage to extract a confession by beating him and by other "third degree" methods of interrogation. As a result, large numbers of slum dwellers of this category go into the police record books. Another type of discrimination in arrests is indicated by a study of traffic offenses in 1960 and 1964 in Mombasa, Kenya, which showed that, in proportion to auto registrations, an Asian was more likely to be arrested and punished more severely than a European and an African less than either group [104].

Most of all, many developing countries suffer from inefficient systems of records and methods of reporting crime. Speaking of Africa, one criminologist has stated: "At different periods the classifications of offenses have changed for the purpose of counting and the area policed has been gradually extended—with obvious consequences for the records" [105]. Reports on crimes are not systematically prepared and are sometimes gathered haphazardly by police officials who are seldom used in governmental planning and who thus cannot be expected to have much knowledge of or interest in criminal statistics. Few developing countries use mechanized systems for collecting statistics or analyzing the data, and hand tallies are always unreliable. A United Nations report elaborates on this problem:

> If statistics pose problems in the developed countries that have reasonably comprehensive and systematic recording procedures, the problems are all the more serious in the developing countries where many services are not nationwide, procedures are not uniform and data are unavailable or sketchy. . . . These problems of efficient recording may indicate the need for a better system, but too often they can be traced to the scarcity of trained personnel or to the difficulty of providing nationwide coverage with limited resources [106].

Consequently increased crime rates, as seen from official statistics, may reflect better reporting procedures, greater public awareness, more police personnel, or other factors. With reference to the situation in Puerto Rico, one study concluded:

> While these statistics, when used with caution, can serve as a crude index of the social changes which are indeed taking place, they cannot, however, provide the kinds of information which allows one to determine how much of the increase is absolute and how much is due to such factors as changes in adminis-

trative practices, the availability of more policemen lately assigned to the Juvenile Aid Division, the community's level of tolerance for certain kinds of acts and behavior patterns, changes in the composition of the population, or variations in the ways individual policemen judge, report and classify certain "offenses." Such official statistics [also] reflect the fact that many areas of social control, previously lodged with the family and other primary institutions such as the schools and the churches, have been transferred to the state through the police and the courts charged with law enforcement [107].

Moreover, since the populations of developing countries are generally increasing at a rapid rate, increases in crime rates should be calculated in terms of population growth if we are to judge whether there has been a real increase. When crime rates are calculated, however, they are usually based on the population at the time of the last census. More adequate rates could be obtained by using estimates of population growth and extrapolating from the last census. It is difficult, of course, to judge the accuracy of any census taken in a developing country. The presence of a permanent statistical unit helps to maintain a basic uniformity between censuses so that data can be compared without serious damage to reality.

Other important aspects of an accurate crime index are the percentages of population distribution by urban and rural areas, the proportion of males in the population, and the percentage of young people. The urban population is in general increasing rapidly in many countries and crime tends to be concentrated there among young male migrants to the city and in the under-25 age group. Most developing countries, particularly the African, have unusually large proportions in the age group under 25, which is most commonly involved in criminal activities. Unless crime rates are calculated primarily on this particular age group, the figures can be misleading. Often the determination of the age of the young offender is a matter of approximation. Since in most countries there is no comprehensive registration of births, the ages of offenders are not precisely known and age groups have to be estimated; sometimes there is no more than a vague division in the records between adults and juveniles [108]. Thus in a country like India, which has either no system at all or an inaccurate one, the age recorded is what the offender says he is or what the police officer judges him to be (medical examinations may be given only if the offender is sent to prison). All of this presents problems. If the offender is caught in association with an adult offender, he may wish to be treated as a juvenile, or, if not, he may report a higher age, preferring the likely shorter prison term of an adult criminal rather than the potentiality of being held for several years as a juvenile. In serious offenses law enforcement officers are likely to put the offender in a higher age bracket, since he cannot often prove otherwise.

Despite these questions about the reliability of official crime statistics, the widespread increase in crime in developing countries indicates that similar crime producing conditions are taking place throughout the world. The reported figures, although not reflecting the true extent of crime, indicate a basic minimum figure which, when large or increasing rapidly, is important. If we knew the actual total crime, the increase would undoubtedly be much greater. Moreover, the social characteristics of those arrested and convicted indicate at least those against whom official action is taken.

NOTES AND REFERENCES

1. Reinhard Bendix, "Concepts and Generalizations in Comparative Sociological Studies," *American Sociological Review*, **28**:532–539 (1963).

2. Emile Durkheim, *Les Règles de la Méthode Sociologique*, translated by S. A. Solvay and J. H. Mueller in G. E. G. Catlin, Ed., *The Rules of Sociological Method* (Chicago: University of Chicago Press, 1938), p. 139.

3. Comparative sociology has been characterized by Eisenstadt as "the investigation of the distribution of social phenomena in different societies, or types of societies, or the comparison of such 'total' societies or of major institutional spheres in terms of their development, persistence, or changeability." Shmuel N. Eisenstadt, "Social Institutions: Comparative Study," in *International Encyclopedia of the Social Sciences* (New York: Crowell Collier and Macmillan, 1968) , Vol. 14, p. 421.

4. Robert Merton, "Foreword," in Robert M. Marsh, *Comparative Sociology: A Codification of Cross-Societal Analysis* (New York: Harcourt, Brace & World, 1967), p. v. Andreski has similarly noted an increasing interest in comparative sociology. See Stanislav Andreski, *The Uses of Comparative Sociology* (Berkeley: University of California Press, 1965).

5. Marsh, *Comparative Sociology*, pp. 5–6.

6. Lois B. DeFleur, "A Cross-Cultural Comparison of Juvenile Offenders and Offences: Cordoba, Argentina, and the United States," *Social Problems*, **14**:483 (1967) .

7. Marvin E. Wolfgang and Franco Ferracuti, *The Subculture of Violence* (London: Tavistock, 1967).

8. Marshall B. Clinard, "The Relation of Urbanization and Urbanism to Criminal Behavior," in Ernest W. Burgess and Donald J. Bogue, Eds., *Contributions to Urban Sociology* (Chicago: The University of Chicago Press, 1965), pp. 541–558, and Paul C. Friday, "Differential Opportunity and Differential Association in Sweden: A Study of Youth Crime," unpublished Ph.D. dissertation, University of Wisconsin (1970) .

9. David M. Downes, *The Delinquent Solution: A Study in Subcultural Theory* (New York: The Free Press, 1966).

10. Hermann Mannheim, *Comparative Criminology* (Boston: Houghton Mifflin, 1965), pp. 92–94; Stephen Hurwitz, *Criminology* (London: George Allen & Unwin, 1952) ; Manuel López-Rey, *Crime: An Analytical Appraisal* (New York:

Praeger, 1970). See also Friday, "Differential Opportunity and Differential Association in Sweden," Durkheim, *The Rules of Sociological Method*, Ruth Shonle Cavan and Jordan T. Cavan, *Delinquency and Crime: Cross-Cultural Perspectives* (Philadelphia: Lippincott, 1968). For comparative surveys of various forms of deviance, but with little on crime, see S. N. Eisenstadt, *Comparative Social Problems* (New York: The Free Press, 1964) and Vytautas Kavolis, *Comparative Perspectives on Social Problems* (Boston: Little, Brown, 1969), Introduction.

11. S. Kirson Weinberg, "Juvenile Delinquency in Ghana: A Comparative Analysis of Delinquents and Non-Delinquents," *Journal of Criminal Law, Criminology, and Police Science*, 55:471–481 (1964); Weinberg, "Female Delinquency in Ghana, West Africa: A Comparative Analysis," *International Journal of the Sociology of the Family*, (March, 1973); Weinberg, "Urbanization and Male Delinquency in Ghana," in Paul Meadows and Ephraim H. Mizruchi, Eds., *Urbanism, Urbanization, and Change: Comparative Perspectives* (Reading, Mass.: Addison-Wesley, 1969), pp. 368–379; Lois B. DeFleur, "A Cross-Cultural Comparison of Juvenile Offenders and Offences: Cordoba, Argentina, and the United States," pp. 483–495, and "Alternative Strategies for the Development of Delinquency Theories Applicable to Other Cultures," *Social Problems*, 17:30–39 (1969).

12. Marsh, *Comparative Sociology*, p. 6.

13. J. J. Tobias, *Crime and Industrial Society in the 19th Century* (London: Batsford, 1967).

14. William Clifford, "Problems in Criminological Research in Africa South of the Sahara," *International Review of Criminal Policy*, 23:18 (1965).

15. Adam Przeworski and Henry Teune, *Logic of Comparative Social Inquiry* (New York: Wiley, 1970), p. 8.

16. DeFleur, "Alternative Strategies for the Development of Delinquency Theories Applicable to Other Cultures," p. 30. Much the same argument has been made by Evans-Pritchard who feels that comparative social science should not range beyond societies that are culturally and geographically similar. E. E. Evans-Pritchard, *The Comparative Method in Social Anthropology* (London: Athlone, 1963).

17. B. B. Hudson, M. K. Barakat, and R. LaForge, "Problems and Methods of Cross-Cultural Research," *Journal of Social Issues*, 15:5–19 (1959).

18. J. M. Stycos, "Sample Surveys for Social Science in Underdeveloped Areas," in R. N. Adams and J. J. Preiss, Eds., *Human Organization Research* (Homewood, Ill.: Dorsey, 1960), pp. 375–388.

19. George P. Murdock, "The Cross-Cultural Survey," in F. W. Moore, *Readings in Cross-Cultural Methodology* (New Haven: HRAF, 1961).

20. Gustavo Lagos, *International Stratification and Underdeveloped Countries* (Chapel Hill, N. C.: University of North Carolina Press, 1963); Simon Kuznets, "Underdeveloped Countries and the Pre-Industrial Phases in the Advanced Countries," in Amar Narain Agarwala and Sampat P. Singh, Eds., *The Economics of Underdevelopment* (New York: Oxford University Press, 1963).

21. For a graphic example of such change, see the description of a small Turkish village in Daniel Lerner, *The Passing of Traditional Society* (New York: The Free Press, 1958), Chapter 1, pp. 19–42.

22. James Bennett, "Criminality and Social Change," in Simon Dinitz and Walter C. Reckless, Eds., *Critical Issues in the Study of Crime* (Boston: Little, Brown, 1968).

23. In actuality, economic progress, according to Culbertson, is not inevitable. He regards change as being more closely linked to population growth, economic efficiency, environmental destruction, and variations in the standard of living. John M. Culbertson, *Economic Development: An Ecological Approach* (New York: Knopf, 1971).

24. *Ibid.,* p. 296.

25. William McCord, *The Springtime of Freedom: The Evolution of Developing Societies* (New York: Oxford University Press, 1965).

26. Irving L. Horowitz, *Three Worlds of Development: The Theory and Practice of International Stratification* (New York: Oxford University Press, 1966) , p. 60.

27. Wilbert Moore, *Social Change* (Englewood Cliffs, N. J.: Prentice-Hall, 1963), pp. 97–101.

28. Population Division, United Nations Bureau of Social Affairs, "World Urbanization Trends, 1920–1960 (An Interim Report on Work in Progress)," in Gerald Breese, Ed., *The City in Newly Developing Countries* (Englewood Cliffs, N. J.: Prentice-Hall, 1969) , pp. 21–53.

29. W. Arthur Lewis, *Development Planning* (New York: Harper & Row, 1966), pp. 68–70.

30. Horowitz, *Three Worlds of Development,* 1966.

31. Fully one-half of the Bolivian national budget was allocated to public and private education. Cuba and Brazil promise universal free education through high school by the 1980's. Ivan Illich, "The False Ideology of Schooling," *Saturday Review,* October 17, 1970, p. 56.

32. René Dumont, *False Start in Africa* (London: Sphere Books, 1966), p. 73.

33. Daniel Lerner, *The Passing of Traditional Society* (New York: The Free Press, 1958) , Chapters 1–3.

34. David Apter, *The Politics of Modernization* (Chicago: University of Chicago Press, 1965).

35. Daniel Lerner, "Comparative Analysis of Processes of Modernization," in Horace Miner, Ed., *The Modern City in Africa* (New York: Praeger, 1967).

36. William Goode, "Industrialization and Family Change," in Bert Hoselitz and Wilbert Moore, Eds., *Industrialization and Society* New York: Mouton, (UNESCO, 1963) .

37. Philip Hauser, "Urbanization: An Overview," in Philip Hauser and Leo Schnore, Eds., *The Study of Urbanization* (New York: Wiley, 1965), pp. 37–38.

38. Moore, *Social Change,* p. 93.

39. Clark Kerr and others, *Industrialism and Industrial Man* (Cambridge, Mass.: Harvard University Press, 1960), Chapter 1.

40. David Horton Smith and Alex Inkeles, "The OM Scale: A Comparative Socio-Psychological Measure of Individual Modernity," *Sociometry,* 29:353–377 (December 1966) .

41. Joseph Kahl, *The Measurement of Modernism* (Austin: University of Texas Press, 1968), p. 21.

42. Gustavo Lagos, *International Stratification and Under-developed Countries* (Chapel Hill: University of North Carolina Press, 1963), pp. 22–30.

43. Kuznets, in Agarwala and Singh, *The Economics of Underdevelopment,* 1963.

44. Criminalité et Dévelopment, Documents Présentés au IV Congrès des Nations Unies pour la Prévention du Crime et le Traitement des Délinquants (Milan: Fondation Internationale Pénale et Pénitentiare Societé Internationale de Défense Sociale, 1970). See also Walter A. Lunden, "The Increase of Criminality in Underdeveloped Countries," *Police*, 6:30–34 (May-June 1962).

45. Interpol has published *International Crime Statistics* for some 20 years.

46. Preben Wolf, "Crime and Development: An International Comparison of Crime Rates," *Scandinavian Studies in Criminology*, 3:107–121 (1971).

47. Comparisons of crime statistics across national borders involves great risks. National statistics are affected by variations in the definition of criminal behavior, by differing judicial procedures, and by alternate procedures for classification of criminal acts. See Marvin E. Wolfgang, "International Crime Statistics: A Proposal," *Journal of Criminal Law, Criminology, and Police Science*, 58:65–69 (March 1967).

48. Fourth United Nations Congress on the Prevention of Crime and the Treatment of Offenders, "Social Defence Problems in Relation to Development Planning," Working Paper Prepared by the Secretariat (New York: United Nations, 1970).

49. *International Review of Criminal Policy*, July 1955.

50. Second United Nations Congress on the Prevention of Crime and the Treatment of Offenders, *Report Prepared for the Secretariat* (New York: United Nations, 1960), pp. 1–18; United Nations Report, *Social Change and Criminality*, Report by the United Nations Congress on Crime and the Prevention of Criminality (Stockholm: United Nations, August 1965) ; B. N. Mullik, *Criminality Resulting from Social Changes and Economic Development* (Government of India, Intelligence Bureau, 1956). Fourth United Nations Congress on the Prevention of Crime and the Treatment of Offenders, Report Prepared by the United Nations Secretariat (New York: United Nations, 1970).

51. United Nations, "Trends in Studies of Juvenile Delinquency," SOA/SD/C.S.1-5, 1966.

52. Walter A. Lunden, "Crimes in Thailand," *Police*, 12:41–48 (January-February 1968).

53. *Ibid.*

54. Andres Aguilar Mawdsley, *La Delincuencia en Venezuela su Prevenion* (Caracas: Ministerio de Justicia, 1961).

55. Oscar C. Blarduni, "Juvenile Delinquency: Sociological and Juridical Considerations," *Revista del Instituto del Investigaciones y Docencia Criminologicas*, 9:11–50 (1965–1966).

56. Franco Ferracuti, "Juvenile Delinquency and Social Change in Puerto Rico," Paper presented for 1966 Meeting of the American Psychological Association, New York.

57. Lenore R. Kupperstein and Jaime Toro-Calder, *Juvenile Delinquency in Puerto Rico* (Rio Piedras: University of Puerto Rico, 1969) , p. 105.

58. United Nations Publication ST/TAO/SER. C/42.

59. Fourth United Nations Congress on the Prevention of Crime and the Treatment of Crime and Delinquency, p. 17.

60. Robert B. Seidman and J. D. Abaka Eyison, "Ghana," in Alan Milner, Ed., *African Penal Systems* (London: Routledge & Kegan Paul, 1969), pp. 59–88.

61. William Clifford, "Juvenile Delinquency in Zambia," United Nations Publication SOA/SD/CS.3, April 30, 1967, p. 15.

62. *Ibid.,* p. 17.

63. Daniel J. Abbott, "Crime and Development in an African City," unpublished Ph.D. dissertation, University of Wisconsin, Madison, Wisconsin, 1971.

64. Aidan Southall and P. C. W. Gutkind, *Townsmen in the Making: Kampala and Its Suburbs* (Kampala: East African Institute of Social Research, 1959), p. 9.

65. Bruce Russett, *World Handbook of Political and Social Indicators* (New Haven: Yale University Press, 1964).

66. *United Nations Statistical Yearbook, 1969,* p. 558.

67. *The New York Times,* July 27, 1971.

68. David H. Bayley, *The Police and Political Development in India* (Princeton: Princeton University Press, 1969), p. 102.

69. Central Bureau of Governmental Service, Government of India, Social Defence in India," A report prepared for the Fourth United Nations Congress on the Prevention of Crime and the Treatment of Offenders, Kyoto, Japan, 1970.

70. Bayley, *The Police and Political Development in India,* pp. 118–120.

71. William Clifford, *Crime in Northern Rhodesia* (Lusaka: The Rhodes-Livingstone Institute, 1960), p. 133.

72. G. Tooth, "Enquête sur la Délinquance Juvénile en Côte-de-l'Or," in D. Forde, Ed., *Aspects Sociaux de L'Industrialisation et de l'Urbanisation en Afrique* (Paris: UNESCO, 1956), pp. 98–103. See also K. A. Busia, "Social Survey of Sekondi-Takorade," in UNESCO, *Social Implications of Industrialization and Urbanization in Africa South of the Sahara* (Switzerland: UNESCO, 1956).

73. Victor D. Du Bois, *Crime and the Treatment of the Criminal in the Ivory Coast,* (VCB-1-'68), Field Staff Reports, Vol. xi, No. 1, West African Series, S. P. Tschoungui and Pierre Zumbach, "Diagnosis of Juvenile Delinquency in Cameroun," *International Review of Criminal Policy,* 20:45–46 (1962); Abdellatif El Bacha, "Some Special Aspects of Juvenile Delinquency in Certain Towns in the Kingdom of Morocco," *International Review of Criminal Policy,* 20:21–23 (1962).

74. G. Mangin, "La Délinquance Juvénile dans Les Territoires d'Outre-Mer," *Rec. Penant,* 1959, pp. 259–303, as reported in G. Houchon, "Les Mécanismes Criminogènes dans Une Société Urbaine Africaine," *Revue Internationale de Criminologie et de Police Technique,* 21:273 (1967).

75. Leticia Ruiz de Chavez, "La Delinquencia Juvenile en el Districto Federal," *Criminalia,* 25:704 ff, Mexico, 1959.

76. Jackson Toby, "Affluence and Crime," in Donald R. Cressey and David A. Ward, Ed., *Delinquency, Crime and Social Process* (New York: Harper & Row, 1969), p. 286.

77. Federal Bureau of Investigation, *Uniform Crime Reports, 1968* (Washington: United States Government Printing Office, 1969), p. 286.

78. *The Challange of Crime in a Free Society,* Report of the President's Commission on Law Enforcement and Administration of Justice (Washington: United States Government Printing Office, 1968), p. 30.

79. Wolfgang and Ferracuti, *The Subculture of Violence,* p. 150.

80. United Nations, *Social Defence Policies in Relation to Development Planning*, Working Paper for the Fourth United Nations Congress on the Prevention of Crime and the Treatment of Offenders, Kyoto, Japan, August 17–26, 1970, p. 16.

81. *Ibid.*, p. 46.

82. Wolf, "Crime and Development," p. 119.

83. *Uganda Argus*, January 26, 1971.

84. *Uganda Argus*, September 28, 1968.

85. *Uganda Argus*, September 19, 1968.

86. *Uganda Argus*, September 19, 1968.

87. Charles Mohr, Dispatch to *The New York Times*, July 27, 1971, p. 2.

88. The *Uganda Argus* was not chosen because of its generally small size (six pages) which prevents the expansion of crime coverage. The *Standard* could easily shift important items to other sections of the paper, but the *Argus* was much more restricted in its ability to displace important governmental and other news.

89. *Uganda Argus*, July 9, 1969.

90. *People*, March 25, 1969.

91. *Uganda Argus*, letter to the Editor, May 5, 1969.

92. *People*, editorial, June 15, 1970.

93. Diario, *El Nacional*, Caracas, Venezuela, September 24, 1968.

94. David Pancho, "Venezuela Presa del Delito," *Revisata Elite*, Caracas, Venezuela, August 24, 1968.

95. R. E. S. Tanner "Some Problems of East African Crime Statistics," in his *Three Studies in East African Criminology* (Uppsala: The Scandinavian Institute of African Studies, 1970), p. 14.

96. Albert D. Biderman and Albert J. Reiss, Jr., "On Exploring the Dark Figure of Crime," *Annals of the American Academy of Political and Social Sciences*, 374:1–15, (November, 1967).

97. United Nations Bureau of Social Affairs, "Juvenile Delinquency in India," SOA/SD/CS.2, 1967, p. 17.

98. *Ibid.*

99. Bayley, *The Police and Political Development in India*, p. 101.

100. *Ibid.*, p. 100.

101. Tanner, *Three Studies in East African Criminology*, p. 9.

102. *Ibid.*, p. 63.

103. In a study undertaken in Colombo, Ceylon, it was found that 163 institutionalized offenders belonged to as many as 153 different gangs and that in the vast majority of these gangs only one member of a possible membership of 22 (in each gang) was in an institution. J. E. Jayasuriya and S. Kariyawasam, "Juvenile Delinquency as a Gang Activity in the City of Colombo," *Ceylon Journal of Historical and Social Studies*, 1:214 (July 1958).

104. Tanner, *Three Studies in East African Criminology*, p. 15. See also Christian P. Potholm, "The Multiple Roles of the Police as Seen in the African Context," *The Journal of Developing Areas*, 3:148 (January 1969).

105. William Clifford, "Problems in Criminological Research in Africa South of the Sahara," *International Review of Criminal Policy*, 23:14 (1965).

106. "Organization of Research for Policy Development in Social Defense," Working Paper Prepared by the Secretariat for the Fourth United Nations Congress on the Prevention of Crime and the Treatment of Offenders, Kyoto, Japan, 17–26 August, 1970, United Nations, New York, 1970, p. 8.

107. Kupperstein and Toro-Calder, *Juvenile Delinquency in Puerto Rico*, pp. 123–124. See also Franco Ferracuti, Rosita Pérez Hernández, and Marvin E. Wolfgang, "A Study of Police Errors in Crime Classification," *Journal of Criminal Law, Criminology and Police Science*, 53:113–120 (March 1962).

108. See, for example, Clifford, "Problems in Criminological Research in Africa South of the Sahara," p. 14.

Chapter 2　The Nature of Crimes
in Developing Countries

Crime presents problems in developed countries far different than those in countries in the process of development. Some of these variations relate to the type of the offenses, some being more common in the developed countries and others less common, or even unique, in the less developed. Other differences lie in the nature of the articles commonly stolen. Two rapidly increasing crimes in developing countries are armed robbery and corruption in government and business. There also appears to be increasing concern about the apparent increase in crimes of violence in developing countries throughout the world [1].

As we have already pointed out, property crimes increase sharply with economic growth and development [2]. The increasing demand for prestige articles for conspicuous consumption is an important factor in the increased rates of theft in developing countries. Young persons are tempted to steal articles or to obtain money to buy items that lend prestige or a sense of modernization. The stealing of bicycles is, for example, a common feature of developing countries in which the bicycle is necessary both for transport and prestige. Other prestige items often stolen by the young are transistor radios and wristwatches. This factor is considered extremely significant in the rise of juvenile crime in Madagascar, where "the important factor leading to juvenile delinquency is the import of foreign products and their sale at high prices. The youth see them displayed in great profusion in the store windows and yet they cannot afford them" [3]. Over a period of time gangs of young offenders develop more and more sophisticated techniques in such offenses as housebreaking, a common offense in the cities of developing countries. They may remove all unattached articles from a house or apartment and, through established channels, dispose readily of these goods for which there is an ever-increasing demand.

Opportunities for theft are much greater in the less developed countries than in the more developed, largely because of a lack of security measures and the habits of most people. On the other hand, elaborate security systems have been devised for the homes of the wealthy; locks and chains to secure all outside doors, locked gates, high walls around the buildings, and the employment of watchmen throughout the night. In the common man's household, however, theft requires little skill, since their dwellings have neither doors nor locks and are poorly constructed. Furthermore, few people are accustomed to safeguarding their valuables in banks. In fact, many wear them, any savings having been invested in jewelry, a practice that often leads to violence in the event of theft. At night most areas are poorly lighted by an occasional kerosene lamp, and firearms are not owned by many. Finally, an important point in cities, single persons or families in which both man and wife work must often leave their meager possessions unguarded during the day. In what is now Bangladesh, for example, the waterways (rivers, streams, and rivulets) are the arteries of trade, commerce, and passenger traffic and consequently become the scene of much crime [4]. The police force is inadequate to meet this type of situation which becomes even worse when adjacent roads are waterlogged and made impassable during the rainy season. For these reasons most crimes in developing countries involve property offenses committed by the poor against the poor. In Haiti, for example, offenses of this kind are most common, the stolen articles being of little monetary value [5]. Theft of food and clothing prevail, but car theft is almost unknown in many of these countries [6]. In Thailand one study of 298 property cases showed that 111, or 29%, totaled less than 200 bahts (about 10 dollars), and 148, or 38.7%, totaled between 200 and 2000 bahts [7]. In the great majority of Kampala property thefts juvenile offenders commit only petty offenses. More than half (55%) of a sample of 102 offenders stole objects worth less than 100 shillings (14 dollars) and 40% of the objects did not exceed 3 dollars in value [8].

Commonly stolen items are light bulbs, pieces of iron, hooks, fittings of all kinds, and pieces of coal and wood, all of which are easily moved and not of great monetary value. Telephone wire is stolen for its copper. The lines are usually accessible, no skill is required, and it can be cut into small pieces for easy sale. Any used auto part, particularly tires and headlights, have ready sales outlets. Even badly worn clothing and shoes can be sold. A breakdown of the objects stolen by a sample of 100 prison inmates from Kampala showed that most of them were relatively small. More than half of the offenders had been sentenced for stealing a coat, a flat iron, a radio, a chicken, a table, a stove, a suitcase, empty sacks, a case of empty bottles, a wheelbarrow wheel, and combinations of used clothing and sheets, and blankets. In addition, others had stolen used tires, auto headlights from a car, and other auto parts, whereas eight of them had stolen used bicycles. Only a tenth of the sample had stolen new goods from a store and another tenth had stolen from an employer. In Douala, Cameroun, in which 80 to 90% of all offenses committed by juveniles are thefts, the order of frequency of stolen articles is small sums of money, clothing, shoes, sewing machines, jewelry and watches, cigarettes, bicycles, and all kinds of foodstuffs [9]. Weinberg found that thefts committed by youths in Accra, Ghana, consisted of portable objects such as food or money, usually of a value under 15 dollars, the money frequently being used to buy food or to attend the cinema. "Theft was a means of subsistence as well as an expressive pursuit of excitement" [10]. The following are some comments on the incidence of the thefts and the reasons given for them by the sample of Kampala prison inmates.

It was during the night when I decided to steal my friend's shirt. I wanted to go home with this shirt. He wouldn't have seen it because I would be wearing it at home in the village.

It was dawn when we decided to go and steal a case of old bottles of soda from a person who lives about a mile away. We had nothing to eat, and that is why we decided to steal these bottles, so we could sell them and get some money.

I was a porter for this company building schools in and around Kampala. As I was helping carry the bricks I saw a wheel of one of the wheelbarrows lying somewhere near the new building, and I picked it up and hid it. Unfortunately, there was one man who saw me hiding this wheel, and he reported me to my employers so I was arrested as I was taking the wheel home. I wanted to have my own wheelbarrow.

The nature of property crime was also coded for a sample of 100 inmates of a prison in Kampala. Only 2% had stolen objects from relatives, but 26% had taken something from friends or neighbors and 28% from strangers. Places of employment were the victims in 23% of the sample, and store thefts occurred in another 4%; 2% were in prison for buying stolen property and information was not available for 16%. The major finding in this distribution is the predominance of theft from individuals, quite often persons well known to the offenders. Given the list of items stolen, these crimes probably represent a rather low level of sophistication and could easily be the work of a single individual.

In many areas of large cities in developing countries stolen goods are sold at reduced prices in markets in which the poor often can find articles they could not otherwise afford and in which the wealthy come to look for bargains. Many of these markets operate with the full knowledge of the police. An offender in Kampala said that he had stolen a radio at a petrol station when no one was watching and that he planned to take it immediately to sell at a nearby market. In Bombay a large proportion of stolen articles are those that can be sold only to shopkeepers and to other dealers in stolen goods. In one study about 40% involved thefts such as scrap iron and various materials used in road construction [11].

One aspect of associated juvenile and young adult delinquency is the phenomenon of "thieves" or "bandit" markets, as they are commonly called. On the Ivory Coast these markets apparently are to a certain extent the result of migrating groups of young people from several regions to the coastal regions of the Gulf of Guinea. A survey was conducted in the Treichville District (Abidjan), where the majority of the migrants from the north live. The bandit markets are formed by groups of thieves whose activities range from picking pockets to stealing parts from wrecked cars and pilfering from stalls and who work in association with dealers who sell a variety of stolen articles. The dealers are, for the most part, the thieves themselves. They work alone and do not appear to belong to organized groups. The bandit markets are so well known that often the victim, even before notifying the police of a theft, rushes to them in the hope of recovering his belongings, usually content to buy them back as cheaply as possible. These markets are run by young male thieves for young male customers [12].

Although confidence games have not been studied much in less developed countries, many forms of this kind of crime probably exist in the urban areas, primarily because of the large uneducated and naïve migrant population. One type of delinquency particularly African involves the "multiplication" of money, wherein skills of charlatanism, magic, and sorcery are used by the swindler to give the victim the impression that he can "grow" money and double it. After his confidence has been gained and the victim puts his own money into a bottle, machine, or some other simple mechanism, the swindler with slight-of-hand movements or other techniques takes his money. Although these cases are not frequently reported because of the victim's hesitation to report them in the face of fear, ridicule, or his desire not to become embroiled with the police, some study has been made of them in Abidjan, where it has been found that the swindlers are generally older persons and almost always from other African countries. An example of this type of fraud is a case in Abidjan of a traveling medicine man who gained the confidence of his victims by demonstrating his powers of making money out of pieces of black paper put into a bottle containing a special "money-making" liquid. Unknown to the victim, these "black papers" were actually real bills painted black with a special liquid that dissolved on contact with the solvent and revealed their real worth. Thus convinced, the victim bought some of the liquid, and the swindler departed before he could use it to make his own money [13].

ARMED ROBBERY

As a country develops, there is an increase in robbery with violence, or the threat of violence, to secure money or material objects. In these robberies knives as well as firearms, automobiles and other more specialized equipment are used in attacks on banks and offices. Public concern with armed robbery has been so great that some countries, such as Uganda, Kenya, and Zambia have advocated the death penalty for it. In 1971 Nigeria publicly executed by firing squads more than 40 persons for armed robbery, before thousands of spectators in some cases. In one case two men were publicly executed in Lagos for robbing a man of $8.58 worth of personal articles [14].

The basic reasons for the increase in armed robbery lie well within the development process. The spread and growth of industrial and business enterprises require the transportation of large payrolls and other funds to local corporations whose security may be limited to a meager force of unarmed private guards. The reward more than compensates the muted risk of capture and imprisonment. Furthermore, as crime in general increases, more persons are committed to prison, and it is from this prison population, trained in criminal techniques and rationalizations, that armed robbery is most likely to come. Prison experience appears to have given them not only the means of securing firearms but the courage to go through with the act. In a study of a sample of 21 persons sentenced to prison from Kampala for kondoism in 1968, all of whom were more than 25 years of age, 62.9% had been in prison before and 38.1% had been in prison two or more times. A study of arrest figures shows likely sophistication in crime for aggravated robbery, that is, serious robbery with violence, or what is termed kondoism in Uganda. Although the majority of men charged in the general categories of personal and property crime were 25 years of age or younger, only 38.5% of the men arrested for aggravated robbery were in this age bracket. Even the age for simple robbery was higher (see Table 4). The older age could well imply a greater likelihood of prison experience.

This type of crime is a serious problem in a developing country that is making extensive economic and social progress. With reference to

Table 4   Arrests for Aggravated Robbery and Other Crimes, by Age, Kampala, Uganda, 1968

Age	Aggravated Robbery		Simple Robbery		All Property Crimes		Crimes Against Person	
	Number	Percentage	Number	Percentage	Number	Percentage	Number	Percentage
25 or younger	10	38.5	179	51.0	1889	56.4	1139	53.5
26 or over	16	61.5	172	49.1	1461	43.6	991	46.5
Totals[a]	26	100.0	351	100.0	3350	100.0	2130	100.0

[a] Totals are less than the total number of arrests recorded by police because age was reported in only 86.8% of the cases.

Malaysia, one of Asia's more rapidly developing countries, one writer has stated:

Armed robbery certainly threatens the rate of economic growth and reduces the benefits of greater productivity for ordinary people. Above all, it creates a widespread sense of personal, public and social insecurity. Though the problem may not seem so great at this juncture of development, we are heading towards that goal [15].

Armed robbery also presents increasingly serious problems in isolated nonurban areas in countries in Asia, Latin America, and Africa. In many ways the situation parallels that of the frontier days in the United States. In India dacoity, or theft with violence, committed by five or more persons, often 20 to 30, is a serious problem and one with a long history. In the large state of Uttar Pradesh, between 1948 and 1958, it was estimated that more than 11,000 dacoities were committed and at least 1500 persons killed [16]. Many Indian police officers are wounded or killed in encounters with dacoit bands. In 1971 in remote areas of the Chambal Valley, an area smaller than Maryland, dacoits committed 285 murders, 352 kidnappings, and 213 robberies [17]. How deeply dacoity is rooted in Indian soil can be gauged from a report of a magistrate in 1802:

Dacoits glory in the dread name they inspire; their names and characters are familiar to all the inhabitants. No one would give evidence against them, and the magistrates are unable to convict them for that reason [18].

Most dacoit bands represent fairly permanent organizations, although sometimes individuals come together temporarily. Leadership

usually is in the hands of those with some prison experience, and recruits are fairly easily made among village youth who are attracted by
the adventure and the money.

There are many legends about the dacoits; many of their exploits
are carried in the press and they are frequent heroes in motion pictures
in which they are seen as "Robin Hoods," attacking rich landlords, helping the poor, and righting wrongs. Operating largely in rural areas in
which there are few police, limited means of communication, and difficult
terrain, dacoits may attack single houses or even entire villages; for example, Debi Singh's gang (a notorious dacoit killed in 1962) was known
to have committed as many as 63 dacoities, 13 murders, 20 attempted
murders, about a dozen kidnappings for ransom, and numerous other
offenses over a period of a decade and a half [19]. The following accounts
in India in 1966 are typical:

. . . a report that 25 bandits, presumably belonging to the gangs of Janga
and Phoola, raided Nadhita village, 15 miles from Agra, killed one person and
kidnapped 13 others for ransom, in the midst of elaborate marriage festivities.
Vengeful dacoits in Etah district shot dead 16 persons, including five women and
four girls. According to newspaper reports, 25 dacoits belonging to the gang of
Mahabira surrounded the houses of two villagers who had given evidence in a
criminal case against the dacoits. They shot indiscriminately at the inmates
without sparing even a one-year old child. [20].

Much of their success lies in fear and intimidation. For aiding
another village attacked by dacoits, one band, for example, shot eight
persons to death, including a woman, attempted to murder another six,
set fire to 15 huts and kidnapped a minor girl.

Armed attacks in developing countries are increasing on private
motor vehicles and buses on the main highways where roads are still
isolated, poorly lighted, seldom patrolled, narrow, and in poor repair.
The following statement of an inmate in an African prison is typical of
this type of offense:

One day some of my friends asked me if I would go with them to a certain
place to do a robbery. They asked me because I was the most experienced driver
in that group and was a very good mechanic. I was promised some money. It
was daytime when we decided to go. We stopped the car of a certain Asian
whom my friends knew well and whom they knew was carrying money from a
bank to his company for his payroll. When he stopped we beat him and took
all of his money, 20,000 pounds. We ran back and each had his share; I got
7000 and gave it to another friend to run his bar. There was another friend
who had not gone with us but who was given a very small amount of money.
He was not satisfied with this so he went and reported us. After two months I
was arrested and here I am. I haven't heard of my friends yet as we scattered so
I do not know where they are now.

LESS COMMON PROPERTY CRIMES IN DEVELOPING COUNTRIES

In a comparative study made of two areas, one in Boston (Roxbury) in the United States and the other in Cairo (Boulac) in the United Arab Republic, some offenses were found to be less common in Cairo [21]. Sex offenses were found to be few in Boulac, as was drunkenness which is ethically and morally condemned by Arab society. Likewise, motor vehicles are not so plentiful and there are fewer opportunities to steal cars and to violate traffic laws. Arrests for offenses against public order accounted for only 2.2% of the arrests in Roxbury and 25.5% in Boulac, the latter involving vagrancy, begging, and collecting cigarette butts. In Boulac, where the collection of cigarette butts is common, juveniles usually work for an adult, generally a woman. The tobacco contents of these butts is reprocessed into cigarettes to be sold to the poor. For this work juveniles receive shelter and meals or money.

Theft of Automobiles and Accessories

Until quite recently auto theft has not been common in developing countries. The increased rate of stealing automobiles and their contents, however, is one of the most striking changes in the nature of offenses accompanying development. As the society develops, the number of vehicles increases and with this increase the number of stolen vehicles is augmented [22]. Some autos are stolen by youths, others by more sophisticated criminals and criminal gangs. This theft of automobiles by the young was felt to be a natural development in a country like Madagascar where boys who, already attracted to mechanical things, especially anything on wheels, with no possibility of owning them, simply get into a parked car and ride until the gas is gone [23]. They then abandon it and take with them anything they find inside. One contributing factor is that people in many less developed countries have not yet developed habits of safeguarding their property. This is changing, for example, in East Africa where the use of protective mechanisms such as car-alarm systems, steering column locks, and hubcaps requiring special tools for removal is rising.

With the initial increase in the number of automobiles, theft is limited by the fact that few people can operate them. In India, for example, where the majority still cannot drive cars are relatively safe from theft. In certain parts of East Africa there is a difference, as cars are often stolen for local sale, for transport out of the country to Zaïre (Congo), or stripped of their parts. In fact, the theft of cars for transportation across international borders is probably the closest approximation to "organized" crime in Uganda today. The car may be repainted, false ownership papers obtained, and some of the border guards bribed. In turn, some form of organization is necessary on the Zaïre side to receive the car and pay for its delivery and disposal.

Sometimes an entire engine of a car being serviced is removed and exchanged for an older engine. More frequently, automobiles are broken into for articles left inside and for their headlights, hubcaps, wheels, and tires, all of which can be readily sold in a country where new articles are expensive and in short supply. Many of these objects have little monetary value and would be difficult to dispose of in a more affluent developed country. Parts are frequently sold to taxicab drivers whose need for replacements is great. The following illustrations are of crimes connected with motor vehicles in Uganda:

Two friends and I stole a car in Kampala at 3 P.M. near the hotel. My friends had a key, and we drive it to _____ Road where we dismantled it and sold its parts to our customers. I got about four hundred shillings, some of which I gave to my sister to pay the house rent and to buy herself some clothes. This was the second time that we had stolen a car. The first time we were not caught.

We stole four tires from a motor car from a petrol station nearby the shop where I was working. It was daytime.

We managed to steal one car engine from a customer's car and sold it to somebody else. This was our common practice. We used to exchange spare parts of some cars brought to us for repairs. We had never been caught except for this time.

One Monday morning as we were going to work my friend suggested that we steal the headlights on the car which was parked outside a mosque. It belonged to an Asian and he had gone to pray. Then my friend went. He pulled or snatched the headlight and ran back to me. He suggested to me that I go and get the second one. I went and tried to pull it. But as I was not experienced in this the headlight lamp fell down and made the noise which warned the owner. My friend ran away and I was arrested. I had never done this before. This friend of mine had told me that we would have sold these lamps for about 50 shillings. This would have helped me to pay back the money I had spent on prostitutes over the week-end.

Violations of statutes governing motor vehicle registration, traffic regulations, drunken driving, and negligent injury to a vehicle or person also present serious problems in developing countries. Many countries, particularly in Africa, have high motor fatality rates in terms of auto registrations. Nigeria and Uganda, for example, have among the highest auto fatality rates in proportion to auto registrations in the world.

Vandalism

Vandalism is another offense common to developed countries but extremely uncommon in countries with low standards of living and in the process of development. A few years ago the senior author tried to describe the extent of vandalism in the United States and Western European countries to a group of Indian judges in Delhi, but they could not conceive of the willful destruction of scarce property or of the slashing or mutilation of objects like tires and bus or theater seats. This attitude toward vandalism, and particularly toward the destruction of badly needed school buildings, is prevalent in less developed countries. Relatively few cases of vandalism were encountered in a study of 7311 arrests in Kampala in 1968.

CRIMES PROBABLY MORE COMMON IN DEVELOPING COUNTRIES

Use of Juveniles by Adult Criminals

Certain crimes may be said to be particularly characteristic of countries in the process of development. Many juveniles are engaged in illegal begging practices, often under the supervision of adults, either their parents or others, who may set certain amounts of money that must be taken in each day. In countries like India which in many states still prohibits alcohol and rations some items such as sugar or grains, especially in times of disaster or famine, juveniles are commonly used by adults in urban areas to transport the illicit alcohol or rationed items. Their services are cheap, and they are less likely to be detected by police.

The child is paid about a rupee per trip and is either given a railway ticket or asked to travel without a ticket. Sometimes an adult accompanies him in another compartment of the same train; sometimes the child is instructed to deliver the bottles to regular customers at particular places [24]. A detailed study of juvenile offenses in the greater Bombay area showed that of the three largest, 56.1% entailed theft, 21.7% food-rationing regulations, and 7.8% prohibition against the sale of alcohol [25]. The violations of food-rationing regulations involved the transportation of illegal grains by juveniles, they also smuggled illicit alcohol by carrying it to outlying areas in milk cans, bicycle tubes, rubber balloons, or bottles. In East Africa, on occasion, young boys are dropped into slowly moving trucks along the major roads leading into the city. They then throw the contents onto the road side to be gathered up by the adult members of the group.

Theft by Servants

Stealing by servants is a common offense not only in the households of the well-to-do and foreign residents but also in those of a rapidly increasing middle class. For the most part household servants are male. There are almost no regulations governing wages and hours of work, and relations between employer and employee are often quite different from the normal. Although stress is put on the personal reliability of all household servants, even the most honest domestic often cannot resist some acts of theft when he finds himself surrounded by readily available items that are completely unobtainable through purchase and that can be disposed of easily. Moreover, a servant can rationalize his acts if he is employed in one of the many foreign households in which extravagance and even waste are often evident. In addition to his rationalizations, the opportunities for theft are constantly present and varied. Ten percent of a sample of inmates in the major prison in Uganda in 1968 were there for stealing from the households of employers (see Table 36, page 236).

Among the objects stolen were money, clothing, radios, and bicycles. Some case histories follow:

I took 200 shillings from my employer. My employer gave me 200 to take to the shops to get change in coins and silver. When I went to the shops I decided not to return. I disappeared with the 200 shillings and didn't go back to my employer for at least two weeks. I bought beer with the money and two dresses for my prostitute. I had never did such a thing. This time I was tempted by satan! I was later arrested by my employer who took me to the police.

I stole 90 shillings from my employer. I was earning 60 a month. One day I received a letter from home saying that I was very much needed by my parents, this was because they had got me a girl to marry. In fact, the wedding ceremony would have taken place on June 9 this year. I was delighted to hear this news. But I had spent all of my 60 shillings. I knew where my boss kept the money so I went and stole the 90 from his money. This would have been enough for my transportation. I then went home without notifying my employer. But he knew my home quite well so after two weeks only he came with the police and I was arrested and brought back to Kampala. I took this money during the daytime. I had never done such a thing before.

I was employed by an African man. I was living near his house, and I used to borrow some plates from him every week-end. I used to get many visitors during the week-ends. I had also a record player and some Congolese records. I had no English records. So I used also to borrow some of his English records. One day he came and claimed that I had stolen his plates and his English records so I was arrested.

My boss had gone home (he was an Asian). I was staying with my brother who refused to feed me so I decided to steal his bicycle in order to sell it to someone. This could have given me money to keep me going for some time.

Thefts by Government Employees

Although limited, available data do suggest that thefts of fees and other funds entrusted to public servants increase with development. A Tanzanian study of all such adjudicated cases from 1960 to 1966 shows such an increase, although the figures might reflect more awareness of the problem and greater possibilities of apprehension [26]. The average convicted person was 24 years old, had been employed by the government for less than two years, stole less than 400 shillings (about $60, in a range of 1 to 140,000 shillings), and gave as his reason for the theft the need to provide school fees for relatives. The penalty for stealing 100 shillings, or more than $14, is two years in prison and 24 strokes. In some developing countries such as India there is the persistent problem of postal employees who remove uncanceled high denomination postage stamps from letters and resell them, presumably to the postal clerk. One letter to a foreign address may carry as much postage as would be earned in two days work. Knowledgable persons, therefore, request hand cancellation of the stamps in their presence.

Food Adulteration

Although food adulteration and the sale of unsafe and unhygienic meats and foodstuffs is a serious problem in the developed world, it is probably far more extensive and has a much more serious effect in the developing countries in which the people are illiterate and have fewer resources. The food inspection facilities are far more limited in these countries, particularly in the refrigeration of meat and other perishable products. One survey in India, based on the work of 40 inspectors, found that in Delhi at least half the foodstuffs sold in the capital were adulterated or below prescribed hygienic standards [27]. Large quantities of food are rotten; milk, which is a staple product, is commonly adultered with water (one reason why Indians prefer to have the cows milked in their presence); in restaurants used tea is dried and mixed with new; flour and milk powder is adulterated with nonnutritious products; vegetable cooking oils are adulterated with mineral oils; papaya seeds are mixed with costly pepper; and brick dust is mixed with chili powder. Most serious of all, however, are the often impure and filthy foodstuffs that are served in restaurants and food shops and at the small stands of food vendors.

Cattle Theft

Cattle theft, a major crime in those developing countries that have large pastoral populations, is akin to the cattle rustling common in the frontier days of the United States, although the underlying reasons differ. Among pastoral people cattle are important status symbols as well as vital sources of food and dung fuel. The Karamajong of East Africa utilize cattle in innumerable ways:

The milk and blood of cattle are drunk; their meat is eaten; their fat used as food and cosmetic; their urine as cleanser; their hides make sleeping-skins, shoulder capes, skirts, bell collars, sandals, armlets, and anklets; their horns and hooves provide snuff-holders, feather boxes, and food containers; bags are made from their scrota; their intestines are used for prophecy, and their chyme for anointing; their droppings provide fertilizer. But cattle are also wealth, and wealth is put to varied uses. Prominent among these are the establishment and development of families, the acquisition of supporters, the achievement of status and thereby of influence in public affairs [28].

In certain parts of East Africa raiding parties commonly steal cattle, often killing members of other tribes in the process. The Ugandan, Tanzanian, and Kenyan governments consider this to be a serious problem; for example, the Dodoth of Northern Uganda, numbering 20,000, conducted 125 cattle raids in 1961 alone [29]. According to police reports, at least 150 people were killed and 25,000 head of cattle changed hands. Forty raids were conducted by the Dodoth and 85 by their enemies; in the balance the Dodoth lost 6500 cattle. Also typical was a 1966 cattle raid in Tanzania of the Wamagati tribe in which 17 persons were killed with spears, clubs, and bows and arrows, although in some raids guns are used. Use is being made of smuggled automatic rifles and submachine guns and even four-wheel drive vehicles, particularly along the borders between Kenya, Uganda, and Sudan [30].

In Madagascar, where there are about 7.5 million people and nearly 10 million cattle, the theft of cattle has become a custom difficult to abolish. In fact, in a way it can be considered a sport, for a man is often obliged to steal a cow or two to prove his virility or to prevent his becoming a social outcast. Anyone imprisoned for the theft of a cow is a hero, and it is not uncommon for him to be met with much ceremony by the people of his village on his release from prison and honored at a feast at which much stolen cattle meat is consumed [31]. India has the largest cattle population in the world and "cattle are all," as one police officer expressed it.

Cattle are as important as children, perhaps more so, and grown men, gnarled by toil, will weep bitterly over the loss of their stock. Some cattle thefts become cases of "cattle napping" when the thief, rather than disposing of the animals himself, lets it be known through an intermediary that they will be returned for ransom [32].

Illegal Begging

Begging only a few decades ago was a recognized form of behavior in many cities of developed countries. For a variety of reasons, such as new laws, stigma, economic changes, secularism, and more adequate welfare measures that aided the crippled and the blind, begging has markedly declined. In the less developed countries, however, begging is still a serious problem in the cities, even though in recent years it has in general been made illegal. Begging is often a highly organized activity generally accepted as a substitute for work. Professional beggars know what kinds of begging are most productive, such as exhibiting deformities, how to dress, and where to beg. Careful attention is paid to dirty dress and the use of certain words and signs. Some of this knowledge is transmitted from generation to generation in begging families.

In the cities of India, a common feature in many bazaar areas, as well as in the main shopping centers, temples, and railway stations, the inevitable beggar makes his daily rounds. The beggar is well aware that many people consider the day well begun if a coin is thrown into a beggar's bowl.

This coin is the means of bodily sustenance to the mendicant. To the giver it is an assurance of spiritual peace. The beggar blesses you. You are fortified by his good wishes. For you the day is free from accidents. Disappointments are put at a distance. You can count on appointments and opportunities, returns and receipts. Alms are twice blessed; they bless him that gives and him that takes [33].

Although a certain type of mendicancy, such as religious begging, has long been common in India, professional begging has become an urban phenomenon for the simple reason that it is a lucrative "trade" [34]. The total beggar population of Delhi was estimated in 1959 at about 3000, or about one in 600 persons, 44.5% of whom were able-bodied. A Bombay survey reported that in the total beggar population of approximately 10,000 about 47% were able-bodied [35]. Many beggars "earn" more than the daily wage of non-beggars. Approximately 90% of the Delhi beggars were full-time. A third of the beggars were children, usually exploited by adults, about 16% begged as religious mendicants, and about 4% suffered from physical and mental handicaps; 500 of them, or one in six, were lepers. A large proportion of the beggars in Delhi are migrants, and members of the various regional groups tend to live together in beggar communities.

Political Offenses

A crime is political whenever the state uses laws or political power to punish or detain persons who are assumed to be a threat to the government and those in control of it. Most governments at one time or another, and in various forms, have had or have political offenders. Considerable evidence suggests that the number confined for political crimes in less developed countries is probably greater than the number held in the average developed country today. Political instability, represented by power struggles between the party in office and various political groups and the part taken by the army in coups and countercoups, inevitably leaves many of the opposition in jail, if they have not already been executed. In less developed countries the possibility of rapid achievement of high status, wealth, and corruption is great for politicians, army officers, and their families and associates. India and many of the developing countries in Africa have security laws that permit the detention of persons for long periods of time without trial for reasons of national security.

Other Offenses

Black markets in money flourish in many developing countries. Much inflation and the instability of indigenous currencies resulting from problems of development frequently put high premiums on pounds and dollars. Numerous individuals exchange money illegally on the streets, and those in business also trade in larger sums.

In countries in which making or selling alcohol is forbidden, as it is in many Indian states and in Moslem countries such as Saudi Arabia, bootlegging is common. In African societies it has long been the custom for villagers to prepare some form of beer or liquor for their personal consumption. Since the brewing of beer and distilling of alcohol in cities such as Kampala often involves unhygienic methods of processing, home brewing is prohibited and controls over the marketing of alcoholic beverages have been established. These regulations are commonly disregarded, and some of the denser slums in Kampala abound with places that make and sell illegal alcoholic beverages, particularly beer and waragi, a popular drink Ugandan made from plantain [36].

Unlawful assemblage and rioting probably occur more frequently in the less developed countries than in the developed. Many riots result from food shortages and political grievances. Others involve disputes between villages, as reported in a typical account by an Indian newspaper release, in one village in the state of Rajasthan, seven people were killed and several injured in a fight between rival groups over the possession of a piece of land [37]. Another common offense in many countries is illegal riding on trains. In one year (1962–1963), for example, in India more than eight million persons, which was only a fraction of the total number, were caught traveling without tickets. Still another common offense, based on India's rigid sex code but difficult to enforce in an urban setting, is "teasing" girls, making offensive remarks, following them, or otherwise annoying them.

Witchcraft is a crime in a number of African countries. Before colonial rule in East Africa most tribes meted out harsh punishment for this practice, and during colonial rule in Kenya, Uganda, and Tanzania antiwitchcraft legislation was enacted [38]. Such penal legislation was continued after independence, and in Uganda, as one example, a law enacted in 1964 provides life imprisonment for any person who directly or indirectly causes the death of another by witchcraft and imprisonment up to 10 years if disease, physical harm, not including death, or the loss of property, is threatened. Excluded from witchcraft are bona fide "spirit worship" or the bona fide manufacture, supply, or sale of native medicines. Sorcery and witchcraft, widespread in Africa in the cities as well as the villages, are based on the belief that behavior is influenced by "spirits" [39]. Unfortunate events, affecting health and social relationships, are often explained as emanating from some force outside the person and as the result of the divinations of another person. Legislation against it is based on the premise that it often leads to fraud, blackmail, and extortion and even the murder of the person who is believed to be practicing it. In addition, the fear of black magic can cause the victim much dread and unhappiness. As a measure of the continued strength of traditional controls in urban areas a sample of 495 Kampala respondents was asked what would happen if a man thought his neighbor was stealing from him and placed a curse on him by witchcraft. More than four-fifths (83.3%) stated that something would happen, and 61.4% felt that the man or his relatives would be harmed.

Gambling is an almost ubiquitous feature of all societies, but rapid industrial development and urbanization may give it strong impetus toward expansion and organization, as Mayorca has suggested of Venezuela [40]. Enforcement of the laws against gambling varies by country, but in some countries, as in Latin America, where certain types of cock fighting are fairly common, it is illegal. Likewise, migrants to African cities are maneuvered into some illegal game of chance and promptly lose their meager funds [41].

WHITE COLLAR CRIME IN GOVERNMENT AND BUSINESS

Crimes committed by businessmen, politicians, and government employees are common in many developed, highly industrialized countries, such as France, Italy, and the United States [42]. Considerable evidence supports the view that such illegal behavior increases as socioeconomic development progresses. Common infringements by businessmen in developing countries include embezzlement and violations of income tax laws and import, export, and currency-control regulations [43]. Lawyers engage in such fraudulent activities as misappropriation of funds in bankruptcy cases and collaborate in making fraudulent claims for damages in various suits. Politicians and government employees engage in criminal practices by direct misappropriation of public funds, indirect acquisition of these funds through padded payrolls, illegal employment of relatives, or monetary payments from appointees. Their illegal activities, however, are usually more subtle. Politicians and government employees make financial gains by granting favors to businesses, such as commissions on public contracts, the issuance of fraudulent licenses or certificates, and tax exemptions or underestimated tax evaluations. A United Nations report presented the following analysis of this problem for developing nations:

> White collar crime may be expected to increase both in size and complexity as the social structure of society becomes more specialized in the course of increasing industrialization and economic development. Penal codes tend to be framed with the more obvious types of crime in mind, such as larceny, burglary, robbery and sex offenses. The white collar criminal is a person of high status, and many of his activities are accepted as part of the business morality practices in Western society. The less developed countries, may expect to experience the effects of white collar crime as their social structure becomes more complex, and they will have to look at their legal system with this development in mind [44].

Political Corruption

Many agree with Huntington that "corruption may be more prevalent in some cultures than in others, but in most cultures it seems to be most prevalent during the most intense phases of modernization" [45]. Myrdal concluded that if conditions in precolonial times were compared with those following independence "the usual view of both South Asian and Western observers is that corruption is more prevalent now than before independence and that, in particular, it has recently gained ground in the higher echelons of officials and politicians" [46]. An Indian study concluded that "rampant corruption in all walks of public life has been adequately proved by the various commissions of inquiry set up from time to time" [47]. Embezzlement and fraud among the élite in Africa is a widespread problem that saps the development potential of the newly independent states [48].

It is generally agreed that corruption of government officials is an acute problem in most developing countries in Asia, Latin America, and

Africa and that many persons have amassed large fortunes in political office [49]. Between 1960 and 1970 the following underdeveloped countries have felt that the situation is serious enough to pass acts against corruption or are carrying out official inquiries: Algeria, Argentina, Brazil, Ceylon, Ghana, India, Indonesia, Nigeria, Morocco, South Vietnam, Syria, Uganda and the United Arab Republic [50]. In 1971 one analysis of Indonesia stated that a key factor in the new national culture is corruption (korupsi).

Today, not only the "bad" people but also the "good" are so deeply implicated in dubious practices that public demands for reform and government cleanup drives seem to have become mainly ritualistic [51].

The economic social, and political significance of *korupsi* should not be minimized. In terms of the national revenue of Indonesia in 1971, an estimated minimum of 25% is siphoned off into corruption.

This rough and ready 25 percent factor for *korupsi* is higher than the 20 percent which is commonly mentioned in Thailand, lower than the 30 percent which is widely assumed in the Philippines. How it compares with percentages in the Western world is for yet more sophisticated generations of computers to calculate. Despite certain noteworthy reforms since 1965, *korupsi* is still on the increase. It has come to be regarded as both normal and necessary [52].

Corruption is one of the most widely pervasive problems of Africa.

Ministers receive from a promoter a gift of money or goods in appreciation for services they have rendered. In the local governments all the advisors want to be part of the public works committees, where side payments are frequent, while no one wants to be on education or health committees [53].

One writer stated that in Africa "venality pervades through and through the fabric of African states. After only a few years in office the top politicians have amassed fortunes worth a hundred times the sum of the salaries received [54].

Another pointed out that the most striking similarity between Nairobi and Kampala politics since independence has been the rise of extensive corruption, the violation of one's duty to the state as a citizen or public official [55]. The attorney-general of Kenya said the following in Parliament in 1968: "It has now become a practice among our government departments that you cannot get a paper or certificate unless you have paid something to an official."

A lengthy account of current corruption in West Africa described payoffs as a way of life in Nigeria, Ghana, Ivory Coast, and Zaïre.

The payoff for a government contract is a frequent business practice in West Africa. . . . There is scarcely a country where the bribe is not considered routine—from customs inspector and visa clerk on up [56].

Although some African politicians transfer large sums from the treasury to their own accounts, the chief source of illegal income is from cuts received on government contracts.

People like municipal councilors and district officers or provincial commissioners can make substantial gains on local contracts and awards of licenses for market stalls [57].

Hardly a wastebasket is bought for an office without some kind of kickback. Tax collections, as well as excise and custom duties, provide other opportunities for graft. Some arrange drastic reductions of taxes or even total avoidance, whereas those who refuse to offer bribes receive stringent assessments. In West Africa corruption has many ramifications, including schools, public works, customs, the police, and even the allocation of jobs, as the following excerpts show [58].

Teachers' salaries are sometimes embezzled by the headmasters or higher officials. Moreover, in the same way as people in other public services, many teachers had to pay for getting appointed, and continue to pay ransom for being kept on the payroll (p. 98).

Officials in charge of public works use lorries and other equipment, materials and man-hours belonging to the state or the municipality to build houses for themselves or hire them to other people. Customs officers have, of course, plenty of scope for speculation: in exchange for bribes they pass goods without levying the duty or at least reducing it substantially, whereas people who give them nothing may have to face interminable delays with the added danger that their goods will be damaged or stolen (p. 98).

Verification of bicycle and car registration, trading licenses and opening hours, enforcement of traffic regulations and hosts of other functions provide the policeman with the opportunities for squeezing out bribes (p. 99) [59].

The allocation of posts in public services (including the most humble) is mostly determined by criteria which have nothing to do with fitness for the job. Apart from a flair for manipulation and intrigue which everywhere in the world always helps the main criteria of selection are kinship and the ability to offer either a bribe or some other services in return—often on the principle of "if you appoint my kinsman, I shall appoint yours" (p. 100).

In developing countries corruption is seldom really regarded as a "crime," even though it is specified as a crime. Many developing countries, for example, have long had traditions of making "gifts" to persons in authority or to gain some personal advantage. Sometimes giving a gift fits accepted custom, but asking for it does not.

According to African traditions giving presents to public functionaries is not only accepted, it is also encouraged; and the public officer should not refuse such tokens of gratitude. If he solicits gifts, it will, of course, be bribery; but if it comes to him unexpected he cannot have a guilty conscience in accepting it. By African standards he will be even ill-mannered to refuse [60].

The extent of the corruption, however, generally grows out of the transition from a traditional to a rapidly modernizing industrial society in which village loyalties have not been replaced by loyalty to an emerging concept of a nation. Because many nations are new, the concept of national interest is weak, whereas loyalty to one's own relatives, friends, and fellow villagers or tribesmen remains strong. A similar situation is found in South Asia, in which strong loyalties to such personal groups as family, caste, ethnic, religious, or linguistic community, and social class invite the type of corruption called nepotism and encourages moral laxity [61].

An African who has reached the top is expected to provide jobs for hundreds of his clansmen, to give decent presents to a vast array of relatives as well as to the clan elders when he visits his village, to make contributions befitting his station to the association of people from his village who reside in the same town as he, to provide in his house food and lodging for kinsmen who come to the town seeking jobs and not finding them for months or even years: to help to pay for the education of the children of his poorer relatives, and last but not least to provide feasts and to defer the costs of sacrifices or funerals (including his own) apart from making donations to the church. As he cannot meet such extensive obligations out of his salary, he is compelled to squeeze bribes, embezzle public funds, take rake-offs and so on [62].

The transition from colonial rule to independence in many developing countries has brought changes that produce corruption. When foreign civil service employees have been forced to leave, their jobs have been filled largely by noncareer civil service employees who are still loyal to their families and clans and who have not yet developed national allegiance. López-Rey points out the importance of the lack among such government officials of the distinction between public administrative function and private interests [63]. Another important factor is the low wages paid most officials, particularly at the lower and middle levels. In new states corruption is relatively easy to conceal because the official rules are neither clear nor enforced and it is difficult to distinguish between traditional gift giving and bribery [64].

The benefits of holding any political office in lands of extreme poverty are enormous, for there is not only the salary but the many possible additional side benefits. In French-speaking Africa a deputy to the legislature may earn a six-months salary equal to the income of the average peasant in a 36-year period [65]. In addition, many officials get preferred housing and other benefits as well as the opportunity to augment their private incomes by political influence, as commonly done in the Philippines [66].

Corruption of officials and politicians in high places can exist only if there is someone capable of corrupting them in these developing countries. This ability to corrupt rests largely in the industrial and commercial classes. In fact, the more a country develops, the more corruption is likely because of the greater possibility of illegal business deals. This explains in part, perhaps, what appears to be an increase in corruption in Indonesia in recent years. It is often essential for businessmen to use illegal policies to complete their deals or to retain their positions among their competitors.

The export-import economy [in Indonesia]—the export of raw materials like oil, rubber, tin, and timber, and the import of manufactured goods like equipment, vehicles, and textiles—accounts for the major part of government revenue and also, therefore, of *korupsi*. Every transaction must be licensed, and every license has negotiable value. Value, that is to the officials who sign it, to the entrepreneurs who use it, and to the innumerable middlemen who interpose their services and exact their cuts.

The experienced Indonesian today has absolutely nothing to learn from the international expert about advances and kickbacks, over-and under-pricing, misrepresentation of quality or quantity, fiscal sleight of hand with regard to hard and soft currencies and multiple exchange rates, rigged bids and concealed commissions, fictitious shipments and falsified invoices, fixing, hijacking, and the highly organized smuggling of contraband cargoes by small speedboats or by fully loaded ocean-going freighters. The military establishment itself is especially knowledgeable. Many of its personnel of high and low degree devote their abundant leisure to such enterprises as keeping the market supplied with tax-free cigarettes, chewing gum, and candy bars, and seeing to it that vast quantities of copra and rubber and timber do not deteriorate while awaiting the prolonged formalities of more legal export [67].

Foreign interests seeking concessions and foreign advisors on government staffs are the source of much corruption in developing countries. Myrdal reports that bribery of high south Asian officials by Western businessmen to get a business deal through or, at all levels, to run their businesses without interference is quite common [68]. One study reports:

Distasteful as this may seem to the uninitiated, it is no secret that no few of the business concerns now at work in Indonesia—Japanese, French, German, Chinese (Taiwan) , at least, if not also American—find that to budget at least 10 percent for anticipated *korupsi* may save them at least another 10 percent in unanticipated drain [69].

The Commission on Corruption in Indonesia in 1970 made careful inquiry into the new large-scale timber industry.

It found that valuable concessions are being handed out illegally to slick foreign operators and their get-rich-quick Indonesian partners whose starting capital is knowledgeability about permits and payoffs. Indonesia's invaluable timber reserves, the Commission further pointed out, are being felled with little concern either for conservation or the assessment and collection of government royalties. [70].

Bribes are seldom given directly but go instead to a middleman who undertakes to pay off all those whose cooperation is necessary for the smooth conduct of production and business.

More generally, when a business transaction is to be settled, an official somewhere down the line of authority will often inform the Western businessman that a minister or higher official expects a certain sum of money. [71].

It might be said that a wealthy country can afford corruption but that a developing one cannot, for corruption diverts national development funds to individual gain and wastes these funds on conspicuous consumption. When corruption takes the form of a kickback or a government contract, it diminishes the total amount available for public development. As a result of bribery, basic long-term national resources are utilized for immediate gain or a factory is located without regard to strategic long-term national goals. The rich may avoid taxation and, in shifting the tax burdens to those less able to pay them, help to create political instability. Bureaucracy presents problems enough, but when it is mixed with graft "the administrative services become a mere machine of extortion, scarcely able to maintain a minimum of public order, let alone to engage in successful economic planning" [72]. When corruption is widespread, people get the idea that only "pull" counts and that much time must be diverted to such contacts. This is particularly important when costly delays result in what is called "speed money" in India. Rather than increasing efficiency, as the famous Santhanam Committee Report on Corruption in India concluded, officials develop the habit of doing nothing at all in the matter until they are "suitably persuaded" [73]. Corruption means that bureaucratic decisions are made in terms of money rather than with the worthwhile objective of a given project for the development of the country.

Corruption also hurts a developing country in its effect on the young men from secondary schools and universities who enter the public service but who do not see a clear road

along which they will travel as far as their abilities will take them in the knowledge that merit will be rewarded and integrity will be the greatest asset.

They see a jungle of nepotism and temptation through which they must hack their way unaided [74].

Most of all, corruption shakes the average citizen's faith in his country's institutions, its élite, politicians, and civil servants. Although the sophisticated may rationalize that corruption, like inflation, is an unavoidable appendage of development, the result is the spread of cynicism and lowered resistance to the giving and taking of bribes [75].

On the positive side corruption can be viewed as an aid to economic growth in the sense that government planners and economic policy makers in developing countries may act too conservatively and not always wisely [76]. It may be argued that corruption secures greater freedom of operation for the private sector, and thus the possibility of more innovation, it results in greater efficiency, reduces uncertainty of investment, and overcomes the indifference and hostility of the government. Corruption can also help to develop a new upper class of efficient, stronger officials who can help the country move toward modernization. In the case of Indonesia

few persons would deny that while there is much corruption by prevailing Indonesian standards, Pertamina (the state oil monopoly) and General Sutowo (the director) are relatively efficient. The obvious conclusion is that *korupsi* may be an essential ingredient in the still obscure formula for creation of a new class of accomplished, propertied, responsible (many would also say reactionary) late twentieth century Indonesians who may make a better show of coping with their gigantic national problems than did their blazingly idealistic—and in the end all too easily corruptible—revolutionary predecessors [77].

It is also argued that many governmental decisions in developing countries would be the same even if there were no corruption. Some of the kickbacks to government officials and politicians are more wisely used to develop the country than the originally intended project. The opportunity for corruption may increase the quality of public servants by bringing more creative and forceful people into poor paying jobs [78]. For those who are denied access to the power system corruption may help to make possible some favorable government decisions.

CRIMES OF VIOLENCE

Most developing countries in Latin America and Africa, as well as a few in Asia, have extremely high rates of criminal homicide (see Table 5). Among the 23 countries with the highest homicide rates only Finland, West Germany, Israel, and Czechoslovakia are developed countries and

Table 5   Deaths by Homicide per 100,000 Population, 1969[a]

	Year	Country	Rate 100,000
1.	1967	Equatorial Guinea	31.1
2.	1965	Nicaragua	29.3
3.	1966	South Africa (African population)	27.9
4.	1967	Colombia	21.5
5.	1968	Guatemala	18.7
6.	1966	Bolivia	11.2
7.	1966	Puerto Rico	6.2
8.	1968	Angola	6.0
9.	1968	Trinidad and Tobago	5.8
10.	1967	Uruguay	5.7
11.	1965	Cuba	5.1
12.	1966	South Africa (Asiatic population)	4.9
13.	1967	Panama	4.8
14.	1969	Southern Rhodesia (European population)	4.3
15.	1968	Kuwait	3.5
16.	1966	South Africa (White population)	3.4
17.	1966	Mozambique	2.6
18.	1968	Ceylon	2.2
19.	1968	Portuguese Guinea	2.1
20.	1967	Philippines	2.1
21.	1968	Finland	2.1
22.	1969	China (Taiwan)	1.3
23.	1967	Federal Republic of Germany	1.3
24.	1969	Israel	1.1
25.	1967	Czechoslovakia	1.1

[a] *United Nations Demographic Year Book, 1970.* Includes deaths by operations of war which accounts, particularly, for the high rate in Equatorial Guinea. Only countries rather than places included.

all of them are near the bottom of the list [79]. These are minimal figures, and if the fact is taken into account that many homicides in less developed countries, particularly the rural areas, go unreported, the differential between them and the countries already developed, in which homicide statistics are more accurate, would be even greater. If Equatorial Africa were eliminated because of the homicides associated with major revolutionary disturbances during 1969, nearly all the highest rates in 1969 would be in Latin American countries. Colombia has one of the highest rates in the world, and the rate in Mexico in 1969 was 24 times higher than that of France or Denmark [80]. It is claimed that in the Federal District of Mexico City the risk of dying from homicide is greater than the risk of being bombed in London during World War II.

In general, the homicide rates of the world are interpreted in terms of culture conflict resulting from social change and to cultural differences in attitudes toward the use of violence. It is impossible to determine, however, how much these high rates are attributable to underdevelopment and how much they are the result of various cultural factors associated with the use of violence to settle disputes. On the whole, Latin American countries have high rates and European countries low: 8 out of the 25 and 5 of the 8 highest are Latin American countries. Finland has a higher rate than any other European country, and Ceylon the highest for Asia [81].

The extremely high rate of homicide in Colombia represents a striking example of large-scale cultural violence, often called *Violencia Colombiana* [82]. There the use of violence has increased fantastically since 1948, when the rate was 11.2 per 100,000, to a high of 51.4 in 1958 and 33.8 in 1960. Like all Latin American cultures Colombia's rate of violence was high, but when a popular political leader was assassinated in 1948 violence spread throughout the country; conservatives and liberals fought bitterly and entire sections of the country fell under armed guerrilla groups. Many groups eventually lost their political meaning and assumed a purely antisocial character; they attacked cars and buses or small villages and killed in a particularly brutal and sadistic manner. Originally rural in nature, these activities permeated the cities, and despite army measures of control the homicide rate continues to be high. Deaths during the last 15 years, in a country of some 10 million persons, are estimated at about 200,000.

Studies in both Puerto Rico and Argentina found that an important element in violence is the desire of the average male to prove his "machismo," or manliness. Persons with Latin American backgrounds are often expected to resort to violence in cases of personal vilification or in marital triangles [83]. When men, even good friends, drink together and exchange insults, a knife fight often ensues in which one or more are killed or injured [84]. In Toro-Calder's study of 98 Puerto Rican male offenders who had committed crimes of violence he found that more than two-thirds (68.3%) had a predisposing sociocultural background in which the following actions were significant.

1. Carrying weapons, for example, machetes, knives, or firearms, is common, accepted, and expected in his group, and these practices are sanctioned by the individual.

2. Fighting and other similar aggressive behavior is common in his social group.

3. Certain situations especially related to gambling, reputation (personal and of his family), and honor are defined as provocative of aggression.

4. The individual has witnessed fights in which weapons have been used and has been involved in such fights, directly or indirectly [85].

Clifford found that the rate of homicide and crimes of violence is much higher in Cyprus than in England and Wales. Such cases grow out of passions of jealousy and revenge which are part of a subculture of violence that exists on that island.

Throughout the years, crimes of honour and those connected with family vendettas have been a feature of Cyprus life. There is some improvement today, but up to recent times there have been so-called "criminal" villages not only steeped in personal feuds and the concomitant violence but also places where assassins could be hired. These murders were almost always connected with family disputes and dishonour by seduction. In such villages the inhabitants do not go out alone at night and they take elaborate precautions against attack through open doors or windows. The linking of these villages with towns and the gradual emergence of better education and more socializing influences have done much to reduce this problem to manageable proportions [86].

Several studies found that offenders who engage in crimes of violence in developing countries are usually young males in their twenties [87]. They are largely unskilled workers from the lower classes and have predominantly rural backgrounds. Wolfgang and Ferracuti concluded that in the high rates of criminal homicide in Mexico the convergence of such factors as male sex, membership in the working class, and a tradition of physical aggression all suggested the existence of a subculture of violence [88]. Between 1928 and 1963 in Mexico 230,432 persons, only 3% of whom were women [89] as is generally found to be the case in most developing countries, were apprehended for homicide.

Various studies in India, Ceylon, and Africa have indicated that criminal homicide is also associated with disputes growing out of long-time personal associations, as is true in the developed countries. An Indian study of a large sample showed that relatives accounted for 26.9% of the victims, whereas friends, acquaintances, neighbors, and co-workers accounted for 50% [90]. Another Indian study showed that murders occur largely within the same caste, if outside the marriage, and involve, for the most part, husband and wife [91]. Of 77 Rajasthani women convicted of murder 53.2% were victim-precipitated [92]. In 81.8% of the cases the victim had some kinship relations with the offender, usually as a member of his immediate family [93]. Three-fourths of the homicides were products of provocation rather than sudden impulse or premeditation, the major being sexual infidelity or ill treatment by the husband or in-laws. Homicides in Ceylon usually occur in the offender's own village and usually involve disputes between relatives or neighbors which are often the result of controversies over property rights [94].

A Uganda study which compared homicides in three districts found considerable variation not only in rates but in the cultural definitions of situations that give rise to violence and the type of weapons used [95]. Of the 501 homicides 159, or 33% grew out of quarrels between members of the intimate family; one-fourth (27%) of all those killed in intimate family disputes were wives. Thirty-seven, or 7.4%, were other relatives and 171, or 34.1%, were friends, fellow-workers, or acquaintances. The remaining 134 cases, or 26.8%, were not identified in the files as having being related to the offender.

People, in general, do not kill strangers except in cases of robbery and other felonies in which material gain is the prime motive. This reveals a strange contradiction. In these societies people are afraid and suspicious of strangers or of those with whom they are not related. Thus, they fear them and think they are safe with those they know and even safer with those to whom they are related, especially biologically. And yet it is through these intimate interpersonal relationships that one is most likely to meet his slayer [96].

The situations from which these homicides developed were, in order of frequency, beer-party brawl (109), domestic altercations (65), provocation by the victim (51), theft (49), mental disorder (43), sexual (39), infanticide (15), dispute over bridewealth (9), dispute over finances (8), dispute over land (7), witchcraft (7), simple quarrel (6), long-standing grudge (5), and mistaken identity (3) [97]. As an example of the difference between developing and developed countries disputes sometimes occur in families in Uganda, where a man is expected to raise the brideswealth for his sons and also to provide them with land on which to build their homes after marriage. Homicide may result when the father either refuses to pay the bride price or if he marries a second or third wife before he settles bridewealth on his mature sons. Bohannon's study of African village homicides found them in traditional settings which define the social relations between the killer and the victim [98]. These relations differ from those of Western societies; for example, a woman might kill her children rather than her husband in a domestic quarrel. Altercations over money are rare, but land disputes or fear of witches are common factors in the precipitation of homicide.

Based on a study of 330 criminal court cases, sexual matters are the primary cause of homicide in northern Sudan (i.e., sexual competition between males, assaults on the honor of men by the sexual impropriety of "their" women, and marital infidelity). The major cause of homicide among Arab women is infanticide induced by illegitimate births. After this comes homicide resulting from drinking sessions in which intoxication is accompanied by gross insult which provokes killing. Third in frequency in the northern Sudan are homicides that result from trespass or violation of property rights in land, water, or animals. These transgressions often cause large-scale fighting between ethnic groups, called *shaklat*, in which multiple killings are the rule [99].

Clashes between village and tribal groups occur frequently in developing countries and often lead to death and injuries. Sometimes these clashes are between factions within a village. In India, for example, in 1963, the police were called in 19,000 cases of rioting in rural areas in which more than 160,000 persons were arrested. In addition, beatings, house burnings, and crop destruction are common measures of revenge; in some cases an entire family or group may be burned alive in a building by opposing village, religious, or caste groups.

One significant study in terms of the contrasts between the proportion of crimes of violence committed in the developed and less developed countries was done in the cities of Boston (Roxbury) and Cairo (Boulac). This study compared an area of high delinquency in a Boston suburb with an area of similarly high delinquency in a Cairo suburb. Both had high population densities, growing populations, poor dwellings, low incomes, and high unemployment. A greater proportion of crimes of violence was found in the Cairo area (Boulac) [100]; in Boulac 34.6% of all arrests were for crimes against the person, in Roxbury, only 8.3%. In Roxbury, two thirds (64.8%) of all arrests for criminal offenses involved property, in Boulac, only one-fourth. The importance of property as a symbol of status in Roxbury and the more important status of the individual in Cairo are given as an explanation of these differences. In Cairo, when a person is threatened by others, he may more quickly resort to force. Similarly, in Iraq, in 1966, among 1416 juvenile offenders, 48.2% were convicted of crimes of violence, which is a considerably higher proportion than in the more developed countries [101].

PROSTITUTION

In most developing countries prostitution is exceedingly rare in rural villages but much more common in the cities. In Burma, Ceylon, Indonesia, and the Philippines, for example, "prostitution exists rather as a phenomenon of the town and urban areas. The close personal relationships, the rigidity of custom and convention, prevent any disapproved practice from flourishing in the villages and rural areas. In the bigger towns, however, the situation is different and, relationships being more impersonal, prostitution can thrive [102].

Since village marriages are generally arranged and the sexual relations of women before marriage strictly regulated, prostitution is severely condemned. Moreover, marriages are generally arranged quite early, marriage and family life are the normal state, and women are dependent on men for their livelihood and social status.

The situation differs in the cities. Men migrate to them without women for the most part, and even in most of the less developed countries the more rigid sex codes inhibit both premarital and extramarital relations, thus providing a demand for the services of the prostitute [103]. Cities like Bombay, Calcutta, Singapore, Bangkok, Manila, Saigon, and, formerly, Shanghai, have lurid histories of prostitution [104]. Although houses of prostitution or brothels with as many as 50 girls are common in Latin America and Asia, this form is disappearing in countries like the United States, where the call girl or streetwalker with a room or hotel arrangement has replaced them. Another of the more prominent aspects of the cities in less developed countries, as in Latin America, is the flagrant practice of prostitution in slum areas, a situation that mothers find particularly disturbing to their children [105].

The women who do migrate to the city often find a welcome relief from strict village codes of conduct. They discover that they can make an independent living selling goods in the market, working at jobs, or becoming prostitutes or "lovers." Women who become "lovers" generally live with a man for some time before moving on to someone else. Unattached women also become common prostitutes, particularly in seaport cities. In the Ivory Coast in 1967 it was estimated that there were between 2500 and 4000 prostitutes, of whom approximately 90% lived and worked in Abidjan, a city at that time of about 400,000 [106]. Prostitution in the cities of Africa and of many less developed countries does not carry with it as much of the stigma associated with this profession in the more developed countries. Consequently it is difficult for the police to eliminate it and generally little is done. The attitude of their village kinsmen toward these women is quite different, as Du Bois relates:

> In view of the indignation, scorn, and outrage which prostitution usually evokes from the established order in the more developed societies of the West, it is interesting to examine the relations between prostitutes and the community at large in the new African states. In the Ivory Coast, at least, there is remarkably little friction between them. While European prostitutes may be looked down upon by other elements of the settler community, this does not seem to

be the case with regard to the African prostitutes. In a developing society such as that of the Ivory Coast, the much more generally accepted gauge for measuring one's position in the community is the material success one has achieved: the possession, for example, of an impressive automobile and stylish and expensive clothes, and the amount of money at one's disposal. A prostitute having these things, and otherwise minding her own business, will command far more respect from her neighbors than the more moral but less glamorous girl who has none of them. Aside from the nature of their work, African prostitutes lead remarkably bougeois lives, which are not too dissimilar from those of their neighbors. Many of them are married and have children; they are good mothers and consider themselves devout Christians. Certainly they do not look upon themselves as pariahs [107].

Similar comments have been made in a study of Accra:

First, it transpired amidst a rising sexual worth of women as well as the rising incentive for prostitutes in the urban community because of the disproportionately large numbers of unattached and single men. . . . Second, prostitution lacked the stigma that characterizes prostitution in Western countries and the United States. In fact, prostitutes in Accra formed a kind of union for their protection. Third, prostitutes could attain an earning range which was difficult to attain in other jobs. In fact, employment opportunities for uneducated women were relatively scarce so that the lure of prostitution persisted [108].

There are indications that many of the prostitutes in the cities of Africa, as well as in other countries, come not only from outside the city but also from abroad, often being recruited, as are many of the prostitutes in Asian cities like Manila, Hong Kong, and Singapore. In the Ivory Coast they come primarily from Ghana, Nigeria, Togo, Mali, and Senegal. To a minor degree, for example, in the cities of Brazil and Argentina, Lebanon, and parts of the Far East, such as Thailand and Singapore, young girls are lured into prostitution, both from within and outside the country, and kept by force, or what is often referred to as "the slave trade" [109]. In Lebanon one study estimated that about 19% of the prostitutes considered themselves victims of deception by pimps or other male acquaintances [110]. There are some indications that "the white slave trade" (although many of them are not white) has not been the product of lurid journalism, as shown in the reports of the International Agreements for the Suppression of the White Slave Trade (1904) and similar international conventions held in 1910, 1921, and 1933. In 1949 the United Nations General Assembly adopted the Convention for the Suppression of Traffic in Persons and Exploitation of the Prostitution of others, and resolutions were adopted by the United Nations Social Commission in 1959 [111]. Increased demand for prostitutes from other countries has been noted, and it is also believed that some of the women, those who have come voluntarily, are happy to escape the censure of their families and villages. They have also gone to other countries for such reasons as earning enough money to set themselves up as vendors, as in Africa or enjoying the courtesan-like status of being the mistress of a local man. The more westernized girls who hang out at bars and dance halls go with anyone who has money to pay them.

Prostitution is much more open and less organized in Africa than it is in the more developed countries. Moreover, the pimp or intermediary is probably less necessary. According to Du Bois, the African prostitute has not become susceptible to organization along European lines, and although she has been known to work for a procurer this custom is not common.

European criminal elements have on occasion made half-hearted attempts to organize the African girls, but these attempts have always failed, mainly because of the African prostitutes' strong ties with their families back in Ghana or Nigeria. These women neither comprehend nor accept a system or "business arrangement" in which a major part of their earnings must be turned over to a faceless entity in distant Europe who presumes to have some sort of hold on them [112].

African prostitutes in some cities, at least in Abidjan, have more organization among themselves than their counterparts in Europe and America, but it is a different type of organization, usually based on three or four large ethnic groups highly formalized and with previously organized arrangements when they run into difficulty with the police. It also furnishes a sort of social security system that takes care of them when they are sick, helps them to safeguard earnings and possessions, and also establishes common prices. Du Bois claims that prostitution among African women is in general not linked to other kinds of criminal activity. In Abidjan the prostitutes are of three types:

1. The small one-room house which opens onto the street. This is both the most ordinary and the lowest type of accommodation offered. A typical example almost always relies on a gasoline lantern for light and is readily identified by the ubiquitous presence of a stringed curtain. When a prostitute is unoccupied, the door is open and she is usually to be found sitting on a chair out in front. When the door is closed and the curtain is tied in a knot across the front, she is busy. Usually the furnishings in such a dwelling are sparse and the bed is coarse and hard. Prostitutes offering this type of accommodation are rarely able to get more than 200 francs per client, and their clients are mostly migrant workers of the lowest economic category.

2. The second type of accommodation is that typically referred to as the "Bracodi" dwelling (so named because of the large brewery of that name in Treichville), and this usually offers greater comforts. Often it has electricity,

possibly a radio, and even white sheets. Women who occupy quarters such as these usually command from 500 to 1,000 francs ($2 to $4), and their clients tend to be skilled and unskilled laborers, minor clerks, and, occasionally, soldiers.

3. The third and most expensive type of accommodation is a private house or apartment in which comparative privacy can be enjoyed by the client. The comforts generally associated with European living quarters are in evidence: electricity, running water, modern beds, perhaps even a television set. Women enjoying such luxurious accommodations are usually able to ask a fee of 2,000 francs ($8), their clients being chiefly the higher-paid African functionaries, Europeans residing in Abidjan, and visiting foreign sailors [113].

Prostitution in India has had a unique history, linked to the Devadasi system of temple dancers. There are frequent references to prostitution as an urbanized and established system more than 2000 years ago. Girls were dedicated to Hindu temples at an early age; became "brides" of God, and were therefore barred from marrying [114]. In this capacity they were to perform various duties for the presiding deity, to dance for him, and to engage in sexual intercourse for the god and for the temple. Even today in India, where it is on a purely economic basis and no longer associated with the temples, many prostitutes claim the Devadasis as their traditional profession. In a study of 425 Bombay prostitutes in 1962, for example, a third of the women interviewed stated that they were Devadasis in the service of the goddess Yellamma; many of them had been dedicated by their families, mainly Harijans or untouchables, in the rural areas [115]. This feature encourages recruitment and furnishes ample rationalizations for the profession, which have become important in a different context in the United States [116]. In addition, certain prostitutes follow a hereditary social profession passed on from mother to daughter among the Beriyas and Deredars [117].

For the most part prostitutes operate only in the large cities and their activities are frequently camouflaged as "dancing girls" who perform for men in their quarters. For many years prostitution was licensed, and there were inspections, but this law was abolished in 1929 and prostitution was made illegal, even though today much of it continues. Along the waterfront in Bombay, for example, there are tolerated areas of prostitution, which have existed since 1880 and in 1962 housed about 13,000 prostitutes. Here multistoried buildings are divided into cubicles, each with a room in the back, and because the doors of some of these brothels are iron-barred they are commonly referred to as "cages." Life in these areas has been described as

large numbers of young and middle-aged men leisurely rambling on the streets and lustfully staring at the women of pleasure; the prostitutes, cheaply dressed in tight clothes and invariably chewing *pan*, sitting in voluptuous postures and indulging in unashamed and pitiably professional coquetry—these are some of the features so patent about the tolerated areas of Bombay. In the nights, life here is highly exaggerated. The gloomy streets with their dark alleys and the dim and diffused lights casting ill-defined, sinister shadows, fire one's imagination with disquieting thoughts. In other parts the place looks as if a fair is on, brightly lit and thronged with made-up faces and men of all ages brazenly bargaining and settling terms with them; groups of people squatting on mid-streets in circles and gambling on card games, heedless of the law or the police [118].

Prostitution in India is almost exclusively a city phenomenon [119]. It was found in the Bombay study that these women were for the most part, migrants, some of them moving to Bombay from long distances [120]. Although 86% were Hindus, nearly half were Harijans, "untouchables," a group outside the normal caste system. Nearly all came from poor families in rural areas, which, of course, is of little significance because most Indian families and city migrants have similar backgrounds. Nearly two-thirds of them had lost both or one of their parents, the majority when they were 10 years old or younger, which is somewhat unusual. They were grudgingly brought up by relatives and later given to city procurers to be dedicated as Devadasis.

The modal age at which the Devadasis left home was 13 to 14 years, the non-Devadasis 15 to 17. Among the non-Devadasis two-thirds were married women, of whom girls widowed at an early age and runaway wives formed a large majority. Nearly all the married respondents were unhappily married, their problems ranging from physical mistreatment, drunkenness, unfaithfulness, or desertion by their husbands, although in some cases there had been some illicit sexual relations on their own part. All the Devadasis and nearly half the non-Devadasis left home for the purpose of prostitution. Although about a third of the non-Devadasis entered the brothels under "involuntary" conditions brought about by deception, kidnapping, or other enforced methods, the other two-thirds entered voluntarily under the persuasion of a procurer who described prostitution as "an easy and paying profession," since all they had to do was to "sleep with men" [121].

It is important to recognize that in India nearly all marriages are arranged and that the dowry, particularly among the lower classes is often of prime importance, with little consideration given to the feelings of the women. Since divorce is frowned on, a woman who finds her marriage impossible has nowhere to go except back to her family, where she is likely to be an outcaste. She cannot marry again, and employment for lower class single women is almost impossible to find. There is sometimes a resort to murder [122], and another alternative in cases of intolerable marital situations may be suicide. In fact, the suicide rates for women in many parts of India are high, which is in decided contrast to the lower rates for women in the developed countries [123]. If the husband dies, the widow also finds herself in a serious predicament, one which might lead to a life of prostitution, since the lot of young widows under the Hindu religion is hard; remarriage is forbidden to women but permitted to men. Whether a woman will go to the city to engage in prostitution as a result of an unhappy marriage or widowhood depends a great deal on the procurer or pimp. In both cases it is the procurer, with his promises of an easy life and much money, who is important.

The procurers, who are mostly women, possibly "retired" prostitutes, are mainly and directly responsible for precipitating the problem by converting these vulnerable women into prostitutes. . . . There are regular vice rackets operating in these rural areas with many women working for them to supply girls to the city brothels. It seems they are very active and alert in spotting and netting the unhappy girls, for the average price of a girl in the vice markets of Kamathipura (brothel area in Bombay) is Rs. 200/. Women traffickers make the operations of the vice rackets easy and least suspicious, rendering vigilance work more difficult. Once the girls go, or are brought, to the brothels, most of them seem to accept prostitution without much protest or hesitation. When they see large numbers of women indulging in it, the grimness and shame attached to prostitution are lost on them and they feel encouraged to taste "the forbidden fruit" and to live on it; it becomes a trade and is no more an immoral and antisocial behavior [124].

Indian prostitutes generally make 10 to 20 dollars a month, although some may make much more. In addition, the brothel keeper often furnishes clothing, jewelry, and cosmetics, which they would ordinarily not have but which are charged to expenses. An Agra study has described the role of the brothel keeper, usually a woman, who has also been a prostitute [125]. In addition to such customary acts as providing medical treatment and protection from police harassment, she also "sends message of love of a girl to the rich customers and schemes to keep them attached to her" [126].

In Beirut there are many differences in the nature of prostitution, compared with India and Africa. A study of a sample of 133 prostitutes revealed that 73% had lived most of their lives in Beirut before becoming prostitutes, the remainder having come from villages and small cities [129]. More than two-thirds were married before entering the profession and, in general, prostitutes had induced them to take up the trade for the gains. Beirut prostitutes are relatively older than one would expect in more developed countries; the average age is 36.3 years and one-fourth are over 45. Although they were recruited at the age of 18.7 years, on the average, they tended to stay for an average of slightly more than 17 years, indicating that prostitution in the Middle East is not a transistory profession. In Beirut, which is a major city in a rapidly developing country, "the socio-economic status of the licensed prostitute, because of the inevitable loosening of moral standards, is undergoing a change. More than 85 percent of the respondents reported that their business had been declining. This is one manifestation that the amateur is beginning to displace the professional prostitute. Outside competition and greater sexual freedom are among the factors responsible for such a change [128].

SOME CONCLUSIONS

Development in a country brings with it a great increase in certain forms of theft, particularly armed robbery. Auto theft can be expected to increase, since the automobile is a major symbol of the modern industrial world. Increased corruption in business and government is also a concomitant of modernization. Eventually such offenses as vandalism, which is characteristic of highly developed countries, will also increase. Check forgery, more embezzlement, and the theft and misuse of credit cards may also be expected to result from growth of the economy.

We can, however, also expect a decrease in some offenses with development. The homicide rates in many countries, which are now generally among the world's highest, will tend to decrease. So will prostitution, which is closely related to the sexual imbalance in cities, the limited employment opportunities for women and their low status. The use of children in crime and illegal begging will diminish along with cattle theft and rioting over food shortages and village disputes. Finally, arrest, imprisonment, and execution for political crimes may be proportionately reduced as greater political stability ensues, even though the record of some of the developed countries in this respect is not good.

NOTES AND REFERENCES

1. Marvin Wolfgang and Franco Ferracuti, *The Subculture of Violence: Towards an Integrated Theory on Criminology* (London: Tavistock, 1967), p. 150.
2. "Social Defence Policies in Relation to Development Planning," Working Paper Prepared by the Secretariat of the United Nations for the Fourth United Nations Congress on the Prevention of Crime and the Treatment of Offenders, Kyoto, Japan, 1970.
3. Report by Lucile Ramaholimaso, Delegate of Madagascar to the Fourth United Nations Congress on the Prevention of Crime and the Treatment of Offenders, Kyoto, Japan, 1970.

4. A. K. Mazmul Karin, "Crime in East Pakistan Since 1947," *International Review of Criminal Policy*, 18:52 (1960).

5. Statement of the Haitian delegate to the Fourth United Nations Congress on the Prevention of Crime and the Treatment of Offenders, Kyoto, Japan, 1970. The delegate indicated that in his judgment development would overcome this type of crime.

6. *Ibid.*

7. W. H. Nagel, United Nations Technical Assistant, "Juvenile Delinquency in Thailand," United Nations Report, p. 121.

8. Eric Paul Kibuka, "Sociological Aspects of Juvenile Delinquency in Kampala 1962 to 1969," Ph. D. dissertation, University of East Africa, 1972.

9. *New Forms of Juvenile Delinquency, Their Origin, Prevention, and Treatment* (New York: United Nations, 1960), p. 20.

10. S. Kirson Weinberg, "Urbanization and Male Delinquency in Ghana," in Paul Meadows and Ephraim H. Mizruchi, Eds., *Urbanism, Urbanization, and Change: Comparative Perspectives* (Reading, Mass.: Addison-Wesley, 1969), p. 371.

11. Hansa Sheth, *Juvenile Delinquency in an Indian Setting* (Bombay: Popular Book Depot, 1961).

12. J. Rouch and E. Berms, "Thieves' Markets in Treichville," in *New Forms of Juvenile Delinquency*, p. 22.

13. Roger Jacobs, with the collaboration of Ernest De Kouassi Ade and Eugene Yro, "La Multiplication des Billets de Banque," Institut de Criminologie d'Abidjan, 1971. See also Jean Pinatel, *La Société Criminogène* (Paris, Calmann-Lévy, 1971), p. 25.

14. *The Wisconsin State Journal*, June 27, 1971. In 1970 Nigeria decreed the death penalty for cases of robbery in which an offender is "armed with firearms or any offensive weapon or is in company with any person so armed, or at or immediately after the time of the robbery the said offender wounds or uses any personal violence to any person." The penalty may be carried out by hanging or by firing squad. "Armed Robbery Tribunals and Executions," *The Daily Times of Nigeria Annual Review 1971* (Lagos: Academy Press, 1972). p. 63.

15. Ibrahim bin Haji Mohamed, "The Need for a Central Agency for Better Coordination against Agencies and to Promote Sound Policies for the Prevention of Crime and the Treatment of Offenders, with Reference to Malaysia," Fourth United Nations Congress on the Prevention of Crime and the Treatment of Offenders, Kyoto, Japan, 1970.

16. *Link* (India), December 7, 1958.

17. *Time*, May 1, 1972.

18. J. C. Curry, *The Indian Police* (London: Faber and Faber, 1935).

19. S. Venugopal Rao, *Facets of Crime in India* (Bombay: Allied 1963), p. 63.

20. *Ibid.*, p. 55.

21. Saied Ewies, "A Comparative Study of Two Delinquency Areas: Roxbury of Boston, Massachusetts and Boulac of Cairo, U. A. R.," *The National Review of Criminal Science* (U.S.A.), 2:1–15 (November 1959).

22. Until 1963 police reports in Uganda did not list auto theft as a separate category but included it under the general category of theft. After 1963 three separate categories specifically related to auto theft: auto theft, theft of spare parts and

accessories from an auto, and theft of other items from an auto. In the United States more than 400,000 automobiles are stolen annually.

23. Ramaholimaso, Report to the Fourth United Nations Congress on the Prevention of Crime and the Treatment of Offenders, 1970.

24. Sheth, *Juvenile Delinquency in an Indian Setting*, pp. 104–131.

25. *Ibid.*, p. 117.

26. Study carried out by Dr. Carl Widestrand, from a private communication.

27. *Times of India,* June 11, 1959.

28. Neville Dyson-Hudson, *Karamojong Politics* (London: Clarendon Press, Oxford, 1966), p. 83.

29. Elizabeth Marshall Thomas, *Warrior Herdsmen* (London: Secker & Warburg, 1965).

30. A communication from Dr. Carl Widestrand.

31. Ramaholimaso, Report to Fourth United Nations Congress on the Prevention of Crime and the Treatment of Offenders, 1970.

32. David H. Bayley, *The Police and Political Development in India* (Princeton: Princeton University Press, Copyright © 1969), p. 114. Reprinted by permission of the Princeton University Press.

33. M. V. Moorthy, Ed., *Beggar—Problem in Greater Bombay* (Bombay: Indian Conference of Social Work, 1959), p. 44.

34. *The Beggar Problem in Metropolitan Delhi* (Delhi: Delhi School of Social Work, 1959) and Moorthy, *Beggar Problem in Greater Bombay*. See also J. M. Kumarappa, *Our Beggar Problem: How To Tackle It* (Bombay: Padma, 1945).

35. *Beggar Problem in Greater Bombay*, p. 38.

36. A. W. Southall and P. C. W. Gutkind, *Townsmen in the Making: Kampala and Its Suburbs* (London: Kegan Paul Trench Trubner, 1957), pp. 57–59.

37. *The Statesman* (New Delhi, India), June 11, 1959.

38. See L. L. Kato, "Re-Thinking Anti-Witchcraft Legislation in East Africa," University of East Africa, University Social Sciences Council Conference, Makerere University, Kampala, December 30, 1968–January 3, 1969. See also Alan Milner, Ed., *African Penal Systems* (London: Routledge & Kegan Paul, 1969), p. 96, and R. E. S. Tanner, *The Witch Murders in Sukumaland—A Sociological Commentary. Crime in Africa Series No. 4,* Scandinavian Institute of African Studies, Uppsala, 1970.

39. Ute Luig, "Accusations of Sorcery as Reflections of Social Problems in an Urban Community: A Case Study," in *Studies of Kampala* (unpublished study).

40. Juan Manuel Mayorca, *Criminologia,* Vol. 2 (Caracas: Graficas Edición de Ante, 1971), p. 155.

41. Southall and Gutkind, *Townsmen in the Making: Kampala and Its Suburbs,* p. 25.

42. Marshall B. Clinard, "White-Collar Crime," *International Encyclopedia of the Social Sciences* (New York: Macmillan, 1968), I, pp. 483–490, and Gilbert Geis, Ed., *White Collar Crime* (New York: Atherton 1968).

43. Carlos Bernardo Klein, "Delito Economico y Desarrollo Economico," *Revista del Instituto de Investigaciones y Docencia Criminologicas,* 8:129–150 (1963–1964).

44. "Causation," *Prevention of Types of Criminality Resulting from Social Changes and Accompanying Economic Development in Less Developed Countries,* A/Conf.

17/3, p. 83. In the light of this statement it is interesting, for example, that at the Fourth United Nations Congress on the Prevention of Crime and the Treatment of Delinquency in 1970, in which the discussion centered on developing countries, almost nothing was said about corruption or white collar crime.

45. Samuel P. Huntington, "Modernization and Corruption," in Arnold J. Heidenheimer, *Political Corruption: Readings in Comparative Analysis* (New York: Holt, Rinehart & Winston, 1970), p. 492.

46. Gunnar Myrdal, "Corruption as a Hindrance to Modernization in South Asia," in Heidenheimer, *Political Corruption*, p. 233.

47. John B. Monteiro, *Corruption: Control and Maladministration* (Bombay: P. C. Manaktla and Sons, 1966), p. 53.

48. René Dumont, *False Start in Africa* (London: Sphere Books, 1966), pp. 72–73.

49. See in particular Ronald Wraith and Edgar Simpkins, *Corruption in Developing Countries* (London: Allen and Unwin, 1953), Heidenheimer, *Political Corruption*, 1970, S. Dwivedy and G. S. Bhargava, *Political Corruption in India* (New Delhi: Popular Book Services, 1967), and Orofre D. Corpuz, *The Philippines* (Englewood Cliffs, N.J.: Prentice-Hall, 1965). See also Lucien M. Hanks, "Corruption and Commerce in Southeast Asia," *Trans-Action*, 8:18–26 (May 1971).

50. Manuel López-Rey, *Crime: An Analytical Appraisal* (New York: Praeger, 1970), p. 193.

51. Willard A. Hanna, *A Primer of Korupsi*, Fieldstaff Reports, Southeast Asia Series, Vol. xix, August 1971, p. 1.

52. *Ibid.*, pp. 6–7.

53. Frank C. Ferrier, "Considérations Sur Certains Problèmes Politiques de l'Afrique Occidentale," in *L'Afrique Occidentale: Développment et Société*, Centre International de Criminologie Comparée, Université de Montréal, 1972, p. 120.

54. Stanislav Andreski, "Kleptocracy as a System of Government in Africa," in Heidenheimer, *Political Corruption*, p. 348. See also Andreski, *The African Predicament* (New York: Atherton, 1968), p. 95.

55. J. David Greenstone, "Corruption and Self-Interest in Kampala and Nairobi," in Heidenheimer, *Political Corruption*, pp. 459–469. This may be the result in East Africa of a conflict between the economic power of the Asians and the Europeans and the political power of the Africans.

56. "In West Africa, Payoff is Way of Life," *The New York Times*, February 29, 1972.

57. Andreski, *The African Predicament*, p. 95.

58. *Ibid.;* the quoted excerpts appear on the pages indicated in the following quotations.

59. It is a common practice in Latin America, particularly in Bolivia and Mexico, for police to collect traffic fines at the place of infraction. This money frequently does not make its way into official police funds.

60. Abraham Kiapi, "Legal Control of Official Corruption in East Africa," University of East Africa Social Science Council Conference, Kampala, Uganda, December 1968, p. 9.

61. Myrdal, in Heidenheimer, *Political Corruption*, p. 238.

62. Andreski, *The African Predicament*, p. 352. See also similar accounts about West African countries, particularly Nigeria, in Ronald Wraith and Edgar Simpkins, *Corruption in Developing Countries* (London: Allen & Unwin, 1963).

63. López-Rey, *Crime*, p. 194.

64. Colin Leys, "New States and the Concept of Corruption," in Heidenheimer, *Political Corruption*, p. 342.

65. Dumont, "Remuneration Levels and Corruption in French-Speaking Africa," in Heidenheimer, *Political Corruption*, p. 455.

66. Albert Ravenholt, "The Peso Price of Politics in the Philippines," in Heidenheimer, *Political Corruption*, pp. 469–479.

67. Hanna, *A Primer of Korupsi*, p. 5.

68. Myrdal, in Heidenheimer, *Political Corruption*,

69. Hanna, *A Primer of Korupsi*, p. 7.

70. *Ibid.* p. 3.

71. Myrdal, "Corruption as a Hindrance to Modernization in South Asia," in Heidenheimer, *Political Corruption*, p. 236.

72. Andreski, *The African Predicament*, p. 109.

73. Quoted in Myrdal "Corruption: Its Causes and Effects," in Heidenheimer, *Political Corruption*, p. 541.

74. Wraith and Simpkins, *Corruption in Developing Countries*, p. 13.

75. Myrdal, "Corruption as a Hindrance to Modernization in South Asia," in Heidenheimer, *Political Corruption*, p. 239.

76. Nathaniel H. Leff, "Economic Development through Bureaucratic Corruption," *American Behavioral Scientist*, 8:8–14 (November 1964) and J. S. Nye, "Corruption and Political Development: A Cost-Benefit Analysis," *American Political Science Review*, 61:417–427 (June 1967).

77. Hanna, *A Primer of Korupsi*, p. 5.

78. David H. Bayley, "The Effects of Corruption in a Developing Nation," in Heidenheimer, *Political Corruption*, pp. 528–531.

79. South Africa might also be included as a developed country, although this would not apply to the large African majority, and it is partly for this reason that the United Nations calculates separate rates for each ethnic group.

80. Alfonso Quiroz Cuaron, "Crime in the Republic of Mexico and the Social Cost of Homicide," *Derecho Penal Contemporaneo*, 29:73–94 (1968). The author estimated the annual social cost of homicide at 34,376 million pesos.

81. Veli Verkko, *Homicides and Suicides in Finland and Their Dependence on National Character* (Copenhagen: G. E. C. Gads Forlag, 1951): Jacqueline and Murray Straus, "Suicide, Homicide, and Social Structure in Ceylon," *American Journal of Sociology*, 58:461–469 (March 1953); Arthur Wood, "Murder, Suicide, and Economic Crime in Ceylon," *American Sociological Review*, 26:744–753 (October 1961). One study found that in general homicide is associated with the degree of urban and industrial development of a country, although there are exceptions. See also Richard Quinney, "Suicide, Homicide, and Economic Development," *Social Forces*, 43:401–406 (March 1965).

82. German Guzman Campos, Orlando Fals Borda, and Eduardo Umana Luna, *La Violencia en Colombia, Estudio de un Proceso-Social, Tomo Primo* (Bogota: Ediciones Tercer Mundo, 2nd ed., 1962), and Wolfgang and Ferracuti, *The Subculture of Violence*, pp. 275–279. See also Pedro Nel Rueda Uriba, "Le Banditisme et La Violence en Colombie," *Revue Internationale de Criminologie et de Police Technique*, 20:117–127 (1966).

83. Jaime Toro-Calder, "Personal Crimes in Puerto Rico," unpublished M. A. thesis, University of Wisconsin, Madison, 1950.

84. Marcos A. Herrera, "El Visteo (Simulated Combat)." *Revista, Del Instituto de Investigaciones Y Docencia Criminologicas,* 9:85–92 (1965–1966); Toro-Calder, "Personal Crimes in Puerto Rico," 1950.

85. Toro-Calder, "Personal Crime in Puerto Rico," p. 121. In his analysis of life in Puerto Rican slums Oscar Lewis described how the women quite frequently carried razor blades in their hair. Oscar Lewis, *La Vida: A Puerto Rican Family in the Culture of Poverty—San Juan and New York* (New York: Random House, 1966).

86. William Clifford, "Notes and Criticisms: Delinquency in Cyprus," *British Journal of Delinquency,* 5:149 (October 1954). A somewhat similar social explanation has been found in a study of homicide in Sardinia. See Franco Ferracuti, Renato Lazzari, and Marvin E. Wolfgang, Eds., V*iolence in Sardinia* (Rome: Mario Bulzoni, 1970).

87. Toro-Calder, "Personal Crimes in Puerto Rico," 1950, and Musa T. Mushanga, "Criminal Homicide in Western Uganda: A Sociological Study of Violent Deaths in Ankole, Kigezi, and Toro Districts of Western Uganda," unpublished M.A. thesis, Makerere University, Kampala, Uganda, 1970, pp. 24–25.

88. Wolfgang and Ferracuti, *The Subculture of Violence,* p. 280.

89. Nino Galvan, *Epidemiological Del Homicidio en Mexico,* 1965.

90. S. Venugopal Rao, *Murder: A Pilot Study with Particular Reference to the City of Delhi* (New Delhi: Government of India, 1968), p. 12.

91. Edwin P. Driver, "Interaction and Criminal Homicide in India," *Social Forces,* 40:153–158 (December 1961).

92. Ram Ahuja, *Female Offenders in India* (Meerut: Menanakshi Prakashan, 1969), p. 122.

93. *Ibid.,* p. 123.

94. Arthur L. Wood, "Crime and Aggression in Changing Ceylon," *Transactions of the American Philosophical Society,* 51, Part B (December 1961), Homicide in Ceylon is about three times greater than the median for those countries that publish such information, being about equal to that of the United States. See also J. H. Straus and M. A. Straus, "Suicide, Homicide and Social Structure in Ceylon," *American Journal of Sociology* 58:461–469 (1953), and C. H. S. Jayewardene, "Criminal Homicide: A Study in Culture Conflict," unpublished Ph.D. dissertation, University of Pennsylvania, 1960.

95. Mushanga "Criminal Homicide in Western Uganda," 1970.

96. *Ibid.,* p. 60.

97. *Ibid.,* p. 63.

98. Paul Bohannan, *African Homicide and Suicide* (Princeton: Princeton University Press, 1960).

99. Carolyn F. Lobban, "An Analysis of Homicide in an Afro-Arab State: Cases from the Democratic Republic of Sudan," Paper presented at African Studies Association Meeting, Philadelphia, Pennsylvania, November 1972.

100. Saied Ewies, "A Comparative Study of Two Delinquency Areas: Roxbury of Boston, Massachusetts and Boulac of Cairo, UAR," *The National Review of Criminal Science* (U.A.R.), 2:1–15 (November 1959).

101. Carl O. Chambers and Gordon H. Barker, "Juvenile Delinquency in Iraq," *British Journal of Criminology*, 11:176–182 (April 1971).

102. Secretariat of the United Nations, "Prostitution in Selected Countries of Asia and the Far East," *International Review of Criminal Policy*, 16:47 (October 1958).

103. For a discussion of prostitution in London of the 1880's and its relation to the more rigid sex code of the day, see Albert Fried and Richard M. Elman, Eds., *Charles Booth's London* (New York: Pantheon, 1968), pp. 124–133.

104. Sean O'Callaghan, *The Yellow Slave Trade: A Survey of the Traffic in Women and Children in the East* (London: Anthony Blond, 1968).

105. See, for example, prostitution in the favelas of Rio de Janeiro, *Child of the Dark: The Diary of Carolina Maria De Jesus*, translated by David St. Clair (New York: Dutton, 1962), and the slums of San Juan, Puerto Rico, Oscar Lewis, *La Vida: A Puerto Rican Family in the Culture of Poverty—San Juan and New York* (New York: Random House, 1965).

106. Victor D. Du Bois, *Prostitution in the Ivory Coast*, Fieldstaff Reports, West Africa Series Ivory Coast, X, No. 2, 1967, p. 1.

107. *Ibid.*, p. 8.

108. S. Kirson Weinberg, "Female Delinquency in Ghana, West Africa: A Comparative Analysis," *International Journal of the Sociology of the Family* (March, 1973).

109. See, for example, Sean O'Callaghan, *Damaged Baggage: The White Slave Trade and Narcotics Trafficking in the Americas* (London: Robert Hale, 1969), and O'Callaghan, *The Yellow Slave Trade*, 1968.

110. Samir Khalaf, *Prostitution in a Changing Society: A Sociological Survey of Legal Prostitution in Beirut* (Beirut: Khayats, 1965), p. 97.

111. *Study on Traffic in Persons and Prostitution* (New York: United Nations Department of Economic and Social Affairs, 1959). See also *International Review of Criminal Policy*, Volume 13 (1958), the entire issue of which is devoted to the problem of prostitution.

112. Du Bois, *Prostitution in the Ivory Coast*, p. 4.

113. *Ibid.*, pp. 6–7.

114. S. D. Punekar and Kamala Rao, *A Study of Prostitutes in Bombay* (Bombay: Lalvani, 1967), pp. 1–4. These girls were not the only prostitutes, since courtesans were also available.

115. *Ibid.*, p. 179.

116. James H. Bryan, "Apprenticeships in Prostitution," *Social Problems*, 12:287–297 (1965).

117. A. S. Mathur and B. L. Gupta, *Prostitutes and Prostitution* (Agra: Ram Prasad, 1965), pp. 136–142 and Appendix B.

118. Punekar and Rao, *A Study of Prostitution in Bombay*, p. 11.

119. Bela Dutt Gupta, *Contemporary Social Problems in India* (Calcutta: Vidyodaya Library Private, 1964), pp. 87–88 and 104–106.

120. Punekar and Rao, *A Study of Prostitutes in Bombay*.

121. *Ibid.*, pp. 181–182.

122. Edwin D. Driver, "Interaction and Criminal Homicide in India," *Social Forces*, **40**:153–158 (1961).

123. Jyotsna H. Shah, "Causes and Prevention of Suicide," paper read at the Indian Conference of Social Work, Hyderabad, December 1959.

124. Punekar and Rao, *A Study of Prostitutes in Bombay*, pp. 182–183.

125. Mathur and Gupta, *Prostitutes and Prostitution*, pp. 35–38.

126. *Ibid.*, p. 36.

127. Khalaf, *Prostitution in a Changing Society*.

128. *Ibid.*, p. 98.

Chapter 3 Urbanization and Crime

Rising crime rates in developing countries are commonly thought of as resulting from social change, particularly rapid social change. This concept is too broad and there is little evidence to support such a relationship. Rather, crime is related to the complexity of developments associated with the world-wide processes of industrialization and consequent urbanization, in which characteristic village life is being replaced by urban living. It is estimated that by 1980 the world's population will total 4300 million and slightly fewer than 1800 million will live in urban areas. Of this total it has been predicted that the population of the developing countries will reach 3100 million, of which 930 million will constitute the urban population [1]. The urban population of less developed countries between 1950 and 1970 increased by 139%, jumping from 284 million to 678 million [2]. In India, often regarded as a nation of villages, the 17.8% living in cities of 20,000 or more in 1961 constituted a larger number of persons than the total population of most countries, a total of more than 75 million urban persons [3]. India had 77 cities with 100,000 or more persons in 1951; in 1961 there were 121.

Because of their greater population growth, the developing countries present a much higher potential for urbanization than the developed countries. The United Nations reports that 85.7% of the world's population growth between 1970 and 2000 will take place in the four less developed major areas: Latin America, Africa, East Asia, and South Asia [4]. It is this large-scale total population increase, primarily in the rural areas, that accounts basically for the increase in the urban population.

This added population must lodge somewhere—if not in the countryside, then in the cities. It is actually lodging in both, and as a consequence squatters by the hundreds of thousands are found not only in the cities but also in the rural areas [5].

China, for example, will have to absorb an average of 6.8 million urban dwellers per year during the next 15 years; India, 6.3 million; Brazil, 3.2 million; Mexico, 1.8 million; Pakistan, 1.4 million; and Indonesia, 1.3 million per year [6]. Not all the increase in urban areas can be attributed directly to migration from the rural setting; slightly less than half is contributed by the urban population's own natural increase [7].

DIFFERENCES BETWEEN URBANIZATION IN LESS DEVELOPED AND DEVELOPED COUNTRIES

It is important to recognize that large cities have existed for thousands of years and others for centuries in many developing countries such as India, the Middle East, and parts of West Africa. On the whole, they were different from the city of today, as Sjoberg has pointed out [8]. They were what he has called "pre-industrial cities." They had no forms of rapid or extensive communication and transportation nor did they have the means of distribution and preservation of food which modern inventions have made possible. Consequently, these cities, although large, tended actually to be clusters of villages. Urban populations were much more permanent and settled than they are today, and there was less migration into the cities from the rural areas. Because of this and because of the absence of media of mass communication as we know it today, there appears to have been less impersonality in social relations. Many parts of West Africa, for example, had long been urbanized, but actually the cities were large groups of clans, and many of the people living there were actually farmers by occupation [9]. This situation was quite different from that existing in the newer cities today, which have actually developed quite rapidly.

Marked differences are found between the economic growth process in the less developed countries and that characterizing the more advanced nations, differences that have had a marked effect on the course of their urbanization [10]. As the literature shows, the correlation between economic growth and urbanization in the developing countries will not necessarily be the same as in developed countries. Although there clearly are common underlying tendencies, the urbanization of developing countries is proceeding more rapidly than did the developed countries. Consequently the extent of the problems in large urban population concentrations, without the adequate national economic bases for employment and rising standards of urban living characteristic of the less developed countries, is often referred to as "overurbanization." According to this viewpoint, industrialization and the rate of economic development have failed to keep pace with urbanization, urban unemployment is extensive, and housing and services inadequate [11]. These factors have significantly affected the growth of crime in urban areas.

"Overurbanization" has been reflected, to take one example, in the constantly increasing degree of concentration of the population in metropolitan Manila. From 220,000 in 1903 the population of Manila proper had soared 500% to 1.1 million by 1960; in the same period the population of the metropolitan area reached 2.1 million. The Institute of Planning of the University of the Philippines predicts a metropolitan population of 5.9 million by 1980 and 11.7 million by the year 2000. Although this large influx of people strains housing, transportation, and welfare facilities, it also represents an available labor pool for commerce and industry. Unfortunately this labor force is largely unskilled and poorly educated. The result is unemployment as well as underemployment, in which three, four, or five men divide a task that could be done by one. Industrial plants are so glutted with employees that many people have gone into service trades, in which they operate food, drink, or cigarette stands, tiny shops, beauty parlors, watch-your-car services, and buy and sell shops, all a far cry from the advertising, banking, and sales that dominate industrialized societies. As a consequence of overurbanization, the major cities of the Philippines, but especially Manila, have been harassed by urban squatters. The national government has been unable to develop a consistent policy toward squatter encroachments on public and private property. Those who live in slum and squatter conditions in Manila constitute more than 30% of the region's population. In the 20-year period from 1948 to 1968 the squatter population multiplied 33-fold, from 23,000 to 767,000 [12].

By 1980, according to a United Nations study, it is estimated that the population of less developed areas will have increased by 645 million rural and 418 million urban inhabitants from the 1960 population [13]. Of this increase, 259 million will be in large cities. This tendency for urban populations to become concentrated in large cities, so characteristic of the more developed countries, is greater in the less developed. It is estimated that the proportion of the population in the cities of developing countries with 100,000 or more increased 83% between 1950 and 1970, compared with 35% in the developed [14]. The proportion in cities of a million or more increased 136% in the less developed and 47% in the developed. In 1960 Latin America had nine cities with more than a million inhabitants, in 1970 there were 15 in this category, and in 1980 it is estimated there will be 26. The number living in cities in 1970, however, was much lower; an urban 26% in less developed, compared with 69% in the developed, 16% compared with 44% in cities of 100,000 or more, and 8% compared with 22% in cities of a million or more [15]. In 1968 there were 153 metropolitan areas in the world with a million or

more inhabitants, 66, or 43.7%, in developing countries: China alone had
18, other Asian countries, 27, Latin America, 16, and Africa, 5 [16].
Among these 153 metropolitan areas 18 had 5 million or more inhabitants; 8 or 44.4%, were in developing countries—one in China, two in
Asia (both in India), one in Africa, and four in Latin America.

The largest or "primate" cities of less developed countries have been
growing at a phenomenal rate. African cities like Addis Ababa, Accra,
Dakar, Abidjan, Nairobi, Kampala, and Kinshasa have doubled or even
trebled in size during the last 10 years. Within the last 20 years the 10
largest cities of India have doubled in population; the population of
Bombay, for example, increased by 70% between 1950 and 1960. Greater
Djakarta grew from 533,000 in 1930 to more than 5 million in 1970.
Naturally this concentration of population and services presents an acute
problem in the developing countries [17]. Abidjan, capital of the Ivory
Coast, provides an example of the tendency of the population, through
migration, to become concentrated in the primate city. In 1940 Abidjan
had 20,000 inhabitants, in 1960, 250,000, and in 1970, 500,000, and is
growing at the rate of 50,000, or 9.5%, a year. By 1975 Abidjan will have
a population of 800,000 and by 1980 more than a million. Du Bois has
described some of the effects of this growth of the primate city:

> An inevitable corrollary of Abidjan's rapid growth as a city has been its
> extraordinary dominance over the country. Like Paris, it is a gigantic magnet,
> drawing in an inordinate share of the country's wealth, people, and talent to
> the detriment of the rest of the nation. As of 1967, 69 percent of all business
> establishments were located in Abidjan, and 85 percent of all salaried workers
> in the country were concentrated there. Because it is both the nation's capital
> and its main port, virtually all of the country's principal business enterprises
> have the major part of their physical installations as well as their headquarters
> in the Abidjan area. Understandably, factories seek to establish themselves here
> because of the port, the availability of storage facilities, and the proximity to
> their sources of supply. Commercial enterprises naturally follow suit, as the in-
> dustrial enterprises which are their principal clients are located in the area [18].

The government of the Ivory Coast is aware of the dangers that such
overcentralization presents: an impetus to an uncontrolled influx from
the rural areas; overcrowded housing conditions; a growing number of
unemployed roaming the streets; an overtaxing of such public facilities
as schools, hospitals, the transportation system; and a rise in the incidence
of delinquency and crime [19]. To offest this overcentralization the government has in recent years taken steps to encourage the establishment of
business and industry in other parts of the country by extending credit
facilities and generous tax advantages to firms willing to establish themselves there. At the same time, it has taken imaginative and energetic

steps to deal with the problems of the rural exodus by improving the living conditions of the people in the interior.

Thus the cities of developing countries, particularly the large primate cities, greatly exceed in importance the proportion of their populations in the total economic, political, and cultural structure of the country. Hoselitz argues that full economic development requires an urbanized environment that will provide, as many cities do, new influences in otherwise tradition-bound societies [20]. Cities are the main gateway toward modernization of a developing country in both technology and the adoption of new practices. Developing countries are frequently judged by the physical and social conditions of their cities, in which the core of their commercial and industrial power and their transportation, distribution, and communication systems lie. The urban man is probably more likely to be the "modern" man [21]. One writer has stated, with reference to Uganda, that "the towns, and especially the national capital, bring together the people of different tribal and language backgrounds and help to produce the more cosmopolitan relations necessary to support a modern nation" [22]. Since they are the point of contact between modernizing influences and African traditions, the cities are "islands of modernization within large areas of traditional culture" [23]. In this sense all cities contribute to nation building because of the "liberating influence of urbanism" [24]. City people are more likely to be more receptive to social change, exposed as they are to a heterogeneous population and seeing as they do the great contrasts between wealth and poverty, between wants that have been stimulated and left unsatisfied, and between what is and what can or should be:

Cities all over the world exhibit the sharp contrasts between the living conditions in well-to-do districts and poor districts. In the developing countries these contrasts are more dramatic. As the criteria for urban construction are established by government, controlled by a small minority not sharing the poverty of the masses, the visible expression is one of unrealistic programs of public and private constructions contrasting with the neglect of social programs [25].

Sprawling slums may stand adjacent to a modern complex of office buildings, dramatizing more vividly potential alternatives to the squalid existence of the slum dweller.

CONCENTRATION OF CRIME IN URBAN AREAS

Delinquency and crime rates are always lower in rural than in urban areas in developed countries and a similar situation exists in the developing [26]. In fact, the increase in crime in less developed countries can be misleading in the sense that it involves a relatively small proportion of the country's total population which is concentrated in urban areas and only in certain parts of them. After studying the urbanization process in Denmark, Christiansen concluded that it could be predicted that countries in which the process of industrialization and urbanization continues, which holds true in most if not all the countries of the world, must expect further increases in crime and delinquency [27].

In the Middle East, Latin America, and Africa pronounced differences have been found between the urban and rural areas in the incidence of crime and delinquency [28]. Clifford has pointed out that juvenile delinquency in Africa south of the Sahara is distinctly an urban problem, as one would expect [29]. An official report in India observed that juvenile crime in an acute form is confined to the cities and, to some extent, the larger towns in which there has been economic distress. It is not a problem of rural areas [30]. United Nations' sponsored studies of juvenile delinquency in India, the United Arab Republic, and Zambia concluded that in all three a high correlation existed between urbanization and official rates for juvenile delinquency [31]. Even if these figures somewhat exaggerate the exact proportion of crime in a country's rural and urban areas, the fact is that the problems of law enforcement and its facilities are concentrated in the cities. Some of this difference may be due to this concentration, but it cannot in itself account for the major difference.

Juvenile delinquency is heavily concentrated in the urban sectors of Puerto Rico [32], and, according to statistical data for several industrial areas in Mexico, juvenile delinquency is related to industrialization and urban growth [33]. In Morocco, as early as 1953–1956, juvenile delinquency, as measured by official reports, was an urban phenomenon [34]. Although only 30% of the country's population lived in urban areas, these areas accounted for 50.7% of the delinquent cases. In Tunis crime is primarily an urban phenomenon; industrialization seems to have led to urbanization and to favor rural exodus, and it is possible to see in this an important factor in criminality [35]. A study of 15,229 criminal cases in Algeria for the years 1966–1967 revealed that 45% had an urban background and 35%, a rural background (20% were unknown); the rural population represented two-thirds of the total population, which meant that criminality was more related to urban areas [36]. In 1966 the districts covered by Cairo and Alexandria accounted for 66.4% of all reported juvenile delinquency cases and 35% of juvenile felonies in the United Arab Republic, whereas in 1961 these two areas represented only 19% of the population [37]. This report concluded that the juvenile delinquency problem remains an urban one; that is, "any attention devoted to it on the levels of prevention and treatment must be directed to the urban sectors of the society of the United Arab Republic" [38]. In Iraq in 1966 9 out of 10 convicted juvenile offenders came from urban areas [39].

Delinquency and crime are not only unduly concentrated in the urban areas of any country but mainly in the largest of these cities, for crime rates tend to vary directly with city size. In the United States, for example, robbery rates are generally more than 20 times greater in the larger cities than in the smaller. Similarly, in the less developed countries cities like Bombay, Calcutta, Bangkok, Seoul, Manila, Caracas, Bogota, Mexico City, Cairo, Lagos, Accra, Abidjan, Kampala, and Nairobi have a much larger share of delinquency and crime than their percentages of population would warrant. In India the rates of reported serious crimes during 1964–1966 in the eight major cities were considerably higher than those of the respective states in which they are located [40], much of which was accounted for by the appreciably higher rates of theft and the slightly higher rates of burglary and robbery. In Korea in 1965 the city of Seoul alone, which reported 62,860 crimes during the year, accounted for 45% of the total for the entire country [41]. Although Beirut in 1965 contained approximately 27% of the total population of Lebanon, 40% of all apprehended cases of juvenile delinquency came from Beirut [42].

It has been estimated as far back as 1954 that in Ghana the total number of cases of juvenile delinquency in the principal towns of Accra, Sekondi-Takoradi, and Kumasi exceed that of the rest of the country [43]. Such delinquency consisted of "prostitution and all that goes with it, 'pimps and zoot boys,' gangsterism, vagrancy and vandalism and offenses against persons and property" [44]. In Zambia, in which nearly all crime is based on property offenses, a disproportionate amount is committed in the three largest cities. Crime rates appear to be increasing at a much more rapid rate in cities, and juvenile crime is generally considered to be related to the size and complexity of urban development, industrialization, and commercialization [45]. In Niger "social problems are numerous in the cities, in particular alcoholism, the use of drugs, juvenile delinquency, etc." [46]. The increased pattern of crime in Mexico City, as contrasted with a village and smaller town, has also been demonstrated [47]. Another study in Mexico found that juvenile delinquency seldom occurs outside the large cities. Thus such formal agencies as the courts are not needed, since family and community controls are effective [48]. About crime in Manila in 1971 one report stated:

While the total volume of crime in the nation increased by 20 percent between 1962 and 1966, the Philippine crime problem has been overstated as a general nation-wide crisis. The crisis seems limited to the Manila area by virtue of its characteristics as a primate city. Incidence of crimes committed in Metropolitan Manila per 100,000 between the given years above as contrasted with the rest of the country is 60 times more for all crimes and 32 times more for index crimes—i.e., crimes which belong to the category of offenses which are usually reported and are of sufficient importance to be significant (murder, homicide, robbery, rape, theft, and physical injuries) [49].

This situation could well have been anticipated from the experiences of developed countries like the United States, where rates for reported burglary are generally two and a half times greater in urban areas than in the rural areas, larceny more than three times greater, and robbery 10 times greater. Studies of crime in France and Belgium by Szabo and in Japan and other places have shown similar marked differences [50].

AGE AND URBAN CRIME

Young males commit most of the crimes throughout the world, and the population of less developed countries consists primarily of the young. As a country outgrows its traditionalism and responds to outside influences and forces inherent in modernization, industrialization, and urban population concentration, its youth are particularly affected. They are the ones who are being arrested, brought before the courts, placed on probation, and committed to institutions. The young who are native to Dakar, for example, are delinquent much younger than those living in the rural areas. Among rural youth juvenile delinquency appears at a much later age but it increases with age.

The young people reject dependence on their families, the schools favor their emancipation, also the mass media, and of the former social systems, almost nothing remains. Traditional rites of coming into manhood have gone, special celebrations are disappearing in importance. Celebrations no longer have the same fullness, . . . and they are now passing to the individual experiences without preparation [51].

In some African countries south of the Sahara 40% of the total population are under 15 years of age and more than 60% are under 21. In Zaïre some 60% of the population are under 25, and between one-third and one-half of the urban population are under 15. Moreover, as in many African countries, the national increase is estimated at 2.5 to 3% per annum, which doubles the population in 30 years and thus further increases the proportion of youth in the population. In a study of juvenile delinquency in Lebanon it was emphasized that the number of young people in the total population was significant; slightly more than 50% were less than 20 years old and about 22% were between 12 and 20 [52].

The urban populations of less developed countries are even younger in composition than the national population, for it is the young who migrate to the cities. In many cities of Africa few old persons are to be seen; one must go to the villages to find them. In some African cities more than 80% of the population are under the age of 40; in Kampala in 1969, for example, 47% were under 20 and 82%, under 45. In many cities, as in Africa, the population could be characterized as consisting of a dominant youth culture in which the older age groups are the minority.

There are some indications that motivations for youth crimes may be somewhat different in the developed and the less developed countries. In the former the behavior of the young may be a product of affluence, with little to challenge them under urban conditions and relatively little pressure on them to work. Long years of schooling may separate them from adults and from any chance of playing a substantive role in society. In the slums of affluent societies the impact of a separate youth culture may have serious consequences. On the other hand, in the less developed and developing countries the impact of urban life on village migrants, detribalization and loss of other ties, and a widespread slum way of life with its often deviant norms and standards on migrants may have great effect on youthful criminality.

URBAN LIFE AND CRIME

As the cities of less developed countries have grown, a new way of life has developed, different from that of the village and similar to that of urban areas in developed countries. This view of large cities in less developed countries today is quite different from the one claimed by Sjoberg [53]. The urban way of life is characterized by extensive conflicts of norms and values, rapid social change, increased mobility of the population, emphasis on material goods and individualism, and an increase in the use of formal rather than informal social controls. This characterization of the city as a way of life developed from sociological studies of Chicago [54]. Epstein studied urbanization and social change in Africa, but although he recognized the existence of personal contacts which involve urban Africans in a network of social relations, he concluded that the towns of modern Africa

satisfy the criteria of Wirth's definition of the city, and there is much in his analysis which has an immediate relevance to African urbanism. Indeed, many of those who have written of the African towns in terms of their poverty, the breakdown of family life, the rise of prostitution, juvenile delinquency and crime, and the problems of psychic maladjustment are describing the phenomena that are fully accounted for in Wirth's theory [55].

This approach has also been recognized in various United Nations reports, one of which stated that urbanization

connotes all kinds of change, in patterns of population distribution, in work habits, housing, leisure pursuits, transactions with widening circles of people and myriad opportunities for crime; it also means a greater complexity of life, impersonality of relationships, subcultures and less immediate controls of behavior. It implies more opportunities for crime with less risk of detection and a disturbing juxtaposition of affluence and poverty [56].

Weinberg reported that processes of urbanization in Ghana affected the central city, the villages from which the people emigrated, and the villages adjacent to the cities. "These changes create conditions which contribute to delinquency" [57]. Bergalli has pointed out in his survey of crime in Latin America that urbanization facilitates rapid expansion in transportation and communication which greatly increases the possibilities of encountering norms that contradict those enforced by the government [58].

Heterogeneity is a striking characteristic of large cities in the less developed countries and naturally brings exposure to a great diversity of norms and values. Like the great cities of the developed countries, exposure to many types of behavior is constant. The following two passages indicate the nature of this great diversity in Delhi, India, and an African city:

Everywhere streets are packed with men dressed in every conceivable costume and headdress from pajamas and *dhotis* of *khadi* to immaculate Western dress; great varieties in height, skin color, eye structure, and facial features reflect the myriad races and ethnic groups left over from the Mongol, Persian, Afghan, and other invasions; in front of small shops selling silver and gold jewelry, cloth, and other objects fat merchants sit cross-legged waiting for haggling customers, their short-sleeved, collarless, long white shirts hanging out; large billboards and sign carriers advertise garish and romantic scenes from the latest Indian movies; the continual squeaking of old-fashioned rubber bulbs serve motorcycle rickshaws and other taxis as horns; horse-driven tongas clatter and whips crack against tired horses pulling excessive loads; and trucks and slow, patient bullocks, the "trucks" of the East, move along in the dense traffic. In the midst of this general confusion, Delhi's huge and dense slum population lives among a squalid chaos of tenements, hovels, shacks, and bazaar stalls scattered through narrow congested streets, alleys and lanes. . . . Slum neighborhoods accommodate increasing mixtures of castes, occupations, and regional origins. Although members of a homogeneous group may live in close proximity and may even predominate in a certain area, housing pressures make it more and more difficult for large numbers of people with similar social characteristics to form exclusive groups [59].

One of the most noticeable features of both African peri-urban areas and African areas inside the towns is the high degree of tribal mixture in the population. It is not unusual to find from twenty to forty different tribes represented in such urban areas, the residents of which are thrown together without regard to their varied cultural backgrounds. Their great heterogeneity contributes substantially to a peculiar type of congestion, the formation of tribal settlements—little pockets of intense over-crowding where members of the same tribe live and find comfort in one another's presence in an otherwise alien environment [60].

In addition to heterogeneity the city simultaneously presents great opportunities for impersonality and anonymity. Although various degrees of intimacy in the local community and in the work place do exist, in the larger city persons experience many impersonal relations in which their identities are not recognized. The teeming streets of large cities, filled with strangers, the numerous impersonal contacts on the way to work or to shop, and the mingling with large crowds at certain citywide events are far different from those of the village. Strangers are almost unrecognizable in the constant flow of people with whom any form of communication may be thwarted by language barriers. When asked whether people in Kampala stole from their own tribe or community, one informant said, "it is hard to tell whether those who steal are of one's own community." This severely weakens the social control mechanisms provided by family and interlocking patterns of friends in the rural home. Within a short distance a youth may enter an environment in which he is completely unknown, and methods of social control such as rumor or gossip become ineffective because information channels seldom exist. The role of this impersonality in crime was shown, for example, in a study of juvenile delinquency in Ghana in which it was found that although sex offenses are rigidly forbidden by native custom and therefore occur infrequently, petty theft from persons outside the tribe and especially from Europeans is regarded as "fair game" and arouses little resultant public resentment [61]. One informant in a Kampala slum stated: "It is a very nice thing if a migrant steals from a rich person in Kampala and when he goes home and shows his money to his parents they congratulate him on this and allow him to keep this money."

Some writers, however, in particular those concerned with urban Latin America, maintain that urban life for migrants does not differ essentially from that of the villages from which they came. This myth of the essential ruralness of the squatter slums or favelas of Rio de Janeiro and the barriadas of Lima has been adequately and effectively disposed of by several studies which probably have application far beyond the cities of Latin America [62]. These researchers have challenged the view that slums are isolated, "quasi-village" settlements, that the residents are unfamiliar with urban institutions, that they are not integrated into urban society, and that many migrants have never lived in small urban areas or had quasi-urban experiences in small towns when visiting or selling produce [63]. Among the favelas of Rio de Janeiro a considerable proportion (51.4%) were born in the city, most are under 19, but nearly one-fourth are in the age group 20 to 49. This means that those who migrate do so to an urban center and find a setting in which there is a permanent core of native urbanites who are long-term residents of the favela and around whom later migrants aggregate [64]. The presence of urban values is seen in the generalized preference for the city among the men and some women. It is forward, not backward, in orientation. The city offers a job market, with some possibilities of upward mobility. Greater freedom can be had in the choice and permanency of relationships with the opposite sex, fewer formalities, and greater opportunities for circumventing traditional bonds and finding structural situations and social enclaves in which such "freedom both from and to" can be enjoyed [65]. More educational opportunities are possible in urban areas, more agencies are available for health and other services, new forms of social entertainment and greater freedom of behavior, are provided, and, finally, there is the free use of urban language which is "rich, funny, ironic, allusive, and largely incomprehensible to outsiders" [66].

Cities of developing countries offer far greater opportunities for theft; in the villages there is often little to steal except agricultural products. Moreover, opportunities are greater for stealing from strangers with a minimum of detection; in the village anonymity can seldom be assured. Consequently the difference between rural and urban crimes against property is generally greater than between crimes against persons. This was found to be true in Venezuela; for example, the conversion of Caracas from a provincial center to a large urban area brought about a change in the nature of the city's criminality [67]. Property crimes became the major recorded offense. Property crime in Ceylon is also associated with urbanization. The urban environment offers means of transportation, the possibility of collaboration with other offenders, fences for the disposition of stolen goods, and protection from interference by law enforcement officials, all of which are difficult to find in a village setting [68]. Urbanization also fosters a concern for material objects simply because all kinds of material goods are more and more in evidence. As young males become transformed from family members into adult citizens, their status is gradually related to their degree of success [69]. Generally this status is measured in terms of their acquisition of material objects [70].

When criminal offenders in Kampala, for example, were asked why persons stole, the following were among the common answers:

They wanted to maintain their girl friends or their prostitutes by buying them good clothes, watches, nice shoes, and paying the rent.

They liked to go to night clubs every week.

They needed it for their careers.

They wanted to have better housing or more money, more luxury things, better clothes, and so on.

In a study of delinquency in a Ghanian city Busia suggested that theft might not be motivated by starvation or other serious needs but rather by the induced desire for more goods [71]. Studies of crime in Arab countries of the Middle East, for example, have been made by the United Nations. The chief offenses in rural areas, which constitute 70% of the population of the region, are murder and assault growing out of personal vendettas and offenses such as illegal pasturage; there is comparatively little property crime. On the other hand, in urban areas the major offenses are theft and other property crime, vagrancy, begging, and sex crimes [72]. Property crime is controlled in rural areas by respect for patriarchal and tribal authority in which honor is the unwritten law.

In the cities former villagers live in slums and often view with resentment the sumptuous villas and modern apartments in which another social class lives in luxury [73]. Young migrants learn crime from street gangs and from older criminals. People who live in cities like Cairo, in contrast to the villages, are judged by the amount of money they have, and thus conflict is created between young people and their migrant parents and relatives.

The decline of intimate communication in an urban setting means that the breaking of rules results in almost none of the informal censure common in the villages; often the police are the only means of control. The broader experiences offered, coupled with increased education, weaken parental authority and other traditional controls not only of the youth but of all persons [74]. A Venezuelan study has commented that the unity of family life in rural areas means that "there are only rare cases of delinquency among the rural youth and possibly many fewer examples of misconduct among the children" [75]. One writer has summarized these problems with reference to Liberia:

The effectiveness of tribe and family as agents of social control has always depended upon the cohesiveness of the particular unit. In the urban areas the cohesiveness increasingly gives way to individualism and the vacuum created by the decline in family and tribal authority has only been filled by the impersonal sanctions of the law [76].

Clifford found that with the coming of urbanization to Zambia the family's ability to exercise close control over the activities of its members diminished and the pressures of a homogeneous community, of common family residence, and of traditional respect for age and authority, dissipated [77]. In India the system of family authority has continued to prevail in the rural areas; disputes rising out of offenses committed by members of the community are generally settled within the family [78]. Only in large towns is recourse to judicial authority regarded as normal procedure. In Morocco the concentration of crime in cities has been explained as a result of the collapse of the traditional family and the transition from a tribal group to a smaller unit, with the subsequent weakening of the family as an institution of social control in urban areas [79]. This decline and its relation to crime has also been seen in Iraq.

The father's old supreme authority over his family has gradually been diminishing. Sons do not obey their father as they used to do and those who marry often now leave their paternal homes and establish new independent homes. On the other hand, the adherence to religion has become weaker, especially among the new generation. Thus the ethical effects of religious teachings on the prevention of crime and delinquency is disappearing. This diminishing social control finds its reflection in the crime situation in town, especially with regard to the migrant. For example, offenses of dishonesty are infrequent among rural communities. The strong tradition regarding such offenses as a disgrace is a preventive factor. However, the tribesman who migrates to town loses his sense of responsibility towards his fellows and is thus more inclined to commit offenses of dishonesty as he has no feeling of identification with those by whom he is surrounded [80].

In village areas of Africa, as in Zambia, for example, the behavior of children is controlled by the informal means of instilling respect for their seniors in the family or tribe. A survey of what villagers believed to be bad behavior in children listed "cursing, fighting, stealing, insolence (answering back), running away, telling lies, laziness, causing damage and illicit sexual intercourse" [81]. Theft has always been regarded as a serious offense. Once it represented food stolen from houses or fields; with modernization it has been money and articles such as clothing and blankets. Probably much of the problem of village theft in many areas today reflects contact with urban standards and values by migrant laborers and an increase in personal possessions which reduces communal family and village ownership. When such behavior does occur, it is dealt with largely by the immediate or the extended family. Recourse is made to the courts only if those outside the family are dissatisfied. Sometimes the delinquent acts are regarded more seriously after initiation ceremonies as well as after marriage.

There is some evidence to support the contention, however, that developing countries, even with varying local conditions, subsequently achieve some uniformity in the concept of crime, thus permitting utilization of the legal code as a reasonable measure of the attitudes toward what constitutes criminal behavior. A survey of urban persons in Zambia showed a tendency to equate serious misbehavior of the young with conduct prohibited by written law, such as stealing, fighting and assault, adultery and promiscuity, sex offenses, burglary, and robbery. This attitude seems to prevail even among those who came from areas in which traditional obligation extends only to relatives and there is no sense of crime attached to stealing from strangers or those outside the tribe [82].

URBANIZATION AND CRIME: A STUDY OF KAMPALA

Uganda is a country with one of the lowest rates of urbanization in Africa. In 1959 an estimated 160,000 people lived in urban areas with populations of 20,000 or more; this represented a level of urbanization of 3%, compared with the world level of 25% or with the overall level for Africa of 13% in 1960 [83]. Uganda's urbanization was then somewhat lower than Tanzania's 3.3% of 1957 and considerably lower than Kenya's 6.9% in 1962 [84]. In 1969 Kampala, the capital and largest city, had a population of 330,000, which represented an increase of 110% over the 1959 population. Kampala accounted for 3.5% of the population of Uganda in 1969. Four other cities in the country have populations of more than 10,000 [85].

Kampala is the main source of reported crime in Uganda; a fourth of all reported crime originates in the capital city. Its rate of total reported crime is seven and a half times the national rate (see Table 6).

Table 6 Property and Personal Crimes Reported to Police—Type by Rate per 100,000 Population[a] and Percent, Kampala and Uganda, 1968

Type of Crime	Kampala			Uganda		
	No.	%	Rate	No.	%	Rate
Property	13,125	32.6	4187	42,892	100	464
Person	5,651	22.1	1803	25,575	100	277
Total	20,574	25.4	6565	80,866	100	874

[a] Rates are based on the 1969 census.

Its property crime rate, which accounts for a third of all reported property crime in the country, is nine times the national average. Reported property crime is two and a half times greater than reported crimes against the person. Moreover, reported property crime constituted 63.8% of the Kampala total, compared with 52.4% of the national total.

Between 1963 and 1968 the rate of reported crime in Kampala increased by 39.1% [86]. Reported crimes in 1963 totaled 10,725, or a rate of 4725 per 100,000; in 1968 there were 20,754, or a rate of 6573. The trends by type of crime in Kampala generally resemble the trends for Uganda in criminal behavior. Table 7 indicates that the rates for all types of crime increased but that those associated with serious violence rose faster than the others. The rate of reported robbery doubled, and aggravated assault was seven times greater in 1968 than in 1963. It should be noted that both types of crime had a comparatively small absolute number of reported violations in 1963, and percentage increases from a

Table 7 Crimes Reported to the Police—Type by Rate per 100,000 Population, Kampala, 1963–1968

Offense	1963			1968		
	No.	%	Rate[a]	No.	%	Rate[a]
Murder and attempted murder	52	0.5	23	144	0.7	46
Manslaughter	4	0.1	2	6	0.1	2
Aggravated assault	246	2.3	108	2326	11.3	743
Common assault	1259	11.7	555	2978	14.5	951
Rape	73	0.7	32	192	0.9	61
Robbery	585	5.5	257	1598	7.8	510
Burglary	2488	23.2	1096	3674	19.9	1173
Theft	4671	43.5	2058	7162	34.9	2288
Receiving stolen property	417	3.9	184	694	3.4	221
Lawful authority and public order[b]	247	2.3	109	619	3.0	198
Miscellaneous	683	6.4	301	1181	5.7	377
Total	10,725	100.0	4725	20,574	100.0	6573
Estimated population	227,000			313,000		

[a] Rates are based on the extrapolation from the 1959 and 1969 population censuses.
[b] Offenses against public order include treason, mutiny, sedition, unlawful association, and rioting. Offenses against lawful authority cover corruption, abuse of office, prejudicing the administration of justice, and certain types of fraud.

small base will be quite high, with only a small increase in the absolute number. Reported robbery represented 7.8% of the total reported crime in Kampala, whereas it is 4.9% of the national total. It appears that robbery, as in the developed countries, is concentrated in this large city where more opportunities are presented.

Characteristics of Arrested Male Offenders

Although only limited data may be available for the entire country, there is even little detailed statistical information on the offenses and characteristics of arrested offenders in African cities. In fact, little is available in most cities of developing countries. This is because such data are not only not readily obtainable but also difficult to compile and tabulate without using some mechanical means. Consequently a more detailed study was made of all male persons arrested in Kampala in 1968. Individual cards were prepared on each male arrest. The available information included the offense, data and location of the offense, and the offender's address, sex, age occupation, and tribe [87]. In general, most information was available for 1968; the largest category for which data were missing was occupation. Among the 8833 male arrests during that year occupation, including those reported as unemployed, was recorded for only 62.3%. For the other categories the percentage of recorded information on offense was 99.8%, sex, 98.9%, tribe, 90.2% and age, 86.8%.

In all 9297 persons were arrested for penal code violations in 1968. Among them 3663, or 39.4%, were arrested for property offenses, 2882, or 31.0%, for personal offenses, and 2752, or 30.6%, for other offenses [88]. Table 8 shows the complete breakdown of arrests by sex and offense. As in all countries, Uganda has a sharp differential in the arrest rate for men and women, the ratio being 23 to 1 in Kampala. Several factors reduced female arrests. First there are more men than women in Kampala; the estimated male-female ratio in Uganda's urban centers is a little less than two to one [89]. A second factor is the restricted role of many African women, even in the cities. Kinship systems of the major tribal groups in Kampala have retained much of their strength. The selection of a sister's marriage partner is still important to the brother and consequently the movements of women are quite controlled [90]. A third factor is the status of prostitution in Kampala. Since the sex ratio is distorted, prostitution is common. In fact, it is one of the most frequent crimes among women, even though the law is seldom enforced. Inadequate institutional facilities to accommodate many female prisoners makes the police reluctant to make arrests except for more serious offenses.

Table 8   Arrests by Type of Offense and Sex, Kampala, 1968

Offense	Male No.	Male %	Female No.	Female %	Total No.	Total %
Murder by shooting	0	0	0	0	0	0
Murder (other than shooting)	43	0.5	2	0.5	415	0.5
Attempted murder by shooting	9	0.1	0	0	9	0.1
Attempted murder (other than shooting)	10	0.1	0	0	10	0.1
Aggravated assaults	1198	13.6	76	20.3	1274	13.8
Common assaults	1383	15.7	124	33.1	1507	16.4
Rape	31	0.4	1	0.3	32	0.4
Other sexual offenses	31	0.4	5	1.3	36	0.4
Aggravated robbery (armed holdups)	31	0.4	1	0.3	32	0.4
Other robbery	398	4.5	2	0.5	400	4.4
Burglary and housebreakings	504	5.7	6	1.6	510	5.5
Shopbreakings	106	1.2	2	0.5	108	1.2
Other breakings	34	0.4	0	0	34	0.4
Theft of motor vehicle	94	1.1	0	0	94	1.0
Theft from motor vehicle (spares, accessories, etc.)	194	2.2	0	0	194	2.1
Theft from motor vehicle (other property)	84	1.0	0	0	84	0.9
Theft of bicycle	98	1.1	0	0	98	1.1
Thefts (all other kinds)	2026	23.0	43	11.5	2069	22.5
Receiving and possession of stolen property	457	5.2	8	2.1	455	5.1
Forgery	89	1.0	1	0.3	90	1.0
False pretences	106	1.2	5	1.3	111	1.2
Counterfeiting	13	0.2	0	0	13	0.1
Riot, unlawful assembly	2	0	0	0	2	0
Arson	10	0.1	0	0	10	0.1
Malicious damage	238	2.7	15	4.0	253	2.8
Corruption	28	0.3	0	0	28	0.3
Idle and disorderly persons	575	6.5	29	7.7	604	6.6
Escape	30	0.3	1	0.3	31	0.3
All other penal code offenses	1005	11.4	54	14.4	1059	11.5
Total	8827	100.0	375	100.0	9202	100.0

Age

Nearly half (47%) of Kampala's population in 1969 was under 20 years of age, and 82% were under 45. Since only 6% of the males arrested were under 18 and 46.1% were over 26, it appears that the criminal population is considerably older in Uganda than in the developed countries (see Table 9). Tanner's study notes that the average age at conviction is between 22 and 25 in East Africa and only a few offenders are under 18 in Uganda [91]. Further data on imprisonment corroborate the arrest figures; 45.6% of the men admitted to the prison in Kampala during 1968 were over 25, and prison data for the whole of Tanzania show that 63.6% of the newly admitted prison population in 1966 were over 25 [92].

Table 9   Male Arrests, Age by Type of Crime, Kampala, 1968[a]

Age	Person		Property		Other		Total	
	No.	%	No.	%	No.	%	No.	%
10–17	104	4.9	241	7.2	118	5.3	462	6.0
18–25	1035	48.6	1648	49.2	1014	45.7	3687	47.9
26+	991	46.5	1461	43.6	1086	49.0	3549	46.1
Total	2130	100.0	3350	100.0	2218	100.0	7698	100.0

[a] Includes only those arrests for which age was recorded.

The age distribution does not vary appreciably by type of crime (see Table 9). Arrests for property crimes have the largest percentage under 18, 7.2%. Compared with the United States, these figures are not unexpected for crimes against the person, but the low percentage of under 18-year-olds arrests for urban property crime differs significantly from most developed countries. Although only 18% of those arrested in 1969 for urban crimes of violence in the United States were under 18, half of those arrested for property crimes were in that age bracket. A special study commission in Sweden found that in 1958 60% of all persons suspected of a crime for the first time were under the age of 15 [93]. Of all persons found guilty of an indictable offense in England and Wales in 1967 some 25% were under the age of 18; in terms of rates per 100,000 population the 14 to 17 age group had the highest rate of 2786.

Migration patterns may be the major reason for the older age of offenders in Kampala. Economic necessity does not compel most African males to migrate to the city until around the age of 17, nor are they usually free to respond to the attractive promise of change from the drab village existence until about that same age. At 18, however, they must begin to pay the head tax levied against all males in Uganda, and money may also be needed then to buy land or to pay a bride-price in marriage. The population in Kampala therefore is disproportionately young, although comparatively few of its residents are under 18. In 1969, 35.4% of the population in Kampala were under 15 years; the comparable figure for Uganda was 46.1. On the other hand, the percentage of the population between 15 and 34 years of age was 46.9 for Kampala and only 30.3 for the country.

The percentages in Table 10 were calculated on the basis of the age group most likely to be arrested. No one under 10 years of age was arrested and 96% of the arrested offenders were males. Both the youngest and oldest groups were under-represented in the criminal population. The 15-to-19-year-old offender group was only slightly larger than the male population in Kampala in that age group. It was the 20-to-34-year-olds who were disproportionately arrested. They account for 51% of the Kampala population that could be arrested, but 68% of those arrested belong to this age group.

Table 10   Male Arrests, by Age, Kampala, 1968[a]

	10–14	15–19	20–34	35+	Total
Percent	1.8	16.2	68.8	13.2	100.0
Number	141	1250	5302	1020	7713[a]

[a] The total here is greater than the total in Table 9 because the offense was missing in certain cases.

Occupational Status

Information on the employment status of the 5812 males in the sample whose occupational status had been recorded was coded in nine occupational categories (see Table 11). These classifications were consistent with several previous social surveys conducted in Kampala [94]. The "selling" classification refers mainly to street vendors who hawk such small items as fried corn or peanuts. Included in the "skilled" category were craftsmen, drivers, mechanics, and similar occupations. "Commercial" was limited mainly to store owners or men who claimed to be store owners. The "professional" category included teachers, military officials, or political leaders.

Table 11   Male Arrests—Occupation by Type of Crime, Kampala, 1968[a]

Occupation	Person	Property	Other	Total
1. Unemployed	23.1	60.5	53.1	49.9
2. Farm	4.3	1.3	2.1	2.2
3. Selling	5.5	2.3	3.0	3.2
4. Unskilled	39.9	23.7	25.7	27.4
5. Skilled	15.2	8.9	10.3	10.7
6. Clerical	7.2	1.6	2.2	3.0
7. Student	3.6	1.0	2.5	2.1
8. Commercial	0.8	0.6	0.9	0.7
9. Professional	0.5	0.2	0.2	0.3
Total	1306	2751	1755	5812

[a] Includes only those arrests for which occupational status was recorded.

Among those arrested slightly more than a fourth were in unskilled occupations and 3.2% were in selling; 10.7% had skilled occupations and only 4% were categorized as clerical, commercial, or professional. A surprising proportion (49.9%) of the arrested suspects reported that they were unemployed, strongly suggesting, on the surface, either a strong relation between unemployment and criminality or the possibility that the police were more likely to arrest unemployed persons. Studies of a sample population of two slum communities (see Chapter 6) and a prison sample showed that the highest unemployment figure was about 19%. Moreover, a 1964 United Nations study of the large Kampala slum area of Kisenyi, which has a high arrest rate and in which every household was surveyed, reported only 2.3% unemployment among all adults 16 and older [95]. In Southall's study in 1956 an unemployment rate of only 6.1% was found for males in Mulago, a densely settled area with characteristics comparable to Kisenyi's and an economic situation that had not markedly changed [96].

At least two possible explanations are valid for the disparity between the unemployment rates of the other samples and that of the arrested suspects. First, arrested suspects may have been hesitant to give their occupations for fear that their employers might be notified and thus imperil their jobs. Second, the arrest data show only 3.2% in the "selling" category, whereas the study of two slum areas in 1968 indicated that an overall 13.2% of the men interviewed gave "selling" as their occupation.

The police officer could have recorded men who carried on this sporadic type of street selling as actually being "unemployed." If many of the skilled workers who were self-employed (such as a carpenter with a small shop in his home) were labeled unemployed, it might also explain a certain portion of the disparity.

The findings were even more suggestive, however, of a possible real relation between unemployment and criminal involvement when type of crime was controlled. Among those arrested for crimes against persons the number reporting themselves unemployed accounted for 23.1%, compared with a percentage of 60.5 of unemployed persons among property offenders (see Table 11).

Crimes Cleared by Arrest

In Kampala 60.6% of the 20,574 crimes reported to the police were offenses against property, 26.5%, or 5455 offenses, were against persons, and 12.9%, or 3685 offenses, were other types. Since the actual proportion of crimes cleared by arrest was not available, such a figure was assumed by calculating the proportion of arrests to crimes known to the police in 1968. The percentages for crimes against the person which were cleared by arrest were much higher than those for crimes against property, a situation also true in the United States (see Table 12). As one might expect, the percentage of crimes cleared by arrest was lower in Kampala than in the country as a whole, the differences being particularly striking in the case of murder and robbery. The city, with its greater density and anonymity, increases the likelihood of offenses occurring between strangers, and identification becomes a problem of greater magnitude. When compared with cities of comparable size in the United States, the proportion cleared was remarkably similar in the case of aggravated assault, rape, burglary, theft, and motor-vehicle theft. The clearance rate for murder and robbery was much higher in the United States, whereas the theft clearance rate was higher in Uganda, even though the United States figure was limited to 50 dollars and over.

Number of Persons Arrested in a Crime

In 1968, 7848 separate crimes associated with the 9309 arrests were recorded in Kampala. As Table 13 indicates, only one person was arrested in 86.2% of the cases, and this percentage does not change by type of crime. This is an unusual finding, since the pattern in developed and most developing countries is in the opposite direction and contrary to most evidence presented in Chapter 7. The most extensive study con-

Table 12   Major Crimes Reported and Offenses Cleared by Arrest, Uganda, Kampala, and the United States

	Uganda, 1968		Kampala, 1968		United States, Cities 250,000 to 500,000, 1970[a]
	Crime Reported	% Cleared by Arrest	Crime Reported	% Cleared by Arrest	% Cleared by Arrest
Murder	1817	60.8	142	37.3	84.1
Rape	1445	60.8	192	63.0	57.6
Aggravated assault	18,432	66.6	2326	61.7	69.5
Theft of motor vehicle	1095	18.4	666	14.9	14.6
Theft	21,082	40.1	5074	35.7	19.3
Robbery	4000	30.0	1598	18.8	27.8
Burglaries, including house and shop	12,078	26.8	3674	20.3	20.3

[a] Federal Bureau of Investigation, *Uniform Crime Reports*, 1970, p. 108. The source of the Uganda figure was police reports. Figures were based on the proportion of arrests to crimes reported to the police in 1968 and therefore were different from the United States figures which consist of the same crimes cleared by arrest.

ducted in a developed nation was done by Shaw and McKay in Chicago. They found that companions were involved in 80% of the 5480 juvenile court cases they studied. Moreover, Kibuka's study of the court records of 723 convicted juvenile property offenders in Kampala found that 569, or 70.7% had committed their offenses alone [97].

Such a high percentage of single offender arrests might be expected for crimes against the person, but the percentage is similar for property

Table 13   Number of Persons Arrested per Crime, Kampala, 1968

No. Arrested	1	2	3	4	5	6	7	8	9+	Total
No. of crimes	6768	838	163	46	19	5	3	3	3	7848
Percent	86.2	10.7	2.1	0.6	0.2	0.1	0.04	0.04	0.04	100

Table 14   Number of Persons Arrested by Type of Crime, Kampala,
1968

No. Arrested	Person		Property		Other		Total	
	No.	%	No.	%	No.	%	No.	%
One	2159	87.7	2735	87.1	1867	83.5	6761	86.3
Two or more	304	12.3	405	12.9	369	16.5	1078	13.7
Total	2463	100.0	3140	100.0	2236	100.0	7389[a]	100.0

[a] The total here is slightly less than the total in Table 12 because the offense was missing in 0.2% of the cases.

crime (see Table 14). The explanation must be found in either the methods of apprehension, procedures for reporting, or the nature of property crime in Uganda. It is difficult to imagine a situation in which only one of two or more arrested suspects would be recorded by the police. It is more likely that the lack of manpower and equipment handicaps the police in apprehending all the offenders personally. Foot-patrol officers are on duty largely during the day, and then there are only 30 to 40 men for all of Kampala, a city of 330,000. The relatively few patrol cars have no radios, and the police generally arrive well after most crimes have been committed. Moreover, a large proportion of apprehensions for property crime are made by the populace, and if more than one person is involved it may be difficult to detain several. A gang may provide one another with protection, and it is thus even less likely that anyone would be arrested. Often a single private guard will be employed to patrol a business establishment or residence, which necessarily limits the possibility of apprehending more than one person.

The low rate of multiple arrest, on the other hand, may indicate a difference in the nature of property crime in a country as underdeveloped as Uganda. Most Africans in Kampala are relatively recent migrants with necessarily limited experience in the methods of committing crimes. The United Nations' Kisenyi Study of 1964 reported that 65.2% of the population had lived there for less than five years [98]. It is reasonable to speculate that theft by a recent migrant would be relatively uncomplicated, such as grabbing an unprotected item. Frequently stolen items are used articles of clothing and small items easy to grab [99]. The newness of urban experience could keep contact with criminal ideas or methods to a minimum for such an offender. Justification and encouragement may, however, have come from companions, even though they did not participate in the actual offense. When a prison sample from Kampala was asked whether they committed their first thefts alone or with others, 75% of the 122 persons responded "alone."

SOME CONCLUSIONS

Almost all the rather sharp increases in crimes against property in a less developed country occur in the cities. Moreover, crime is concentrated in the primate cities, or in a few other large urban areas, even in those less developed countries that remain predominantly rural in nature. The marked differences between the nature and the speed of the urbanization process in the developing countries today, compared with those of the past, make this problem even more acute.

The cities of developing countries contain a much greater proportion of young, unskilled, migrant males than the developed countries do. Since the economic and industrial development of the urban areas is usually incapable of absorbing more than a small portion of this influx into productive, financially rewarding occupations, the remainder must seek survival in marginal types of work, help from relatives, or funds from their villages or tribal areas.

To a migrant the contrasts in the way of life in a large city in a developing country represents a much greater difference than it would in the developed. Increased crime in less developed countries can be expected primarily because in these countries young people predominate, the growing cities attract the young, and it is the young who are most noticeably affected by the way of life in the city and who are drawn more easily into criminal activities.

NOTES AND REFERENCES

1. United Nations, *Urbanization in the Second U.N. Development Decade* (New York: United Nations, 1971).
2. Kingsley Davis, "The Role of Urbanization in the Development Process," *Conference Papers,* Rehovot Conference on Urbanization and Development in Developing Countries, Rehovot, Israel, 1971, p. 5.
3. Roy Turner, Ed., *India's Urban Future* (Berkeley: University of California Press, 1961).
4. United Nations, *Growth of the World's Urban and Rural Population, 1920–2000* (New York: United Nations, 1969), Tables 35 and 36, Chapter IV.
5. Davis, "The Role of Urbanization in the Development Process," p. 5.
6. United Nations, *Growth of the World's Urban and Rural Population, 1920–2000,* Annex, Table B., p. 9–33.

7. Davis, "The Role of Urbanization in the Development Process," pp. 4–5.

8. Gideon Sjoberg, *The Preindustrial City: Past and Present* (New York: The Free Press, 1960).

9. Frank C. Ferrier, "Population et Urbanisation de L'Afrique Occidentale," *L'Afrique Occidentale: Développpment et Société,* Centre International de Criminologie Comparée, Université de Montréal, 1972, pp. 43–46.

10. Philip M. Hauser and Leo F. Schnore, Eds., *The Study of Urbanization* (New York: Wiley, 1965), p. 36.

11. Manuel López-Rey, *Crime: An Analytical Appraisal* (New York: Praeger, 1970). He states that in spite of widespread planning, urbanization is proceeding more rapidly than the improvement of social and economic conditions, with the possible exception in some countries of health services and in others of social services (p. 232). Also, when they concentrate their efforts on the urban area of a capital, some African countries, particularly, show all the usual harmful effects of over-urbanization (p. 232). This concept, however, has been challenged by a number of writers, one reason being that most of the Central and South American countries, as well as many in Africa have no great pressures on the land in the countryside. See N. V. Sovani, "The Analysis of 'Over-Urbanization,' " in Gerald Breese, Ed., *The City in Newly Developing Countries* (Englewood Cliffs, N. J.: Prentice-Hall, 1969), p. 327. Another approach to the problem of overurbanization is suggested by Lerner. In some developing countries the rate of urbanization is disproportionately large compared with the country's percentage of literacy. Thus countries like Egypt show a large growing surplus of urban over literate populations. See Daniel Lerner, *The Passing of Traditional Society* (New York: The Free Press, 1958), pp. 65–68.

12. Alejandro Melchor, "Urbanization in the Philippines," *Conference Papers,* Rehovot Conference on Urbanization and Development in Developing Countries, Rehovot, Israel, 1971, p. 7.

13. "World Urbanization Trends, 1920–1960," in Breese, *The City in Newly Developing Countries,* p. 44.

14. Davis, "The Role of Urbanization in the Development Process," p. 13.

15. *Ibid.,* p. 12.

16. *The International Atlas* (Chicago: Rand McNally, 1969), Tables I–12 and I–23.

17. Lagos, for example, in 1962 consumed 50% of the electricity and 56% of the telephones in all Nigeria. Economic Commission for Africa, *Workshop on Urbanization in Africa,* Addis Ababa, April 25–May 5, 1962, United Nations, SEM/URB/AF/1.

18. Victor D. Du Bois, *Social Aspects of the Urbanization Process in Abidjan,* Fieldstaff Reports, West Africa Series, Vol. X, No. 1, 1967, p. 6.

19. Abidjan in 1966 was host to an international conference dealing with crime. Travaux du XVIe Cours International de Criminologie, Abidjan, September 12–24, 1966 (Paris: Picon et Durand-Auzias, 1968).

20. Bert F. Hoselitz, *Sociological Aspects of Economic Growth* (New York: The Free Press, 1960), p. 170.

21. Alex Inkeles, "Making Men Modern: On the Causes and Consequences of Individual Change in Six Developing Countries," *American Journal of Sociology,* 75:208–226 (September 1969).

22. Alvin H. Schaff, "Urbanization and Development in Uganda: Growth Structure and Change," *The Sociological Quarterly*, 8:120 (Winter 1967).

23. "Urbanization in Africa: Some Spatial and Functional Aspects," *Items*, 25:27, Social Science Research Council (September 1971).

24. A. A. Laquian, quoted in T. G. McGee, "Catalysts or Cancers? The Role of Cities in Asian Society," in Leo Jakobson and Ved Prakash, Eds., *Urbanization and National Development* (Beverly Hills, Calif.: Sage, 1971), p. 177.

25. Jorge E. Hardoy, "Policy and Planning Related to Rapid Urbanization," *Conference Papers*, Rehovot Conference on Urbanization and Development in Developing Countries, Rehovot, Israel, 1971, p. 5.

26. Marshall B. Clinard, "The Relation of Urbanization and Urbanism to Criminal Behavior," in Ernest W. Burgess and Donald J. Bogue, *Contributions to Urban Sociology* (Chicago: University of Chicago Press, 1964), pp. 541-559. See also Marshall B. Clinard, *Sociology of Deviant Behavior* (New York: Holt, Rinehart & Winston, 1968), 3rd ed., and Edwin H. Sutherland and Donald Cressey, *Principles of Criminology* (Philadelphia: Lippincott, 1960), 6th ed., pp. 154-157.

27. Karl O. Christiansen, "Industrialization and Urbanization in Relation to Crime and Delinquency," *International Review of Criminal Policy*, 18:8 (October 1960).

28. Philip M. Hauser, Ed., *Urbanization in Latin America* (New York: International Documents Service, Columbia University Press, 1960), and UNESCO, *Social Implications of Industrialization and Urbanization in Africa South of the Sahara* (Lausanne: UNESCO, 1956).

29. William Clifford, "The Evaluation of Methods Used for the Prevention and Treatment of Juvenile Delinquency in Africa South of the Sahara," *International Review of Criminal Policy*, 21:17-32 (1963).

30. *Urbanization in Asia and the Far East*, Proceedings of the Joint UN/UNESCO Seminar, Bangkok, Thailand, August 8-18, 1956 (UNESCO) 1958, XX.57.V7A, Chapter IX, p. 233. See also *A Report on Juvenile Delinquency in India* (Bombay: The Children's Aid Society, 1956), p. 8.

31. United Nations, "Juvenile Delinquency in India," June 1967, SOA/SD/CS.2, "Juvenile Delinquency in the United Arab Republic," September 1966, SOA/SD/C.S.1, and "Juvenile Delinquency in Zambia," April 1967, SOA/SD/CS.3.

32. Lenore R. Kupperstein and Jaime Toro-Calder, *Juvenile Delinquency in Puerto Rico* (University of Puerto Rico: Social Science Research Center, 1969) and Isabel Suliveres, "Juvenile Delinquency: Theoretical Implications for Puerto Rico," in Isabel Suliveres, Ed., *Manual de Lecturas para el Aidestramiento de Officiales Probatorios Juvenile*, Centre Investigaciones Sociales, Facultad de Ciencias Sociales, Universidad de Puerto Rico, 1969.

33. Hector Solis Quiroga, *Jornadas Industrialies*, 4A, pp. 123-160 (January–March, 1957).

34. Abdellatif El Bacha, "Quelques Aspects Particuliers de la Délinquance Juvénile dans Certaines Villes du Royaume du Maroc," *International Review of Criminal Policy*, 20:21-23 (December, 1962).

35. Abdelwahab Bouhdiba, *Criminalité et Changements Sociaux en Tunisie* (Tunis, University of Tunis, Les Memoires du Ceres, 1965), p. 79.

36. Ministre de la Justice, République Algérienne Democratique et Populaire, "Criminalité et Mesures de Prévention," report presented at the Fourth United Nations Congress, Kyoto, Japan, 1970.

37. United Nations Bureau of Social Affairs, "Juvenile Delinquency in the United Arab Republic," mimeo, SOA/SD/CS.1, 1966, p. 1.

38. *Ibid.*, p. 24.

39. Carl D. Chambers and Gordon H. Barker, "Juvenile Delinquency in Iraq," *The British Journal of Criminology*, 11:176–182 (April 1971).

40. D. N. Dhanagare, "Urbanism and Crime," *Economic and Political Weekly*, 4:1–4 (July 1969). He found some variations in the type of offense.

41. Chung-Hyun Ro, "Seoul," in Aprodicio A. Laquian, Ed., *Rural Urban Migrants and Metropolitan Development* (Toronto: Intermet Metropolitan Studies Series, 1971), p. 161.

42. Mustafa El Augi, *Délinquance Juvénile au Liban* (Beirut: Publications du Centre de Recherches, 1970), pp. 28–29.

43. James Riby-Williams, "The Treatment of Juvenile Delinquency in the Gold Coast of West Africa," *International Review of Criminal Policy*, 6:7 (July 1954).

44. *Ibid.*

45. Clifford, "Juvenile Delinquency in Zambia."

46. M. Bako, "Urbanization et Développment," *Conference Papers*, Rehovot Conference on Urbanization and Development in Developing Countries, Rehovot, Israel, 1971, p. 4.

47. Ruth Shonle Cavan and Jordan T. Cavan, *Delinquency and Crime: Cross-Cultural Perspectives* (Philadelphia: Lippincott, 1968), pp. 42–70.

48. Norman S. Hayner, *New Patterns in Old Mexico* (New Haven: College and University Press, 1966), pp. 170–171.

49. Melchor, "Urbanization in the Philippines," p. 7.

50. Denis Szabo, *Crimes et Villes* (Louvain: Catholic University of Louvain, 1960). See also *Urbanization in Asia and the Far East*, UNESCO, Chapter IX, and Szabo, *Criminologie* (Montréal: Les Presses de L'Université de Montréal, 1965).

51. Simone Hugot, "Les Problèmes de la Délinquance Juvénile à Dakar," Ph.D. dissertation, Centre de Recherche Psycho-Sociologique, Dakar, Senegal, 1968.

52. Augi, *Délinquance Juvénile au Liban*, p. 23.

53. Gideon Sjoberg, *The Preindustrial City* (New York: The Free Press, 1960).

54. Louis Wirth, "Urbanism as a Way of Life," *American Journal of Sociology*, 44:1–24 (1938). Wirth's statement was based, in part, on Georg Simmel, "The Metropolis and Mental Life", in Paul K. Hatt and Albert J. Reiss, Jr., Eds., *Reader in Urban Sociology* (New York: The Free Press, 1951), pp. 563–574, and Robert E. Park, *The City* (Chicago: University of Chicago Press, 1929). Other terms, such as *mass society* or *secular*, which generally reflect the same process, have been used. For a discussion of secular societies see Howard Becker, *Man in Reciprocity* (New York: Praeger, 1956), pp. 169–197. See also Marshall B. Clinard, *Sociology of Deviant Behavior*, pp. 86–98.

55. A. L. Epstein, "Urbanization and Social Change in Africa," in Breese, *The City in Newly Developed Countries*, p. 255.

56. *Social Defence Policies in Relation to Development Planning*, working paper prepared by the Secretariat, Fourth United Nations Congress on the Prevention of Crime and the Treatment of Offenders, Kyoto, Japan, 1970 (New York: United Nations, 1970).

57. S. Kirson Weinberg, "Urbanization and Male Delinquency in Ghana," in Paul Meadows and Ephraim H. Mizruchi, Eds., *Urbanism, Urbanization, and Change: Comparative Perspectives* (Reading, Mass.: Addison-Wesley, 1969), p. 377.

58. Roberto Bergalli, *Criminologia en America Latina: Cambio Social Normativa y Comportamientos Desviadas* (Buenos Aires: Ediciones Pannedille, 1972).

59. Marshall B. Clinard, *Slums and Community Development: Experiments in Self-Help* (New York: The Free Press, 1966), pp. 140–141, and p. 142.

60. Peter C. W. Gutkind, "Congestion and Overcrowding: An African Problem," *Human Organization*, 19:130 (1960). See also Hilda Kuper, Ed., *Urbanization and Migration* (Berkeley: University of California Press, 1965).

61. G. Tooth, "Survey of Juvenile Delinquency in the Gold Coast," in *Social Implications of Industrialization and Urbanization in Africa South of the Sahara*, pp. 86–91.

62. Anthony and Elizabeth Leeds, "Brazil and the Myth of Urban Rurality: Urban Experience, Work and Values in 'Squatments' of Rio de Janeiro and Lima," in Arthur J. Field, Ed., *City and Country in the Third World* (Cambridge, Mass.: Schenkman, 1970), pp. 229–285.

63. The traditional view of "rural" urban slums is, for example, presented in William Mangin and Jerome Cohen, "Cultural and Psychological Characteristics of Mountain Migrants to Lima, Peru," *Sociologus*, 14:81–88 (1) (1966).

64. Leeds and Leeds, *Brazil and the Myth of Urban Reality*, p. 235.

65. *Ibid.*, p. 261.

66. *Ibid.*

67. Elio Gomez Grillo, *Delinquencia en Caracas* (Maracaibo: Editorial Universataria de la Universidad del Zulia, 1971).

68. Arthur L. Wood, "Crime and Aggression in Changing Ceylon," *Transactions of the American Philosophical Society*, 51, Part 8, December 1961.

69. Daniel Lerner, "Comparative Analysis of Processes of Modernization," in Horace Miner, Ed., *The City in Modern Africa* (New York: Praeger, 1967).

70. For a graphic example of the similar process in the United States see Robert S. Lynd and Helen Lynd, *Middletown* (New York: Harcourt Brace, 1929). See also Lionel Tiger, "Bureaucracy and Urban Symbol Systems," in Miner, *The Modern City in Africa*, 1967.

71. K. A. Busia, "Social Survey of Sekondi-Takorade," in Hauser, *Social Implications of Industrialization and Urbanization in Africa South of the Sahara*, 1966.

72. Muhsen Abbes, "Juvenile Delinquency: Prevention in the Pre-Delinquent Stage," Third United Nations Seminar for the Arab States on the Prevention of Crime and the Treatment of Offenders, 1964, SD/ESOB/WP.1/2.

73. *Ibid.*, p. 7.

74. *Social Change and Criminality*, report to the Third United Nations Congress on the Prevention of Crime and the Treatment of Offenders (Stockholm: United Nations, 1965).

75. Tulio Chrossone, Ximena Rodriguez de Canestri, Omar Arenas Candelo. and Nilda Hernandez, *Trastornos de la Conducta Juvenil* (Caracas: Pulicaciones de la Facultad de Derecho, Universidad Central de Venezuela, 1968), p. 34.

76. Gerald H. Zarr, "Liberia," in Milner, *African Penal Systems*, p. 194. Houchon has also surveyed criminality in Africa and has concluded that urbanization is related

in these ways: detribalization which leads to family breakdown, greater education which has brought about changes in perceptions of social class without proper outlets, and the absence of organized leisure time leading to the formation of gangs. Guy Houchon, "Les Mécanismes Criminogènes dans Une Société Urbaine Africaine," *Revue Internationale de Criminologie et de Police Technique*, 21:271–277 (1967).

77. Clifford, "Juvenile Delinquency in Zambia," pp. 26–31.

78. S. C. Varma, "Juvenile Delinquency and Its Prevention in Rajasthan," *Social Defence* (New Delhi), 3:25–31 (1967).

79. Abdellatif El Bacha, "Quelques Aspects Particuliers de la Délinquence Juvénile dans Certaines Villes du Royaume du Maroc."

80. M. N. Kadhim, "Some Aspects of Participation of the Public in the Prevention and Control of Crime and Delinquency in Iraq," paper from the Fourth UN Congress on the Prevention of Crime and Treatment of Offenders, Kyoto, Japan, 1970, pp. 4–5.

81. Clifford, "Juvenile Delinquency in Zambia."

82. See William Clifford, "The African View of Crime," *The British Journal of Criminology*, 4:477–486 (July 1964).

83. United Nations, *Report on Survey of Present Land Uses and Master Plan Programme for Kampala* (Kampala: United Nations Regional Planning Mission, 1969), p. 22.

84. Kenya's urbanization is at least double that of Uganda, but its reported crime rate is one-half less. This difference may be an artifact of data collection and reporting, but it could be the subject of a comparative study.

85. Three of the cities are administrative centers for districts that cover large territories. Their summaries of crime reported to the police include offenses from the rural areas in the district. To include them in the study it would have been necessary to record every crime in their books in order to separate the urban crime from the rural.

86. The five-year period between 1963 and 1968 is a relatively short time for which to consider trends, but analysis is constrained by the limits of the data. The year 1963 was chosen because it was the first year that could reasonably be judged to be politically normal within the time span of the available data. If the trend in crime rates is based on 1960, there would have been a 15% drop in the reported crime rate by 1968, but this was the unstable period leading up to independence and therefore was not used.

87. Tribal background was tabulated but not included here, since the 1969 census did not include tribe and the only other available data for comparison was the 1959 census, which was inadequate.

88. Arrests are entered in police districts in a "crime report book" or a "minor crime book." The original plan was to gather a complete set of statistics from each police district for 1960, 1964, and 1968. Normally four or five crime books are filled in each police district during the year, but even in 1964 complete information in one or two of the five books could not be found at most stations. It was then decided independently to collect data for 1968 on all arrests and on the majority of the crimes reported. In the police districts major offenses against the penal code were reported in one book and minor penal code and ordinance violations in another. In this study, however, the distinction between the two types

of offense was eliminated, and all penal code violations were included because of the arbitrary distinction between similar types of behavior. The nature of a blow during a quarrel, for example, may be the only differentiation between common and aggravated assault.

89. Josef Gugler, "Urbanization in East Africa," Markerere Institute of Social Research Kampala, 1966, p. 8 (mimeographed).

90. David Parkin, *Neighbors and Nationals in an African City Ward* (London: Routledge & Kegan Paul, 1969), pp. 92–96.

91. R. E. S. Tanner, "Rural Crime in East Africa—Some Theoretical Issues," R. D. R. Paper No. 34, Kampala: Makerere Institute of Social Research, 1966.

92. Annual Report, Prison Department, Tanzania, 1966.

93. Cited in Paul C. Friday, "Differential Opportunity and Differential Association in Sweden: A Study of Youth Crime," unpublished Ph. D. dissertation, University of Wisconsin, 1970, p. 111.

94. Two extensive studies of urban life were being conducted by Josef Gugler and Regina Solzbacker and the occupation code was adapted from their interview schedules. It was impossible, however, to determine the percentage in each of these categories in the general population of Kampala.

95. United Nations, *Recommendations for Urban Development in Kampala and Mengo,* Kampala, TAO, Uganda, 1964, p. 153.

96. Aidan Southall and P. C. W. Gutkind, *Townsmen in the Making: Kampala and Its Suburbs* (London: Kegan Paul Trench Trubner, 1957), p. 240.

97. Eric Paul Kibuka, "Sociological Aspects of Juvenile Delinquency in Kampala 1962 to 1969," Ph. D. dissertation, University of East Africa, 1972.

98. *Recommendations for Urban Development in Kampala and Mengo,* p. 95. Other data from research on two slum communities found that persons interviewed had lived in Kampala for less than five years.

99. See Chapter 4 for a more detailed discussion of the types of article stolen.

Chapter 4   Crime and the Problems of Migration to the City

The process of industrialization in Europe was generally accompanied by a gradual drift of the population to the towns and cities. Although this same process is found in some developing countries, what is taking place today in many of them, particularly in Africa, is quite different from the process that took place in nineteenth-century England. Then people came to the city from adjoining small towns. Today in developing countries in Africa urbanization has mainly proceeded not by a series of such stages but by a "sharp leap" from a small village to a distant urban center [1]. The Uganda study found that 60% of a sample of criminal offenders and nonoffenders had migrated directly to Kampala and that approximately 80% of both groups had either come directly or had made only brief stops in other communities. On the other hand, studies in Colombia have found that migrants often travel to a smaller city en route to a larger one [2].

Migrants to the city receive their initial training in developing their value systems in a comparatively homogeneous village setting. In this home environment expectations are accepted by most members of the community. Deviations from the daily routine are unusual, and formal censure quick and compelling. When asked about the manner in which crime was handled in their own villages, three slum dwellers in Kampala replied:

When a man steals from his community where he is known he can even be killed.

It is always condemned, for example, if someone had been charged with theft, it is difficult for him to marry in our tribe. Thieves are sometimes hanged in our tribe.

We look at this person as a bad person who wants to spoil the good name of our community so we try to find a way to stop him.

In the village the individual expects his kin to respond to his needs in times of crises. The urban environment in developing countries undermines this communal base of rural living without often supplying substitutes, such as unemployment compensation, as is done in industrialized countries. On the other hand, there is evidence, of an increase in the growth of tribal, regional, and other voluntary organizations in some urban areas. In general, according to one migrant to Kampala, "it is hard for people to improve things because few really care. Each one is after himself." The migrant is confronted with a heterogeneous maze of norms and values. The growth of the economy spurs occupational diversification and new life styles emerge. McCord says:

> Exposure to a city's wiles, its contrasts and strange experiences, opens new vistas to the ex-villager. He learns that other styles of life exist, other religions, and political authorities other than those of his own village. Because he must, he learns to tolerate attitudes and habits which clash with his own [4].

THE PULL OF LARGE CITIES FOR MIGRANTS

The major cities of developing countries consist primarily of migrants from the rural areas, a migration which is taking place throughout the world and for varied reasons [5]. Although this city growth is generally attributed to an economic "push" from an overpopulated agricultural area, we must not underestimate the great significance of the "pull" factor of city life in the total process. New industries are developing in these large cities, more diverse occupational opportunities are available, wages are often higher, and better employment as well as educational opportunities are offered [6].

Industrialization and the concomitant development of a money economy often necessitates movement to the city for economic objectives. Young men leave their families to tend their land while they try to secure work in the city, thus creating a large pool of unattached males whose main goal is to accumulate money [7]. In the Kampala study, for example, a sample of 578 migrants was questioned about their reasons for migrating to the city. Approximately 78% of the responses suggested that search for employment was a major factor, and the next most frequent responses, which accounted for 7 and 8% of the replies, were for schooling and to visit friends and relatives, respectively. One reason for this need for money is that the colonialists in many parts of Africa levied head taxes as revenue measures and, indirectly, to force workers into unpleasant factory jobs, a practice that has continued since independence. Industrial employment often represents the only source of funds for these tax payments for those without cash crops; the alternative is a jail sentence.

Urban life, however, offers even more than this incentive. The attraction of "city lights" lies not only in jobs and cash but in facilities like better lighting and water, transportation, education, hospitals, and the excitement of the city and its "civilization." A Korean study of the factors that cause people to migrate to a city like Seoul found three of the top seven were "pull" factors: education, cultural resources, and desire for urban life [8]. Among the chief reasons given for migration to Freetown, as Banton pointed out, was the "attraction of the town as a center of civilization where novel material benefits are available" [9]. In Niger it was reported that although many were attracted for financial gains others spoke about the "enriching experiences of the city" and that

people of the city see many things to enrich their lives even though they cannot read or write; in the city where it is civilized one dresses well, speaks well, sees new things; in the countryside one is bored, while in the cities there are the cinemas, the dance halls, the week-end activities [10].

In Africa it has been pointed out that city living has a "particularly strong appeal for individuals whose mental horizon has been bounded by the bush enclosing their village." [11]. This has been said about the attractions even of the slums of Ghana:

What never ceases to surprise the outsider is that rural-urban migrants from green, forest-covered mountains find the city with its shanty-town periphery not merely more lively than the village but visually more beautiful. They refer to buildings, neon signs, and even the roads and advertisements [12].

The city's anonymity also offers greater opportunity for social, economic, and political advancement to groups traditionally discriminated against in the villages, as, for example, the millions of depressed people like the Harijans (untouchables) and low-caste Indians.

The introduction of general secondary education in rural areas, as in Africa, has had a powerful impact on the young. Persons with even three or four years of schooling, and particularly any secondary education, are unwilling to remain in their villages, and each year the urban labor markets are flooded with young men who never again will be satisfied with the subsistence farming of their fathers [13]. Unfortunately they are frequently unable to find jobs and often become associated with deviant groups. A study in Zambia, for example, showed that delinquents in Lusaka had a higher educational level than that of the country as a whole [14]. Education presumably brings prestige and the guarantee of a job as well as escape from tradition and a status previously fixed at birth.

It offers a possibility of advancement through merit. In this connection, Professor Mabogunje of the University of Ibadan has pointed out that the development of African cities was long held up because they were regarded largely as markets for European consumer goods rather than production centers, with subsequent restrictions on educational development. In most African countries, after independence, "the flood gates of migration from rural to urban areas seem to have been thrown wide open" [15].

"URBANIZING" THE MIGRANTS

Literature on absorption problems of migrants has dealt extensively with persons who move from one country to another. A close parallel is seen in developing countries in which persons from various tribes, linguistic groups, or regional backgrounds move to the larger cities. The migrant must often acquire a new local language and frequently a European language [16]. One study even suggests that lack of communication, due to an inadequate or nonexisting knowledge of Spanish, is a contributing factor in producing maladjustment and subsequent crime in urban areas of Mexico. Because of the high rate of migration from rural to urban areas, many of the immigrants speak only their Indian dialects [17]. If the city happens to be located in an area in which the dominant culture is quite different, the city itself presents ways of life markedly different from village life. In this sense, much of what has been written about the absorption of immigrants into a country applies to in-migration to a city in less developed countries. We might use Eisenstadt's measures of successful absorption of an immigrant into a foreign country to apply to an in-migrant to a city in a less developed country: (a) the extent to which new roles are learned; (b) a successful social participation in the new social organization of the city, (c) a limited amount of deviant behavior such as crime, (d) limited expression of personal and group values and, (e) an identification with the values of the receiving community [18].

Migration to metropolitan cities affects people in different ways. Some migrants are short-term, goal-oriented, or periodically employed persons who leave their families on small plots of land and are not committed to urban living. This migrant characteristically comes for a specific reason, such as acquiring sufficient money with which to buy more cotton land. A Kampala study shows that only 20% of these migrant workers stay more than five years [19]. Others stay longer but do not break their rural ties because of family, tenure of family land, and a strong attachment to traditional village life. They return to the village periodically and may eventually even remain. Still others become "urbanized"; their village ties weaken, they adopt urban occupations and life styles, what income and property they have is largely urban, and they bring their families to the city which they regard as home [20]. Any length of stay in the city and absence from the village, however, results in every African's becoming detribalized as soon as he leaves his tribal area, "even though he continues to be acted on by tribal influences, he lives in different kinds of groupings, earns his livelihood in a different way, comes under different authorities" [21].

The urbanizing effect of migration to the city represents a shift in the balance between ties with and outside the city. A migrant population becomes genuinely urban or has been "effectively urbanized once this shift has become decisive, so that its extra-town ties have collectively shrunk to negligible proportions as compared with its within-town ties" [22]. As a measurement of the decline of such outer ties we can use location of kin and friends, regularity of country visiting, location of property, and response to questions such as where a person's real home is located and where he would choose to live [23]. Organized communities of people in urban areas who come from the same rural locations may, of course, inhibit the shift of emphasis to urban ties. Still another measure of urbanization is the increased complexity of role structures. Southall's study of Kampala found that in general town life is characterized by role relationships that are more narrowly defined, more specific, more unequally distributed between peers, more extensively developed in latent role structure, more numerous as a whole in relation to persons who are themselves living at a high spatial density, and more fleeting.

These migrants constitute an extremely heterogeneous population, coming as they do from diverse regions and tribal groups and having different language and religious backgrounds. In one small area of a large African city as many as 20 to 30 tribal groups, with extremely varied cultural backgrounds, might be represented [24]. In India there would also be the caste groups, in Latin America, regional and racial groups. Some enclaves can maintain a semblance of their former unity, but even this often breaks down with more and more migration, the impersonality of the city, and increasing housing pressures. Few common norms and values are left as the migrants are confronted with conflicting urban standards. Marris has found that as an economy develops it diversifies more quickly in the larger African cities than elsewhere. As people make their living in many different occupations, with varying rewards and degrees of security and prestige, further diversification occur in the patterns of life.

Family relationships acquire a different emphasis and different value according to occupation and income. Groups within society segregate—physically, into different neighborhoods; socially into different kinds of association; psychologically, into attitudes toward life [25].

One writer has attributed the marked increase in crime in Bangkok to the fact that many rural migrants to the cities, finding themselves in a conglomeration of people, chiefly alien and removed from their rural and familial types of control, lose their inhibitions. The traditional family systems are disrupted and parental control over the young is weakened [26]. Grillo notes the disorienting effect in Caracas of pressing recent migrants into huge housing projects in which they are surrounded by those with distinct life styles, customs, and levels of amiability [27].

Migrants face severe difficulties in acquiring skills needed for effective living in the urban environment. Education is the main source of status-building skills, and nonstudents in the Kampala sample were questioned on their reasons for quitting or not attending school. Uganda has only private tuition at the primary and secondary levels of education, and 57% said that they did not have enough money. Another 15% attributed their lack of education to the death or illness of their parents and, ultimately, a shortage of funds. Thus it may be quite difficult for the poorly skilled and trained migrant to break out of the cycle and advance to better economic and social positions.

Problems of Identity

The migrant frequently lacks a sense of community within the social structure of the large city, particularly if he has made no long-term commitment. The transient nature of his stay in the urban milieu, along with the decrease in his familial support, prevents him from developing a sense of commitment to a community. He becomes bewildered by the city's impersonality, the anonymity of the municipal government, and often even by the place in which he has been fortunate enough to find work. His foremost concern, he feels, must be his achievement in the urban status hierarchy [28]. The African worker, in particular finds the transition to a series of discontinuous impersonal relations, with employers, landlords, policemen, traders, and officials, an abrupt one. Adapted in childhood to work, comfort, and recreation in a comparatively small but comprehensive face-to-face group, he often finds his craft and other skills either useless or undervalued and his environment strange and even hostile.

The early patterns of domestic, kinship, and neighborhood relations are often excluded; the self-reliance and group solidarity for shared production and sustenance under a subsistence economy are little guide to the foresight, economizing, and bargaining required in the new patterns of wage income and the need to buy most goods, in which unfamiliar modes of expenditure for livelihood and display are offered and even enforced [29]. The presence of relatives can be a source of stability and direction for a while, but their willingness to help the rural cousin diminishes as they themselves become caught up in the urban mobility system [30]. Generally there is little else to mitigate his plight unless he finds a situation in which social ties play an important role among tribal, regional, caste, and other groups. In a study of Kampala, for example, tribal ties among many migrants were found to persist in effective kin or "brother" relations and marriage arrangements [31].

Economic Problems

Financial matters absorb a large part of the migrant's attention and may even bring about undesirable activities. Shortage of money is a major problem for most migrants to large cities because of unemployment, partial employment, or the higher living costs. Even if he is employed, he is often overwhelmed with the realization that in a cash economy he must pay for his housing and for almost everything he consumes, even fruits and vegetables which he had either grown or bought cheaply. Although a moneyless subsistence was possible in the village, in the city goods are scarce and closely guarded. He finds it equally hard to realize that cheap housing seldom can be built, even for the labor [32]. He experiences, too, the breakdown of the traditional security of tribal customs in which he had the right, in time of need, to make demands on the tribe and the extended family. With this source denied him, he may resort to crime, partly because it "may be less discreditable by the communal doctrine of tribal society under which the disadvantaged are allowed to share in the property of the more affluent" [33].

Although urban unemployment is produced by the complex factors that bring people to the city, its extent, and the seriousness of the problem are governed by the length of time the migrant is willing to stay, how he can survive without work, and the extent to which friends and relatives can offer him support. A Uganda study showed that although the majority of a sample of unemployed had been looking for work less than six months, one-fourth had been looking for more than a year [34]. Some walked several miles each day, seeking employment. Some relied on sporadic income from the sale of crops or livestock back in their villages or from gifts. Even with no help, many migrants remain in the city, chronically impoverished, often with transient jobs, unable to increase their earning capacity or to face up to a return to the more regular and disciplined life of the rural areas from which they have come. The city may cause particular disillusionment among those whose expectations are too high, for items that often considered necessities are regarded as luxuries in the village. One African study found that three-fourths of the members of urban migrant households felt that people worry more about money than they had in the village; only one-fourth achieved their expected economic goals [35].

In a United Nations report on crime and delinquency in Arab countries it was emphasized that migrants become aware of their own deprivation when they see the wealth of the city and that these feelings of deprivation lead to antagonism toward society, an antagonism kept alive "by a feeling of oppression and absence of social justice which was considered to be one of the major elements of delinquency among both adults and juveniles in these countries" [36]. Residents in Kampala expressed similar feelings when they were asked why people stole. One simply said that "stealing is just caused by a feeling that one should be as rich as the others without any job to get money from," and another said that people steal for money and to make the rich poor also.

Because of the uncertainty of living conditions, migrants are often unable or unwilling to take their families with them, but when they do establish themselves as a family they find it almost impossible to accommodate young migrant relatives or friends who follow them to the city. Housing and food prices they find almost prohibitive, children often cannot find school placements or suitable jobs, and the division of labor in a family accustomed to sharing responsibilities for cultivating the land has little meaning [37]. Although polygamy may be traditionally the rule, it is uncommon in cities because it is impractical and costly and because not even the higher status associated in rural areas with multiple wives applies.

Most African migrants who come to the city without wives must choose between the alternatives of a temporary wife who will live with him and cook for him, a girl friend, or a prostitute for whose attention he has to pay cash. Respondents in the Kampala study had various comments on the typical relations between men and women in slum areas:

You could hardly term it a "relationship." This is because the place is full of only prostitutes, so their relationship with men is never firm or lasting.

Only those people who get married in the countryside and then come here have firm marriages. Others have none; there are many prostitutes in the area.

If a man has money, then many women stick to him like ticks.

Women are after money. Once you have no money they quit and look for a richer man.

I found my wife sleeping with another man in my own bed. So I beat her and dismissed her.

I had gone for a trip and when I came back I found that she had loved other men so I dismissed her.

Those marriages arranged at home are firm, but those arranged here are not.

The woman migrant is usually seeking a marriage partner, but she often sees a new aspect of the position of women. She sees that she can be more emancipated and sophisticated in the city and that she can earn an independent livelihood by casual work, trade, or prostitution. She can even own property. The authority of the husband is weakened, and this in turn separates the wife from economic and social dependence on her husband's family [38]. Other women migrate to the city to find freedom from the traditional role of a wife which often borders on servitude compared with the life style of the more sophisticated, urban women [39]. They flatly reject the institution of marriage and prefer less binding temporary relationships with men.

Urban Slums

Whether the urban migrant moves alone or with his family, he is generally forced to live in squatter communities, shantytowns, or in the stabilized slums of the older parts of the city. He is soon resocialized to a different life style from that of his home village. A fourth of the migrant householders surveyed in a study in Ghana stated that one of the major problems of urban life was the slums, the bad housing, and the poor sanitation [40]. The greatest impact on the new migrant comes from this slum way of life, in which the physical problems are less threatening than the sociological aspects that are reflected in various deviant behavior patterns such as alcoholism, illegitimacy, prostitution, delinquency, and crime. [41].

In both developed and developing countries the majority of reported crime and delinquency is committed by slum dwellers and much of it occurs in the slum areas. The vast tracts of slums in the cities are considered one of the prime sources of criminal behavior in Venezuela [42]. As another example, a sample of urban residents in Ghana placed the blame for most crime on rural-urban migrants and regarded the squatter, shanty slum areas as the source of the criminal activities [43]. The migrant nuclear family in India settles in the city slums, where they are economically hard-pressed and socially outcast. The family "gradually loses its ideals of community welfare and sentiments of cohesive family life. Marriage-bonds are loosened and sex-partnership becomes the sole aim of marriage" [44]. Often both parents try to work, but they lack the support of other family members who were always available to care for the children in the village, and the "neglected or the destitute child is either victimized by adults for their anti-social activities or takes to law violation activities as an easy means of supporting himself" [45]. With reference to the relation of rural migrants to crime in San Juan, Puerto Rico, one study has stated:

Many of these migrant families, driven to the city in hopes of better conditions, are forced into slum-type existence, and the children grow to adulthood in an environment of social, economic and emotional deprivation. . . . Lack of adequate living space and the absence of recreational facilities force these youngsters to spend much of their time in the street looking for something to do, someone to talk to, and someone to "play" with. At the same time, their street life is frequently, though not always consciously, oriented toward seeking some sort of recognition and status in their peer group and some means of acquiring money and/or material possessions to which their middle class counterparts have ready access. Thus, their independence from informal social controls imposed by the family, their almost complete freedom of action, their sense of fatalism, their abject hatred of authority figures, their rationalized distrust of and dis-association from the middle class and their ready access to crime, vice, alcohol and drugs easily provide the opportunities and impetus for illegal and delinquent activities. Under these circumstances, it is not unexpected that such deviant behavior is becoming more frequent, but what is more, is tolerated to a considerable degree and thus tends to ilicit the tacit approval of the community [46].

CRIME AMONG YOUNG MIGRANTS

Reports from developing countries are filled with the high incidence of crime and delinquency among young migrants. A United Nations summary report for the world, for example, stated:

The tendency of rural youth to seek excitement in the city frequently ends in juvenile delinquency. There is no doubt that urban ideas and influences now reaching into the countryside are causing widespread restlessness among the rural youth: some of them are reported to migrate hundreds of miles in search of the excitement of the town and the prestige of urban life and employment [47].

A Ghanian study found that the majority of offenses in the larger cities were committed by the young from country areas. This phenomenon is common, since there is no significant relation to a particular tribe or religion [48]. The Republic of Central Africa reported that it is faced with a serious crime rate in urban problem areas, crimes primarily committed by youthful migrants from rural areas [49]. The prevalent offenses are stealing, particularly pickpocketing and car thefts. Only 25.9% of the fathers and 27% of the mothers of juveniles accused of theft in Cairo had been born that city [50]. The remainder, who were migrants, had come predominantly from the country rather than from other urban areas. Similarly, the relation of crime to the migration of young people to the city has been shown in a Peruvian study [51]. In Zambia it was found that nearly half the delinquents were migrants who had become "detribalized." "Few of them had any real understanding of the traditions and customs of the tribes to which they belonged" [52]. In the Upper Volta cities the typical migrant has been described as a young boy who does not want to stay on the land, who has had very little schooling, and who has become attracted to city life because of its excitement, the movies, and its variety of activities. He has no means of livelihood so he starts out by stealing or buying packages of cigarettes or small trinkets which he hopes to sell back in the village. This type of activity really does not enable him to live and he does not want to go back a failure, so he stays on in the city. His first thefts are simply utilitarian to get something to eat and to live. As an adolescent he teams up with others of his ethnic or village group and thus crminal groups develop [53].

A study made in India in 1967 analyzed the problem of the migrants and its significance in the increase of juvenile delinquency in that country [54]. In the city of Bombay it was felt that the urbanization and industrialization process attracted growing numbers of people to the cities from the villages and resulted in a gradual loss of ties and the subsequent disintegration of controlling social forces which lead to increased crime and delinquency.

They (the old family group) are replaced by the nuclear family consisting of parents and children cut off from other relatives and a neighborhood in which the mores are not homogeneous and the behavior of one person is a matter of relative indifference to others. . . . The family and the neighborhood are, therefore, no longer competent to control their members [55].

Despite evidence of this kind, it is important to recognize that the cities of developing countries grow mainly from migration, and although offenders come from this population it must also be recognized that it also contains many nonoffenders. In the Kampala study a group of young offenders, aged 18 to 25, was compared with a control group of nonoffenders of the same age. Both groups were made up almost entirely of migrants with no significant statistical difference between the groups but with a slightly higher proportion of migrants (90 and 83%) among the nonoffenders [56]. Migration appears to affect some individuals in more pronounced and different ways than it does others. Another important question is whether the juvenile migrant who comes into conflict with the law is different from those who remain in the countryside. In other words, are some predisposed to delinquency before they depart from the village and thus have already established a personality pattern for a delinquent way of life? The sheer numbers of these youthful migrants would seem to invalidate this explanation. A United Nations report has stated that "there are so many basic socio-economic factors at play in the rural area forcing the individual to leave it, that such a personal or psychological explanation of migration is completely overshadowed" [57].

Although ethnic heterogeneity in African cities is a factor in detribalization, these tribal or cultural differences have less effect in producing delinquency than the general influences of city life. Whenever the young are part of migrant families, the general impotence of parents to control them is a source of dismay to many urban Africans [58]. Traditional premarital controls become even more ineffective; young women are frequently induced into prostitution or have illegitimate children. A Lagos study found that in the urban family age loses its authority when the experiences of one generation become irrelevant to the next [59]. Only a quarter of the young people were found to have the same occupation as their fathers. Group festivals of tribal life are replaced by individual beer drinking parties. Many young males are left with little external control over their behavior, for the criminal law, the police, and other law-enforcement agencies of urban society may not be regarded as legitimate sources of authority. Those migrants who do remain with their families or friends from the same tribe experience more pressures to conform to conventional norms. Mayer found that when there were direct relationships with tribesmen indirect relations were also implied.

These consist in the consciousness that each man still has kin or friends in the same community at home. Thus indirect or third-party sanctions emanating from home do much to regulate the men's interaction while they are in town [60].

CRIME AND INITIAL ADJUSTMENT OF MIGRANTS IN KAMPALA

In the Uganda study migrants represented 83% of a sample of 164 offenders, aged 18 to 25, imprisoned for property offenses committed in Kampala and 90% of a control group of 206 nonoffenders [61]. The control group consisted of a sample of young males living in the two slum areas that were studied (see Chapter 5). The control group was assumed to be from the same social class and type of area in Kampala from which the sample of offenders had come. Three options were available in the selection of an offender sample. One method, the interview (because of the high rate of illiteracy, the use of a questionnaire would have been impossible) of a sample of the general population by using self-reported crime as the measure of deviance, had several shortcomings. First, several social scientists at the university who have had extensive field experience warned against such procedures because they might produce biased answers for large portions of the data. Second, at the time of the research the animosity between the Bugandans, who represented the largest single tribal group in the city, and the government was at a high level. An alternative method of obtaining a sample of offenders would have been to interview arrested offenders at police stations, but this was discarded for several reasons. There appears to be a strong fear of police and police practices in Uganda, and it is doubtful if a sufficient rapport could have been established. Furthermore, information concerning the nature of the offense was needed and many would be reluctant to discuss this subject before trial and sentencing. Manpower and time limitations also reduced the practicality of this procedure.

It was decided to select a sample of institutionalized property offenders from the Murchison Bay Prison in Kampala who had been sentenced during the three-month period, March to June 1969. Although institutionalized samples have been criticized in the developed countries because they may reflect the characteristics of those most likely to be imprisoned rather than offenders in general, several factors in the social, judicial, and penal systems of Uganda mitigate this source of error. In the United States, for example, blacks and the poor are more likely to be imprisoned for an offense than the white middle-class person because of the differential power distributions among the classes. Class biases are reduced in Kampala, for most Africans still belong to the lower classes. Well-developed probation systems can also affect the composition of prison populations. If a large portion of convicted offenders was put on probation, a bias could enter the sample and limit the generality of conclusions. Probation is still not really approved in Uganda, since it is not regarded as punishment. Moreover, Uganda's probation service is not highly developed. Only 1.1% of convicted offenders were put on probation in 1967 and another 4.4% received suspended sentences or were cautioned.

A factor that caused greater concern was that 48.7% of those convicted were fined. Available statistics did not record the sentence by type of crime. In 1967, however, there were twice as many court cases for offenses against persons or for violations of regulations as for offenses against property—22,750 to 11,102 [62]. Data gathered in this research indicate that more severe penalties were given for crimes against property. Although 22.6% of those sentenced to imprisonment in the country received a sentence of one month or less, none of the property offenders, aged 18 to 25, processed at Murchison Bay Prison in 1968, received a sentence of less than two months. It can be assumed that nearly all of those fined had committed minor assaults or transgressions against municipal ordinances. Although some property offenders were fined, the sample would perhaps represent only those judged to have committed a more serious property crime. The penal system has several features that further enhanced the validity of the sample. Convicted offenders from Kampala are initially taken to a classification center near the city, then dispersed to a variety of institutions throughout the country. Since the city does not possess a jail for short-term offenders, all persons convicted of a crime must pass through the classification center. Normally, each offender spends at least two weeks at this center before being sent elsewhere.

The offender sample was restricted to male property offenders aged 18 to 25. The lower limit of 18 was imposed by prison policy, and the upper limit was chosen because of the widespread finding that the major portion of crime is committed by those under the age of 26. Cases were not excluded from the sample because the length of sentence was quite short. It might be argued that a sentence of less than six months does not indicate an offense of sufficient seriousness to warrant inclusion in the offender sample. It is doubtful, however, whether distinctions such as felony and misdemeanor or length of sentence represent more than artificial administrative decisions [63]. They give no indication of intent or motivation. Only 3% of the sample were given sentences of less than three months and 15% were given less than six months. The criticism does not affect a large portion of the sample. At several points men were transferred to the prison farms after two days and consequently a total of 39 offenders was missed; because of selection methods no substitutions could be made. They composed 19.2% of the total number of possible subjects admitted during the interview period. There were no refusals and the men appeared to be cooperative. The final sample constituted 164 male property offenders from 18 to 25 years of age. To determine whether the sample was representative of all young property offenders admitted to the prison data from the admission records were collected on all young property offenders admitted in 1968. The distributions for religion, education, and tribe were quite similar.

Some developing countries reveal a pattern of step migration, wherein migrants move first to a small town, then to a large city. In a study of several hundred males aged 15 and over, for example, who moved to Ouagadougou in Upper Volta and Niamey in Niger, it was revealed that less than one-third had moved directly to Ouagadougou and about one-half to Niamey, the rest having had two or more intermediate moves [64]. Most of the Kampala migrants, both the offenders in a prison sample and the nonoffenders, had moved directly to the city from their original homes (see Table 15). In fact, there was no significant differences between the two groups. Moreover, responses of the extent of previous urban experience revealed a significantly greater proportion of offenders to have lived only in a village before moving to Kampala (see Table 16). Seventy-one percent of the migrant offenders and 48.6% of the migrant nonoffenders had a village setting as their only points of reference. The village migrants' lack of familiarity with urban living appears to have had a possible relation to patterns of association that ultimately ended in their arrests.

Table 15   Number of Moves in Migration to Kampala—Offenders Versus Nonoffenders

	Offender		Nonoffender	
	No.	%	No.	%
1	82	60.3	111	60.0
2	32	23.5	37	20.0
3 or more	22	16.2	37	20.0
	136	100.0	185	100.0

$x^2 = 1.07$
df = 2
NS

Migrants who lack friends or the means to rent shelter must gravitate toward the makeshift sheds or vacated market stalls in which homeless transients congregate. Those with some funds can find cheap rooms in less desirable sections, often near bars where beer is brewed and sold illegally and where criminal patterns are likely to be encountered. Although all offenders did not come from such surroundings, most of them undoubtedly found themselves faced with this situation.

Both criminal offender and nonoffender migrants were asked if a relative or friend from their tribal groups had helped them to get food,

Table 16   Previous Residence Before Migration to
Kampala—Offenders Versus Nonoffenders

	Offender		Nonoffender	
	No.	%	No.	%
1. Village	96	70.6	90	48.6
2. Town[a]	23	16.9	54	29.2
3. City[a]	17	12.5	41	22.2
	136	100.0	185	100.0

[a] "Town" had a population of less than 10,000 and "City" more
than 10,000.
$\chi^2 = 15.48$
df = 2
$P < .001$

shelter, money, or employment when they arrived at Kampala. The responses are shown in Table 17. Nonoffenders received aid from at least
one member of their own tribe, a relative or friend, in 75% of the cases,
whereas the offenders received such help only 59% of the time, a difference that was statistically highly significant. One out of four offenders, as
compared with 15.7% of the nonoffenders, received no help at all.

Table 17   Responses to the Question, "When You First Arrived in
Kampala, Did You Get Help from Someone?"

	Nonoffender		Offender	
	No.	%	No.	%
1. Family or other relative	101	54.6	61	44.9
2. Friend—same tribe	39	21.0	20	14.7
3. Friend—different tribe	16	8.7	20	14.7
4. None	29	15.7	35	25.7
Total	185	100.0	136	100.0

$\chi^2 = 16.47$
df = 3
$P < .001$

Offenders who had no form of assistance sometimes had to seek material help outside the tribal network, and this absence of tribal or kin orientation could have been a critical event in the total career pattern for many of them. In telling how he met his best friend, one respondent describes the situation of many migrants. "He was a migrant and had nowhere to stay. I met him at around 10:00 P.M. at night and he asked me whether I could give him some help, say accommodations. I agreed and led him to my own home. From then on we began to be friends." When they receive no help, one study of unemployed in Kampala, for example, quoted several migrants as saying that they were "trying to raise their bus fare home because they did not want to become thieves and they saw no alternative if they had to stay on in town" [65].

Crime and Migrants' Contact with Relatives and Tribal Members in the City

For many migrants the extended family remains a source of security against the conflicting pressures of urban life [66]. In the Ugandan study only 4% of the control group of nonoffenders indicated that they had no contact with relatives in Kampala [67] (see Table 18). The offenders' pattern of interaction was statistically significantly different. One third of the offenders who had relatives in Kampala completely shunned them, whereas only 4% of the nonoffenders did the same. Twenty-five percent of the nonoffenders, compared with 34.2% of the offenders, reported having no relatives in Kampala. More than half the offenders (55.4%) had

Table 18   Contact with Relatives in Kampala—Offenders Versus Nonoffenders

	Nonoffenders		Offenders	
	No.	%	No.	%
Contact with relatives	148	96.1	72	66.7
No contact with relatives	6	3.9	36	33.3
Total with relatives	154	100.0	108	100.0
No relatives in Kampala	52	25.0	56	34.2
Total	206	100.0	164	100.0

$\chi^2 = 40.88$
$P < .001$
$df = 1$

no access to this potential form of reinforcement for law-abiding behavior. It is possible that a portion of the offenders were rejected by their families and relatives because of their involvement in deviant activities. Moreover, some came to the city because of conflict with relatives in the village. Nevertheless, the avoidance of kin in Kampala removed a potential source of unfavorable definitions for criminal behavior.

Restricting friendships to members of one's own tribe may serve to reduce urban influences that might call into question important values or traditions concerned with property crime. Tribal members have greater potential for exercising control in the city, since they are much more likely to communicate with important family members at home. These ties with the village may provide a strong emotional force in the life of the urban dweller. Respondents were asked to name the tribe of their three best friends. A numerical scale of diversity was constructed on the basis of their responses [68]. The degree of diversity in tribal friendships between offenders and nonoffenders was significantly different. (The actual tests and levels of significance for all items used in the comparison of offenders and nonoffenders and the communities with a high and low crime rate in the Kampala study are summarized in Appendix A. Some test results are included in the tables, but in general specific figures are not included in the text.) When the scores were dichotomized into high and low, 41% of the offenders had a high diversity of tribal friendships, whereas only 26% of nonoffenders were high. Along with avoiding their kin in the city, offenders had a greater tendency to find friendships outside their tribes.

Crime and Migrant Contacts with Village Home

It might be presumed that a continued relation with his village could serve as a stabilizing influence on the life of the urbanite by presenting definitions unfavorable to criminal behavior. In his study of Africans in East London, South Africa, Mayer, for example, notes that one way in which traditional migrants preserved their unity and sense of identity in the city was by frequent visits to the rural home [69]. In the Uganda study, however, this type of expected relationship between crime and village contacts was not found. Kampala offenders and the control group were asked whether they ever visited their relatives in the village. The results are shown in Table 19 [70]. There is no significant difference between offenders and nonoffenders. Actually, 69.6% of the offenders, as opposed to 76% of the nonoffenders, reported that they visited their relatives in the village. In some cases, however, the failure to maintain ties with rural kin might not have been because of a lack of interest. One

Table 19   Visits to Relatives in Home Village—Offenders Versus Non-offenders

Visit	Nonoffenders		Offenders	
	No.	%	No.	%
Visited	155	76.0	105	69.6
Did not visit	49	24.0	46	30.4
Total with relatives	204	100.0	151	100.0
No relatives in village	2	1.0	13	7.9
Total	206	100.0	164	100.0

$\chi^2 = 2.14$
$df = 1$
NS

offender remarked, for example, that "I feared my parents for I had told them that I had come here to Kampala to work for money, but I had failed to get a job. Thus I had no money. How could I appear before them without a single coin?"

Two other questions treated the respondents' relation with the village. The first questioned whether he had any land at home or could expect to receive any from his kin. Since land is a source of status and possible income, land ownership could be a vehicle for bringing an individual into contact with his kin and his traditions. In times of crises possession of land would provide alternative means of support, were the person willing to return to its cultivation. There was no significant difference statistically between offenders and nonoffenders on possession of land in the village, although the percentage of offenders who claimed to own land (43.9) was higher than the percentage of the nonoffenders (36). The offenders did not disproportionately represent the dispossessed, since almost half of them had some land of their own. This result suggests that the offenders were not economically more deprived than the ordinary nonoffender and that their offenses were not motivated for this reason [71]. The second question asked if the respondent intended ever to return home permanently. Intent to return home permanently at some time would seem to imply that the respondent feels he will be accepted by his kin and that he has not rejected village life as an unacceptable alternative to urban life. Likewise, the item on intent to return to the village permanently produced no significant differences between samples, but again the offenders (53%) more often gave the traditional response that they would return home than the nonoffenders (41.2%).

SOME CONCLUSIONS

In many developing countries migration to the cities, as compared with the history of developed countries, is not by intermediate stages but by a sharp leap from village to a distant urban center. The urbanizing of village migrants presents serious problems of identity, economic stress, and problems of living in urban slum areas. Most of all, there is ample evidence that one of the greatest hazards for a rural migrant is to engage in crime or prostitution.

The Kampala study showed that a crucial factor in the involvement of the migrants in criminal activities is their initial adjustment to the city. Those who later engaged in crime were less likely to have had a relative or a friend to help them on their arrival to adjust to the city. Moreover, they were less likely to have maintained contacts with relatives and tribal ·members in the city.

On the other hand, the differences between offenders and non-offenders on all three measures of village contact were not significant. The offender did not appear to be more likely to be cut off from his rural past or from the support that rural ties might bring him. The offenders, moreover, tended to be more isolated in the urban environment. The maintenance of rural ties therefore does not appear to reduce the likelihood of criminal involvement; the events and patterns of initial contact and association in the city appear to be the major determinants of behavioral choices.

NOTES AND REFERENCES

1. A. L. Epstein, "Urbanization and Social Change in Africa," in Gerald Breese, Ed., *The City in Newly Developing Countries: Readings on Urbanism and Urbanization* (Princeton: Princeton University Press, 1969), p. 254.

2. William L. Flinn, "Rural to Urban Migration: A Colombian Case," Land Tenure Center, Madison, Wisconsin RP. No. 19, and William L. Flinn and James W. Converse, "Eight Assumptions Concerning Rural-Urban Migration in Colombia: A Three Shanty-town Test," *Land Economics*, **XLV**:84–104 (November 1970).

3. Kenneth Little, *West African Urbanization: A Study of Voluntary Associations in Social Change* (Cambridge: Cambridge University Press, 1965); P. C. Lloyd, *Africa in Social Change: Changing Traditional Societies in the Modern World* (Baltimore: Penguin, 1967): William Mangin, "Latin American Squatter Settlements: A Problem and a Solution," *Latin American Research Review*, 2:65–69 (Summer, 1967).

4. William McCord, *The Springtime of Freedom: The Evolution of Developing Societies* (New York: Oxford University Press, 1965), p. 36. See also Pandharinath Prabhu, "Bombay: A Study on the Social Effects of Urbanization on Industrial Workers Migrating from Rural Areas to the City of Bombay," in *The Social Implications of Industrialization and Urbanization* (Calcutta UNESCO, 1956), pp. 49–107, and William L. Flinn, "Process and Effects of Rural-Urban Migration in Colombia: Two Case Studies in Bogota," in F. F. Rabinovitz and F. M. Trueblood, Eds., *Latin American Urban Research* (Beverly Hills, Calif.: Sage Publications, 1971), pp. 70–98.

5. Breese, *The City in Newly Developed Countries*, pp. 79–84.

6. Michael Banton, *West African City: A Study of Tribal Life in Freetown* (London: Oxford University Press, 1957), p. 214.

7. Walter Elkan, *Migrants and Proletarians* (London: Oxford University Press, 1960). See also Lloyd Rodwin, *Nations and Cities* (New York: Houghton Mifflin, 1970), p. 5.

8. Study by Man-Gap Lee, Seoul National University, as reported in Young-Hee Rho, "The Place of Metropolitan Areas in the Korean Situation," *Conference Papers*, Rehovot Conference on Urbanization and Development in Developing Countries, Rehovot, Israel, 1971, p. 3.

9. Banton, *West African City*, p. 214.

10. Translated from M. Bako, "Urbanization et Développment," *Conference Papers*, Rehovot Conference on Urbanization and Development in Developing Countries, Rehovot, Israel, 1971, p. 3.

11. Little, *West African Urbanization*, p. 11. See also Horace Miner, Ed., *The City in Modern Africa* (New York: Praeger, 1967).

12. John C. Caldwell, *African Rural-Urban Migration: The Movement to Ghana's Towns* (New York: Columbia University Press, 1969).

13. Adame Curle, *Educational Strategy for Developing Countries* (London: Tavistock, 1963).

14. William Clifford, "Juvenile Delinquency in Zambia," A United Nations study to assess the real extent of juvenile delinquency as well as the extent to which changes in the delinquency rates may be due to economic, social, and/or psychological causes, United Nations No. SOA/SD/CS.3, April 30, 1967.

15. Akin L. Mabogunje, "Urbanization Problems in Africa," *Conference Papers*, Rehovot Conference on Urbanization and Development in Developing Countries, Rehovot, Israel, 1971, p. 2.

16. Joseph H. Greenberg, "Urbanism, Migration and Language," in Hilda Kuper, Ed., *Urbanization and Migration in West Africa* (Berkeley: University of California Press, 1965), pp. 50–59. For a study of Kampala see Carol Meyers Scotton, *Choosing a Lingua Franca in An African Capital* (Edmonton: Linguistic Research, 1972).

17. Antonio Sanchez Galindo, "The Penitentiary Center of the State of Mexico as an Institution for Study," *Derecho Penal Contemporaneo*, Mexico, 30:79–101 (1969).

18. Shmuel N. Eisenstadt, *The Absorption of Immigrants: A Comparative Study Based Mainly on the Jewish Community in Palestine and the State of Israel* (London: Routledge and Kegan Paul, 1954).

19. Elkan, *Migrants and Proletarians*, 1960.

20. Philip Mayer, *Townsmen or Tribesmen, Conservatism and the Process of Urbanization in a South African City* (London: Oxford University Press, 1961), and Leon E. Clark, Ed., *From Tribe to Town: Problems of Adjustment* (New York: Praeger, 1959).

21. Mary Gluksman, "Seven Year Research Plan of the Rhodes-Livingstone Institute of Social Studies in British Central Africa," *Rhodes-Livingstone Journal*, 4:12 (1945).

22. Philip Mayer, "Migrancy and the Study of Africans in Town," *American Anthropologist*, 64:580 (1962).

23. Mayer, *Townsmen or Tribesmen*, p. 9.

24. Aidan Southall and P. C. W. Gutkind, *Townsmen in the Making: Kampala and Its Suburbs* (London: Kegan Paul Trench Trubner, 1957).

25. Peter Marris, *African City Life* (Kampala: Uganda Press Trust, 1966), p. 67.

26. Walter A. Lunden, "Crime in Thailand," *Police*, 12:47 (January–February, 1968).

27. Elio Gomez Grillo, *Delinquency in Caracas* (Universidad del Zulia, Faculated de Humanidades y Educaión, 1970), p. 178. See also Lloyd Rogler, "Neighborhoods and Slums in Latin America," *Journal of Inter-American Studies*, 9:507–528 (1967).

28. Lloyd, *Africa in Social Change*, pp. 125–142. For an analysis of the same subject in Latin cultures see Joseph Kahl, *The Measurement of Modernism: A Study of Values in Brazil and Mexico* (Austin: University of Texas Press, 1968); his findings indicate that achievement may not be so strong in the Latin culture.

29. Daryll Forde, "Introductory Survey," in *Social Implications of Industrialization and Urbanization in Africa South of the Sahara* (United Nations: UNESCO, 1956), p. 49. See also Philip M. Hauser, Ed., *Urbanization in Latin America* (New York: International Documents Service, 1961).

30. Peter Marris, "African City Life," *Nkanga*, 1, (1968).

31. David Parkin, *Neighbours and Nationals in an African City Ward* (London: Routledge and Kegan Paul, 1969), and Aidan Southall, "Kampala-Mengo," in Miner, *The City in Modern Africa*, pp. 297–332.

32. Caldwell, *African Rural-Urban Migration*, p. 171.

33. Gerald H. Zarr, "Liberia," in Alan Milner, *African Penal Systems* (London: Routledge and Kegan Paul), 1969, p. 194.

34. C. R. Hutton, "Unemployment and Labour Migration in Uganda," unpublished Ph.D. dissertation, Makerere University, Kampala, Uganda, 1968.

35. Caldwell, *African Rural-Urban Migration*.

36. Draft Report of Third United Nations Seminar for the Arab States on the Prevention of Crime and the Treatment of Offenders, Damascus, September–October 1964, October 4, 1964, p. 9.

37. C. Sofer, "Urban African Social Structure and Working Group Behavior at Jinja, Uganda," in *Social Implications of Industrialization and Urbanization in Africa South of the Sahara* (Lausanne: UNESCO, 1956), p. 602.

38. Peter Marris, "Motives and Methods: Reflections on a Study in Lagos," in Miner, *The City in Modern Africa*, pp. 44–55.

39. Southall and Gutkind, *Townsmen in the Making*, p. 79.

40. Caldwell, *African Rural-Urban Migrants*.

41. Marshall B. Clinard, *Slums and Community Development: Experiments in Self-Help* (New York: The Free Press, 1966), Chapter I.

42. Juan Manuel Mayorca, *Criminology* (Caracas: Graficas Ediciones de Arte, 1971), pp. 124–25.

43. Caldwell, *African Rural-Urban Migrants.*

44. Hansa Sheth, *Juvenile Delinquency in an Indian Setting* (Bombay: Popular Book Depot, 1961), p. xix.

45. *Ibid.,* xix.

46. Lenore R. Kupperstein and Jaime Toro-Calder, *Juvenile Delinquency in Puerto Rico* (Rio Piedras: University of Puerto Rico, 1969), p. 123.

47. United Nations, *Report on the World Situation,* Publication No. 1957. IV. 3, pp. 141–142. Also see *New Forms of Juvenile Delinquency: Their Origins, Prevention and Treatment,* London, August 8–20, 1960, A/Conf. 17/7 p. 46.

48. G. Tooth, "Survey of Juvenile Delinquency in the Gold Coast," in *Social Implications of Industrialization and Urbanization in Africa South of the Sahara* (Lausanne: UNESCO, 1956), pp. 86–91. This study found no differences in psychological abnormalities between offenders and a control group.

49. Statement made at the Fourth United Nations Congress on the Prevention of Crime and the Treatment of Offenders, Kyoto, Japan, August, 1970.

50. United Nations Bureau of Social Affairs, "Juvenile Delinquency in the United Arab Republic," mimeo, SOA/SD/C. S.1, 1966, p. 35.

51. Caravedo Baltazar, "Pathologii Social en el Peru," cited in *Current Projects in Prevention of Crime,* 3:139 (1963) (Washington, D. C.: U. S. Government Printing Office, 1963). It was felt that this migration was an outgrowth of changes in the entire social structure of the society rather than individual pathology.

52. Clifford, "Juvenile Delinquency in Zambia," p. 33.

53. Pierre M. Lagier, "Criminalité et Justice en Afrique Occidentale," in *L'Afrique Occidentale: Développement et Société* (Montréal: Université de Montréal, 1972), pp. 384–385.

54. United Nations, "Juvenile Delinquency in India," a study to assess the real extent of juvenile delinquency as well as the extent to which changes in the delinquency rates may be due to economic, social, and/or psychology causes, XOA/SD/CS.2. June 16, 1967.

55. Sheth, *Juvenile Delinquency in an Indian Setting,* p. xviii.

56. For a discussion of the offender and nonoffender groups see pages 00 to 00.

57. "Urban Juvenile Delinquency," *Prevention of Types of Criminality Resulting from Social Changes and Accompanying Economic Development in Less Developed Countries,* Second United Nations Congress on the Prevention of Crime and the Treatment of Offenders, London, August 8–20, 1960. p. 9.

58. Ellen Hellman, "Life in a Johannesburg Yard," in Simon and Phoebe Ottenberg, *Cultures and Societies of Africa* (New York: Random House, 1960), p. 556.

59. Peter Marris, *Family and Social Change in an African City: A Study of Rehousing in Lagos* (London: Routledge & Kegan Paul, 1961), p. 136.

60. Mayer, *Townsmen or Tribesmen,* p. 287.

61. A Kampala study of 102 juvenile property offenders found them to be highly mobile, not only having migrated to the city from the rural areas but also having

moved from one place to another. Only four persons in the sample had lived in one place during the five years before their arrest. See Eric P. Kibuka, "Sociological Aspects of Juvenile Delinquency in Kampala 1962 to 1969," Ph.D. dissertation, University of East Africa, 1972.

62. *Uganda Statistical Abstract, 1968,* Government Printer, Entebbe.

63. Edwin H. Sutherland and Donald Cressey, *Criminology,* (Philadelphia: Lippincott, 1970), 8th ed., p. 17.

64. Joel Gregory, "Les Migrations Modernes en Afrique Occidentale," in D. Ian Pool, "La Population de L'Afrique Occidentale," *L'Afrique Occidentale,* p. 13.

65. Carol Hutton, "Unemployment and Labour Migration in Uganda," unpublished Ph.D. dissertation, Kampala Makerere University, 1968, p. 86.

66. Peter Marris, "African City Life," *Nkanga,* 1:5 (1968).

67. It would have been better to have solicited information on the frequency of contact with relatives. Such an item was initially included in the interview schedule, but an undetected typing error on the offender schedule made it impossible to use this data.

68. The responses were coded zero if no friend were mentioned, one if the friend was from the same tribe, and two if he were from a different tribe:

$$\text{score} = \frac{3 \times (\text{sums of responses})}{\text{number of friends mentioned}}.$$

It was necessary to develop the scale in this manner because some respondents mentioned only one or two friends.

69. Mayer, *Townsmen or Tribesmen,* p. 284.

70. Frequency of contact was not recorded because of a clerical error in the schedule.

71. In a study of crime in the Cameroun the authors arrived at a similar conclusion concerning juvenile delinquency. S. P. Tschoungai and Pierre Zumbach, "Diagnosis of Juvenile Delinquency in Cameroun," *International Review of Criminal Policy,* **20**:45–46 (1962).

Chapter 5   The Social Organization of Slums
and Criminal Behavior

Nearly all large cities, whether in developed or developing countries, have slums, and these slums constitute the most important and persistent problem of urban life today. An ever-present phenomenon of the rapidly expanding cities of Africa, Latin America, and Asia are the extensive slum communities of squatters and shantytowns in and around their peripheral areas as well as those that still exist in their older sections. Families in Bangkok crowd together in "pile villages," which are groups of poorly constructed shacks raised on wooden stilts along the waterfront. The small lanes of Calcutta, Dacca, and Lagos are lined with tin shacks, bamboo huts, and straw hovels, all set amid filth and scented with the odors of open drains. Impoverished shantytowns and squatter shacks built from junk cover the hillsides of Rio de Janeiro, Lima, Hong Kong, and other Asiatic, African, and South American cities. No slums are denser than some of those of Hong Kong and Singapore, where a single large room may house 10 to 20 families, each occupying only "bed space," two-tiered, with almost no personal privacy possible. Indian slums have existed for centuries and are known by many words: *bustees, jompris, juggies, ahatas, cheris, katras,* and *chawls.* Similarly, in Latin America slum and squatter communities are common and variously referred to as *jacales* or *colonias proletarias* in Mexico; *favelas, mocambos, algados,* or *vilas de malocas* in Brazil; *callampas* in Chile; *villas miserias* in Buenos Aires; *barrios clandestinos* in Colombia and Peru; *ranchos* in Venezuela; *kampongs* in Indonesia; and *bidonvilles* in French-speaking Africa [1].

Slums can be classified along a continuum. They differ in physical setting, overcrowding, permanence of the inhabitants, degree of organization among the residents, and types of problem presented [2]. In some slums unique circumstances affect the residents. Physically they may be mere shantytowns, collections of hovels made of scrap materials, hastily erected on unauthorized land and without even the basic comforts of water and sanitation. Others may range from substantial multistoried tenements to palatial old houses formerly occupied by wealthy citizens. Regardless of physical structure, most slums are overcrowded far beyond the minimum standards of health and decency. Slums can also be regarded in terms of the attitude of the slum dweller toward social mobility by assimilation or acculturation into the social and economic life of the community and the measure of socioeconomic handicaps and barriers to such movement [3]. Each of these variables provides two general classifications: "slums of hope" and "slums of despair." The former are characterized by the attitudes of the residents, whether they expect to improve their situations and whether there are opportunities for advancing out of the slums. Slums of hope are generally the homes of recent immigrants to the community, whereas those of despair are populated by groups of longer residence. Laquian has suggested a number of more detailed variables that may be used in classifying slum and squatter communities:

(a) spatial location (central city or peripheral area) ; (b) degree of physical deterioration of dwellings and surroundings; (c) extent of overcrowding and congestion of dwellings and people; (d) relative age of the settlement; (e) type of land occupied (valuable land or marginal land) ; (f) adequacy of urban services (water, fuel, light, medical, and welfare services); (g) community organization or disorganization; (h) ethnic or class homogeneity or heterogeneity; (i) extent of deviant behavior (crime, juvenile delinquency) ; (j) apathy and social isolation; (k) disease rates and extent of health and sanitation; etc. [4].

People dwelling in old established slum areas and newer squatter communities constitute a large proportion of the large cities of all developing countries (see Table 20). In Calcutta in 1961 it was estimated that 2.2 million, or 33% of the population, lived in slums. The latest survey in 1968 of the extent of the slum population in metropolitan Manila revealed that there were about 127,852 squatter families (767,112 persons) and 55, 907 families (335,442 persons) living in slums, a total of 183,759 families, or 1.1 million persons out of a total population of approximately 3 million [5]. In Dakar in 1969 approximately 30% of a population of approximately 500,000 lived in *bidonvilles*. Of a total population estimated at 730,000 in Guayaquil, Ecuador, 360,000, almost half, were living in squatter settlements in 1968 [6]; in Lima, Peru, approximately 36% of a population estimated at 2.8 million in 1968 lived in squatter settlements [7]; and the percentage in Caracas was 35. One regional planner has briefly outlined the basic problems which have led to the growth of slum areas.

Table 20 Population in Slums and Uncontrolled Settlements as a Percentage of the Population of Major Cities in Selected Less Developed Countries

Country	City	Year	City Population	Population in Slums and Uncontrolled Settlements	
				Total	As Percentage of City Population
Africa					
Senegal	Dakar	1969	500,000	150,000	30.0
United Republic of Tanzania	Dar-es-Salaam	1967	272,800	93,000	34.0
Zambia	Lusaka	1967	194,000	53,000	27.0
Americas					
Brazil	Rio de Janeiro	1947	2,050,000	400,000	20.0
		1957	2,940,000	650,000	22.0
		1961	3,326,000	900,000	27.0
	Belo Horizonte	1965	872,300	119,799	14.0
	Porto Alegre	1962	680,000	86,465	13.0
	Recife	1961	792,000	396,000	50.0
	Brasilia	1962	148,000	60,000	41.0
Chile	Santiago	1964	2,184,000	546,000	25.0
Colombia	Cali	1964	812,810	243,840	30.0
	Buenaventura	1964	110,660	88,530	80.0
Ecuador	Guayaquil	1968	730,000	360,000	49.0
Mexico	Mexico City	1952	2,372,000	330,000	14.0
		1966	3,287,334	1,500,000	46.0
Panama	Panama City	1968	373,000	63,000	17.0
Peru	Lima	1957	1,260,729	114,000	9.0
		1961	1,715,971	360,000	21.0
		1969	2,800,000	1,000,000	36.0

(Continued)

Table 20 (continued)

Country	City	Year	City Population	Population in Slums and Uncontrolled Settlements	
				Total	As Percentage of City Population
	Arequipa	1957	117,208	10,500	9.0
		1961	135,358	54,143	40.0
	Chimbote	1957	33,000	6,600	20.0
Venezuela	Caracas	1961	1,330,000	280,000	21.0
		1964	1,590,000	556,300	35.0
	Maracaibo	1966	559,000	280,000	50.0
	Ciudad Guayana	1966	86,000	34,000	40.0
Asia and the Far East					
Afghanistan	Kabul	1968	475,000	100,000	21.0
China	Taipei	1966	1,300,000	325,000	25.0
India	Calcutta	1961	6,700,000	2,220,000	33.0
Indonesia	Djakarta	1961	2,906,000	725,000	25.0
Iraq	Baghdad	1965	1,745,000	500,000	29.0
Malaysia	Kuala Lumpur	1961	400,000	100,000	25.0
Pakistan	Karachi	1964	2,280,000	752,000	33.0
		1968	2,700,000	600,000	27.0
Philippines	Manila	1968	less than 3,000,000	1,100,000	35.0
Singapore	Singapore	1966	1,870,000	280,000	15.0

SOURCE: *Improvement of Slums and Uncontrolled Settlements*, Report of the Interregional Seminar on the Improvement of Slums and Uncontrolled Settlements, Medellin, Colombia, February 15–March 1, 1970 (New York: United Nations, 1971).

When census or United Nations figures were not available for city populations in the years required to correspond with the data on slums and uncontrolled settlements, figures were derived from the most accurate base data and growth rates. The term "city population" has generally been taken to include the population of the urban agglomeration.

The existing stock of housing cannot cope with a population growing rapidly through natural increase and tides of immigration. Given the cost of conventional construction, the nation lacks resources to increase that stock at the same rate as the population is increasing. Since new housing is expensive, it goes primarily to the wealthier families and a rising middle class, except for a small amount of expensively subsidized housing for the poor. . . . In a sense, with the exception of servants, all of the urban poor live in marginal housing. Those crowded into housing that has filtered down to them are occupying the marginal units of the conventional stock. And those that live in self-constructed settlements settle on land which from the point of view of location, topography, or tenure is marginal in the sense that it is at or just beyond the margin of the conventional land market. Marginal housing goes up on hillsides that are too steep for conventional development, or on floodplains; it spreads beyond the build-up margin of the city; and it takes over land whose owners cannot or will not enforce their claims (private owners in some cases, public in others) [8].

The slums in developing countries are particularly regarded in physical terms: they are overcrowded, seriously congested, and seriously lacking in services and facilities. Such physical aspects alone, however, do not make the slum, and poor housing per se does not produce crime and other forms of deviant behavior. The problems of the slum are produced by the conditions that have developed there. The slum represents a way of life all its own, with its own social organization and a subculture with its own set of norms and values [9]. In turn, these values are reflected in the social ills of crime, prostitution, or drug addiction, poor health practices, bad sanitation, a growing social isolation from the greater urban world, and a general apathy and lack of participation in self-help activities at the community level [10]. One author has well summarized the problem: although he was writing specifically about developed countries, his comments apply equally to the less developed.

Certainly there is much evidence to substantiate the argument that the incidence of poverty, disease, vice, and crime is far greater in slum districts than in other parts of the metropolis. What the picture overlooks, however, is that the housing problems of slum occupants are generally inseparable from family and community disorganization, poverty and disease. Human lives as well as houses are blighted in these areas. Merely moving occupants into better dwelling units will not cure other physical and social ills. Empirical evidence, in fact, is accumulating to show that improved housing does not have many of the social benefits initially attributed to it. . . . Yet the belief that delinquency, prostitution, alcoholism, crime, and other forms of social pathology automatically inhere in the slums and will die if their demolition continues to persist [11].

Even with the provisions of improved physical conditions for slum dwellers in the developed countries the slum way of life continues. In fact, in most slum clearance projects, where similar income groups have been relocated, whether in Chicago, New York, San Juan, Caracas, or London, extensive deviant behavior and poor health and sanitation practices still exist [12]. A study of a high-rise apartment slum clearance project in a large United States city, for example, revealed widespread delinquency and crime [13], and a Puerto Rican discussion of housing projects uncovered untold friction and social problems [14]. Another study found that the isolation and impersonality of the housing projects in San Juan contribute to juvenile delinquency [15]. Slum clearance projects bring together a new group of strangers who destroy whatever community feelings and informal social controls previously existed in the slum areas. Substitutes are usually formal controls administered by an external housing agency which attempt to deal with the residents' problems with regulations that often result in counter-reactions. A social scientist who studied a slum clearance project in Puerto Rico wrote of the tremendous implications in the lives of these slum people. It meant "moving from small houses to apartment buildings, from wooden construction to concrete buildings, from squatters rights to tenancy, from shifting day by day to planned administration." The planner faces the problem that many people are not ready for this change and do not want to make it in this particular manner. "Those who do make the move are frequently not those who could profit most by the change" [16]. Slum shantytowns have many advantages compared with public housing projects, according to another Puerto Rican study which found the former to be a self-sustaining community in which rural newcomers found new ways in a neighborhood of friendliness, strong kinship ties, and cooperativeness. In contrast, the management of public housing projects crushes leadership, old kin and neighborhood ties are broken up, and the climate is one of frustration, suspicion, and resentment [17].

Although it is not hard to understand the problems of the slums in less developed countries, it is often difficult to understand that they actually perform real economic and social functions as a "natural" part of rapid urban growth rather than a pathological phenomenon. Slums reflect the larger processes of industrialization and urbanization which apply to a series of interdependent relationships with certain segments of the city's population as well as with the city as a whole.

Researchers on the slum or squatter way of life have shown that these areas are uniquely suited for the "shock absorber" role they have to assume to tide over rural migrants from their old ways to the modernity of urban man. As areas in transition themselves, they provide a comfortable abode for the formerly rural migrant finding his way in urban society [18].

Turner has pointed out that uncontrolled urban settlement is the result of normal processes of urban accommodation under the exceptional conditions of contemporary urbanization. "By this hypothesis, squatter and other forms of uncontrolled urban settlement are not the 'official aberrations' they so commonly are assumed to be. They are the perfectly natural response to an abnormal situation" [19]. In a study that undoubtedly indicates the functions of the slum almost everywhere in less developed countries the slums of Calcutta were found to have several functions of major importance in the urbanization process.

1. They provide housing at rents that are within the means of the lowest income groups.

2. They act as reception centers for migrants by providing a means of assistance in the adaptation to urban life.

3. They provide within the bustee a wide variety of employment in marginal and small-scale enterprises.

4. They provide a means of finding accommodation in proximity to work.

5. Their social and communal organization provides essential social support in unemployment and other occasions of difficulty.

6. They encourage and reward small-scale private entrepreneurship in the field of housing [20].

In developing countries slums provide the city with cheap unskilled labor and cheap housing, they make possible an association of migrants from similar tribal and regional groups, and they educate village migrants into the ways of urban living [21]. With this unskilled and semiskilled labor city growth, particularly in developing countries, is realized. Slum dwellers export their labor and "import" goods and services from other parts of the city. Though individual purchases may be small, the total consumption of these consumer commodities is significant. Without such a population cities could not survive. In less developed countries the development of slums belongs to urban development as a natural aspect of growth, not as a "cancer" on the body social. Thus the development of slums can be accepted as an expected social phenomena; the slum community may be regarded as a community in development, "receiving its share of urban community services, and contributing its own services to the development of the greater urban area" [22]. Moreover, in their relation to the process of urbanization slums contribute to the modernization of a country, and the rural person becomes slowly transformed into the urban man [23].

In less developed countries shantytowns and other self-help construction constitute sizeable total contributions to the country's wealth. The thousands of shacks erected, the lanes and roads developed, all require materials and labor for which the government has not been required to expend its often meager resources. Even the local markets in which stolen goods are made available to slum residents at low prices provide a certain service to the residents of the area. On the other hand, slums of developing countries are counterproductive, since limited government resources must be allocated to maintain them, meager as this maintenance usually is. Lerner points out that the social conscience of a modernizing society will not allow, nor can its self-protection afford, the kind of death bred by squalor [24]. "Every such new urban agglomeration makes substantial demands upon the resources of its environment: more police and fireman, more hospitals and schools, more housing and related facilities"[25]. Thus, even though slums contribute to the growth of a country in their own unique ways, they simultaneously swallow valuable resources. In all probability no methods could ever be devised to ascertain the true balance sheet. Barbara Ward has commented on the larger social and political effects of the extensive slum living in less developed countries.

All over the world, often long in advance of effective industrialization, the unskilled poor are streaming away from subsistence agriculture to exchange the squalor of rural poverty for the even deeper miseries of the *shantytowns, favelas,* and *bidonvilles* that, year by year, grow inexorably on the fringes of the developing cities. They . . . are the core of local despair and disaffection—filling the *Jeunesse* movements of the Congo, swelling the urban mobs of Rio. . . . Unchecked, disregarded, left to grow and fester, there is here enough explosive material to produce in the world at large the pattern of a bitter class conflict . . . erupting in guerrilla warfare, and threatening, ultimately, the security even of the comfortable West [26].

SLUMS AND CRIMINAL BEHAVIOR

In all countries, regardless of their development, the majority of the *reported* crimes are committed by urban slum residents [27]. In the United States, for example, in crimes such as burglary, robbery, murder, aggravated assault, and forcible rape, the criminal offender, as well as his victim, are likely to be slum residents and the site of the crime, a slum community. Studies of cities of developing countries appear to show similar correlations. The presence of squatters and slum dwellers in Manila is associated with high incidence of juvenile delinquency and crime. The district of Tondo which has more than half of Manila's squatters accounted for 35.8% of the reported crime victims in 1965; it also has the highest percentage of crimes against persons among the district of Manila [28]. A 1969 government report from Kuala Lumpur reported an increase in crime, juvenile delinquency, and a wide variety of social problems [29]. Here squatter areas were found to be the seedbeds in which "thugs, secret societies and other racketeers" carry on their activities. Studies of the Indian cities of Bombay, Kanpur, and Lucknow also demonstrated that juvenile delinquency, juvenile vagrancy, and crime were associated primarily with slum areas [30], as did a study of slums in Lima, Peru, and Mexico City [31].

Another study of criminal and other deviant behavior in the central city slums of Lima, Peru, showed a concentration in the slum areas [32]. In a study of crime in Caracas Grillo points out that it occurs primarily in the "ranchos," or slums, which have sprung up as a result of the heavy rural migration to the city and the city's insufficient economic expansion [33]. The growth of these large sprawling shantytowns is directly related to the growth of crime. From these environments a subculture develops, a subculture based on the social disintegration of community life and the development of criminal attitudes and predispositions. In San Juan, Puerto Rico, the homes of those who commit delinquent and criminal acts are concentrated in certain parts of the city, largely in slums but also in *caserios* or slum rehousing projects [34]. Some slum areas in San Juan, such as La Perla, have a long history of delinquency and prostitution, a situation that is also characteristic of the districts long known as "Buenos Aires" and "Little Tokyo" [35].

The "criminalizing" effect of slums is potentially strongest on those younger persons who migrate to these high crime areas and who are simultaneously becoming emancipated from village and home ties. There is strong evidence that the slum neighborhood, rather than the individual or family, provides the milieu for juvenile delinquency and crime. Here the stolen goods are sold; here the attitudes of antagonism toward the police and outside authorities are developed. Gang delinquency, in the form of theft or assault, may be a natural means of adjusting not only to the social roles, behavior patterns, and norms of the groups but also to the slum neighborhood to which the gang delinquents belong.

This characterization of the slum criminality is based on reported conventional crime. If one had the statistics and could include white collar crime among middle and upper class politicians and government officials, among businessmen and lawyers one might get a different picture of the distribution and concentration of crime in developing countries.

Crime and the Kampala Slums

In the Uganda study a comparison was made of the crime rates in Kampala, both for slums and nonslum areas, in terms of the types of crime, residence of the offender, area of offense, and crimes reported to the police [36]. The slums ranked consistently higher than the nonslum areas on all the variables, which strongly supports the hypothesis that most types of crime have higher rates of incidence in the slums. Rates for crimes against the person were approximately 50% higher in the slums, probably because of the presence of a subculture of violence among slum people, which predisposes them to handle conflict by violent means, and the result of congested living conditions that throw persons of diverse backgrounds together [37].

These slums produced more violence and more property crime within their boundaries, but they also produced an even greater number of persons who were arrested for property crimes (see Table 21). Both the rates for the place in which the offense occurred and the residence of the offender were higher in the slums. In general, the slum rate was approximately 50% higher than the nonslum rate for most types of crime and data. The rate of those giving the slums as residence when arrested for property crime was even higher; in fact, it was 118% greater than those who gave addresses in a nonslum area. Moreover, the slum dwellers tended to commit crimes against someone in their own communities more often than the nonslum dwellers (see Table 22). One Kampala informant stated: "On the whole, the slum dwellers are always living in fear of having their things stolen." The difference, however, was not quite so great for property crime as for personal and other offenses. Two-thirds (66.6%) of the slum dwellers were arrested for crimes against persons in their own areas, compared with about 54% of those from nonslum areas. Only a slightly larger number committed theft in their own areas than nonslum dwellers: 35.8% compared with 30.2.

Table 21   Rates of Crimes Reported and Arrests per 1000 Population by Residence of Offender and by Area of Offense, Slum Versus Nonslum by Type of Offense, Kampala, 1968

Type of Data	Slum			Nonslum		
	Person	Property	Other	Person	Property	Other
Arrests:						
Residence of offender	12.9	19.0	13.8	8.5	8.7	7.2
Area offense	13.6	12.4	10.5	8.3	8.0	6.5
Crimes reported	20.2	41.6	12.2	13.8	27.4	8.4

Table 22 Residence of Offenders and Place in which Offenses Occurred for Slum and Nonslum Areas, by Type of Offense, Kampala, 1968

Type of Offense	Slum			Nonslum		
	Percent[a] Same	Percent Different	Total	Percent[a] Same	Percent Different	Total
Person	66.6	33.4	898	54.1	45.9	846
Property	35.8	64.2	1376	30.2	69.8	955
Other	41.0	59.0	934	30.9	69.1	706

[a] The percentages in this column indicate the proportion of offenders in that category who committed offenses in their own communities.

SLUM AREAS WITH HIGH AND LOW CRIME RATES

Numerous studies have suggested that the central figure in the criminogenic urban environment of developing countries is the rural migrant, squeezed out of his home by a burgeoning family or seeking the city as a source of escape from the dullness and rigors of his village life, as well as of greater opportunities for advancement. His success or failure in adapting to this new urban world seriously affects his chances of becoming engaged in criminal activities. These chances appear to be greater in some areas than in others, for although crime rates are high in most slum areas they are not in all of them. A study of the slum areas in Kampala, for example, showed considerable variation in the rates of reported crime, which tended to group in high and low categories. For those slums that had higher crime rates the average was 81.7 reported property crimes per 1000 population; it was 10.7 in the low crime rate slums. The possibility of a successful adjustment is likely therefore, to be affected, by the type of local slum community the migrant enters. Some slum communities appear to be more adept than others in establishing barriers against the criminality so often characteristic of much urban life.

In the Uganda study an effort was made to find some answers to the important question why two slum areas differ in their crime rates [38]. Finding two such areas in Kampala with approximately equal physical conditions and economic status was not easy. Decisions on physical similarity and population were simplified by a United Nations study of land use in Kampala [39]. It estimated population for the city's 100 subsections with aerial photographs for the less dense areas and by individual canvassing in the highly dense sectors. United Nations researchers had divided the city into more than a hundred units, calculated each sector's population density, and estimated and rated their physical living conditions on a three-point scale. Density was measured as low (fewer than 20 inhabitants per acre), medium (20 to 60), and high (more than 60). General living conditions were also divided into high, medium, and low levels, based on the condition of the roads and lanes, water facilities, and living units. It was decided that the two communities selected should be high on population density and low on general living conditions.

It was even more difficult to ascertain the extent of crime in local areas. Two separate methods were used to determine the level of property crime in each local slum area—a subjective rating and official statistics (see Table 23). With the help of experienced observers a list was drawn up of all well-recognized low-income residential slum areas in the city. Supervisory police officers and probation officials were asked to rank them according to degree of criminality. A total of 11 separate ratings for each area was added to give an overall rating index for ranking communities in degrees of criminality. In addition, rates of property crime were calcu-

Table 23 Subjective Ratings of Extent of Crime and Reported Property Crime Rates per 1000 Population by Local Areas in Kampala

Area	Sum of Subjective Ratings	Rank on Subjective Ratings	Rate of Reported Property Crime	Rank on Reported Property Crime
Kisenyi	15	1	64.5	8
Katwe	38	2	79.0	2.5
Kivuula	47	3	75.0	4
East Katwe	49	4	79.0	2.5
Namuwongo	61	5	19.4	12
Mulago	71	6	108.3	1
Nakulabye	104	7	56.2	9
Kibuli	108	8	11.2	15
Kamwokya	110	9	12.1	14
Bwayise	112	10	73.0	6
Nsambya	129	11	5.4	16
Nakawa	130	12	20.4	11
Ndeeba	136	13	14.1	13
Kibuye	146	14.5	65.0	7
Mengo	146	14.5	76.0	5
Kiswa	152	16	47.7	10

lated for each of the areas. This required an estimate of the population and the amount of property crime. The United Nations study helped to give the approximate number of inhabitants in each area. Estimates of the amount of property crime were not so readily available. The smallest unit for police reporting was the police station, which always included several local areas in its jurisdiction. The only possible method of gathering this information was to consult the station records for each crime reported by the smaller subdivision; fortunately place of offense was recorded by area, not by street address. Consequently data on each crime reported to the police in 1968 were transferred to code sheets and punched on computer cards. Rates of reported property crime were then calculated on the basis of the United Nations population estimate.

The local slum area selected for a high degree of criminality was Kisenyi, which ranked first in subjective judgments of criminality and eighth in rate of reported property crime. Kisenyi has been considered one of the most criminal areas in Kampala for many years and had been so described in a study 15 years earlier [40]. It also met the criteria of high density and poor physical conditions. It has the greatest concentration of prostitutes in the city, a wide selection of bars, places in which illegal beer is sold, gambling and dancing establishments, and drugs (mostly marijuana). Fifteen years ago Southall stated that in Kisenyi the "most frequent source of diversion is certainly the many disputes which arise from some kind of cheating or theft, and often results in fights. . . . In every case the sight of violence draws a large crowd within a few seconds" [41]. Located adjacent to the bus station, major markets, and the business center, it attracts recent arrivals, especially if they have no relatives or friends to help them.

The selection of the second community proved to be more difficult. The area had to have living conditions comparable to those in Kisenyi but a much lower rate of crime. Two communities, Kibuli and Namuwongo, met the requirements statistically. Although Kibuli had a lower rate of reported property crime than Namuwongo, it had the disadvantage of being the recent subject of an intensive anthropological investigation. All members of the community had been interviewed at least once, some three times, and the investigators were still in the field. Namuwongo ranked fifth on the subjective ratings of the extent of crime and twelfth on rates of reported property crimes. Its rate of 19.4 reported property crimes per 1000 inhabitants is less than a third of Kisenyi's. The area had been developed more recently, partly as a result of extensive Kenyan migration after World War II. It is situated directly behind the railroad tracks bordering the industrial sector of Kampala. Since it was not included within the city limits until boundary changes were made in

1967, Namuwongo had received little attention from agencies concerned with the physical improvement of urban conditions.

Investigation revealed that the physical surroundings in Namuwongo were comparable to and even worse than those in Kisenyi. Namuwongo was not serviced by the water board in Kampala and had only one water-pipe and one well for the entire area. Kisenyi has much better water service; 19% of the residents had taps in their yards or homes [42]. One of Kampala's major markets is situated in Kisenyi, whereas Namuwongo has none [43]. Three recognized primary and secondary schools serve Kisenyi. Children from Namuwongo's community school are permitted to compete for entrance into Kampala secondary schools, but the community school is not officially recognized as part of the Kampala school system. A major health clinic borders Kisenyi, but residents of Namuwongo must travel two to four miles to the Nsambya or Mulago hospitals. In terms of utilities and social services the high crime community fared much better than the low.

Each community was divided into 15 sections in accordance with maps provided by the United Nations survey teams. Most interviewers questioned respondents in one or two sections in both communities, but some worked in only one community. Interviewers with experience in both communities were asked to make comparisons on a section by section basis, rating such variables as cleanliness and sturdiness of housing, cleanliness of general area, and amount of water. On all factors of housing, cleanliness, and available water Kisenyi was rated better than Namuwongo. On sturdiness of housing, sections of Kisenyi were favorably rated almost three times as often as sections of Namuwongo. Since the selection of sections was not totally random, there is a possibility of systematic error and the comparison of the best of Kisenyi with the worst of Namuwongo. Most sections of Kisenyi, however, are included among the units of comparison. These findings are meaningful in that they concur with the information gathered from official sources. Respondents in both communities were also asked to give their views on the standards of health and cleanliness where they lived. The differences between the two communities were not statistically significant, at the 0.05 level. The number responding "bad" was 44.9% in Namuwongo and 52.7 in Kisenyi. On the basis of amenities, such as water and electricity or schools and interviewer's ratings, Kisenyi was in a better physical position than Namuwongo. Even living conditions possibly were slightly better in the high crime area.

The reported arrest and crime data permitted more detailed comparisons: (a) between crime rates in the two communities and (b) between the two communities and the average crime rates for the slum and nonslum areas. Kisenyi's rate of reported property crime was three times that of Namuwongo, but its rate of reported crimes against the person was only 50% higher (see Table 24). Although the latter difference was fairly large, it was much smaller than the difference for property crime. A low rate of property crime is not necessarily inconsistent with a high rate of crime against the person. Namuwongo, as we point out later, is a more homogeneous area, and, as Wolfgang and Ferracuti have said, "homicide is most prevalent, and the highest rates of homicide occur, among a relatively homogeneous subcultural group" [44]. This statement is not meant to imply that Namuwongo is more violent than Kisenyi but rather that a homogeneous group may have ties of friendship or tribal similarities that reduce the amount of property crime but still have culural definitions that define violence as a normal method for handling disputes.

Table 24   Rates of Crimes Reported to the Police and Arrests per 1000 Population by Area of Offense and Residence, Type of Crime, and Community, Kampala, 1968

		Area			
	Type of Crime	Kisenyi	Namu-wongo	Slum	Non-slum
Arrests:					
Area of offense	Person	19.1	9.1	13.6	8.3
	Property	19.4	4.2	12.4	8.0
Residence of offender	Person	23.6	8.8	12.9	8.5
	Property	33.9	8.7	19.0	8.7
Crimes reported	Person	30.6	20.2	20.2	13.8
	Property	64.6	19.5	41.6	27.4

Kisenyi's rate of arrest for crimes against property and crimes against the person was higher than the average for slums, being 57% higher in property crime (see Table 24). With respect to the area in which the offense was committed Namuwongo's rate of crimes against the person was double its rate of crimes against property, whereas the rates of property crime and crimes against the person are nearly equal to Kisenyi. On the other hand, according to residence of the offenders and crimes reported to the police, the rates of crimes against property and the person are nearly equal in Namuwongo, whereas rates for property crime were generally much larger than rates for crimes against the person in Kisenyi.

Among the suspects arrested for crimes against the person and who gave an address in Kisenyi 56.2% had committed the criminal offense in that district, which is considerably less than Namuwongo's 76.7% (see Table 25). Among those arrested for property offenses 29.2% of the Kisenyi offenders and 35.8% of the Namuwongo offenders had committed their offenses in their respectives areas.

Table 25   Percent of Arrests by Place of Residence and by Type of Offense, Kampala, 1968

Areas of Arrest	Kisenyi		Namuwongo		Slum		Nonslum	
	%[a]	Total	%[a]	Total	%[a]	Total	%[a]	Total
Person	56.2	290	76.7	133	66.6	898	54.1	846
Property	29.2	428	35.8	120	35.8	1376	30.2	955

[a] The percentages in this column indicate the proportion of those arrested who gave a specific sector of Kampala as place of residence and also committed the offense in the sample place.

A study of 723 convicted juvenile property offenders found that, with the exception of two areas in Kampala, they tended to commit their offenses in the areas and often in the same neighborhoods in which they lived [45]. In another sample of 102 property offenders Kibuka found that not only were nearly all offenses committed in the local neighborhood in which they lived but 69% of them knew the victims well [46].

The Sample of Respondents

To test various hypotheses derived from a theoretical model a represent-ative sample of persons to be interviewed was selected from each of the two areas. In the cities of developing countries representative sampling in such low-income communities, in which the concentration and distri-bution of houses is almost totally unplanned, serious difficulties are often presented. Fortunately, since both areas included densely populated sec-tors, data were available from a United Nations study that included maps identifying each building, its use, and the number of household residents. The "households" ranged from a single individual in one room to one family occupying several rooms. Information about household composition and space usage was based on what members of a family, for example, regarded as a "household." Because of this available detailed information, the level of sophistication in the sample was far beyond the original expectations.

The ultimate goal in the sample was to find a representative group of males 18 years or older. The sample was restricted to males because the East African woman's role is still largely limited to the local community, with only a slightly expanded role in the urban area [47]. Leadership positions are typically held by males, and even in the city, among most tribal groups, a payment to the bride's family is still expected. Since crime, with the exception of prostitution, is largely a male activity, the characteristics of the male population were the primary concern in the investigation.

Initially the plan was to take a random sample of buildings and then interview a member of a randomly selected household, but this would have resulted in an over-representation of single household units and would have biased the sample toward the residents with larger homes. Consequently it was decided to attempt a pure random sample. All households in Kisenyi and Namuwongo, 1914 and 2314 respectively, were numbered, and a sample of 350 numbers for Kisenyi and 400 for Namuwongo was drawn from a random table of numbers for which substitutions were provided [48]. To ensure generational differences and to prevent the sample from consisting merely of males who happened to be home during the day interviewers were instructed to seek the youngest male 18 years or over in households with even code numbers and the oldest male in households with odd code numbers. Several problems affected the composition of the original sample of 750 cases [49] (see Table 26). The final sample of 534 cases, 250 from Kisenyi and 284 from Namuwongo, was

Table 26 Outcome of Original Community Samples of 697 Cases Interviewed, Kisenyi and Namuwongo

	Kisenyi	%	Namuwongo	%
Interviewed	250	71.4	284	81.8
Refused	10	2.9	10	2.9
Women only	31	8.9	8	2.3
Buildings vacant or destroyed	5	1.5	9	2.6
No African resident	17	4.9	0	0.0
Language problems	8	2.2	0	0.0
Never located	29	8.2	36	10.4
Total households	350	100.0	347	100.0

Table 27   Age Distribution of 534 Males Interviewed in Kisenyi and Namuwongo

Age	Kisenyi No.	Kisenyi %	Namuwongo No.	Namuwongo %	Total No.	Total %
18 to 25	100	40.0	106	36.9	206	38.6
26 plus	150	60.0	178	63.1	328	61.4
Total	250	100.0	284	100.0	534	100.0

divided by age into those between 18 and 25 and those 26 or older. The results are shown in Table 27.

Before entering an area for interviews attempts were made to reach the chief government official directly responsible for the area. The project was explained to him so that he could allay fears if he were to be questioned by the residents. He was asked not to make a formal announcement of the study to the community, however, to prevent community members from interpreting it as a government-sponsored study. Emphasis was put on the sponsorship of the investigation by the university, for the importance of education is well recognized in African cities and people have a great deal of respect for the university. In general, cooperation was good; there were only 20 refusals among the 534 actually interviewed. The need to interview a specific member of a household frequently required several visits before final contact was made. Since lack of time was the only factor that affected any household's finally being omitted, the sample being a random one, it was felt that significant errors would not be introduced.

The Framework for Studying Slum Community Organization

To study the relation between community organization and the difference in rates of property crimes in these two slum areas a scientific framework was necessary. The selection of various factors within the social structure to be investigated was based on theoretical interests and the findings of previous research on the subject. It was hypothesized that effective control of property crime, especially within a slum community, requires sufficient knowledge of and friendship between neighbors so that there will be (a) a general tendency to reject stealing from neighbors, (b) neighbors will help informally to guard one another's property, (c) strangers can be readily identified, and (d) residents will give help if someone is attacked.

These bonds must be quite strong, because economic and other pressures to steal can be very great on slum dwellers. Certain social structures appear to facilitate the growth and the maintenance of such unity, whereas others seem inimical to its existence. In this connection Landecker has suggested four types of integration which are characteristic of any social group—normative, cultural, communicative, and functional [50]. This is the frame of reference used in the analysis of slum community social organization.

No effort was made by Landecker to suggest connections for the four types of integration, but in the Uganda research the suggested model was that whenever there was a high degree of communicative integration

Research Model for Types of Integration

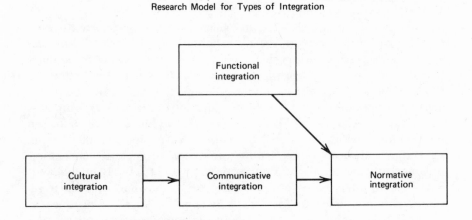

there would be less crime. If persons have similar cultural backgrounds, their abilities to communicate are normally enhanced because they have many similar experiences and are not overly suspicious of everyone. This does not reject the possibility of severe cleavages; in the heterogeneous urban environment, however, similarities receive added importance as forms of support. A high degree of cultural integration would increase the probability of friendships and a more solid communicative integration, all of which act as effective forms of social control over crime. Functional integration can affect the degree of normative integration, that is, the rate of property crime in the community, in two ways. First, the person would be more likely to come into contact with unfavorable definitions of crime and, second, if the person has a job, power, or status gained through contacts outside the community, he would be less likely to jeopardize them by arrest and imprisonment.

Normative Integration

Normative integration is defined as the degree to which group conduct conforms to cultural standards. Relying on the work of Angell, Landecker has suggested that a crime index covering the important forms of criminal behavior could be used as one measure of this variable [51]. Thus the principal measure of normative integration was the rate of property crime within the community, but also used were the respondents' perceptions of this community. People were asked about the likelihood of property being stolen in their communities and the amount of fighting and drunkenness in the area. There was a highly significant statistical difference in the responses between the two communities for both items. Respondents were asked "What do other people think of this area?" Although slightly more than half the Namuwongoans replied, "Don't know," the difference between the responses was striking: 83% of the men from Kisenyi felt that the perceptions of outsiders of their community was quite negative (see Table 28). They were also asked what they thought of their own community. Again the differences were striking (see Table 29). A much larger proportion of Kisenyi, 46.5 versus 18.5%, felt that their residential areas were "not a good place." A person's perceptions of his surroundings most likely stem from and are influenced by the nature of his inter-

Table 28   Responses to the Question, "What Do Other People Think of This Area?" Kisenyi and Namuwongo

		Kisenyi		Namuwongo	
		No.[a]	%	No.[a]	%
1.	Bad place (drunkards, murderers, fighting, prostitution, adultery)	182	83.1	59	43.7
2.	Not clean enough	3	1.4	6	4.4
3.	Good place	29	13.2	27	20.0
4.	They wish to improve it	4	1.8	16	11.9
5.	Only for Luos	0	0	22	16.3
6.	Other	1	.4	5	3.7
	Total	219	100.0	135	100.0
	Don't know or no response	55	22.0	156	55.0

[a] In several instances there were multiple responses to the item. All responses were summed together and the numbers are accordingly larger than the sample size.

Table 29   Responses to the Question, "What Do You Think of Your Community?" in Kisenyi and Namuwongo

	Kisenyi		Namuwongo	
	No.	%	No.	%
1. Good place	56	24.3	80	37.0
2. Satisfactory	23	10.0	29	13.4
3. Standard of living is too low	4	1.8	15	7.0
4. Not a good place (dirty, theft, unemployment, under-developed)	107	46.5	40	18.5
5. Improvements are necessary (lights, roads, buses, etc.)	18	7.8	34	15.8
6. Nothing, except to live in	22	9.6	18	8.3
Total	230	100.0	216	100.0
Don't know or no response	22	8.9	61	21.5

action in his community. Kisenyi's residents saw their area as being much more criminal than those in Namuwongo believed theirs to be. The following are typical comments of those living in Kisenyi:

Each one looks after his property as best he can.

I have often been threatened by thieves in Kisenyi.

Each one guards his house in Kisenyi and theft is still rampant, particularly at night.

Nothing is good in Kisenyi. We came here because we could find no better houses at a cheap price. But now I like it here, but still nothing is good. No one can come here and feel secure.

It teaches someone how to be tough and careful because one is constantly worried about his property.

I fear the place. I can't even walk at night. I am only here because the rent is cheap, or there are people of my tribe.

On the other hand, the following comments were made about Namuwongo:

Namuwongo has cheaper rents and few problems of theft.

If one stays out of trouble one will stay very well in Namuwongo.

People like to stay here because there are few troubles, or at least few troubles like theft and fights.

There are fewer troubles like theft, quarrels, or drunkenness here.

A series of items relating to attitudes toward the degree of deviance associated with various acts was given to the respondents. It was hypothesized that values and attitudes would reflect the differences in behavior between the two communities. The items were selected from a study of deviance in a triethnic community in the United States [52]. Neither the young nor the old in the two areas differed significantly in disapproval of theft: more than 80% of those under 25 and 80% of those over 25 from the two communities considered stealing to be wrong. The situations presented in the items, whether it was right to steal from the rich or to steal to feed one's family, would seem to be conditions under which theft would be most acceptable, but they were strongly rejected in both communities. The greater prevalence of property crime in Kisenyi cannot be explained by a difference in attitudes toward theft among its population. The residents of Kisenyi did not consider theft an acceptable alternative, but they did not successfully implement their convictions. Moreover, the young from Kisenyi had significantly fewer negative attitudes toward fighting, prostitution, and wife beating. The difference in attitude toward these acts among the young would be expected, since they live in an area in which prostitution and fighting are common. These findings further support the basic proposition that the difference in crime rates lies in the differential social organization of the communities and the impact this organization has on the ability of community members to control the behavior of others.

Cultural Integration

Cultural integration refers to the internal consistency of the cultural standards of a group. This integration is lacking when group values and expectations make conflicting demands on its members. In most urban areas of African countries communities that are entirely culturally integrated are not numerous, since several culturally distinct ethnic groups often live in small pockets throughout the cities. If the local community is to be the unit of analysis, it would be fruitless to attempt to determine the internal consistency of each cultural group. A more significant measure would be the number and proportion of different cultural groups represented.

Cultural integration appears to be quite important in relation to criminal behavior rates. Cavan and Cavan, for example, described a barrio in a Mexican village with a low rate of crime [53]. The barrio residents had a common Indian tradition which differentiated them from the rest of the village and their unity was strengthened by their concerted efforts to remain isolated and to maintain their own style of life. Although it is an example from a rather highly developed country, the case of the Japanese in the United States relates to this point, for even when a family lived under physical slum conditions their crime rate remained remarkably low [54]. Through isolation and a strong cultural tradition they maintained a high degree of social control within their own community.

Although similarity of cultural background is significant, success or failure in adjustment to an urban environment can also be affected by concious attempts to preserve beliefs and traditions. Lewis studied a barrio in Mexico in which the residents survived the more disruptive aspects of urban life by emphasis on their common traditions, aided by regular visits to their home villages [55]. Similar results were found in a study of migrant adaptation in Brazil [56]. In Parkin's study of Kampala he stated that "the need for ultimate social security is one of a number of reasons for maintaining strong links with the rural home" [57]. Large associations grew up in Lima, Peru, to help migrants from certain regions in the interior [58].

Tribal Homogeneity

The principal means of measuring cultural integration in the two communities studied was tribal homogeneity, which refers to the number of tribes and their proportional representation within a local community. When there are fewer tribes, the chances are greater that individual members will receive more consistent definitions of traditionally accepted behavior. Other factors also determine whether the individual will achieve a consistent and stable set of norms and values that might inhibit criminal behavior, such as frequent contact with "kin" in both the city and the village, which helps to reinforce basic traditions, and restriction of close friendships to members of his own tribe, which has the effect of reducing the normative dissonance characteristic of the city. Any community in which many persons maintain greater contact would be expected to have a higher degree of cultural integration and a lower property crime rate.

The degree of tribal homogeneity was calculated by a mathematical technique suggested by Lieberson [59]. As applied to the two communities, it gives the probability of encountering two persons from a different tribe if they were randomly chosen from the population. This was a much greater probability in Kisenyi (.906) than in Namuwongo (.724).

Although this finding demonstrates the greater homogeneity in Namu-wongo [60], actually it understates the differences in homogeneity between the two communities. Men from 34 different tribes were included in the Kisenyi sample, men from 25 tribes in the Namuwongo. The dominant tribal group in Namuwongo, the Luo, represented 48% of the population in the area, whereas the largest proportion for any tribe in Kisenyi was only 23.5%. People in Kisenyi were quite aware that tribal heterogeneity was characteristic of their area.

It is a place for all tribes who have failed to live in good areas because of lack of jobs.

It is a place which brings all tribes together.

It unites all different tribes.

Tribal Diversity in Friendships

Restricting friendships to members of one's own tribe may serve to reduce heterogeneous urban influences that might result in questioning important values or traditions against property crime. Tribal members have greater potential for exercising control in the city, since they are much more likely to communicate with important family members at home. These ties with the village presumably provide a strong emotional force in the life of the urban dweller.

Respondents were asked to name the tribes of their three best friends. A numerical scale of diversity was constructed on the basis of these responses [61]. The F score for the young was not statistically significant, whereas for those over 26 it was highly significant. The older men from Kisenyi had a much greater diversity in their relations than those from Namuwongo, but the youth from both areas were equally likely to select a friend from a different tribe. Friendship ties provide a greater degree of freedom of choice and are a better reflection of the tendencies to move away from traditional alignments. It might be argued that the more restricted friendship patterns among the older males in Namuwongo would follow naturally from its greater tribal homogeneity, but this line of reasoning cannot be applied to the youth because young men from Namuwongo were just as likely to have nontribal friendships as young men from Kisenyi.

Contact with Relatives

No significant statistical differences were found between the two slum communities, in either the younger or the older groups, in their contacts with their relatives in Kampala. In all cases at least 90% of those who had relatives in Kampala reported that they were in touch with them. These responses emphasized the continued strength of family ties, even in the urban area. The interview item did not measure the closeness or the importance of the relationships but only that a small minority of the respondents avoided relatives altogether [62].

The item that questioned contact with relatives in the village showed no significant differences between the two communities for either age group, and only 29% of the total community sample reported that they never visited relatives in their home villages. Although relations with family and kin are an important element of African urban life, this element does not appear to affect differentially the ability of the local community members to control property crime.

Communicative Integration

Communicative integration refers to the extent to which contacts permeate the group [63]. Communication patterns have been emphasized in studies of slum areas in the United States, particularly in the work of Suttles [64]. Communicative integration operates both on individual and organizational levels. At the individual level it refers to the everyday interactions that occur among residents of the community. The nature of these relationships can be analyzed on three dimensions: scope, depth, and exclusivity. "Scope" means the number of acquaintances an individual can relate to within the community on a basis that goes beyond simple recognition of a common geographical origin. "Depth" means the degree of commitment members have to one another, and a behavioral indicator would be the degree to which people are willing to sacrifice or inconvenience themselves for another person. "Exclusivity" means the degree to which friendships are limited to members within the community. The level of communication can be critical in the exercise of social control within a community. Rogler compared highly deviant slum clearance projects in Puerto Rico with the less criminal squatter settlements of Lima [65]. In the Puerto Rican case the main characteristic of the relations between neighbors was a basic animosity expressed by constant bickering. People without ties based on kinship or mutual interests were randomly distributed in apartment units. In the Lima squatter settlements, on the other hand, the cooperative struggle for survival in the face of government opposition bound the residents into unified communities. After a planning period of as much as a year, a thousand slum dwellers might occupy an undeveloped section of government land in one night [66]. The squatter settlements also exhibited a lower rate of crime than the older central city slums of Lima. Although Israel can no longer be regarded as a developing country, its rapid social change makes it something of an appropriate case. Community cohesiveness, measured by ethnic homogeneity and the degree of commitment to a collectively shared purpose, was shown to be associated with low delinquency rates, and it was a more important influence on delinquency rates than the rural-urban differences [67].

The stability of a population could affect its ability to attain a particular level of communication. In the case in which a significant portion of the population remains for only a short time the formation of binding ties and commitments through organizations is severely hampered. Moreover, communication on a more formal level, by participation in voluntary organizations, can have a potent effect on the tone of the social environment [68]. It provides the opportunity for relationships to develop between groups within the total community. Depending on their goals, they could be a primary source of community cohesiveness.

Reasons for Moving to Community and Length of Residence

One of the most critical decisions affecting the urban experiences of any individual is the selection of a place to live and the motivation behind the decision. Table 30 shows the reasons given by the community sample for their choice of Kisenyi or Namuwongo. The men from Namuwongo much more frequently moved there because of friends or relatives (55.2 versus 36.8%). The factors surrounding the movement to Kisenyi more

Table 30 Responses to the Question, "Why Did You Move to Your Community?" Kisenyi and Namuwongo

	Kisenyi		Namuwongo	
	No.	%	No.	%
1. To live with friend, relatives, or member of tribe	92	36.8	153	55.2
2. Cheap housing	61	24.4	60	21.7
3. Find a job	26	10.4	17	6.1
4. Near place of employment	47	18.8	19	6.9
5. Born there	3	1.2	5	1.8
6. Chance	18	7.2	4	1.5
7. Told it was a good place	3	1.2	19	6.9
Total	250	100.0	277	100.0
Don't know or no response	16	6.4	6	2.1

often reflected a response to the exigencies of urban life: employment, chance, cheap housing. The men from Kisenyi were more often compelled to establish a base where they had no immediate support from relatives or friends. It is these chance factors that often determine the types of norms and values a person will be exposed to in the city.

If there is a high turnover in a local community's population, it is more difficult to achieve control over people's behavior and to develop more permanent lines of communication within the group. The difference between the two communities on mobility, measured by the number of times they had changed residence in Kampala, was statistically significant. This was true for both the younger and older groups, but it was stronger for those over 25. The men from Kisenyi tended to change residence in the city more often than the men from Namuwongo. There were, however, no significant differences between the two communities on length of residence. Only 30% in Kisenyi and 35% in Namuwongo had lived in their communities for more than five years.

Respondents were asked, "If you had the opportunity to move to some other section in Kampala, would you leave here?" The chi squares showed no statistically significant differences in responses between the communities: one-third in both communities, 39.2% in Namuwongo and 37.4% in Kisenyi, indicated that they would move. Even though the respondents in Namuwongo said that they were as willing to move as the Kisenyi men, fewer of them actually did so. The men from Kisenyi had the higher rate of residential change in Kampala.

Individual Relationships

Effective control of property crime within a community depends, in part, on mutual knowledge and friendship among members. Isolated individuals who have few bonds with the people around them are less likely to support neighbors when trouble develops. As one respondent of Kisenyi stated, "even when people see theft occurring they simply say that they are killing him and they go on their own way. No help is offered. Each one to himself, that's what they do." A large proportion of isolates in the community makes identification of strangers more difficult, but when everyone is known within a sizeable radius of any house a thief cannot move under the cover of anonymity [69].

The scope of individual relationships was measured by asking, "How many different places are there in your community where you know people and go by to visit every once in a while?" Although the differences between the two areas were statistically significant for both age groups, they were much stronger for the older group. In general, men from

Namuwongo reported more homes in which their relationships with the occupants was such that they visited them. The situation in Kisenyi was reflected in the comment of a respondent: "No two neighbors can sit down to talk about how to reduce theft. Everyone is for himself."

To measure the strength of the bonds among community members, respondents were asked, "Will a person's neighbors give him any help if he loses his job?" and "Are the family relations between men and women living together firm and lasting here?" The purpose was to elicit general feelings about the nature of human interaction in their communities. The first item measured responsiveness in time of financial crises and was chosen because the economic factor is one of the most critical uncertainties in the slum areas of developing countries. The differences between the two communities on willingness to give financial help to others was not statistically significant by age groups. Only 20.8% of the men in Kisenyi and 33.8% of the men in Namuwongo could state that a man would receive help from his neighbors in a financial crisis. Even in Namuwongo, where the unity appeared to be greater, many were pessimistic about receiving help, one saying that people give help to no one "because everyone struggles for himself and they are people of my economic status." Another said that they give help only if they have been "very good neighbors." This would seem to be in sharp contrast to the village setting in which a man generally can ask for help as his right.

The second question investigated not only the stability but also the strength of a primary bond, the family unit, on the assumption that more tightly knit families might reduce mobility and provide more effective discipline for children. Hellman states, "The breaking up of the family is one of the first results of slum residence" [70]. In one African study delinquency appeared to be concentrated in homes with severed family relations and a lack of emotional stability [71]. The differences in responses on relations between men and women were striking and highly significant statistically. Both young and old in Namuwongo perceived a greater firmness and stability in the relations between men and women in their communities: 85% for Namuwongo, compared with 40% in Kisenyi. One respondent from Kisenyi typified the situation there: "A person married today will be a bachelor tomorrow. There is no love. People may marry to get sexual enjoyment for a day or two." Another said that the family is weak because many women are not properly married and there is much prostitution. The persistent strength of the family in Namuwongo stems in part from the value placed on it by the migrant groups residing there. Among these groups the bride-price is still high, and the families have a stronger interest in the selection of part-

ners and the stability of the marriage. Furthermore, informal social controls can be brought to bear on the family when there is a greater degree
of social organization in the community. One of the leaders in Namuwongo claimed that if a man had a family back in the village and began
living with a woman leaders in the community would sometimes bring
the family to Kampala [72].

The third area of individual relationships is the exclusivity that
measures the degree with which close friendships are limited to members of the community. Respondents were asked where their three best
friends lived. A four-point scale was constructed to rate the individual
from high to low on exclusivity [73]. There were no significant statistical
differences between communities in either age group. The distribution
on the scale was almost evenly split in both areas—half had few friendships outside the community and the other half had many. Even though
interaction among community members appeared to be higher in Namuwongo than in Kisenyi, the residents of Namuwongo had close friends
outside the community as often as the subjects from Kisenyi. Perhaps
mobility and work patterns have a uniform distributive effect on the location of friends. The pressure for living space may also force close village
friends to live in separate parts of the city. Thus the two aspects of individual relationships which considered the nature of interaction within
communities (scope and depth) were statistically significant. On the other
hand, the degree of relation with outsiders (exclusivity) was not significant.

Participation in Organizations

Voluntary organizations are often an important part of African urban
life. Lloyd, for example, states:

> Yet the townsmen do not live as discrete atoms; they have formed an enor-
> mous number of new associations, through which they express not only those new
> interests occasioned by urban life and employment in the modern sector, but also
> those interests severed in the rural area by the indigenous associations [74].

Internal voluntary organizations and participation in them have several
possible unifying effects on a community. Members may develop a greater
sense of identity with the community than those who simply reside there,
especially if the goal of the organization is the betterment of living conditions. Work on projects that improve the physical nature of the area
require both social psychological and physical inputs which could deepen
commitment. Acquaintanceships resulting from membership may extend
the links of friendship and serve further to bind members to the com-

munity. They may also make possible entrance into the larger urban world, as Rogler has pointed out in regard to Latin American slums.

The degree of a slum neighborhood's incorporation into the city may well depend upon the cooperative arrangements formed among families, particularly as they are organized into viable and politically oriented associations [75].

Organizations can also act as buffers against the confusing and disconnected experiences of urban life.

Internal organizations may be self-help, recreational, political, ethnic, or religious. Respondents were asked to name their organizational memberships and were considered active members if they had attended a meeting in the last six months [76]. Namuwongo was statistically significantly higher than Kisenyi on participation in local community organizations, but the strongest difference was in the older group. Twenty percent of the Namuwongo and only 7% of the Kisenyi respondents reported active participation in some local organization. Of particular importance are the tribal unions found in many parts of Africa. [77]. The dominant group in Namuwongo, the Luos, had a strong union that provided its members with numerous local community services [78]. It established a credit union to help parents educate their children, organized sports teams, and even arranged for the dead to be buried in the tribal homeland. Thus the community with the lower crime rate appeared to have a higher degree of organizational unity.

Religion is an integral part of urban life in much of Africa [79]. Wiley, for example, in a Zambian study found that the greater percentage of adult life spent in cities was positively associated with a positive attitude toward religious organizations [80]. The data on attendance indicate that there were large significantly statistical differences between the two communities, yet there appears to be a strong religious life in both communities [81]. Forty-four percent of the respondents in Kisenyi reported weekly attendance with little difference by age group, but 66 percent of both age groups from Namuwongo claimed weekly attendance. Regular attendance at a religious service could have several functions of social contact. Contact with other community members could enhance the sense of belonging, non-criminal values would be reinforced through the services, and attendance may represent to a degree a public commitment to the values expressed acting as a restraining force against pressures to contravene these values.

In conclusion, the cohesiveness within Namuwongo was further demonstrated by the fact that when an interviewer entered a local area many of the residents frequently gathered round the first man to be interviewed. An impromptu meeting would occur to decide whether to permit the interview. Once a favorable decision had been obtained, there was no trouble at any of the remaining households in the area. The only similar response in Kisenyi came from a small concentration from another African country: they steadfastly refused entrance to the interviewers.

Functional Integration

Functional integration was originally defined as the interdependence of group members by the division of labor. Although this may be a relevant variable in a large city, it has limited use within the boundaries of a small urban community. There is probably a low degree of economic specialization within small local communities of African urban areas. The concept is more useful if modified to refer to integration into the larger urban society, implying that the more ties an individual has with the larger urban society the less likely he will be to contravene common conduct norms. Ties could come by occupation or by membership in non-local organizations or political parties. In a study of delinquency in Cordoba, Argentina, for example, DeFleur developed a theory based primarily on a concept similar to functional integration as used here [82]. She hypothesized that the low institutional involvement of the lower class does not provide the experiences necessary to internalize societal norms. The lower class has low rates of participation in political, educational, economic, and religious institutions. As a result, the youth lack the direction necessary to restrict contacts with delinquent boys.

On the whole, functional integration did not distinguish between high and low crime rate communities. It was hypothesized that the community with the greater proportion of men functionally integrated into the large urban community would have a lower rate of property crime. Functional integration was divided into two parts: socioeconomic integration and participatory integration. Variables included under the first were education, occupation, and home ownership. The second consisted of participation in urban organizations and civic participation.

Socioeconomic Integration

The principal factors used to measure socioeconomic status were education and occupation [83]. There were no differences between the two communities on the education of the younger males, but there was a strong relationship for the older males. The older generation in Kisenyi, the high crime community, was better educated than were the older people from the low crime community. Community cohesiveness apparently does not depend on a higher level of education among members. The lowest educated group in the community sample, the older males from Namuwongo, was the primary source of unity and control in the low crime rate community. There was also a consistent trend for the respondents from the high crime community to have an equal or even higher socioeconomic position as measured by occupation [84]. The younger men from the high crime rate community clearly tended to have higher occupations. There was, however, no significant difference between the two communities on the general occupations of either age group.

The housing in both slum areas consisted primarily of inexpensive and poorly constructed, mud-covered wooden frame buildings with tin roofs. Presumably any home ownership has implications of communicative integration; the owner would probably tend less to move around Kampala or to return to his village, and this would add stability to the community. A significant statistical relation was evident between the older persons of the two areas on home ownership. Twenty percent of the older men from Namuwongo owned their own homes versus 6.8% of the older group in Kisenyi.

Participatory Integration

Two separate approaches were utilized to investigate participatory integration that measured contacts with organizations and activities and presumably reinforced values of conformity. The first was participation in organizations such as labor unions, political parties, and various city-wide cooperatives that have a broader membership than the local community. The second, civic participation, investigated the respondent's participation in national ceremonies, contact with officials, and use of governmental agencies. Civic participation was measured by asking the respondents whether they had attended an Independence Day ceremony or spoken with a councilman about a problem. There was a total of seven items on civic participation in the interview schedule.

No significant differences showed between the two communities on participation in urban organizations for either age group. Twenty-two percent of the men in Namuwongo and 18% of the Kisenyi men reported active memberships in at least one urban organization. There was also no significant difference between the two communities in civic participation for either the younger or the older groups [85]. The percentage in the category of low civic participation was 63.5 for Namuwongo and 62.4 for Kisenyi. With the exception of Independence Day ceremonies, minimal participation in activities of this kind would be expected of a poorly educated migrant population. These general results fit somewhat the Mexican findings of Cavan and Cavan [86]. The members of the *barrio* derived their strength and solidarity from their isolation from the dominant groups outside their communities. By remaining aloof they preserved customs and values contradictory to criminal involvement and gained a sense of purpose and belonging in their lives. This finding is also consistent with a study of three *barrios* in Colombia which differed in both age and internal cohesion. The measures of participation in non-local organizations did not distinguish between three slums studied [87].

SOME CONCLUSIONS ABOUT SLUM SOCIAL ORGANIZATION AND CRIME

As in developed countries, most crime is concentrated in slum areas. Members of some urban slums in developing countries appear to be more successful in their attempts to control criminal behavior. The two communities with differences in rates of property crime also showed differences in community integration and in the residents' perceptions of their communities. The men from the high crime community were much more likely to believe that there was much crime, fighting, and drunkenness in their community. There were no significant differences between either age groups in the two communities on whether theft was wrong. This common approbation of theft suggested that most inhabitants opposed stealing but that one community was better structured to implement its feelings.

In terms of cultural integration, the high crime rate area was the most diverse in tribal background. The diversity in tribal friendship proved to be the most statistically significant factor: the men from Namuwongo restricted close friendships more to members of their own tribes. Those from the high crime rate area had fewer negative attitudes toward fighting, prostitution, wife beating, or illegal beer brewing, but there was no difference in their negative attitudes to stealing. The analysis of communicative integration in the low crime community indicated, particularly among those over 25, more visiting, less mobility, and greater participation in local community organizations, including religious groups. The high crime rate area was less likely to have stable family relationships. There was no difference, however, in the willingness to give financial help to others. A large, approximately equal, portion of both communities said that they would leave if they had the chance; however, men from Namuwongo actually changed residence in Kampala less often than those from Kisenyi. The low crime rate area was able to maintain a sufficient degree of communicative unity to control property crime in spite of a fairly rapid turnover in population. In terms of functional integration there was no significant statistical difference in the links members of the community had to the larger urban areas in organizational and civic participation. Occupation and education levels were significantly higher for young males in the high crime community. The older generation in Namuwongo owned their homes much more often than the older males in Kisenyi.

Several tentative conclusions are particularly important and warrant further investigation. First, although urbanization and industrialization in less developed countries erode traditional authority and negate the usefulness of knowledge possessed by elders, those in the older group appear to play a vital role in determining the character of urban slum communities. Second, a higher average socioeconomic status does not necessarily increase the ability of members of a community to control behavior within its boundaries, nor does a fairly rapid change in population automatically destroy cohesiveness. The latter finding may call into question some of the assumptions concerning the critical variables in slum areas in cities of both more and less developed countries. Finally, with respect to functional versus communicative integration and control of property crime, internal relations and patterns of behavior within the local community are the more important and appear to be somewhat independent of linkages outside the community.

NOTES AND REFERENCES

1. The United Nations has sought a more nonvaluative term than slum or squatter and has thus substituted "transitional urban settlements" in the sense that their inhabitants are undergoing social and economic change, often from a rural to an urban way of life.

2. Marshall B. Clinard, *Slums and Urban Community Development* (New York: The Free Press, 1966), Chapter 3.

3. Charles J. Stokes, "A Theory of Slums," *Land Economics*, 38:187–197 (August 1962).

4. Aprodicio A. Laquian, "Slums and Squatters in South and Southeast Asia," in Leo Jakobson and Ved Prakash, Eds., *Urbanization and National Development* (Beverly Hills, Calif.: Sage Publications, 1971), pp. 185–186.

5. Aprodicio A. Laquian, *Slums Are for People* (Honolulu: East–West Center Press, 1971), p. 12.

6. *Plan Tentativo de Actividades de la División para el Desarrollo de la Communidad*, Comité para la Rehabilitación y Urbanización de los Barrios Suburbanos de Guyaquíl, 1968.

7. Horacio Caminos, John F. C. Turner, and John Steffian, *Urban Dwelling Environments* (Boston: Massachusetts Institute of Technology Press, 1969).

8. William Alonso, "Planning and the Spatial Organization of the Metropolis in the Developing Countries," *Conference Papers*, Rehovot Conference on Urbanization and Development in Developing Countries, Israel, 1971, pp. 2–3.

9. Gerald D. Suttles, *The Social Order of the Slum: Ethnicity and Territory in the Inner City* (Chicago: University of Chicago Press, 1968).

10. Marshall B. Clinard, *Slums and Community Development: Experiments in Self-Help* (New York: The Free Press, 1966), Chapter I. Although slums constitute the most important and persistent problem of urban areas in developing countries, and often of the country itself, the number of sociological studies made of them is limited. Most of those that have been studied have been in Latin America. W. P. Mangin, "Latin American Squatter Settlements: A Problem and a Solution," *Latin American Research Review*, 2:65–69 (Summer, 1967); A. B. Hollingshead and Lloyd H. Rogler, "Attitudes Toward Slums and Public Housing in Puerto Rico," in Leonard J. Duhl, Ed., *The Urban Condition* (New York: Basic Books, 1963), pp. 229–245. See also Oscar Lewis, *La Vida: A Puerto Rican Family in the Culture of Poverty—San Juan and New York* (New York: Random House, 1966), Lloyd H. Rogler, "Neighborhoods and Slums in Latin America," *Journal of Inter-American Studies*, 9:507–538 (October 1967), and José Matos Mar, "The 'Barriados' of Lima: An Example of Integration into Urban Life," in Philip M. Hauser, Ed., *Urbanization in Latin America* (New York: International Documents Service of Columbia University Press, 1961), pp. 170–190.

11. John C. Bollens and Henry J. Schmandt, *The Metropolis: Its People, Politics, and Economic Life* (New York: Harper & Row, 1965), pp. 255–256.

12. Marshall B. Clinard, "Urbanization, Urbanism, and Deviant Behavior in Puerto Rico," in Millard Hansen, Ed., *Social Change and Social Policy* (Rio Piedras: Social Science Research Center, 1968), pp. 24–36; Gerald Suttles, "Deviant Behavior as an Unanticipated Consequence of Public Housing," in Daniel Glaser, Ed., *Crime in the City* (New York: Harper & Row, 1970), pp. 162–176; Terence Morris, *The Criminal Area: A Study in Social Ecology* (London: Routledge and Kegan Paul, 1958); and Lee Rainwater, *Behind Ghetto Walls: Black Families in a Federal Slum* (Chicago: Aldine, 1970).

13. William Moore, Jr., *The Vertical Ghetto: Everyday Life in an Urban Project* (New York: Random House, 1969). See also Suttles in Glaser, *Crime in the City*, pp. 119–137.

14. Rogler, "Neighborhoods and Slums in Latin America."

15. Isabel Suliveres, "Delincuencia Juvenil: Implicaciones Teoricas para Puerto Rico," in Isabel Suliveres, Ed., *Manual de Lecturas para el Adiestramiento de Oficiales Probatorios Juveniles* (Rio Piedras: Centro de Investigaciones Sociales, Facultad de Ciencias Sociales, Universidad de Puerto Rico, 1969).

16. Kurt W. Back, *Slums, Projects, and People: Social Psychological Problems in Puerto Rico* (Durham: Duke University Press, 1962), pp. 106–107. For similar results in a housing project in Lagos see Peter Marris, *Family and Social Change in an Africa City: A Study of Rehousing in Lagos* (London: Routledge & Kegan Paul, 1961).

17. Helen Safa, "Puerto Rican Adaptation to the Urban Milieu" in Peter Orleans and William Russell Ellis, Jr., *Race, Change and Urban Society* (Beverly Hills, Calif.: Sage Publication, 1971), pp. 153–190.

18. Laquian, *Slums Are for People*, p. 35, by permission of The University Press of Hawaii. See also Laquian, "Slums and Squatters in South and Southeast Asia" in Jakobson and Prakash, *Urbanization and National Development*.

19. John F. C. Turner, "Uncontrolled Urban Settlement: Problems and Policies," Working Paper No. 11, Agenda Item No. 4, Inter-Regional Seminar on Develop-

ment Policies and Planning in Relation to Urbanization, Organized by the United Nations Bureau of Technical Assistance Operations and the Bureau of Social Affairs, University of Pittsburgh, November 24–27, 1966, p. 17, as quoted in Laquian, *Slums Are for People*, p. 34, by permission of The University Press of Hawaii.

20. Robert J. Crooks, "Urbanization and Social Change: Transitional Urban Settlements in Developing Countries," *Conference Papers*, Rehovot Conference on Urbanization and Development in Developing Countries, Rehovot, Israel, 1971, p. 8.

21. The social function of the slums of the United States has also been described in these terms: "Clearly, any attempt to regard the slum as only a residential habitat for the working class, as merely a locus of poor housing and low rent, or as mainly a harbor for many forms of social pathology, neglects its prime significance in rendering possible a meaningful life in a society which is oriented to different values and to different patterns of social relationships." Marc Fried and Joan Levin, "Some Social Functions of the Urban Slum," in Bernard J. Frieden and Robert Morris, Eds., *Urban Planning and Social Policy* (New York: Basic Books, 1968), p. 72.

22. Charles A. Frankenhoff, "The Economics of Housing Policy for a Developing Economy," Puerto Rico, Social Science Research Center, University of Puerto Rico, 1967, mimeo., p. 150; C. A. Frankenhoff, "Elements of an Economic Model for Slums in a Developing Economy," *Journal of Economic Development*, 16:36–38 (1967). See also Laquian ,"Slums and Squatters in South and Southeast Asia," in Jakobson and Prakash, *Urbanization and National Development*.

23. Laquian, *Slums are for People*, pp. 25–26.

24. Daniel Lerner, "Comparative Analysis of Processes of Modernization," in Horace Miner, Ed., *The City in Modern Africa* (New York: Praeger, 1967), p. 25.

25. *Ibid.*

26. Barbara Ward, "The Uses of Prosperity," *Saturday Review*, August 29, 1964, pp. 191–192.

27. Clifford R. Shaw, Henry D. McKay, et al., *Juvenile Delinquency and Urban Areas* (Chicago: University of Chicago Press, rev. ed., 1969); Terrence Morris, *The Criminal Area: A Study in Social Ecology* (London: Routledge and Kegan Paul, 1958); Shankar S. Srivastava, *Juvenile Vagrancy: A Sociological Study of Juvenile Vagrants in the Cities of Kanpur and Lucknow* (New York: Asia Publishing House, 1963); J. J. Panakal and A. M. Khalifa, *Prevention of Types of Criminality Resulting from Social Changes and Accompanying Economic Development in Less Developed Countries*, Reports of the Second United Nations Congress on the Prevention of Crime and the Treatment of Offenders, London, August 8–20, 1960; and Glaser, *Crime in the City*, 1970.

28. City of Manila and National Science Development Board, *Manila: Its Needs and Resources* (Manila: Office of the Mayor, 1966), Chapter 9, as reported in Aprodicio A. Laquian, *Rural Urban Migrants and Metropolitan Development* (Toronto, Canada: Mission, 1971), p. 144.

29. "Rehousing and Resettlement of Squatters in Kuala Lumpur," October 1969, Report by the Sub-Committee on Squatter Rehousing and Resettlement, National Operations Council, 1969, as cited in Laquian, *Rural Urban Migrants and Metropolitan Development*, p. 106.

30. Srivastava, *Juvenile Vagrancy*, and Hansa Sheth, *Juvenile Delinquency in an Indian Setting* (Bombay Popular Book Depot, 1961), p. 150.

31. H. Rotondo, J. Mariategui, B. Bambaren Vigil, B. Garcia Pacheco, and P. Aliaga, "Studies in Social Psychiatry in Urban and Rural Areas," extract in *Excerpta Criminologica*, No. 90, 1962, p. 380, and David Garcia Estrada, "Tepito," *Criminalia*, 32:375–383 (1966).

32. William Mangin, "Latin American Squatter Settlements: A Problem and a Solution," *Latin American Research Review*, 2:65–69 (Summer, 1967).

33. Elio Gomez Grillo, *Delincuencia en Caracas* (Caracas: Universidad del Zulia, 1970), pp. 75, 97, and 124.

34. Theodore Caplow, Sheldon Stryker, and Samuel E. Wallace, *The Urban Ambiance: A Study of San Juan, Puerto Rico* (Totowa, N. J.: The Bedminster Press, 1964), p. 62. See also Lenore R. Kupperstein and Jaime Toro-Calder, *Juvenile Delinquency in Puerto Rico: A Socio-Cultural and Socio-Legal Analysis* (Rio Piedras: Social Science Research Center, 1969), and Clinard, "Urbanization, Urbanism and Deviant Behavior in Puerto Rico," in Hansen, *Social Change and Social Policy*, 1968.

35. Lewis, *La Vida*, 1966.

36. Areas were classified slum and nonslum on the basis of physical characteristics. Generally the social and physical characteristics of communities were closely related. In this sense the distinction does not have the same meaning as it has in developed countries. Within a given sector a slum area had a density of 150 or more inhabitants per hectare and a low rating on living conditions. The nonslum areas totaled 104,650 and the slum areas 71,665. Had it been possible to use a sociological definition of slums, in terms of a way of life, the slum population might have exceeded the nonslum and the rates would have been even higher in the slums.

37. For a discussion of the characteristics and influence of such a subculture see Marvin E. Wolfgang and Franco Ferracuti, *The Sub-Culture of Violence* (London: Tavistock, 1967).

38. Too often community investigations are limited to one area and criminogenic features are imputed from a study of a single case. See, for example, Ellen Hellman, "Life in a Johannesburg Slum Yard," in Simon and Phoebe Ottenberg, Eds., *Cultures and Societies of Africa* (New York: Random House, 1960). Many of the early community studies in the United States were of this nature.

39. United Natitons, *Report on Survey of Present Land Uses and Master Plan Programme for Kampala* (Kampala: United Nations Regional Planning Mission, 1969).

40. Aidan Southall and P. C. W. Gutkind, *Townsmen in the Making: Kampala and Its Suburbs* (London: Kegan Paul Trench Trubner, 1957). Kisenyi means "swamp," and a portion of it is reclaimed land from the swampy margin of the Nakivubo river.

41. *Ibid.*, p. 24.

42. United Nations, *Recommendations for Urban Development in Kampala and Mengo*, Kampala, TAO/Uganda/1, 1964, p. 98.

43. *Ibid.*, p. 26.

44. For a detailed discussion of this phenomenon, see Marvin Wolfgang and Franco Ferracuti, *The Subculture of Violence* (London: Tavistock, 1967).

45. Eric Paul Kibuka, "Sociological Aspects of Juvenile Delinquency in Kampala 1962 to 1969," Ph.D. dissertation, University of East Africa, 1972, p. 239.

46. *Ibid.,* p. 339.

47. Preliminary analysis of a community adjacent to Namuwongo indicated that many women had hardly left the neighborhood since their arrival in Kampala (reported by Regina Solzbacher).

48. A building with six separate households could have sampling units 871 to 876. The interviewer was instructed to give the number 871 to the first household at which he found someone at home and, moving to the right, to number the remaining households. If household 873 had been selected, the family two doors to the right of the initial contact would have been interviewed.

49. There was a turnover of population, especially in the high crime community of Kisenyi. The United Nations survey was conducted in August 1968, and by the time this research was begun, only six months later, 14 buildings had been torn down or abandoned. Because of time pressure, two peripheral sections of Namuwongo were removed from the sample, and the original number of households selected was reduced from 400 to 347.

50. Werner S. Landecker, "Types of Integration and Their Measurement," *American Journal of Sociology,* **61**:332–340 (January 1951). Neither the size nor the type of the group is specified, but the city is used as a basic example.

51. Robert C. Angell, "The Social Integration of Selected American Cities," *American Journal of Sociology,* **47**:575–592 (1941).

52. Richard Jessor, Theodore Graves, Robert Hanson, and Shirley Jessor, *Society, Personality, and Deviant Behavior: A Study of a Tri-Ethnic Community* (New York: Holt, Rinehart and Winston, 1968).

53. Ruth Shonle Cavan and Jordan Cavan, *Delinquency and Crime: Cross-Cultural Perspectives* (New York: Lippincott, 1968), pp. 45–49.

54. Arthur Lewis Wood, "Minority Group Criminality and Cultural Integration," *Journal of Criminal Law Criminology and Police Science,* **37**:498–510 (March–April, 1947). Another example of emphasis on traditions as an adaptation to the urban experience is found in a study of East London, South Africa. Philip Mayer, *Townsmen or Tribesmen: Urbanization in a Divided Society* (Capetown: Oxford University Press, 1962).

55. Oscar Lewis, "Urbanization without Breakdown," in Dwight Heath and Richard Adams, Eds., *Contemporary Cultures and Societies of Latin America* (New York: Random House, 1965).

56. Eugene Wilkening, Joao Bosco Pinto, and José Pastore, "The Role of the Extended Family in Migration and Adaptation in Brazil," Land Tenure Center, University of Wisconsin, R. P. 23, August 1967.

57. David Parkin, *Neighbors and Nationals in an African City Ward* (London: Routledge and Kegan Paul, 1969), p. 186.

58. William Mangin, "The Role of Regional Association in the Adaptation of Rural Migrants to Cities in Peru," in Dwight Heath and Richard Adams, Eds., *Contemporary Cultures and Societies of Latin America,* 1965. Mayer describes how one portion of African migrants to the South African town of East London escaped disruptive influences of urban migration by frequent visits home and systematic rejection of contact with nontraditional influences. Mayer, *Townsmen or Tribesmen,* 1962.

59. Stanley Lieberson, "Measuring Population Density," *American Sociological Review*, **34**:850–862 (December 1969).

60. The clustering of tribe *within* the communities was also distinctly different. Although Namuwongo does contain a sizeable number of tribal groups, the tendency for the migrants there to gather into homogeneous enclaves was greater than in Kisenyi. Within some small sections of Namuwongo, Luos made up 75% of the respondents. In another small section of Namuwongo which represented 10.7% of the sample, the Banyaruanda totaled 78% of those interviewed. On the other hand, in no small section of Kisenyi did one tribe constitute more than 57% of the sample, and the total number of respondents interviewed in that section was only seven.

61. The responses were coded 0 if no friend was mentioned, 1 if the friend came from the same tribe, and 2 if he came from a different tribe:

$$\text{score} = \frac{3 \times (\text{sums of responses})}{\text{number of friends mentioned}}.$$

It was necessary to develop the scale in this manner because some respondents mentioned only one or two friends.

62. Parkin, *Neighbors and Nationals in an African City Ward*, p. 186. Parkin notes in his study of Kampala that tribal ties among the many migrants persisted in effective kin or "brother" relations and marriage arrangements.

63. The concept is more individualistic than communal in Landecker's definition which deals with the comprehensiveness of interpersonal communication.

64. Suttles, in Glaser, *Crime in the City*, 1970. See also Herbert Gans, *The Urban Villagers: Group and Class in the Life of Italian-Americans* (New York: The Free Press, 1962).

65. Rogler, "Neighborhoods and Slums in Latin America."

66. Mangin, "Latin American Squatter Settlements: A Problem and a Solution."

67. Shlomo Shoham, Nahum Shoham, and Adnan-el Razeh, "Immigration, Ethnicity, and Ecology as Related to Juvenile Delinquency in Israel: An Explorative Study," *British Journal of Criminology*, **6**:401–409 (October 1966).

68. For a thorough analysis of the role of tribal associations in adapting to urban life, see Kenneth Little, *West African Urbanization* (Cambridge: Cambridge University Press, 1965).

69. A Uganda newspaper during this period described a robbery in one of the denser heterogeneous areas of Kampala. The gang smashed the door with a rock, beat the occupants, and stole what they could find. No one responded to their pleas for help.

70. Hellman, "Life in a Johannesburg Slum Yard."

71. William Clifford, "Crime and Culture—An African Study," *Canadian Journal of Corrections*, **8**:157–166 (1966).

72. This information came from a personal interview with the head of the community school in Namuwongo.

73. The same procedure as that employed for "tribal diversity" was used in developing the scale [61].

74. P. C. Lloyd, *Africa in Social Change: Changing Traditional Societies in the Modern World* (Baltimore: Penguin, 1967), p. 193.

75. Rogler, "Neighborhoods and Slums in Latin America."

76. Organizations were classified as "local" or "urban," urban implying that the membership is drawn from all parts of the city. Numerical scales were constructed for each category based on the number of active memberships. Attendance at a religious service was treated separately. It was felt that the regular congregation had a different kind of involvement than the usually small number who belong to church organizations and direct the affairs of the church.

77. Post notes that these unions are prevalent in West Africa and play a vital role in aiding the adjustment of new migrants to cities. Ken Post, *The New States of Africa* (Baltimore: Penguin Books, 1964), p. 80.

78. Margaret Jellicoe, "Credit and Housing Associations Among the Luo Migrants of Kampala," Makerere Institute of Social Research (mimeo), Kampala, 1969.

79. Hilda Kuper, *Urbanization and Migration in West Africa* (Berkeley: University of California Press, 1965), p. 12. See also Lloyd, *Africa in Social Change,* pp. 258–260.

80. David S. Wiley, "Social Stratification and Religion in Urban Zambia: An Explanatory Study in an African Suburb," unpublished Ph.D. dissertation, Princeton Theological Seminary, April 1971.

81. The F scores were significant at the 0.001 level for both young and old: the men from Namuwongo tended to be much more active churchgoers.

82. Lois B. DeFleur, "A Cross-Cultural Comparison of Juvenile Offenders and Offenses, Cordoba, Argentina, and the United States," *Social Problems,* 14:483–495 (1967). See also Lois B. DeFleur, *Delinquency in Argentina: A Study of Cordoba's Youth* (Pullman: Washington State University Press, 1970).

83. The correlation between education and occupation for the total community sample was low (.25). The majority of the men in the sample had either no education or only some level of primary schooling. Only 19.4% of the total sample in Namuwongo and 31.2% in Kisenyi had received any secondary education. For those with a primary education or less, education appears to have little bearing on their occupations—skilled or unskilled. Only 13.4% of the men in Namuwongo and 21.6% of the men in Kisenyi had occupations higher than skilled labor. Thus at this stage of development, when the educational system is rapidly expanding on the primary level but job openings are scarce, there appears to be little relation between the two factors for the lower class urban Ugandan.

84. Eugene Havens and Elsa Ugandizaga, *Tres Barrios de Invasion* (Bogota: Ediciones Tercer Mundo, 1966). In this study of Colombia three slum communities show marked differences in occupation and life style. These authors found that the older slums had the more settled and prosperous populations.

85. A scale of civic participation was developed by summing responses to the items and trichotimizing the scores into low, medium, and high participation. To a certain extent these findings confirm the validity of the scale. It was first used in a study of a slum and a more settled government housing estate in Mombasa. The latter had a much higher rate of civic participation. Since two slum communities responded identically in Kampala, it may be measuring the variable for which it was originally intended. See Richard E. Stren, "Report on Housing Survey of Mombasa, 1968," Dar es Salaam, University College, 1968, mimeo.

86. Cavan and Cavan, *Delinquency and Crime,* pp. 45–49.

87. Havens and Ugandizaga, *Tres Barrios de Invasion,* p. 74.

Chapter 6   Poverty, Differential Opportunity, and Criminal Behavior

Attempts have been made to explain crime in developed countries as being the direct result of economic deprivation or, more indirectly, of the inability of persons to achieve the economic and educational goals of a society by legitimate means. These approaches have included such conceptual frameworks as poverty, anomie, and differential opportunity. In general they would regard the individual deviant or criminal as a person who has been unsuccessful in a goal-oriented society.

POVERTY AND CRIME IN DEVELOPING COUNTRIES

By definition, developing countries are poor countries. It seems logical to associate their poverty with their criminality or to attribute their increasing criminality to their poverty, as many have attempted to do in the developed countries. This approach in particular has been stressed by the Economic and Social Council and the Secretariat of the United Nations, whose general view has been that crime problems lie deep in the processes of economic and social development and must be resolved within them [1]. López-Rey has pointed out that in developing countries "governments still rely excessively on the thesis that improvement of material conditions will considerably reduce, if not eradicate, crime and juvenile delinquency" [2]. Moreover, many countries with a socialist system of government emphasize a similar economic explanation for their crime. In a 1970 report, for example, rising crime in Algeria was attributed to inadequate economic development [3].

It is thought that criminality begins with need and that it can be reduced to the extent that the causes related to underdevelopment can be successfully attacked and the educational and technical level of the country raised. It has been anticipated that these developmental measures should reduce criminality. If, as it is claimed, crimes are committed by those who cannot afford the simple needs and amenities of life, the basic cause of crime, from an economic point of view, is low income and inadequate capital formation. It can be concluded, therefore, that when people are no longer poor crimes and other forms of deviant behavior will largely disappear. Massive sums of foreign capital and general economic development will generally alleviate most of the crime and similar problems in a country in the process of development.

It is not surprising that poverty and social inequality have been assumed by some to explain the general increase in rates of crime and delinquency in developing countries, in view of the fact that economic deprivation has long been considered a basic cause of the social problems in the more developed societies [4]. Many economic writers and social workers, including earlier writers like Henry George, Karl Marx, Charles Booth, Jane Addams, and William Bonger, have recognized the importance of economic factors in social life. In this view society's failure to provide adequate goods, services, and housing for everyone permits crime and other forms of deviant behavior to develop, and economic fluctuations and the maldistribution of wealth contribute to these deviations.

It is important therefore to appraise the validity of this model of the economic man who steals because he is poor, because he has had bad housing, or because others have more of society's goods than he has. Without question, poverty in any country, developed or developing, seriously affects health, life expectancy, infant mortality rates, housing, quality of family life, community as well as individual living, and educational opportunity. Above all, individual and collective poverty limits social participation, particularly in political, social, and economic spheres. There are, however, several objections to the concept of poverty as a basic explanation of criminal behavior, whether the country is highly developed or in a low state of development.

Poverty can mean insufficiency in relation to a certain standard of living, sharp inequalities of income distribution, inability to achieve certain aspirational levels, or a subculture of behavior patterns and attitudes. This insufficiency can refer to a particularly low level of subsistence, as in many Asian and some African countries. From this point of view the "poor" person will obviously vary with the standard of living in both time and place. A poor person in Western Europe or the United States has infinitely more material goods than a poor person in Africa or India. Poverty may also be regarded as a relative concept in terms of comparative incomes, and marked inequalities of income distribution in which the poor represent the lowest segment in income range. There is therefore a great deal of difference between poverty as a relative concept based on the standard of living and as a relative concept in terms of inequality of income. According to the latter, the poor, by definition, would always be with us. Equally applicable to less developed countries is the view that it is important to "keep distinct the difference between poverty as the inability to obtain a specific level of living and inequality as the relative sharing of the economic and social output. The two can be moving in different directions" [5]. Poverty can be examined in still another sense, not defined in absolute terms, but in relation to the aspirations and expectations of a culture and its capacity to produce the goods to satisfy these expectations.

Still another view of the concept of poverty is that it may represent a culture or subculture of certain behaviors and attitudes. Poverty in this sense consists of shared sets of values, behavior traits, and beliefs that set it apart from the more affluent segments of a society, a condition developing from socialization in an environment of economic uncertainty and limited financial resources. Oscar Lewis has referred to this condition as the "culture of poverty" which he felt to be worldwide [6]. It might be well, however, to speak more appropriately of "culture and poverty," since there are groups of poor in diverse geographical and national locations, with different opportunity structures [7]. Certainly there is considerable difference in the values of the poor in rural compared with urban areas. López-Rey has acknowledged that social and economic conditions play a certain role but one that should never be magnified and transformed into the explanation of all crime [8].

It is true that most persons arrested, prosecuted, and imprisoned for crimes, both in the developed and the less developed countries, do come from the lower socioeconomic groups. This would seem to indicate that the social structure usually associated with poverty has a relation to the kinds and rates of crime. The proportion of deviants from the lower socioeconomic groups would be much smaller were the samples more representative. Studies in developed countries, without exception, indicate that persons from the lower socioeconomic groups are more likely to come to the attention of agents of social control such as the police and to be labeled as criminals than are those from the more affluent groups. Yet it is interesting to note that a distribution of a large sample of juvenile offenders arrested in Bombay revealed that only one-fifth (19.3%) were very poor, one-half (50%) were poor, 15.2% were fairly well off, and 1.2% very well off [9]. It is interesting that the distribution in cases of delinquency studies in Lebanon was not too dissimilar. Among 2880 cases of juvenile delinquency studied between 1963 and 1965 12% came from very poor families, 33% from poor families, 42% from families whose earnings were sufficient to meet their basic needs, and 2% from rich families [10].

It is also important to note that criminal behavior, in the form of occupational or white collar crime such as business crimes and political corruption, appears to be quite extensive among the more economically well-to-do groups in most societies, but these offenders are seldom prosecuted and few persons are imprisoned [11]. This type of crime appears to be equally common, perhaps even prevalent, in less developed countries in which the power élite is often beyond the law and in which political corruption is particularly common [12]. Crime figures seldom include these cases. Were the true knowledge of all crimes available, it might be difficult to say whether crime is greater among the poverty stricken or among the affluent.

It cannot be concluded that crime is related to the poverty and bad housing found in slum areas, in particular, the slum areas of developing countries. The high crime rates of slum areas are produced by general social conditions rather than the physical buildings and surroundings [13]. In fact, wherever slum clearance or relocation projects have been attempted, the results have been disastrous in the reduction of deviance. In the United States, for example, as well as in Caracas and San Juan, some of the highest rates of deviance are found in slum clearance projects. A British sociologist concluded that the physical characteristics of an area have little relevance to crime and delinquency except as an indirect determinant of the area's social status. The delinquency rates remained high even after the construction of new government housing projects [14].

Moreover, the crime rates of many highly developed countries negate the hypothesis that an increasingly high standard of living and the provision of a variety of social services diminish crime. In fact, a stronger case can be made for the relation of affluence to crime [15]. Criminal behavior has not markedly decreased. It has even increased over the last century even though there has been a constant rise in the living standards in such Western European countries as Sweden, the United Kingdom, and Germany. Today the two countries with the highest per capita income—Sweden, in which there is also a fairly equitable distribution of wealth, and the United States—have particularly serious crime problems. After surveying crime from a worldwide view Middendorff concluded that improvement in living conditions, or what is called a better standard of living, does not necessarily, by itself, reduce juvenile delinquency [16]. Consequently, it might be well to adopt a

theoretically consistent interpretation of the significant fact that crime has probably increased throughout much of the Western world during the last one hundred and fifty years, despite the obvious and indisputable increase in the economic well-being of nearly everyone everywhere. The unparalelled economic and social progress of the last century and a half has given the ordinary worker a much better economic position than he ever enjoyed in the past but it has also brought new pressures and demands that often result in criminality [17].

It might be argued, however, in the case of the less developed countries, that an increase in per capita income could mean little as far as reflecting an actual increase in the standard of living, since national income may go primarily to the élite and wealthy groups within the country. Actually poverty is too simple an explanation for a more complex process of socialization into criminal norms. Norms that permit and even sanction acts of theft must generally have been incorporated into a person's life organization by intimate contact with others who transmit deviant cultural, neighborhood, and occupational norms. After surveying the crime situation in Latin America, Bergalli has stated:

It is simplistic to apply a pure economic model to the explanation of crime. If poverty was a cause then all states in Latin America should have a much higher crime rate than the United States, whose income per capita is much greater than any Latin American country [18].

DIFFERENTIAL OPPORTUNITY AND CRIME IN DEVELOPING COUNTRIES

One frame of reference, partly economic in nature, that may be relevant to an explanation of crime in developing countries is the concept of anomie. To some sociologists criminal behavior results from a state of anomie, or the clash between institutional means and cultural goals in the access to a given success goal by legitimate means [19]. Merton, the proponent of this formulation, points out that most modern societies emphasize material success in the form of the acquisition of wealth by education, as an accepted status goal, but at the same time they fail to provide adequate institutional means or norms for members of the lower class and the poorer groups to achieve these goals [20]. These people are often referred to as being anomic, in the sense that they are powerless to achieve money, higher education, and the general affluence of the society. Such people become frustrated by the system and may resort to stealing or other adaptations to achieve status goals.

The model of anomie has been vigorously criticized as an explanation of deviant behavior in modern societies [21]. Consequently the tendency to drop or to modify the theory on the basis that "anomie was perhaps never there" is increasing. It is possible, however, that anomie is more applicable as a partial explanation for some of the social forces leading to increased crime in countries undergoing rapid development; for example, in developing societies goods in considerable amounts and varieties are suddenly made available to the general population. Under colonial rule these goods had been available only to foreigners and a small group of local persons. Despite independence and development, the low living standards still give these material possessions, as well as a higher standard of living, a high status value in an urban context. Access to higher status by education is often unattainable, and when it is possible the economy is often insufficiently developed to make use of those persons who do manage to obtain it. Similarly, in many developing countries the rising crime rates among young males can be linked to the impact of ownership of such things as transistor radios, "mod" clothes, and automobiles. The relative deprivation by those who feel disadvantaged may be correlated with the crime rates in countries in the process of development. In a study of juvenile delinquency in Mexico one writer reported that a leading cause of the high rates was the gross difference between the incomes of the rich and the poor [22]. In his discussion of affluence and adolescent crime in developed countries, however, Jackson Toby has adopted a reverse position, namely, that secularism, the emphasis on distribution of goods, and the stimulation of the mass media, such as television, for material goods has "thrown light on why the sting of socio-economic deprivation can be greater for the poor in rich societies than for the poor in poorer societies" [23].

Building largely on Merton's concept of anomie, another widely known theory, that of differential opportunity, which has been developed basically to explain the growth of delinquent gang behavior among urban youth, has been expanded to account for crime in general and for other forms of deviance [24]. According to Cloward and Ohlin, delinquent gang behavior grows wherever legitimate means to the attainment of the success goals, such as economic and higher educational opportunities, are blocked. The disparity between what lower class youths are led to want and what is actually available to them becomes the source of a major adjustment problem. Cloward and Ohlin suggest that adolescents who form delinquent subcultures have internalized an emphasis on conventional goals. They are faced with limitations on legitimate avenues of access to these goals, and since they are unable to revise their aspirations downward they experience intense frustrations. As a result they may explore nonconformist alternatives [25]. This theory likewise incorporates Sutherland's differential association theory that deviant adaptation such as crime to achieve success goals depends upon access to illegitimate means. The individual must have an opportunity to acquire the techniques and he must have rationalizations for his crime [26].

According to the differential opportunity theory, the primary means of attaining economic success goals is education. By education the individual acquires the skills, the life style and mannerisms, and the values necessary to advancement in a modern society. Because of insufficient income, poor school facilities, and inadequate preparation, lower class persons have limited access to education and therefore to the possibility of a better paying occupation which is critical to his achievement wealth and status. Many lower class persons react to these restrictions on opportunity by adopting illegitimate means such as crime to attain their goals, their choice depending on their exposure to these means.

On the whole, this theory of crime, based on the alienation and the frustrations of the lower class, has not been subjected to many actual tests in developed countries. Whenever they have been tested, the results have been confusing. One study claimed to show this association, but the methodology was poor [27]. A more convincing but still inconclusive study was done by Luchterhand and Weller [28], and Friday, in a Swedish study, found evidence that differential opportunity, if linked with other factors, has considerable value as an explanation [29]. On the other hand, a large-scale test by Short and Strodtbeck in Chicago discovered that blocked opportunity scores do not predict criminal behavior [30]. The behavior of delinquent boys is more determined by the immediate context of status within the gang rather than the detached, culturally determined goals of success. Still another study, done in London, revealed that the differential opportunity hypothesis does not offer a satisfactory explanation [31]. Delinquency in the working class is not a product of alienation but results rather from a process of dissociation from middle-class contexts in school, work, and recreation.

Almost no specific research has been done on the application of the theory of differential opportunity to less developed countries, although certain related data and claims are available from a few places [32]. In a city like Bombay, for example, where many juveniles are neither employed nor going to school, it might be expected that nearly all of those arrested would come from this group. In actuality one study of a large sample showed that 11.9% were in school, 16.3% were employed full time, and 18.9% were employed part-time, or a total of approximately one-half the total group [33]. An Argentine article has stressed the importance in less developed countries of considering differentials in the access to education or training and to opportunities for economic, social, and cultural advancement [34]. These stresses are particularly great in societies that are undergoing a transition from traditional to modern stages of development and may well lead individuals to delinquent acts. Several African studies have claimed that crime is related to a lack of economic and educational opportunity; in his study of crime in South

Africa Freed related delinquency to the lack of education among the Africans. He states that the "facilities for Native education on the Reef were inadequate, and opportunity for schooling existed for only a third of the children" [35]. Freed also found low occupational status strongly associated with crime. A study of juvenile delinquency in Southern Rhodesia linked the increase in gang delinquency to differentials in the opportunities for increased educational and economic opportunities [36]. Consistently, gang members were unemployed youths from poverty-stricken backgrounds who had little opportunity to attend school. On the other hand, a comparison of delinquents and nondelinquents in Lusaka revealed no difference in the economic level or in the occupational status of the father [37]. The delinquents were lower in educational attainment than the nondelinquents but higher than the average educational level of the country as a whole.

None of these studies, however, really systematically tested the theory by exploring in detail the educational and occupational backgrounds of offenders and nonoffenders. The Uganda study attempted to discover if there were a real relation between differential opportunity and criminal behavior. The analysis considered several critical factors in the theory of differential opportunity—occupational and educational differences, material and educational aspirations, and perceived opportunity. The offender sample (164) consisted of persons from Kampala who had committed property offenses, aged 18 to 25; the nonoffender control group consisted of 206 young males of the same age from two slum communities in Kampala [38].

Many members of the developing middle class of white collar workers in business and government still often retain characteristics similar to the lower prestige laborers in life style, recreational patterns, and basic values [39]. Even though the gulf between the African élite and the ordinary African may be wide, status distinctions are beginning to show in the lower class. Education and occupation are replacing the tribe as a primary determinant of position in the urban environment [40]. Yet the tribe is not totally divorced from the differentiating process because certain groups tend to become associated with specific occupations [41]. Occupancy in government housing estates is determined by income and occupation, although not completely without regard to tribal origins [42]. Status differences are being recognized increasingly, and they affect various facets of social interaction between class and occupation groups.

Occupational and Educational Differences

Occupation was divided into three levels: low (unemployed, farm, or part-time selling), medium (unskilled and skilled), and high (clerical,

Table 31   Occupational Level—Offender and Nonoffender

	Nonoffender		Offender	
	No.	%	No.	%
Low	60	29.1	44	26.8
Medium	101	49.1	108	65.9
High	45	21.8	12	7.3
Total	206	100.0	164	100.0

$\chi^2 = 16.0$
$df = 2$
$P\ .001$

commercial, professional, and student). The differences between offenders and nonoffenders had a high degree of statistical significance (see Table 31).

At the lower end of the occupational scale there was little difference between offenders and nonoffenders; it was in the medium and high level of occupation that the differences were quite pronounced. There was little difference between the two groups in the percentage unemployed. Only 13% of the offenders reported themselves to be unemployed at the time of their arrests, whereas 17% of the nonoffenders put themselves in this category. Although unemployment does not appear to be a critical distinguishing factor, it is prominent in the rationalizations given by the offenders for their thefts. Unemployment may be a basis for justifying theft, but it cannot be considered a "cause" behind the decision to commit the crime. The major occupational category in which the offenders were disproportionately represented was the middle level; 65.9% of the offenders versus 49.1% of the nonoffenders held jobs in the unskilled and skilled categories. This finding conflicts with the 49.9% of the unemployed recorded for Kampala arrests (see Chapter 1) and makes one doubtful of the accuracy of police reporting of this status.

Western criminologists have suggested that unemployment is not an absolute condition, and therefore has little relation to criminality [43]. In a study of youth crime in Sweden, for example, Friday found no relation between unemployment and youth crime [44]. The young unemployed in his sample expressed little concern with their future and appeared to be confident in their abilities to secure employment eventually. If a large percentage of the labor force is unemployed the jobless feel less frustration than if the economy is strong and most persons have jobs. Since employment is difficult to obtain in most African cities and few have steady wage employment, joblessness may not be as social psychologically demeaning. To a certain extent this might account for the lack of a significant relation between unemployment and criminal involvement in Kampala. Moreover, being unemployed in a developing country does not necessarily mean that a person is suffering real financial hardship and, conversely, being self-employed, for example, as a street vendor, does not mean that such a person is better off than the unemployed. Actually on occasion persons who are employed have greater opportunities for crime, as in the case of theft by servants.

Highly significant educational differences were revealed between offenders and nonoffenders. The differences, however, were of inadequate education rather than no education at all. The proportions of offenders and nonoffenders who had received no education were quite similar; 16 percent of the nonoffenders and 22.6 percent of the offenders were totally uneducated. In this connection, several authors have argued that school dropouts in Africa who cannot find jobs in the city present a special problem because they refuse to return to the village [45]. This view received support from the Kampala data: it is not the uneducated who are disproportionately represented but rather the poorly educated who more often commit property crime. Among the nonoffenders, 43.3% had more than a primary education, compared with only 18.9% of the offenders. Twelve percent of the nonoffenders were attending school when interviewed, whereas only 1% of the offenders were in school at the time of their arrests. Since education is the primary means of advancement, participation in the system may offer hope that some students will hesitate to jeopardize themselves by engaging in crime. Students are perhaps more in contact with noncriminal patterns and less with criminal patterns. It is possible, of course, that those with limited education are more likely to be convicted.

Material Aspirations

The theory of differential opportunity assumes a generally high level of aspiration for material success among all segments of the population and that those who commit crime are those who cannot achieve such goals legitimately. Such assumptions, as applied to developed countries, have been questioned, since there is doubt that such goals are accepted by everyone in a complex urban society. The all-pervading importance of monetary and education goals, for example, does not appear to be accepted by all groups, in particular by lower class gang boys [46].

On the other hand, in less developed countries aspirations among the general urban population, which have been referred to as the revolution of rising expectations [47], may more likely include material elements. In the Uganda study measures were constructed to test both material and educational goals among offenders and nonoffenders. Desire for a better standard of living was measured by responses to the question: "A man has a steady job as a factory worker and has two rooms for his living quarters. He makes 200 shillings (28 dollars) a month and has a wife and three children. There is space for him to grow some food. Should a man in Kampala have more than that?" Educational goals were ascertained by asking how much education the respondent would want for himself and for his son if the opportunity were there. It was hypothesized that the offenders would have equal or higher material and educational aspirations than the nonoffenders [48].

Nonoffenders responded affirmatively more often than the offenders to the hypothetical question of the need for a certain level of material satisfaction, but the difference was not statistically significant (see Table 32). That offenders did not appear to have significantly different aspirations from nonoffenders indicated a more universal acceptance of material goals. Approximately half of each group wanted more than the basic set of living conditions suggested by the question. Although there was little difference between the two samples in terms of material aspirations, this does not necessarily indicate that desire for material goods has no influence on property crime. Urban life offers a range of activities or possessions unimagined in the village. In the rationalizations offered for

Table 32   Desire for a Higher Standard of Living than that Described in Hypothetical Situation, Offenders and Nonoffenders

	Nonoffender		Offender	
	No.	%	No.	%
Yes	109	52.9	75	45.7
No	97	47.1	89	54.2
Total	206	100.0	164	100.0

$\chi^2 = 2.2$.
ff = 1, NS.

theft by offenders the theme of desire for more luxuries was repeated frequently. Many steal because they

... want to maintain their girl friends (prostitutes) by buying them good clothes, watches, nice shoes, and paying the house rent;

... want to go to nightclubs every week;

... want more money or a better place to live;

... want luxury things such as better clothes and going to night clubs or providing special articles for girlfriends.

There were highly significant differences in educational aspirations. Forty-two percent of the nonoffenders and only 14.4% of the offenders wanted a university education, but only 15.7% of the offenders and 11% of the nonoffenders wanted less than the equivalent of a Cambridge Certificate (high school diploma). These high goals underscore the respected position held by education even among the poorest citizens in African countries. The disparity in educational aspirations could, of course, be the result of the difference in the level of learning between offenders and nonoffenders. To test this theory education was trichotomized into low, medium, and high. With education controlled, offenders still tended to have less ambition, especially at the extremes in education. In the low and high categories the nonoffenders had significantly higher goals than the offenders, but the difference was greatly reduced for those with a medium level.

On the degree of education for their sons the patterns of responses was similar to their personal patterns for those with low and medium education, but a discontinuity was evident in the high-level group. The more highly educated offender and nonoffender groups desired a high educational level for their sons, even though offenders in this category wanted less for themselves. This suggests that although the offenders' personal aspirations were lower they still appreciated the value of higher education. Thus the offenders' "aspirations" may reflect realistic acknowledgment of possibilities rather than the conclusion that, because they expressed lower educational goals they were not motivated to choose illegitimate methods for material advancement to compensate for the lack.

Perceived Opportunity

The respondent's perceptions of his own opportunities, both legitimate and illegitimate, were further measured with a battery of items that required the subject to agree or disagree with statements concerning his past and future opportunities in the social structure as well as others that implied knowledge of possible illegitimate opportunities. The hypotheses were that offenders more than nonoffenders would perceive (a) that they had had less chance of achieving success, (b) that illegitimate means to success are necessary, and (c) express greater knowledge of contacts in illegal activities. From previous studies in developed countries which utilized this method as a measure of the theory of differential opportunity items were selected that fitted the African situation. These items were derived from Short and Strodtbeck [49] and Friday [50]. Items were then factor-analyzed (the factors with their loadings are presented in the Appendix). One, the lack of opportunity, expressed the concept of differential opportunity, the perception of fewer chances to succeed than others. The other was the need for illegitimate means. This encompassed both a belief in the necessity to use illegal methods to earn enough money and an awareness of illegal contacts.

No significant difference was found between offenders and nonoffenders in their understanding that they had fewer chances to succeed than others [51]. Since few could claim to have had exceptionally good opportunities, the degree of perceived blockage from opportunities was the same for offenders and nonoffenders. The degree of perceived blockage for both groups, however, was fairly high. Sixty percent of the nonoffenders and 65% of the offenders agreed to the statement that "Your parents cannot give you the chances that most young people want." Both samples came from backgrounds that provided limited opportunities; 59% of the offenders and nonoffenders listed their fathers' occupation as "farmer" and only 12.2% of the fathers had received more than six years of education.

The Use of Illegitimate Means

The factor classified as "need for illegitimate means," reflected the respondent's judgment of the possibility of success in the economic system by legitimate means. The difference between offenders and nonoffenders was statistically highly significant at the .001 level. Offenders felt much more strongly that success was made possible only by some kind of unlawful behavior. With the item, "It is hard to earn much money without doing something illegal," 56% of the offenders and only 36% of the nonoffenders agreed. If not a motivating force, this attitude could definitely provide a suitable rationalization for theft. Moreover, since opportunities for employment are associated with education, its level may be inversely related to the need for illegitimate means, the educated presumably having greater access to legitimate channels, as the correlations between education and need for illegitimate means indicated. However, the correlations were low. The lower correlations for the offenders may have been the result because only a small percentage had gone beyond the primary school. Nonetheless, the critical feature that distinguishes offender and nonoffender samples is not past opportunities and their effect on present chances but the attitudes toward the present system. Offenders had a greater tendency to view it as "corrupt" and to feel that their only recourse was to utilize illegitimate means.

The responses on need for illegitimate means contrast with the responses of offenders and nonoffenders about success by hard work. Approximately 95% of each group agreed with the statement "If a person works hard he can get ahead." Both groups of respondents generally believed that with sufficient effort a person could advance himself, yet nepotism is generally widespread on all occupational and governmental levels in Africa. Approximately 80% of both groups agreed that such influence was necessary to get well-paid jobs. These conflicting ideas underscore the paradoxes created by the superimposition of urbanization and independence on a traditional value system. There is a refusal to relinquish belief in hard work but a realistic appraisal of the opportunity structure.

One may question whether the attitudes of offenders existed before arrest or were developed after conviction and imprisonment. Studies in Western nations suggest the latter possibility. Friday's study of differential opportunity and differential association in Sweden found that offenders under the age of 21 had a more pessimistic view of their future chances than those over 21 [52]. He interpreted this to mean that official sanctions may have altered the younger group's evaluation. The older group had a better perspective on its position in the occupational structure and were less threatened by arrest. In a study of adjudicated juveniles in the United States Lambert states that data show it (anomie) to be more pronounced after adjudication [53]. The data in the present study were not constructed directly to investigate this subject, but the absence of differences on lack of opportunity between the two groups appears to indicate that the offenders' perceptions were independent of adjudication.

Perception of Differential Opportunity in Two Slum Communities

To explore further the relation between differential opportunity and criminal behavior the response patterns to the questions on opportunity were analyzed for the residents of the two Kampala slum communities, one with a high and the other with a lower crime rate (see Chapter 5). Although there were no significant statistical differences between offenders on lack of opportunity, strong differences in this factor appeared between the two communities. The men from the high crime community perceived that they had received fewer opportunities for advancement than the men from the area with the lower crime rate. Moreover, the need for the use of illegitimate means to attain success highly differentiated the two communities for both younger (under 26) and older (26 or more) men. In Chapter 5 it was noted that men from both communities expressed equal disapproval of theft, even under crises situations, but the men from the high crime rate area felt much more strongly that advancement could come only by illegitimate means. Thus both measures of differential opportunity were distinguished clearly between the communities.

Viewed as a control group, the average responses of the young men from both slum communities did not differ significantly from those of the offender group; however, there were significant differences on the use of illegitimate means.

To understand this relation more fully means for the two factors on differential opportunity for offenders and the young of both communities are shown in Table 33. The means of the young men of the high crime rate community and the offender group were essentially equal on lack of opportunity but are distinctly different from the mean of the young males in the low crime rate area. On need for illegitimate means, however, the offenders vary considerably from the young males from both communities.

This pattern of responses suggests an important element that might be crucial in distinguishing the control group from the offenders. The three groups, young males from areas with high and low crime rates and the offenders, were distinctly different on need for illegitimate means, but both the young from the high crime community and the offenders

Table 33   Differences in Means for Factors on Differential Opportunity, Offenders Versus Nonoffenders

Factors	Nonoffenders		Offenders	Young
	Namuwongo	Kisenyi		Kisenyi and Namuwongo
Lack of opportunity	3.255	2.980	2.988	3.121
Need for illegitimate means	4.312	3.600	3.280	3.966

felt equally that they had fewer opportunities and chances for success. The distinguishing factor between the youth of the high crime community and the offenders was the offenders' greater disenchantment with the honesty and openness of the economic system. Although the sense of the disadvantage is important, the need for illegitimate means appears to be the critical element in perceived opportunities.

The theory of differential opportunity which emphasizes that crime arises from blockage to success within the economic and social system because of disadvantages in social background, was therefore only partly supported in the Uganda study. It did not distinguish between offenders and nonoffenders but only between high and low crime communities. However, the need to use illegitimate means to break the law to achieve certain ends was significant between offenders and nonoffenders as well as between the two slum communities.

SOME CONCLUSIONS

The theory of differential opportunity claims that the poverty of the lower classes prevents them from using legitimate means, such as education, to acquire valued goods, thus giving them no alternative but to engage in illegitimate activities. Whether they actually commit crimes depends on their access to the structures of illegitimate opportunity. The logical conclusion is that opening up avenues of educational and economic opportunity will reduce criminality. The experience of economically developed countries, however, has been the opposite. The supposed panaceas have not reduced criminality. With discouraging regularity the higher general standards of living, better distribution of wealth, and new urban housing programs ultimately appear to have little or no effect on crime rates. Scientific studies have also documented an extensive amount of criminality among economically successful middle and upper income groups.

Nonetheless, the enormous proportion and extensive poverty of lower classes in the cities of developing countries, as well as the great emphasis that has been put on rising expectations, warranted a test of the theory, even though tests in the United States, England, and Sweden have been largely inconclusive. The major conclusions of the Kampala study were that absolute deprivation did not distinguish between offenders and nonoffenders: approximately similar proportions of offenders and nonoffenders were unemployed or had no education. The offenders were overrepresented in the class that had a few years of education or low level jobs. It is possible that this educational minimum was sufficient to obtain a low-income job but that expectations had been raised. Questions on material aspirations, however, revealed no differences, but educational aspirations were markedly higher among the nonoffenders.

There were no differences in perceptions of insufficient help from parents or the inadequacy of their own background experiences. Perceptions of blocked access to better positions in the employment structure, however, sharply distinguished offenders and the control group. A high level of cynicism toward the nepotism and corruption in business and government was expressed by the offender population.

The theory of differential opportunity also stresses access to illegitimate means, and it this aspect that may represent the key, rather than the blocking of economic and educational opportunities, to an understanding of criminality in less developed countries. The heterogeneity, complexity, asymmetry, anonymity, impersonality, and individuality of urban life create situations not only for young migrants but for those in positions of economic and political power in regard to motivations, opportunities, rationalizations, and the lack of effective legal controls to support the breaking of formal laws. The illegitimate opportunity structures for particular offenses in each class determine the form of deviance.

NOTES AND REFERENCES

1. United Nations, *International Action in the Field of Social Defence, 1966–1967,* Prepared by the Secretariat of the United Nations (Doc. E/CN/5/C2/Rs, 1966), and Related Documents, and United Nations, *Progess Report on the Programmes in the Field of Social Development* (E/CN.5/409/Add.4, 1967).

2. Manuel López-Rey, *Crime: An Analytical Appraisal* (New York: Praeger and London: Routledge and Kegan Paul, 1970), p. 21.

3. Report au IVème Congrès des Nations Unies Pour la Prévention du Crime et le Traitement des Délinquants, Ministère de la Justice, République Algérienne Démocratique et Populaire, Imprimerie Officiel, Alger, 1970.

4. See, for example, for a developed country, Louis A. Ferman, Joyce L. Kornbluh and Alan Haber, Eds., *Poverty in America; A Book of Readings* (Ann Arbor: University of Michigan Press, 1965), p. 5.

5. S. M. Miller and Martin Rein, "Poverty, Inequality and Policy," in Howard S. Becker, *Social Problems: A Modern Approach* (New York: Wiley, 1966), pp. 436–437. For a discussion of the distinction between the economic definition of poverty primarily in terms of a given level of income and as a sociological phenomenon see Robert J. Lampman, *Ends and Means of Reducing Income Poverty* (Chicago: Markham, 1971).

6. Oscar Lewis, *La Vida* (New York: Random House, 1965).

7. Eleanor Burke Leacock, Ed., *The Culture of Poverty: A Critique* (New York: Simon and Schuster, 1971).

8. López-Rey, *Crime*, p. 186. It is often assumed that the poverty that results from economic depressions associated with the business cycle produces increased rates of deviance. From the extensive evidence available it can be concluded that the business cycle has little or no direct relation to crime.

9. Hansa Sheth, *Juvenile Delinquency in an Indian Setting* (Bombay: Popular Books Depot, 1961), p. 243. These definitions were in terms of Indian standards of living.

10. Mustafa El Augi, *Délinquence Juvénile au Liban* (Université Libanaise: Publications du Centre de Recherches, 1970), p. 61.

11. Edwin H. Sutherland, *White Collar Crime* (New York: Holt, Rinehart & Winston, 1949, reissued, 1960), Chapter 2; Marshall B. Clinard, *The Black Market* (New York: Holt, Rinehart & Winston, 1952); and Marshall B. Clinard, "White Collar Crime," *Encyclopedia of the Social Sciences* (New York: Crowell-Collier and Macmillan, 1968).

12. See Chapter 2.

13. See Chapter 5.

14. Terrence Morris, *The Criminal Area: A Study in Social Ecology* (London: Routledge & Kegan Paul, 1957).

15. John K. Galbraith, *The Affluent Society* (Boston: Houghton Mifflin, 1958).

16. Wolf Middendorff, "The Origin of the 'New Forms' of Juvenile Delinquency," in *New Forms of Juvenile Delinquency: Their Origin, Prevention and Treatment* (United Nations Publication A/Conf. 17/7), p. 41. Switzerland, the third wealthiest, appears to have no serious crime problem, whereas the fourth wealthiest, West Germany, has. In Japan both juvenile and adult arrests, including those for theft, have been decreasing since 1960. The official explanation in 1970 was that "economic prosperity has solved the problem of poverty as well as the stability of the social condition of the nation" (Ministry of Justice, *The Trends of Juvenile Delinquency and Procedures for Handling Delinquents in Japan*, Japan, 1970). This contradicts the general worldwide experience and, in particular, that in the United States and Sweden. This decline may be related to the long postwar readjustments which have reached full development and also to changes in arrest policies.

17. George B. Vold, *Theoretical Criminology* (New York: Oxford University Press, 1958), p. 176, restates Morris Ploscowe's theory.

18. Roberto Bergalli, *Criminologica en America Latina* (Buenos Aires: Ediciones Pannedille, 1972), p. 66.

19. Anomie is used here in a different sense from that proposed by Durkheim, to whom the concept represented "normlessness." See Emile Durkheim, *Suicide* (translated by John Spaulding and George Simpson: New York: The Free Press, 1951).

20. See "Social Structure and Anomie" in Robert K. Merton, *Social Theory and Social Structure* (New York: The Free Press, 1957), pp. 161–194, and Marshall B. Clinard, "The Theoretical Implications of Anomie and Deviant Behavior," in Marshall B. Clinard, Ed., *Anomie and Deviant Behavior* (New York: The Free Press, 1964), pp. 1–56.

21. Clinard, *Anomie and Deviant Behavior*, 1964, for criticisms.

22. Luis Rodriguez Manzanera, "Juvenile Delinquency in Mexico," Ph.D. dissertation, University of Rome, 1968, p. 43.

23. Jackson Toby, "Affluence and Adolescent Crime," *Task Force Report: Juvenile Delinquency and Youth Crime*, The President's Commission on Law Enforcement and Administration of Justice (Washington: U. S. Government Printing Office, 1967), p. 143.

24. Richard A. Cloward, "Illegitimate Means, Anomie, and Deviant Behavior," *American Sociological Review*, 24:164–176 (1959).

25. Richard Cloward and Lloyd Ohlin, *Delinquency and Opportunity: A Theory of Delinquent Gangs* (New York: The Free Press, 1960), p. 86.

26. Edwin H. Sutherland and Donald R. Cressey, *Criminology* (Philadelphia: Lippincott, 1970), 8th ed.

27. Irving Spergel, *Racketville, Slum Town, Haulberg: An Exploratory Study of Delinquent Cultures* (Chicago: University of Chicago Press, 1964).

28. Elmer Luchterhand and Leonard Weller, "Delinquency Theory and the Middle-Size City: A Study of Problem and Promising Youth," *The Sociological Quarterly*, 7:413–423 (1966).

29. Paul C. Friday, "Differential Opportunity and Differential Association in Sweden: A Study of Youth Crime," unpublished Ph.D. dissertation, University of Wisconsin, 1970.

30. James F. Short, Jr., and Fred L. Strodtbeck, *Group Process and Gang Delinquency* (Chicago: University of Chicago Press, 1965).

31. David M. Downes, *The Delinquent Solution: A Study in Subcultural Theory* (New York: The Free Press, 1966).

32. One theory that has been tested in a less developed culture is that of Albert K. Cohen, *Delinquent Boys: The Culture of the Gang* (New York: The Free Press, 1955). He states that gang delinquency is a consequence of hostility and protest by lower class boys to middle-class values as represented, for example, by a middle-class oriented school system. To determine the extent to which this theory explains the patterns of juvenile delinquency in an urban community in Argentina, a study was made of the degree to which features of the social order result in adjustment problems for lower class boys and delinquency in Cordoba. Data were collected on a sample of 273, based on an examination of the social class structure, values of middle and lower classes, characteristics of the family at two different social levels, and the school system. Data concerning the patterns of delinquency were drawn from juvenile court case records and interviews with offenders, judges, police, lawyers, and legislators. It was found that important elements in the social setting, which encouraged the development of the delinquent subculture in Cohen's theory, were not present in Cordoba: the schools, for example, do not provide a frustrating experience for lower class boys. For this reason it was predicted that if the Cohen theory is valid, in that the subculture is a response to problems of status frustration generated in the schools, it should be unlikely that such subcultures would be widely found in this setting; however, delinquent subcultures were found in Cordoba. See Lois B. DeFleur, "Alternative Strategies for the Development of Delinquency Theories Applicable to Other Cultures," *Social Problems*, 17:30–39 (Summer, 1969), and DeFleur, *Delinquency in Argentina: A Study of Cordoba's Youth* (Pullman: Washington State University Press, 1970).

33. Sheth, *Juvenile Delinquency in an Indian Setting*, p. 142.

34. Victor José Irurzun, "Differential Structure of Education and Opportunities as a Crime-Producing Factor" *Revista del Centro de Estudios Criminologicos,* Mendoza, Argentina, 3:27–32 (1968).

35. Louis F. Freed, *Crime in South Africa: An Integralist Approach* (Capetown: Juta, 1963), p. 212.

36. P. Ibbotsom, "Survey of Juvenile Delinquency in Southern Rhodesia," in UNESCO, *Social Implications of Industrialization and Urbanization in Africa South of the Sahara* (Switzerland: UNESCO, 1956), p. 170–172.

37. William Clifford, "Juvenile Delinquency in Zambia," a study to assess the real extent of juvenile delinquency as well as the extent to which changes in the delinquency rates may be due to economic, social, and/or psychological causes, United Nations Publication SOA/SD/CS.3, April 30, 1967.

38. In order to increase the confidence that differences between offenders and non-offenders were more valid, the level of statistical significance was set at 0.01.

39. P. C. Lloyd, *Africa in Social Change: Changing Traditional Societies in the Modern World* (Baltimore: Penguin, 1967), pp. 127–128.

40. David Parkin, *Neighbors and Nationals in an African City Ward* (London: Routledge and Kegan Paul, 1969), p. 70.

41. Lloyd, *Africa in Social Change* p. 110. See also Walter Elkan, *Migrants and Proletarians* (London: Oxford University Press, 1961).

42. Parkin, *Neighbors and Nationals in an African City,* pp. 52–60.

43. See, for example, Donald R. Taft and Ralph England, *Criminology* (New York: Macmillan, 1964), 4th ed., pp. 120–127.

44. Friday, "Differential Opportunity and Differential Association in Sweden," 1970.

45. Lloyd, *Africa in Social Change,* p. 117, and K. A. Busia, "Social Survey of Sekondi-Takoradi," in Ibbotsom, *Social Implications of Industrialization and Urbanization in Africa South of the Sahara,* pp. 74–86.

46. Marshall B. Clinard, *Sociology of Deviant Behavior* (New York: Holt, Rinehart & Winston, 1968), 3rd ed., p. 159, and David Bordua, "A Critique of Sociological Interpretations of Gang Delinquency," in Marvin E. Wolfgang, Leonard Savitz, and Norman Johnston, Eds., *The Sociology of Crime and Delinquency* (New York: Wiley 1962), pp. 289–301.

47. Irving Louis Horowitz, *Three World of Development: The Theory and Practice of International Stratification* (New York: Oxford University Press, 1966), pp. 4–5.

48. Questions such as the above could produce distorted results if respondents lacked "empathy," the ability to imagine oneself in a situation other than one's own. Respondents could conceivably desire a much better life but not make the psychological transfer to the situation demanded by the questions. They would then tend to understate their aspirations. Interviewers reported no problems of this nature, and most respondents wanted more education than they had. This would seem to imply that the item met its intent.

49. Short and Strodtbeck, *Group Process and Gang Delinquency,* 1965.

50. Friday, "Differential Opportunity and Differential Association in Sweden," 1970.

51. This finding was different from that of Rosa del Olmo and several others who conducted an extensive study of juvenile delinquents and nondelinquents in Caracas which included perceived opportunities. The students from lower class

schools expressed a strong awareness of the limited opportunities available to them. Inmates of juvenile institutions expressed less concern for limited opportunities, but many of them were reported to have low I.Q.'s. Nonetheless, the class differentials in perceived opportunities were clearly evident. Hernan Mendez Castellano, Miguel Bolivar, Rosa Del Olmo, Carmen Morales, and Beatriz Poleo, "Investigation Sobre la Teoria de Contencion en Los Trasternos de Conducta de los Adolescentes," *Relacion Criminologica*, No. 6, March–June 1971.

52. Friday, *"Differential Opportunity and Differential Association in Sweden,"* pp. 208–210.

53. Virginia Lambert, "An Investigation of the Relationship of Delinquent Self-Conception of Adjudication for Delinquency," unpublished Ph. D. dissertation, University of Wisconsin, 1969, p. 1967.

Chapter 7   Differential Association and Criminal Behavior

The theory of differential association has been widely used as a frame of reference to explain criminal behavior in the more developed parts of the world, particularly in the United States. Originally proposed more than 30 years ago by Edwin H. Sutherland, it states that criminal behavior is developed by normal social processes common to all learning [1]. Like all behavior, crime is learned from friends and associates and is often influenced by the areas in which one lives. Most criminal associations are of an intimate group nature, such as juvenile gangs, adult criminals or business organizations. Any diversified society has conflicting definitions of legal codes, some of which favor violations and others do not. Whether an individual becomes a criminal depends on the balance and nature of his contacts between these two types of definition or, more specifically, on the relative frequency, duration, priority, and intensity of his association with criminal and anticriminal patterns. More specifically, a person becomes criminal by intimate association with others who present favorable definitions of criminal behavior, and these associations are in excess of and of a quality different from his experience with noncriminal definitions. The content of this learning includes the techniques of committing the offense, specific rationalizations, and motivations. The importance of the criminal association and consequent learning depends on how early these contacts start, how frequent they are, over how long a period, and the extent to which certain favorable models, such as one's best friend, engages in criminal behavior.

Although this theory has been criticized, it appears to fit the facts of socialization and learning theory in general and has been found to agree with the framework of operant conditioning or reinforcement theory in psychology as it does with set theory as well [2]. In fact, it seems to fit the facts about the nature of criminal behavior better than any other. A number of studies have confirmed it [3]. A few have either criticized it or have claimed that it does not stand up under research [4]. Criminological theory in both the United States and Europe has increasingly emphasized social and group factors in the explanation of delinquency and crime; however, too many European criminologists still tend to consider biological and psychological factors to be much more important. Differential association found consistent support in a cross-cultural study that investigated samples of delinquents and nondelinquents from San Antonio, Texas, and Monterrey, Mexico [5]. Despite the many differences between the cultural groups, the same basic factor differentiated the delinquents from the nondelinquents in all samples.

Among the developing countries India provides a classic example of differential association in the criminal tribes which for many centuries have lived by antisocial activities [6]. Today about 198 of these tribes or ethnic groups, such as the Bawaria, Bhantu, Habura, Kanja, Karwal, and Sansiya, constitute a population of about six million, and the total losses from their crimes are great. The more accepted theory is that these groups developed long ago from native populations that were unable to resist various invaders and either found refuge in isolated areas or became nomads. They were forced into menial occupations and treated like untouchables, segregated on the outskirts of villages; today, however, they live in groups in urban areas. Over the years each tribe took up some means of thievery to supplement its earnings, partly because of various periods of political instability, and these patterns became established ways of living.

Many efforts were made under British rule to deal with them by passing various Criminal Tribe Acts which enabled local governments to declare any tribe guilty of the systematic commission of crime, to direct the registration of all tribal members, to require each member to report to the police at stated intervals, and to notify the police of changes of residence. These acts were repeated after independence (such groups are now officially known as excriminal tribes), but other measures of control and rehabilitation have often been instituted, usually without much affect.

These tribes have great cohesiveness, their own social codes, rules of allegiance, and councils. Usually they wander about in groups or gangs of 10 to 20 families under the direction of a leader; on occasion several groups may join forces. Among the duties of the leader are the recruitment of gang members from the tribe, planning the operations, making arrangements with "fences" to dispose of stolen property, using women as lures to obtain information about property, and deciding whom to sur-render when the gang is traced by the police.

Even in the commission of crimes each caste and tribe had its own rituals, omens, taboos, methodology and peculiarities. Some tribes committed only dacoi-ties, some only highway robbery, some were expert in burglary, some committed petty thefts in railway trains or at bathing ghats or in fairs, some only picked pockets, some were shop-lifters, some counterfeited coins and some were con-fidence-tricksters [7].

Children are trained in crime from generation to generation by giv-ing them lessons, for example, in various forms of stealing. They learn how to remove articles deftly from places like bathing ghats and religious gatherings and to hide money cleverly, as under their tongues. The women help in many ways by committing crimes on their own and sup-porting their men and children in their illegal activities.

COMPANIONS, GANGS, AND CRIME

Criminal associations may be formed with individual companions or in youth and adult gangs. Studies in Western and other more developed countries have found that learning crime from one's peers, particularly in the form of youth groups, is the strongest determining factor in crimi-nal involvement, especially in urban areas [8]. Youth gangs have been reported as playing an extensive part in crime in countries as far apart as the United States, England, France, Germany, Sweden, Japan, and South Africa. With the greater freedom of movement in urban areas in de-veloped countries and the growth of secondary socializing agencies, such as schools, children spend less time with their families and more with friends of the same age and interests. In Japan in 1968, for example, a study of 10,750 juveniles, which represented about one-tenth of those arrested (not including arrests for minor offenses, traffic violations, and accidents) revealed that almost half (46.8%) had broken the law with another person. The younger they were, the higher the percentage of com-panions; at the ages of 14 to 15 it was 53.8%, from 18 to 19, 41.8%. For major penal offenses the figure was 31.4%, theft, 32.2, robbery, 35.7, bodily injury, 29.0, and rape, 34.5. In adult cases the figure for major crimes with companions was 15.0%; in robbery, 23.5% [9].

Delinquent youth groups and gangs do not appear to be confined to developed countries. One survey reported that "the more important new type of juvenile delinquency found in nearly all parts of the world is the formation of juvenile gangs which commit delinquent acts" [10]. The

literature on delinquency in various parts of Africa repeatedly emphasizes the development in urban areas of groups of youths who steal or
engage in other delinquent acts. After conducting his own study in Kinshasa and surveying the work of other studies of youth crime in French-
speaking West Africa, Houchon has concluded that group life, either
with a companion or in gangs, is important in delinquency [11]. In Dakar
between 1953 and 1961 there was an increase in offenses committed in
groups, particularly by young persons with a median age of 12 years [12].
A study of delinquency in Kinshasa noted an increasing tendency toward
theft and violence, particularly in the more organized juvenile gangs [13].
In the two major cities in the Cameroon regular groups of children without jobs or other means of support normally engaged in some sort of
delinquent behavior. In Douala, the largest city, young delinquents between the ages of 10 and 20 committed their offenses with other persons
in 47% of the cases; in Abidjan, Ivory Coast, about 42% of the juvenile
offenders had companions [14]. In each case the number of associates was
generally quite small, and the younger the boy the less likely he would
work alone. A study of youth offenders in Accra, Ghana, most of whom
were migrants, showed that those "who became delinquents were exposed
and susceptible to the influence of delinquent associates. Whether mani-
fested in stealing or prostitution, delinquency is learned predominantly
from association with other delinquents" [15].

A summary report prepared for the United Nations on Asian crime
pointed out how extensively juvenile groups are involved in crime.
Juvenile gang activities were reported as being extensive in Colombo,
Ceylon [16], and a study of 382 juvenile offenders in Bangkok showed
that 238, or 62%, committed their acts in groups [17]: 37.2% with two
persons, 16.2% with three, 9.4% with 4, and 9.4% with more than four.
Only 3.9% of the juveniles belonged to gangs with which an adult was
associated. According to Nagel, this was once the traditional type of gang
in Thailand, whereas the modern gang consists only of youths. The group
factor in these offenses is shown by the fact that 229 of these youthful
offenders either had criminal friends or had committed the crime with
criminal friends. Official statistics in Thailand distinguish between robbery and gang robbery in which three or more persons participate. The
latter has increased much more rapidly than robbery or other serious
crimes. The 1959–1963 average for reported gang robberies each year was
2538, for the two years 1964–1965 it was 3344, or an increase of 31.8%.
A Malaysian report on youth crime stated:

> The youth from the slums allies himself with others in similar circumstances
> and together they as a group find the strength to reject the value system of
> society replacing it with one of their own [19].

A study of a sample of delinquents in Chile found that 92% had been arrested for theft and that 72% had committed their offenses as part of a gang [20]. In a Caracas study it was found that an average of two persons usually attack and rob a victim; sometimes there may be three or four and occasionally as many as five [21]. David also noted that delinquency in urban Venezuela is primarily performed in a group context [22].

SOCIAL PROCESS AND SOCIAL STRUCTURE IN GANG BEHAVIOR

Family, kinship, and community ties are weakening in the less developed countries, a process that is followed in an urban environment by the growth of "peer groups" such as criminal youth gangs. After studying delinquents in Dakar one researcher reported that only a small proportion of the members of delinquent youth groups were socially maladjusted [23]. Commenting on the situation in less developed countries, one United Nations report states that although peer groups may fill the social vacuum in many legitimate and constructive ways in the conditions of urban slums they often operate as gangs that "roam the streets, committing petty crimes, sometimes supporting themselves by predatory means, conducting warfare against other gangs and often serving as the tools of professional criminals" [24]. Gang behavior among juveniles in cities of some parts of Africa, for example, represents a response to the breakdown of controls and former organizational structure. Writing on the effects of urbanization on rural Bantus in South Africa, Williamson reported a breakdown in primary controls following detribalization and the introduction of cash economy, accelerated mobility, personal anonymity, and new leisure-time pursuits. "One aspect of nonconforming behavior has been gang life among the (African) juvenile offenders" [25].

Gangs and groups that have directed their activities toward crime furnish the means of training new members and of assisting those already accepted to develop their skills and to dispose of stolen property. Rationalizations or techniques of verbalization for their delinquent behavior in the face of adult disapproval and legal sanctions are largely developed in gang associations. A study by Weinberg of 67 female offenders who engaged in prostitution and theft in Accra found that:

> Techniques for deviant behavior were learned from their companions by informal tutelage. About 91 percent were directly or indirectly influenced by companions toward deviant behavior even though many committed their offenses alone and were arrested alone. Thieves learned where to seek out their victims, how to steal from a stall in the market-place and how to cope with the police.

Novices in soliciting learned how to fend off men as well as how to attract them, they learned where to congregate and how to cope with the police, the courts and the authorities. The solitary or lone offenders generally stole from their parents and guardians [26].

The effectiveness of delinquent gangs lies in the fact that by mutual excitation illegal activities are made attractive to the individual; for example, an adult Zambian offender with a long record of offenses reported that at the age of 12 he had belonged to a juvenile gang which would

go into an Indian shop and ask for change in order to see where the money was kept. They would then show some interest in the blankets which the shop sold and would ask to see one of them. When the blanket was produced they would open it over the counter so that it would cover the drawer where the money was kept. It was then only necessary to divert the man's attention to other blankets still on the shelves and whilst he was getting these they would put their hands under the blanket on the counter pretending to examine it but in fact stealing the money from the drawer [27].

The position, or social status, of gang members is measured by standards different from those of conventional adult groups. A gang member often achieves high status by displaying courage and skill in the commission of a crime, by having a long record of delinquencies, and, even better, by having been incarcerated in a correctional institution. In less developed countries status within the gang is secured almost entirely by stealing and seldom for the vandalism so common in developed countries. In David's study in Argentina, for example, he pointed out that since any young person is influenced by his peer or reference group the juvenile delinquent cannot be regarded solely as an individual. To influence him he must be removed from his reference group or an attempt must be made to sway the entire group [28]. The importance of the peer group has also been elaborated on by an Indian researcher:

Their craving for status drives them to seek "herd" approval, and to allay feelings of deficiency and inferiority they indulge in anti-social activities. The gang gives them life. . . . Gang code, gang loyalty, delinquent group behavior and hostility to authorities cannot but flourish [29].

In a study of 50 gangs in Kinshasa many were found to have individual identities. Each gang has its distinguishing symbol, some special article of apparel, a particular greeting, and a unique hair style. Younger boys learn from the older ones. Gang violence generally takes one of three directions, "against members of the same age of rival gangs; against strangers in the neighborhood, usually to steal from them; and, finally, against girls with the aim of taking advantage of them" [30]. On the other hand, a sample of juvenile offenders whom Sheth studied in Greater Bombay showed that the gangs to which the juveniles belonged were in a formative, rudimentary stage, and that gang loyalty and solidarity were short-lived [31]. Many of the gangs, however, were headed by adults who used the younger members as adjuncts to their own criminal activities. Juvenile vagrants in India frequently engage in various kinds of crime and in these acts nearly all have companions. Such affiliations range from a strong gang life to loosely affiliated groups. A study of 300 from Lucknow and Kanpur showed that 40.7% had companions, though neither regular nor fixed, 33.7% had some connection with a gang, 22.3% led an active gang life, and 3.3% were unclassified [32].

The nature of the activities indulged in by the vagrants of this group is such where a compact gang life is indispensable. For example, activities like picking one's pockets or systematic stealing, etc., which require training and experience, can successfully be carried on only in a well organized gang [33].

In Varanasi (Benares) a detailed study was made of groups of juveniles by the use of interviews, participant observation, and group interaction analysis. It was found that 60% of all groups studied were antisocial but had loose organization without definite leadership. Among the organized gangs 80% engaged in stealing [34].

One of the few studies of gang behavior in a developing country comparable to those done in the United States is Weinberg's, who found that among the 99 male delinquents he interviewed in Accra almost all (94%) were either directly influenced by delinquent associates or congregated at the meeting places of delinquents [35]. Their delinquent behavior was a group practice learned in the process of interacting with peers, a process in which they acquired the techniques and rationalizations of stealing and procuring. Some gang behavior demonstrates a great deal of solidarity, as shown in the following case:

Akuetah, a thirteen-year old delinquent, had lived with his mother until he was eight and was then sent to his father. He fought with other boys and was expelled from school, whereupon he returned to live with his mother and grandmother. He became friendly with four older boys who had also dropped out of school; they formed a gang and engaged in predatory practices almost daily. Their routine consisted mainly of stealing money for food or for the evening cinemas. When their mothers left home in the morning for petty trading, they decided upon their activities for the day. Each boy took his turn at stealing enough for the entire group. They also practiced collective stealing. One gang member would buy some article from a woman in the market place and then return to tell her that the person who had sent him was dissatisfied with the product. The woman would follow the boy to see the person and, as soon as she left her stall, the other boys would raid it and steal money and merchandise while the lead boy would flee into the crowd [36].

On the other hand, some group associations in Accra were found to be loose in structure and the thefts less organized.

Kwami stole money from his mother and, with an associate whom he met while playing soccer near his house, habitually stole from the market place. The two planned an operation in which one would ask the lady at a stall about the cost of articles while the other tried to steal money from the box. When successful, they shared the loot, although the boy who did the actual stealing received the larger share. Kwami said they also stole tin-meats and sweets, which they either consumed or sold. With the stolen money, Kwami and his companion bought clothes and attended movies [37].

From the research that has been done on delinquency in Cairo [38], it appears that the kind of group to which a juvenile attaches himself is an important contributory factor to his subsequent delinquency. This study found that the characteristics of criminal gangs differed from those of noncriminal groups. In the first place, the average size of the gang was smaller than the noncriminal and the difference between the two averages was found to be statistically significant. Second, a multiplicity of socially deviant activities such as truancy from school, homosexuality, theft, smoking, and gambling act as bonds to hold gang members together. Even if these activities do take place in the noncriminal groups, they are only occasional and incidental. Third, the two groups differed markedly in their recreational habits. The gang groups' activities were characterized by some kind of violence and danger, whereas the noncriminal groups tended to avoid them. The former frequented cafés, disreputable clubs, and the like, whereas the latter favored social clubs and recreational institutions. Gang members also appeared to have extensive relations with members of other gangs. In gang theft there is a pattern of organization of labor for collecting and disposing of specific objects, and this organization is carried out in a cultural atmosphere permeated with antisocial values. Each gang appears to have its own headquarters and an area of operation in the city, an area not to be trespassed on by members of other gangs. Smaller cliques existed within these gangs, and the loyalty to these cliques often transcended the loyalty to the gang itself. Although extensive, the relationships of the gang members appear to be neither lasting nor deep.

As part of a larger study 63 "hard-core" juvenile offenders were questioned in Cordoba, Argentina, about the nature and characteristics of their gangs [39]. These gangs were relatively small, many had no clearly established leadership, and membership was generally open to any boy who was vouched for and who was willing to engage in the groups' activities. The gangs supported strong interest in sports and fought regularly with boys from other neighborhoods. The most frequent lawbreaking was theft, and the stolen items were either used or sold, the proceeds being spent on movies, drinking, and girls.

ADULT GANGS

Although our discussion has been concentrated on juvenile and youth gangs, there are, of course, adult gangs similar to those of the developed countries. Reference has already been made to crime committed by adult groups, armed robbery in particular (see Chapter 2). Some are of a nature unique to the country. Secret societies, which murder, rob, kidnap for ransom, and engage in general extortion and intimidation, have existed in the Chinese community of Malaysia for many years. The membership, however, is no longer restricted to Chinese and now includes Malays and Indians [40]. In 1969 the police reported 226 active secret societies and gangs of adults which had a total membership of about 12,000. Most of the serious large-scale crimes are committed by this group. Members range from age 16 to 26, although some younger ones are associated with them. They present a major law-enforcement problem, and special measures devised by the authorities include forced registration, restricted residence, and banishment from the city.

Youth gangs in less developed countries work more closely with adults in committing thefts than they do in the developed countries. In certain urban areas of Latin America, for example, gangs of young and older males are more common than those composed only of minors [41]. This may be due partly to the lack of a fully developed sophisticated youth culture in the cities of the developing countries and the awareness that articles can more easily be disposed of by adults. A study of offenses in Bombay, for example, revealed that the majority of juveniles engaged in theft worked either with or for adults. This is shown in part by the articles stolen, since a large percentage of them, such as metals, railway accessories, and similar articles difficult to resell to individuals would be of use only to established dealers or receivers of stolen property (see Table 34). Some children who work under the orders of their parents or other adults transport liquor or narcotics and steal from coal yards. In Varanasi (Benares) some juvenile gangs were supported by organized adult criminals who engaged in black marketeering and "protection" rackets with shopkeepers and businessmen. In a study of 300 juvenile

Table 34   Articles Stolen by Juvenile Offenders in Greater Bombay

	Percentage of Total
Metals	34.5
Scrap-iron, iron sheets, iron moulds, fishhooks, iron balls of water-tank, brass pieces, brass taps, brass bolts and nuts, brass utensils, lead covers of gutters, metal pipes, and wires	
Cash and costly articles	20.6
Coins, rupee notes, purses, checks, jewelry, watches, fountain pens, spectacles, cameras, bicycles	
Clothes	11.0
Saris, dhotis, ready-made clothes, cloth	
Railway accessories	6.7
Hides, bulbs, iron rods, battery cells, electric fans and their parts	
Edibles	5.9
Grains, vegetables, coconuts, tea, tins of chocolate	
Miscellaneous articles	13.3
Water boilers, petromax lamps, leather bags, advertising posters, books, carpets, gunny bags, shaving brushes, spare parts for motors, electrical equipment, glass, soda water bottles, chappals, goats	
Unknown	8.0
Total	100.0

Derived from Hansa Sheth, *Juvenile Delinquency in an Indian Setting* (Bombay: Popular Book Depot, 1961), 107.

vagrants in Lucknow and Kanpur it was shown that most of the juveniles made important contributions to adult gangs.

They are more active and agile, and therefore better suited for certain types of activities, for instance, pocket picking, shoplifting and other small thefts as they can manage to escape easily without being apprehended. They get easy entrance into shops and houses as house servants. In this connection it is important to mention that the majority of sky-light thefts and "cat-burglaries" are committed by juveniles who are especially trained for the purpose and act according to the instructions of their senior.

They have easy access to places generally out of bounds for adults (especially in female sectors). Thefts and similar incidents at the time of fairs, where pilgrims are deprived of their belongings, are some of the doings of these juvenile craftsmen. They are adept in removing clothes and articles especially of females bathing in the river. "River Bank" fairs in both the cities have come to be associated with a certain amount of notoriety in regard to such activities.

Even when caught they get a mild chastisement from the public and leniency from the law; and quite often they are let off without any punishment. . . . Partnership with juveniles means more profit to the adults as at the time of the distribution of booty a juvenile partner usually gets the minimum share. They cannot escape with the booty. They can travel by rail freely and do not bother for tickets. They can enter any compartment including those reserved for women. They make themselves serviceable in many other ways as well. They are used as passive agents in homosexual practices and further exploited by senior members in a game of dice or cards [43].

DIFFERENTIAL ASSOCIATION AND CRIME IN KAMPALA

It appears that many of the property crimes in Kampala are not committed by groups of individuals but by single persons. In the Kampala study, for example, in 86.2% of all arrests only one person was involved. In another study in which 102 juvenile property offenders in Kampala were interviewed, nearly all of the respondents attributed their criminal behavior to "bad company" [44]; however, 67% reported that they committed their offenses alone, 27% reported two to three companions, and 7% acknowledged four or more associates. The 67% included 14 servants who were therefore generally alone [45]. There was no significant difference in the number of companions and the value of property stolen [46]. The groups to which offenders belonged were loosely structured, membership being casual and quite short-lived.

Assuming the accuracy of the police statistics, which might not be the case (as discussed on pages 000-000), this situation may be explained in part by the nature of the conditions under which an object is stolen and in which a companion might not be necessary. Many of the articles were used clothing or similar objects taken from a neighbor or simply because they were readily available. To commit many of these offenses required little in the way of criminally sophisticated techniques. To the extent that much of the theft in developing countries consists of small low-cost items this pattern may be generalized in all. Another reason for the failure to arrest other offenders in a group is the lack of police time and interest in petty theft. Kibuka found, moreover, that the offenders' relations were generally casual rather than permanent, thus making it difficult for the police to apprehend them [47].

The prevalence of individual theft, however, does not negate the impact of friends or gang members on the decision-making process which ultimately ended in a theft. Support for his motives and the rationalizations for his acts may have been learned from others. Although police statistics may not show this group influence, it is revealed by a detailed comparison of the role of differential association in a group of offenders and nonoffenders in Kampala.

Criminal Association with Friends

In the Kampala study a scale was constructed to measure the extent of differential association with friends who had been in trouble with the police. This scale included various friendship patterns: friends with whom the person had associated most often, known the longest, known first, known best, known at all, and knew at present. Reiss and Rhodes attempted empirically to test the theory of differential association by having respondents rate their friends on a conformity-deviance scale [48]. Since it included only present friends, the possibility of critical associations at an earlier period was not treated. Short constructed a scale to distinguish among the friendship variables of intensity, duration, priority, and frequency [49]. In replicating Short's study, Voss developed a six-item index of differential association which encompassed connections with deviant persons in both present and previous relationships [50]. This index was chosen as one of the principal measures of differential association and includes the following items:

1. Think of the friends you have been associated with *most often*. Were (or are) any of them ever in trouble with the police?
2. Think of the friends you have known for the *longest* time. Were (or are) any of them in trouble with the law at the time you first knew them?
3. Think back to the *first* friends you can remember. Were any of them in trouble with the law at the time you first knew them?
4. Have any of your *best* friends ever been in trouble with the law while they were your best friends?
5. Have *any* of your friends ever been in trouble with the law?
6. Are any of your *present* friends in trouble with the law?

Respondents were given four categories to choose from: most, several, few, none. These choices were scored 1 to 4, respectively. All items showed high intercorrelations, the sixth somewhat lower (see Table 35). The responses indicated that the subjects tended to answer "several" in all items or "none." Apparently they made little distinction between types of friendship. The question on "present" friends appears to have been threatening, and many responded "none" who had used "several" on the first five. Since intercorrelations were so high, it was decided to build a scale of differential friendships by summing the responses to the

Table 35   Correlations Among Items from Scale of Differential Friendships

	Most Often	Longest	First	Best	Any
Most often[a]					
Longest	.70				
First	.61	.70			
Best	.63	.68	.69		
Any	.69	.68	.63	.68	
Present	.47	.56	.56	.57	.54

[a] Headings refer to the nature of relations the respondent had with friends who had been in trouble with the police.

six items. The sums were reduced into a scale ranging from 1 to 6. The resulting index does not cover all the possibilities of associations that could present criminal patterns, but it did distinguish between offender and control samples at the 0.001 level.

A group of 164 offenders was compared with 206 nonoffenders, all of whom were 18 to 25 years old. A significant statistical difference between the two groups showed up on the scale for differential association with those friends who had been in trouble with the police, the offenders more often having close friends known to the authorities (see the appendix). In the urban areas of developing countries the close friends of a migrant may replace kin or family as the most important socializing factor. When friends have been in trouble with the police, they instill negative feelings about private property, the police, and the law. If a friend has also served a term in prison, he can provide even more rationalizations for criminal behavior. A number of the Ugandan offenders' descriptions of their offenses demonstrated the role of companions in many property crimes even of a less sophisticated nature.

I picked some money (twenty shillings) from a lady's handbag. She had neglected her bag and I suspected there was money, so I decided to snatch it from her. I did this because I had seen my friends do it very often. It was daytime at the bus park in Kampala.

We took this tape recorder and a pair of trousers. We would have sold them to customers. We had done such things for quite a long time. I learned it from my friends whom I met in the city.

I was trying to steal some three shirts from a shop. It was day time at around 10 o'clock, when I went to a certain shop. Formerly, we had done exactly the same thing with a friend. That time my friend was arrested, but I pleaded not quilty and was acquitted. So, I wanted to try my luck once more. I had some customers to buy the shirts I would steal. As I was marching out from the shop with the three shirts the assistant shopkeeper made an alarm and I was arrested.

Together with three friends of mine we planned to steal some bags of nuts from our employer. They packed them and since I was going out in our employer's car with the driver they asked me to take the parcel to our usual place. Unfortunately, this time I was seen by our employer as I was taking the parcel to the lorry. So I was arrested. We had done this almost daily for about a year—but we had never been arrested. We had our customers who used to buy them.

So far, in a developing country like Uganda, only a limited number of offenses compared in sophistication with that seen in developed countries. Almost all offenses of a sophisticated nature in the Kampala study, however, were committed in association with companions, often of the gang type. These offenses demonstrated the kind of planning and techniques that required more than one person to carry them out. Presumably these techniques had been developed over a period of time, perhaps having been devised by others, possibly with prison experience, and transmitted to the group. With more sophisticated group tutelage it appears that crime in places like Uganda may become more and more skillful. We can, for example, predict that the more progress made in a developing country, the more crimes will resemble the following. In the first case the offender had stolen cars and committed armed robbery as a member of a gang.

I stole a car during the daytime on _____ Road in Kampala. This car belonged to an Asian. Previously, I had given 500 shillings to the driver (chauffeur) of that car. He then gave me the key and I copied its model. So I went back and made exactly the same key. So one day when I saw that he had parked his car on _____ Road, about ten in the morning, I stole it. It was the owner who was driving, not the chauffeur. I had planned to steal the car. You know, such things take a long time to plan. We have to trace the car for quite a long time. This time was I who was to trace this car. I did it quite satisfactorily and got it. Later, along with seven people one of them my brother, we chased a car which was taking money from a bank for about twenty miles. We were well equipped with pangas (large knives like machetes). It was about 11:00 in the morning. We used a car which I had stolen. We beat this Asian and took his 1,800 shillings. This was on _____ Road. Another time, we were five people in the group, all friends. We chased and stopped an Asian's car on _____ Road. We were all equipped with pangas. It was about 11:00 in the morning. We took about 9,000 shillings from the man. We used the same car I had stolen before. We knew that the car was taking money. This takes months and months until we study or trace the movements of these people. For each case it took two months to trace the factory owners, or to know where, when, how, in what car they transferred the money. In some cases, we bribe the driver or cooperate together. This time it was all our business. We did everything ourselves. We did not use the drivers of those managers to tell us when they would be taking the money. We were discovered because of the Malayain (prostitutes) who reported us! I happened to be a friend of a young, nice looking and attractive lady. She used to spend nights with me and I always had sex with her. She was a very nice woman. But I didn't know that she was a member of the C.I.D., for she loved me very much for about two months. Then one day she took the duplicates of the keys of my car to the police. She reported me. I was finished. Then one evening as we were drinking in a bar with my friends we saw two policemen come in, and they arrested us. It was easily found out that it was the same group which had done all the crimes. But I pleaded not guilty and now I am serving a four-year sentence for theft of a motor car. I learned it from my friends. My brothers had done this for quite a number of years. I was persuaded to join them. We had a brother of ours who sells spare parts of different vehicles so we used to give him all the money we stole. He would use this money to buy spare parts. I hear he is still doing well in our business. But I am afraid he may not have enough money with which to buy more spare parts. He depended too much on our financial help. This business was paying us quite well. But when I go back it seems that I may do the same work (stealing) because all my business (garage) will be in its worst situation. So it seems it will take me years to bring it to the former standards. The best way will be to steal.

I stole a suitcase about three o'clock in the afternoon from a stranger. We have a group of people who do and plan this sort of thing. I had to do it because I was so used to doing it that I couldn't do any other job. I was doing it almost daily. I could sell the property found in these suitcases, clothes, watches, etc. We used to tell passengers all sorts of lies, that we could look after their suitcases while they went out in the latrine or tell them to look at something for awhile or staring at the traffic lights while we snatched away the handbag from their hands.

I was in charge of the company's store and was keeping the key. We conspired with a colleague who agreed to take the key to the blacksmith who could make a duplicate of our key. He got the duplicate. So one afternoon at lunch time he opened the store (with my knowledge) with the new key and stole some two bicycles, a radio, and about ten axes. Later on as we had arranged, we sold them and I got 1700 shillings. I had done the same thing previously in another company.

Criminal Record of Relatives

Relatives are also possible sources of positive definitions of criminal behavior. The Uganda respondents were asked how many of their relatives had been in trouble with the police [51]. Although no significant statistical difference between the offender and nonoffender was found in this item, 78% of the nonoffenders, in contrast to only 67% of the offenders, reported that none of their families had ever been arrested or questioned. Since only five % of the population of Uganda live in urban centers, most relatives live in a village setting which tends to preclude criminal involvement or at least arrest. For this reason relatives may not be the probable sources of criminal definitions that urban peers who have internalized deviant norms are.

Criminal Experience in Rural Areas

Studies of criminal association of the young in urban areas have generally been measured by asking questions about the criminal patterns of the respondent's friends in the city [52]. The scope of the analysis in the Uganda study was expanded beyond close friends because in some rural areas of Africa patterns of theft are said to vary from common to occasional. Tanner found, for example, that among pastoral people in East Africa a good year invites the envy of others who have less good grazing and water, which often leads to cattle raids from neighboring communities with whom there has been continuous tension [53]. Youths raised in agricultural communities in which such events have occurred may have been influenced by favorable definitions of theft and may thus be more receptive to criminal suggestion when they come to the city.

Moreover, as Sutherland suggests, the earlier the experience with illegal behavior patterns, the more important that encounter is in determining subsequent illegal behavior. "Priority is assumed to be important in the sense that unlawful behavior developed in early childhood may persist throughout life" [54]. In the Uganda study it was thought that village experiences might be important determinants of subsequent urban behavior, since a large percentage of migrants move to Kampala around their eighteenth birthdays. Such experience of theft carried to the city by the young may affect the way in which they respond to urban situations such as the suggestion that they engage in theft. For this reason the respondents were asked whether the men in their village stole from other villages or strangers. No significant statistical differences were found between offenders and nonoffenders. However, 60% of the offenders, and 70% of the nonoffenders, claimed that at least some of the men did steal from other villages or strangers. These responses imply that theft may be more common in rural areas than is generally acknowledged. The number of persons involved may be proportionately lower than in the urban sector, but most villages appear to have had some experience with theft. The lack of significant difference between samples suggests that this pattern may be evenly distributed throughout many rural areas.

Differential Attitudes Toward Deviance

In the Uganda study a series of questions on attitudes toward types of "deviant" activity also attempted to determine whether the offenders' value judgments differed from those of the nonoffenders. It was expected that offenders would view these acts more positively than the non-offenders, even though both groups came from similar migrant situations. The items presented to the respondents included attitudes toward theft under various conditions, fighting, smoking marijuana (bhang), getting drunk, wife beating, prostitution, illegal beer brewing, and bribery. The responses to the questions were factor-analyzed, and three distinct patterns resulted, in two of which there were significant differences between the two groups. In the first offenders were more likely to view with favor stealing from the rich and stealing to feed one's family. This was a different finding from the study of two Kampala slum communities in which there was no significant statistical difference between the high and low crime communities for either age group in the degree to which they were opposed to theft in all forms [55]. It is impossible to determine whether the offenders had these attitudes toward theft before they broke the law, but the attitudes at least demonstrated the rationalizations that are used to justify property crime. One offender stated: "If one steals from Europeans or Asians, it is very good and they (family and friends) appreciate it. But very bad from your own people."

Similarly, offenders were more likely to approve of a man's getting drunk every time he visits a bar and a woman deciding to become a prostitute in order to buy better clothing. Attitudes toward illegal beer brewing and a policeman's acceptance of a bribe not to close an illegal brewing place showed no differences. Since brewing beer in villages is an integral part of the African tradition, it is understandable that little difference would occur on this factor. Many regard attempts to make the brewing of beer illegal in urban areas as an unwanted interference of government under urban conditions. The only item in this group that the majority of respondents in both groups considered "not wrong" was beating one's wife. Traditionally, African culture views a male as the absolute head of the household.

Differential Urban Activities

The Uganda research tested a series of items as a measurement of certain activities, based on a similar set used by Short and Strodtbeck [56]. The offender and nonoffender respondents were asked how often they and their friends engaged in a series of activities which, when factor-analyzed, resulted in two clusters. The first included fighting and gambling, the second dancing, "sitting around," and getting drunk. There was no significant statistical difference in fighting and gambling but there was for the second group of activities. Although dancing and drinking are normal activities, their greater frequency among offenders could imply that offenders have a life style somewhat different from that of nonoffenders. Frequent attendance at certain bars would probably increase the chances of exposure to criminal contacts. Moreover, the regular pursuit of these activities could indicate a somewhat different kind of participation in the urban environment.

SOME CONCLUSIONS

A major principle formulated by students of criminal behavior is that it is learned by processes of differential association. As in developed countries, there is ample evidence that the major social groups that transmit and perpetuate criminal norms in developing countries are youth and adult gangs. Although group activities have been found to vary by degree of organization, size, and nature of behavior, delinquent groups retain a strong level of influence over criminal behavior in developing countries. The dynamic and supportive function it fills makes this influence a particularly powerful instrument of control over the activities of individual members; young gang behavior offers some support for the destructive effect of urbanization on kin and family structures.

In the Kampala study the offenders' close friends had been in trouble with the police to a greater extent than had the friends of non-offenders. Studies in developed countries have also indicated that the recreational patterns of criminal offenders differ substantially from those of noncriminal groups, a finding suggested by the Kampala study. The typical offender reveals that although he has not broken his ties with his village completely he has adopted strong urban preferences and behavior patterns. He is neither fully urban nor traditional but rather appears to be a marginal man cut off from supportive kinship ties. As we pointed out in our discussion of migration, the offender tended to have had fewer urban experiences; he had been alone on arrival, had fewer contacts with relatives or tribal friends in the city, and thus tended to have fewer contacts with persons who might be expected to reinforce noncriminal backgrounds and more with places in which criminals might congregate. He is more likely to be isolated from urban groups that might possibly enable him to reject criminal behavior, and he is more likely to have friends who have been in trouble with the police.

NOTES AND REFERENCES

1. Edwin H. Sutherland and Donald Cressey, *Criminology* (Philadelphia: Lippincott, 1970), 8th ed. pp. 77–100.

2. Robert L. Burgess and Ronald L. Akers, "A Differential Association-Reinforcement Theory of Criminal Behavior," *Social Problems*, 14:128–147 (1966); Melvin L. DeFleur and Richard Quinney, "A Reformulation of Sutherland's Differential Association Theory and a Strategy for Empirical Verification," *Journal of Research in Crime and Delinquency*, 3:1–22 (1966); and Donald R. Cressey, "The Language of Set Theory and Differential Association," *Journal of Research in Crime and Delinquency*, 3:1–22 (1966); and Donald R. Cressey, "The Language of Set Theory and Differential Association," *Journal of Research in Crime and Delinquency*, 3:22–27 (1966).

3. Albert J. Reiss, Jr., and A. Lewis Rhodes, "An Empirical Test of Differential Association Theory," *Journal of Research in Crime and Delinquency*, 1:5–18 (1964); Daniel Glaser, "Differential Association and Criminological Prediction," *Social Problems*, 8:6–14 (1960); Henry D. McKay, "Differential Association and Crime Prevention: Problems of Utilization," *Social Problems*, 8:25–37 (1960); Harwin L. Voss, "Differential Association and Reported Delinquent Behavior: A Replication," *Social Problems*, 12:78–85 (1964); and C. R. Jeffery, "Criminal Behavior and Learning Theory," *Journal of Criminal Law, Criminology, and Police Science*, 56:294–300 (1965). See also Edwin H. Sutherland, *The Professional Thief* (Chicago: University of Chicago Press, 1937), Menachem Amir, *Patterns of Forcible Rape* (Chicago: University of Chicago Press, 1971), and Marvin E. Wolfgang and Franco Ferracuti, *The Subculture of Violence* (London: Social Science Paperbacks, Tavistock, 1967).

4. Sutherland and Cressey, *Criminology*, 1970, contains a discussion of the criticisms of the theory.

5. C. M. Rosenquist and E. I. Megaree, *Delinquency in Three Cultures* (Austin: University of Texas Press, 1969).

6. D. N. Majumdar, *Races and Cultures of India* (Bombay: Asia Publishing House, 1958), pp. 362–375; Clarence H. Patrick, "The Criminal Tribes of India with Special Emphasis on the Mang Garudi: A Preliminary Report," *Man in India*, 48:244–257 (July–September 1968); C. B. Mamoria, *Social Problems and Social Disorganization in India* (Allahabad: Kitab Mahal, 1960), pp. 228–237; S. V. Rao, *Facets of Crime in India* (Bombay: Allied, 1967), pp. 45–53; and J. J. Panakal and S. D. Punekar, "Challenge to Society: A Study of the De-Notified Communities" (in preparation).

7. Mamoria, *Social Problems and Social Disorganization in India*, p. 229.

8. Sutherland and Cressey, *Criminology*, pp. 71–92; Clifford Shaw and Henry McKay, *Juvenile Delinquency in Urban Areas* (Chicago: University of Chicago Press, 1970), rev. ed.; James F. Short, Jr., and Fred L. Strodtbeck, *Group Process and Gang Delinquency* (Chicago: University of Chicago Press, 1965); Malcolm W. Klein, Ed., *Juvenile Gangs in Context: Theory, Research, and Action* (Englewood Cliffs, N. J.: Prentice-Hall, 1967). See also *New Forms of Juvenile Delinquency: Their Origin, Prevention and Treatment*, general report by Wolf Middendorff, Judge, Federal Republic of Germany, Second United Nations Congress on the Prevention of Crime and the Treatment of Offenders, London, August 8–20, 1960 (New York: United Nations Department of Economic and Social Affairs, 1960), p. 43. Fyvel has

examined gang delinquency in a number of countries. See T. R. Fyvel, *Trouble-makers: Rebellious Youth in an Affluent Society* (New York: Schocken, 1962). See also a study of French gangs in Philippe Parrot and Monique Gueneau, *Les Gangs d'Adolescents* (Paris: Presses Universitaires de France, 1959), and Edmund W. Vaz, "Juvenile Delinquency in Paris," *Social Problems*, 10:23–31 (1962). Studies have been made as well of adolescent delinquents in Sweden; for example, by Dick Blomberg, *Den Svenska Ungdomsbrottslighten* (Stockholm: Falu Nya Boktryckeri AB, 1960).

9. Ministry of Justice, *The Trends of Juvenile Delinquency and Procedures for Handling Delinquents in Japan*, 1970, p. 20.

10. Middendorff, *New Forms of Juvenile Delinquency*, p. 43.

11. Guy Houchon, "Les Mécanismes Criminogènes dans Une Société Urbaine Africaine," *Revue Internationale de Criminologie et de Police Technique*, 21:271–277 (1967).

12. Evelyn Pierre, J. P. Flamand, and H. Collomb, "La Délinquance Juvénile à Dakar," *International Review of Criminal Policy*, 20:27–35 (December 1962).

13. Paul Raymaekers, "Pre-Delinquency and Delinquency in Leopoldville (Kinshasa)," *International Review of Criminal Policy*, 20:53–58 (1962).

14. Middendorff, *New Forms of Juvenile Delinquency*, p. 20.

15. S. Kirson Weinberg, "Juvenile Delinquency in Ghana: A Comparative Analysis of Delinquents and Non-Delinquents," *Journal of Criminal Law, Criminology and Police Science*, 55:480 (December 1964).

16. J. J. Panakal, in *Prevention of Types of Criminality Resulting from Social Changes and Accompanying Economic Development in Less Developed Countries*, United Nations Department of Economic and Social Affairs, 1960, p. 30.

17. W. H. Nagel, "Juvenile Delinquency in Thailand," United Nations Report, 1967, pp. 120–121.

18. *Ibid.*

19. Ibrahim bin Haji Mohamed, "The Need for a Central Agency for Better Coordination among Agencies and to Promote Policies for the Prevention of Crime and the Treatment of Offenders with Reference to Malaysia"; paper presented at the United Nations Congress at Kyoto, Japan, August 1970, p. 2.

20. E. Brucher Encina, "Enfance et Jeunesse Antisociales en Chile," *Hygiène Mentale*, 53:216–220 (1964).

21. Elio Gomez Grillo, *Delinquencia en Caracas* (Maracaibo: Editorial Universataria de La Universidad del Zulia, 1971).

22. Pedro David, *Sociología Criminal Juvenil* (Buenos Aires: Ediciones Depalma, 1968), pp. 131–132.

23. Pierre, Flamand, and Collomb, "La Délinquance Juvénile à Dakar," 1962.

24. United Nations, *Report on the World Social Situation* (New York: United Nations Sales No. 1957, IV. 3), pp. 141–142.

25. R. Williamson, "Crime in South Africa: Some Aspects of Causes and Treatment," *Journal of Criminal Law, Criminology, and Police Science*, 48:187–188 (July–August 1957). See also P. C. W. Gutkind, "Congestion and Overcrowding: An African Problem," *Human Organization*, 19:129–134 (Fall, 1960).

26. S. Kirson Weinberg, "Female Delinquency in Ghana, West Africa: A Comparative Analysis," *International Journal of the Sociology of the Family* (March, 1973).

27. William Clifford, *Profiles in Crime* (Lusaka: Ministry of Housing and Social Development, Social Welfare Research Monograph No. 3, 1964), p. 31.

28. David, *Sociología Criminal Juvenil*, p. 95–97.

29. B. K. Bhattacharya, *Juvenile Delinquency and Borstels* (Calcutta: Shankar 1962), p. 4.

30. Paul Raymaekers, "Prédélinquence et Délinquance Juvénile à Leopoldville," *International Review of Criminal Policy*, 20:52 (December 1962).

31. Hansa Sheth, *Juvenile Delinquency in an Indian Setting* (Bombay: Popular Book Depot, 1961), p. 230.

32. Shankar Sahai Srivastava, *Juvenile Vagrancy: A Socio-Ecological Study of Juvenile Vagrants in the Cities of Kanpur and Lucknow* (New York: Asia Publishing House, 1963), pp. 121–122.

33. *Ibid.*, p. 123.

34. Inder Jeet Singh, "Juvenile Subculture in Varanasi," *Social Welfare*, 16:4–5, 28 (1969).

35. S. Kirson Weinberg, "Urbanization and Male Delinquency in Ghana," in Paul Meadows and Ephraim H. Mizruchi, Eds., *Urbanism, Urbanization, and Change: Comparative Perspectives* (Reading, Mass.: Addison-Wesley, 1969), pp. 368–379.

36. *Ibid.*, p. 372.

37. *Ibid.*, pp. 376–377.

38. United Nations Bureau of Social Affairs, "Juvenile Delinquency in the United Arab Republic," mimeo, SOA/SD/CS.1, 1966, p. 28. This study was conducted by the National Center for Social and Criminological Research, Cairo.

39. Lois B. DeFleur, "Alternative Strategies for the Development of Delinquency Theories Applicable to Other Cultures," *Social Problems*, 17:30–39 (1969).

40. Abdul Hamid bin Muhamad, "The Prevention of Crime and Treatment of Offenders in Malaysia," Government of Malaysia Report to the Fourth United Nations Congress on the Prevention of Crime and Treatment of Offenders, Japan (Kyoto), 1970, p. 5.

41. David, *Sociologia Criminal Juvenil*, p. 132.

42. Singh, "Juvenile Subculture in Varanasi," 1969.

43. Srivastava, *Juvenile Vagrancy*, pp. 125–126.

44. Eric Paul Kibuka, "Sociological Aspects of Juvenile Delinquency in Kampala from 1962 to 1969," Ph. D. dissertation, University of East Africa, 1972, p. 373.

45. *Ibid.*, pp. 342–343.

46. *Ibid.*, p. 326.

47. *Ibid.*

48. Reiss and Rhodes, "An Empirical Test of Differential Association Theory," 1964.

49. James F. Short, "Differential Association and Delinquency," *Social Problems*, 4:233–239 (Winter, 1957).

50. Voss, "Differential Association and Reported Delinquent Behavior: A Replication," 1957. Items were also derived from Paul C. Friday, "Differential Opportunity and Differential Association in Sweden: A Study of Youth Crime," unpublished Ph. D. dissertation, University of Wisconsin, 1970, Chapter 8.

51. "Trouble with the police" does not necessarily mean theft or personal crime. It could cover offenses against poll taxes, bicycle registration, or other ordinances.

The question, unfortunately, did not distinguish between types of crime so that probably a much higher proportion of relatives, perhaps 90% or more, were not involved in a major offense.

52. Short, "Differential Association and Delinquency," 1957; Voss, "Differential Association and Reported Delinquent Behavior," 1957; Friday, "Differential Opportunity and Differential Association in Sweden," 1970.

53. R. E. S. Tanner, *Three Studies in East African Criminology* (Uppsala: The Scandinavian Institute of African Studies, 1970), p. 54.

54. Sutherland and Cressey, *Criminology*, p. 75.

55. See Chapter 7, page 000.

56. Short and Strodtbeck, *Group Process and Gang Delinquency*, p. 83.

Chapter 8   The Police and Prisons
in the Developing Countries

The police and the prisons have similar functions in both developed and developing countries, but the role of the police and the conditions of the prisons differ markedly. Since the scientific literature on these issues is limited, considerable reliance must be placed on materials from scattered studies in a few countries. Whether these observations would be equally applicable to most developing countries is a matter of conjecture; it is our opinion, however, that they would probably have considerable significance.

THE ROLE OF THE POLICE IN DEVELOPING COUNTRIES

During the last 10 years an ever increasing amount of literature on the role of the police has been produced by sociologists and political scientists in developed countries, particularly in the United States and Great Britain [1]. Research has been conducted on a wide variety of subjects: the often ambiguous roles that police play in enforcing laws while, at the same time, attempting to safeguard the individual, their wide discretionary powers in making arrests and the way in which they exercise this power, the informal practices they use to uncover crime and the extent to which they threaten the rights of the offender, their relations with the public, public attitudes toward them according to different economic and ethnic groups, the role of the police in maintaining certain economic and political groups in power, and their relations with other agencies of criminal justice administration.

    With one or two exceptions, comparable studies are unavailable for developing countries. Although numerous historical accounts have been written about police forces in various countries and many books, manuals, and similar materials describe their formal organizational structures and duties, the study that is most like those on developed countries is Bayley's on the police in India [2]. It is the work on which we must rely heavily for much of this discussion. Although it deals only with India, it probably can be reasonably assumed that many of the issues and problems are quite similar to those of other developing countries and that it is particularly applicable to those countries that have only recently become independent of colonial rule.

Colonial powers generally left an efficient police force, so essential to maintaining control of vast land areas with a limited force of administrators. The Indian police force today appears to be particularly well led and reasonably efficient, even though now accountable to elected officials. The total Indian police force of 500,000 represents a greater ratio of police to population than those in other more developed countries: India has one policeman for 848 persons, Great Britain, 565, the United States, 526. In terms of area India has one policeman per two square miles, the United States one per 15.2, and Great Britain one per 0.81. If we eliminate the armed police reserve, the Indian police ratio to population is smaller than those of the other two countries. Using rates of clearance of crimes by arrests as a measure of effectiveness, Indian police are appreciably better than they are in the United States or Great Britain.

The Legacy of Colonial Rule

At present police do not contribute adequately to the national development of countries previously under colonial rule, largely because they have been greatly affected, and to some extent handicapped, by the ideologies and police practices of the colonial administrations. Their job had been to protect the property, person, and future prospects of the Europeans and those local groups who were dependent on them for power and livelihood. Police action in those parts of Africa and India that were formerly British currently reflect an illogical mixture of the effects of British colonial practices. In the Police Act of 1861, for example, the British introduced into India a civil police with a philosophy derived from the pioneer efforts of Sir Robert Peel and others in England. Although this approach emphasized the British liberal tradition of subordination to the rule of law and popular accountability, the exigencies of colonial rule required a much more passive relation between the police and the public in India than it did in Great Britain. With constantly rising independence movements and increased group frictions the police had to make ever greater efforts to contain the population by a strict law-and-order approach and ever more repressive measures. The situation has not materially changed even now, according to Bayley's account.

One can understand that the British might not have felt much urgency about reforming the Indian police during the last hundred years of their rule, especially during the twentieth century when they were preoccupied with containment of political self-assertion. But the philosophy of containment and passivity, quite proper as far as it goes, has endured after independence. Despite the fact that the unhappy relations between police and public have been documented again and again, reform has been approached through patchwork expedients. Pay has been raised, new officers established, fringe benefits improved, supervision reorganized, and new regulations unveiled. The effect has been predictable. In the words of one recent police commission, the situation "appears to have remained more or less the same since independence" [3].

Independence did bring revolutionary changes in the political system of developing countries, but it generally had little effect on the structure and philosophy of police administration. The police are still generally used as a paramilitary force to deal with internal problems. As an example, the British colonial authorities separated the police into two parts, the regular police with duties similar to those at home and an armed police reserve ready to crush riots related to independence and other divisionary movements by extreme force. Today in India the armed police reserves number two-fifths of the 500,000 Indian police. In many African countries the police forces are larger than the military and far more influential. In Ghana in 1964 the police force numbered 21,000 and the military, 8000; Liberia had an army of 3500 and a security force of 20,000; Nigeria before its civil war had 23,000 police and only 8300 troops; Upper Volta and Niger each had thousand-man armies and 50% larger police establishments; Chad had an army of 400 and a police force of 1950; and Gabon had 600 and 900, respectively [4]. Bayley has suggested that the Indian police reduce the armed police and develop more trained officers capable of assuming initiative in day-to-day affairs.

The police constable must cease to be a spear-carrier in the background of the police drama; he must become a major actor standing in center stage. Development of a more efficient, responsible constable probably would involve lesser expenditures on the armed police. This would happen for two reasons. Savings might thereby be realized that could be applied to the recruitment and training of new constables. Also emphasis in administration, both police and civil, would be encouraged to shift from containment to prevention. The fact that the armed police exist in such overwhelming numbers inhibits the more creative utilization of the armed constabulary [5].

Similarly, a study of the Nigerian police, made in 1966, began by stating that a carry-over from colonial rule "the relationship between the police and the public in this country cannot be said to be cordial" [6]. Newspapers contained many articles about the arbitrary exercise of police power and other irregular behavior. The changes in behavior which tended to widen the gap between the Nigerian public and the police were

(1) the exaggeration by the police of evidence in court, (2) the use of unnecessary violence, (3) fatuousness in dealing with public demonstrations, (4) ineptitude in handling the public on occasions of public demonstrations, (5) incivility to members of the public, and (6) unnecessary delay in attending to complaints [7].

A later study showed that the Nigerian public was particularly disturbed by the lack of courtesy shown by the police in discharging such duties as traffic control, making arrests, and taking statements.

New and Increased Police Duties

In most developing countries the police have moved far from the original "law-and-order" functions associated with crime control and now have contacts with citizens in various new roles. Because of technological changes and government policy, they have many new regulatory functions. Because of their centralized organization in most African countries and the availability of their manpower the police are often assigned tasks that in the United States and Western Europe would be handled by specialized agencies and portions of the bureaucracy. Licensing of commercial enterprises, supervision of trade, management of prisons, protection of the currency, enforcement of exchange controls as well as immigration and passport inspection, border patrol, and refugee settlement are often handled directly by the police force. In Tanzania, for example, police are expected to aid in village development. In the Ivory Coast the Surété Nationale is responsible for migrant labor. In the Sudan there is a special division of railroad police [8].

In India the police must deal with prohibition laws, the hoarding of foods and grains, land redistribution, the purity of gold ornaments, and even payment of dowries. Although traffic and registration enforcement have not reached the level of Great Britain, the British public's main contact with police, this problem is growing in all developing countries. In Delhi, from 1950 to 1962, registered auto vehicles increased from 108,000 to 170,000, and there were 160,000 registered bicycles, although the police estimated the number of unregistered bicycles at 240,000. To enforce bicycle registration, as well as safety regulations, police must organize frequent check points; in one evening 4000 bicyclists in Delhi were stopped and their tires deflated because of faulty equipment. As these newer contacts with the police increase, so also will hostility toward them.

The police forces in many developing countries have not been materially increased in relation to population since their independence. The proportions of police to population in some of the African countries during the late 1960's were as follows: Nigeria one policeman to 2500 persons, the Ivory Coast 1 to 2000, Mali 1 to 3330, Upper Volta 1 to 3800, Algeria 1 to 1200, Sierra Leone 1 to 1500, and Liberia 1 to 2000. If Africa on the whole is only approximately 10% urbanized and if, for analytical purposes the same ratio of one policeman for every 400 to 500 persons in the developed countries is accepted, serious difficulties can be predicted for many of the African countries as urbanization increases [9].

Yet, as their cities have grown in size and affluence, the police have had to assume many duties other than those associated with crime control; for example, traffic control and checking registrations. Furthermore, because of new responsibilities associated with independence, the police spend much time acting as guards for important foreign dignitaries and in traveling to various parts of the country with a far greater number of public officials. Referring to the extra duties imposed on the police of Delhi, one newspaper stated:

V.I.P. visits and national days like Independence Day and Republic Day take away thousands of policemen from their normal work and if these events coincide with a session of Parliament and one or two major demonstrations or a fire, then a number of police stations are left with only a handful of men each [10].

Except for heads of state, much of this protection represents only ostentation, and is not really needed. One writer stated that in Seoul, Korea, the inadequacy of protective services in the city becomes readily apparent when it is considered that the police force has other duties aside from crime detection and control.

With their outmoded equipment, limited transport capabilities and general lack of training and support, it is a wonder that the police forces in Seoul and other cities in Korea are doing as good a job as they are performing at present [11].

Public Attitudes Toward the Police

The need for a changed role for the police is reflected in the findings of an Indian public opinion survey based on 3600 interviews of the public in urban and suburban areas by the Indian Institute of Public Opinion, which showed that the average citizen regarded the police as "unsympathetic, unfriendly, and untrustworthy" [12]. In general the survey revealed special distrust of the police with respect to their impartiality and honesty. A large number of those interviewed said that they expected the police to be authoritarian, rude, inconsiderate, corrupt, prone to use unnecessary and frequently even brutal force, sometimes in collusion with criminal offenders, and often uneven in their dealings with the public. The Indian policeman is not regarded as a friend of the public and this lack of trust is not likely to encourage contacts with them. Although these opinions were frequently associated with personal or near-personal experiences rather than derived from commonly held stereotypes, the survey did reveal that respondents were likely to believe almost any negative comments about the police. The situation is somewhat circular: because public cooperation is given grudgingly and unenthusiastically, the police invariably tend to approach the public as a hostile group. Similar attitudes are expressed toward them in many other developing countries, and certainly they have been found in studies in the United States. Bayley feels that suspicion of the police may be worldwide [13]. In Nigeria, for example, police cooperation with the public is difficult because people are still afraid of them, believing that questioning by a police officer is the first step toward arrest [14]. A later study indicated much the same attitude of public distrust, misunderstanding, and fear [15].

A Ugandan informant commented on the difference between the actions of village elders and the police:

The police are less trusted in Africa. They are quite unlike the village elders where everything is asked gently and in a friendly manner. There is no slapping or any form of rudeness.

After interviewing 102 juvenile property offenders in Kampala Kibuka concluded that the law-enforcement authorities, especially the police, commanded low respect among offenders and their families.

The offender saw the police as representing an oppressive, corrupt, and inhuman aspect of society. They particularly singled out the police cruelty towards suspects and police intimidation to coerce the suspect to make confessions [16].

Surveys in India showed that in general people expressed a willingness to seek out the police when they encounter a situation that is unusual, criminal, or indicative of danger. Two-thirds of the respondents, however, thought that their neighbors hesitated to go to the police even when they needed help. "The Indian public is substantially unwilling to volunteer assistance, in the form of information to the police. They would rather not become involved" [17]. People in developing countries hesitate to become involved with the police primarily because of personal inconvenience, such as delays in making out reports or the possibility of being required to appear in court. When a man has a hard time earning a meager living and might have to travel a long distance to make a court appearance, he does not want to face these additional hardships. Nevertheless, the police in less developed countries devote a large part of their time to the public interest, and it is the public that can influence the success or failure of police work. In India the police continually complain of the lack of public cooperation, even admitting that because the public is uncooperative they must resort to other means of obtaining convictions, "expedients which may be improper or bordering on impropriety and which, when found out, like another turn of the screw, invite misunderstanding by magistracy and public" [18]. Although they may not be entirely to blame for this predicament, they are certainly the most accessible point at which initiative may be taken in transforming police-public relations.

In spite of a more favorable ratio of police to population, suspicion of Indian police methods is so ingrained in the public that it refuses to cooperate as long as the courts continue to go to endless lengths to obtain evidence of impropriety. "The result is a feeling of victimization on the part of the police" [19]. Many Indians are convinced of police brutality, the proportion varying from 7 to 37% in the sample. The percentage of persons who had actually seen these beatings varied from 43% in a Kanpur urban sample and 22% in Bangalore to 13% in Mysore. Press accounts often refer to brutal methods against suspects in accounts of officer dismissals. Although Bayley concludes that there is brutality, he says it is not so common as it was during British rule and that this problem also exists in the United States.

The Indian study showed that police contacts were much greater on all strata of the urban population, since city living itself provides more opportunities for purposeful face-to-face relations [20]. Approximately 3 in 10 male adults in the larger cities have had personal experience with the police, whereas the ratio is only 1 in 10 in the rural areas. Moreover, urban people were three times as likely to have witnessed improper police action. Urban populations judge police more harshly because of the higher rate of police contacts and also because the general climate in the cities is more favorable to the expression of opinion. Contrary to findings in the United States, attitudes toward the police did not vary significantly by social class.

Investigation of the relations between the people and the police turned up somewhat unexpected results in the Uganda study. The 528 men in the Kampala sample were asked whether people in their neighborhoods liked or disliked the police. It was hoped that fear of possible recrimination would be reduced by the use of a more indirect question in which the respondent would not have to give his own opinion. Among the 528 persons interviewed 50% responded "liked," 35% chose "uncertain," and only 14% selected "dislike" as the category that best reflected community feelings. When asked for the reasoning behind their statements, the majority noted the protective function of the police. Although the people are dubious about the crime-detecting skills of law enforcement officers, they recognize their role as the formal barrier between themselves and the numerous forms of personal violence that threaten their lives.

Social Isolation from the Public

The police in developing countries are generally more socially isolated from the public than the police in the United States and particularly in Great Britain. Fewer than half the people interviewed in India, even in the rural areas, recognized or knew the name of any particular policeman [21]. This isolation is related to their behavior on duty and also to the custom, quite common in many developing countries which have been under colonial rule, for police officers and their families to live in special houses and barracks in the manner of military personnel. All officers and about half the regular staff of the Indian police force live in government housing, isolated from civilians. All armed police live in barracks, a practice highly approved by police officials. It is felt that these men are thus somewhat removed from the temptation of leniency or corruption and that it builds an *esprit de corps* that can help to overcome the effects of former alliances. A Nigerian police study found that this concentration of police officers in barracks puts them in a class apart and reduces social contacts with the general public [22].

In India, as well as in most developing countries, the police tend to emphasize the apprehension of offenders rather than the prevention of crimes or accidents. These officers know that the public could contribute materially to crime prevention by taking sensible precautions, but the police do little to help the public in these matters in the way of advice or any demonstration of concern. As a result, the public has little opportunity to see any display of active sympathy by the police [23]. If the police in developing countries are to prevent crime, they must keep open the various avenues of communication with those citizens who are most hostile to them or who criticize them the most but who could also be the most effective in combating criminal activities in their own areas [24].

Organizational Problems

In the less developed countries it is important to know more about who is being recruited, what effect membership on the force has on the lower ranks, what relations actually exist between the lower and upper ranks, and how police decisions are made. Little is currently known about these organizational problems, as Bayley views the situation in India. Some police forces consist primarily, for example, of persons from certain tribes, ethnic groups, or areas.

In the Sudan, the northern Nubas have traditionally found police service attractive and have formed the basis of many units. In Kenya, partially because of historical events as well as government planning, neither of the two major tribes, the Kikuyu and Luo, dominate the army or the police. The police is heavily Kamba while the army is primarily Kamba and Kalenjin [25].

Bayley states that little is known about the Indian organizational police structure in terms of who joins the force as constables, what families, castes, and regions they come from, or what their aspirations are. His study in Delhi state demonstrated a tremendous gap between supervisors and line personnel in terms of "democratic job perspectives." Although police staffs demonstrated the greatest awareness of democratic norms, police constables showed the least. Among the five agencies studied the greatest gap between supervisors and line personnel was found in the police, which was perhaps a tribute to the excellence of the officer corps as much as a criticism of the constables. Socialization to nation-building and development-supporting attitudes may be occurring in the lower ranks, but it

may not be immediately apparent to the educated, city-bred officers, policymakers, or scholars who are cut off from the constables by styles of life, language, worldly experience, and position. On the other hand, it may not be occurring at all. At lower levels the police organization may have been captured by the men it recruits; the organization exhibits their proclivities rather than successfully engendering new patterns of thought and action [26].

A 1970 Rand study of various city police departments in the Philippines concluded that the police operate with their own criteria, the crime rate having little impact either on their organization or their behavior, that the police performance, as measured by the arrest rate, does not decrease the crime rate, and that, finally, the arrest rate does not depend on such factors as training, education, or the higher pay of personnel [27].

A good example of an African police force is the Ugandan, whose organization and administration is typical of a country that for some time was under British colonial rule. The Ugandan police force is organized as a nationally unified vertical body whose centralized force is directed, coordinated, and controlled from the top but whose divisional administrative units, or central coordinating offices, are divided into regional, district, station, substation, and police-post levels [28]. At the top of this hierarchical structure the inspector general of police is the overall commander of the force. Immediately below him is the deputy inspector general, beneath whom are the five senior assistant commissioners, four of whom are in charge in the four main departments of the force. These four divisions are the uniformed or general-duties branch, whose duties are to prevent the commission of crime and make arrests, the criminal investigation department (C.I.D.), which is responsible for detecting crime, making investigations, and doing forensic laboratory work, the special or armed force which deals with riots and the special branch which handles subversive matters. The inspector general of police, and his top senior officers and their specialized supporting staffs constitute the Ugandan police force.

The district commanders are responsible to the regional commanders for the direction and control of the police in the administrative districts, of which there are 18. Each district police commander is assisted by senior officers from each department of the force at that level of operation, and this pattern is repeated at the station, substation, and outpost levels. Police stations and substations do not necessarily follow the administrative division of the country or districts: rather they are opened in areas the inspector general of police thinks necessary after duly considering all factors relating to the maintenance of law and order and the protection of life and property. The Ugandan police force employs a small but growing number of women police officers, slightly fewer than 100 in 1970. They are fully integrated into the service and work mainly in the cities and primarily with juveniles.

Uganda has a comparatively small police force even for an East African country. The total manpower in 1968 was 6234, including the signal and traffic branches, when the population was about nine million. This represented one officer for every 1300 to 1400 persons, one of the lowest rates in the world, whereas Kenya, Uganda's neighbor, reported a ratio of one to 700 inhabitants. The world average at this time was one to 500 [29]. The difference between Uganda and Kenya may be the result of their colonial experiences. Relying more heavily on traditional social control measures and having fewer Europeans and foreign investments to protect, the Ugandan police force received less attention than its Kenyan counterpart. The Ugandan police force did increase from 5057 to 6234 between 1964 and 1968, a 23.3% growth, but since this was thought to be inadequate it was suggested in the Second Five-Year Plan, in 1966, that the police force be increased by 3000 to a total of 10,000. Even with this increase Uganda would still have only one policeman for 880 persons, and if the projected needs are raised 10% annually it would mean an additional 7000 ordinary policemen by 1973 [30]. This increase will be difficult to achieve not only because of the big item of salaries but the additional equipment and special housing that would be required. With reference to the need for more police, Uganda's Second Five-Year Plan for 1966–1971 reported that

not only is the police small in relation to the population—and three years ago it was smaller still—but it has to cope with an increasing volume and sophistication of crime. . . . Unfortunately, more complex, more urbanized and more wealthy societies breed more crime, not less. The accelerated rise in incomes and wealth which the Second Plan will start will further add to the work of the police, not least because urban population can be expected to increase twice as fast as total population [31].

Despite the fact that Uganda has one of the lowest ratios of policemen to population in the world, the people do not often seem to think so, as is true of many developing countries, in which there have been periods of political unrest.

It is reported from Uganda that many of the local people are under the impression that it is a very highly policed state. The explanation of this is interesting and a good instance of the type of special problems with which the authorities of a developing country have to contend. As is frequent in many new countries which are still settling into being one nation, there have been areas of political unrest in various parts of the country. Extra policemen had to be posted in when there were real threats to the maintenance of law, and the posting of these extra policemen was interpreted by the local inhabitants as extra recruitment on a large scale. This impression was exaggerated by the fact that many of the people in the more remote parts of the country were also coming into contact with an organized police force for the first time. Thus a major problem for those responsible for the police force is to assess the relationships between the newly developed force and the people whom they are serving, where there is no tradition of this type of social control [32].

Following independence the police force in Uganda was almost completely "Africanized." In 1968 there were only three European superior officers, compared with more than 70 in 1962. In recent years there has also been a constant upgrading of requirements for entering the police academy, and at present a minimum of seven years of schooling is required [33]. This level of education is far above the average grade attained by the general population. The police are trained at special centers, one school for lower ranking personnel and a police college for advanced and promotion courses. Basic training lasts 32 weeks. As government employees with stable incomes and a comparatively high educational and training level, the police have a substantially higher status than the police in the United States. As they do in most countries, the Ugandan police play a contradictory role with respect to the people. They protect citizens from criminal attack, but at the same time they must enforce such unpopular regulations as the collection of head taxes. To many Ugandans these tax laws represent unjust and heavy burdens and also the possibility of being imprisoned for failure to pay them.

Police manpower is concentrated in urban areas in which they have a greater degree of legitimacy than they have in the rural areas. Although the ratio for the country in 1969 was one police officer for every 130 persons, the number of police in Kampala was 665 or one for 642 persons [34]. Tanner states that in a "detribalized" and urban area like Kampala the police are less of an alien imposition. They "symbolize the new conception of nontribal central government and for this reason the people may be willing to use the police more than in the country" [35]. Even though police manpower is concentrated in the cities, their peripheral duties reduce the number of men available to protect the citizens. The depletion in manpower is reflected in a statement in 1968, by a resident of one area in Kampala, that the "residents of Mulago, sometimes assisted by police, have started patrolling the Mulago area at night in a bid to stop theft and other criminal activities in the area" [36]. In Kampala an unknown but sizeable number of policemen are occupied in the protection of ministers and other government officials. Another significantly large group spends its time in traffic control, for the number of passenger cars in the country has increased 31% since independence, and most of the 32,800 vehicles are in urban areas. Because of increasing problems in time-consuming traffic control, the Uganda authorities are giving serious consideration to the possibility of setting up a separate traffic department. Police manpower problems are further complicated by the difficulty of supplementing them with mechanized equipment.

In carrying out their functions the police have the use of ancillary equipment, particularly laboratories and various types of motor vehicles, equipped with radio and telecommunication facilities. This kind of resource, being expensive and in relatively short supply in every country, is in particular short supply in developing countries, including Uganda. Therefore most efficient usage of such equipment as is available assumes a particular importance in these countries [37].

The traditional custom of publicly beating and sometimes murdering an apprehended thief complicates the role of the police in the control of crime in Uganda, as it does in a large part of Africa [38]. Thieves who fall into the hands of a mob are often seriously injured with fists, clubs, or stones and many have been killed. In one case in Kampala in 1968 seven thieves were beaten to death. In fact, a large proportion of all property offenders are apprehended by the public and not the police.

One African researcher described the prevalance of beating thieves: "I have personally several times risked myself to save a thief from being killed by a mass beating in Kampala and I have heard people say that all thieves should be killed and left on the side of the road for others to see and learn" [39]. On occasion public beatings have occurred in certain homicide cases, and even the driver of an automobile which has injured someone is not safe. This kind of public punishment is common elsewhere in Africa. "The sight of an angry mob pursuing a petty motorbike thief in Nigeria and beating him senseless is an unforgettable one. Arrest and quick removal by the police are all that may save a man's life in some cases" [40].

The traditions of the people underlie this custom. In village areas in which people are poor and their few possessions mean much to them apprehended thieves have always been beaten. Much personal satisfaction is derived from this performance, particularly if others are watching. It is also feared that offenders might not be dealt with severely enough if they were simply turned over to local authorities. In fact, it is generally the custom, at least in the urban areas, to beat a thief and then turn him over to the police. In the Kampala study, for example, when respondents of two local communities were asked what they considered the most effective way of stopping theft—beating a thief or turning him over to the police, 45% chose both techniques—beat him and then give him to the police. Only 19% felt that the suspect should be beaten and not turned over to the police. An Abidjan account vividly describes what can take place.

Toward a thief the public shows neither compassion nor mercy. He is immediately surrounded, seized, and then led off to the police station to the rhythmic chanting of "Thief! Thief!" (Voleur! Voleur!) His torment begins on the way, for every bystander, however unconnected with the actual incident, feels himself personally involved, and this general feeling of empathy with the victim gives the public license to vent its wrath on the alleged malefactor. People surge around the thief, shout insults, rush up to strike him, and hurl garbage at him. Generally a thief makes no effort to defend himself against such attacks, realizing that any effort to do so would be futile and would probably only further enrage the mob.

When the thief is finally delivered to the police station by the angry mob, he probably has a feeling of profound relief, but at the police station he encounters a climate just as hostile. For persons caught in the act of committing a crime, or against whom circumstantial evidence is abundant, there is a natural presumption of guilt, and the accused is treated as such. He is stripped down to his undershorts, photographed, fingerprinted, and entered on the police records. Then he is led into an inspector's office and subjected to intense questioning. Any recalcitrance on his part invites a blow from the investigating officer. Little wonder, then, that most such inquiries promptly lead to a confession [41].

A much publicized variation occurred in 1972 in the Central African Republic when President Bokassa ordered soldiers to beat 45 imprisoned thieves [42]. The result was three dead inmates and the rest wounded, some severely. Both the dead and the wounded were put on public display for six hours.

Police and the Nature of Power Groups

In those developing countries in which there is some form of democracy the police do not always play a completely neutral role. The very nature of their activities is important in maintaining the power of the wealthy landowning and industrial groups, foreign and domestic. They also help to keep the dominant political party in power by making it difficult for political opponents to obtain parade and speaking permits and even to use armed force when crowds try to redress social wrongs. They also keep under surveillance those suspected of any type of subversive activities. In their quest for law and order the Indian police, for example, have become especially sensitive in the past to the activities of leftist politicians, watching them closely and occasionally dealing with them more severely than with other groups [43]. They are also often power-making forces in the sense that they have helped to overthrow political regimes, as, for example, in Ghana, Sierre Leone, and Uganda.

The Police and National Development

National development can be greatly affected by the manner in which the police operate. Police of developing countries are particularly important because they have great power and are highly visible; they probably come into contact with more citizens than the personnel of any other government agency, they possess almost a monopoly on the use of force, are responsible for safeguarding many important societal values, and are closely identified with the law. Because they are not merely passive agents of government, they can affect the nature of social regulation of the people and can reinforce whatever stabilizing processes are present. By developing a feeling of national loyalty they can help to overcome particularistic loyalties or allegiance to subnational groups. A government may encounter serious difficulties in building support for its programs if its police are corrupt, abuse their power, or make few positive contributions. The conclusion reached in Bayley's study of the Indian police was that they had failed to play a sufficiently active role in nation building or in development in general. He felt that this was regrettable and suggested a number of specific contributions that could be helpful not only to India's program but to those of other countries.

Police may serve as living proof of the possibility of creating a truly national instrument of government; they may be one of the few agencies acting in the name of the nation even though composed of individuals from many subnational groupings. The police serve a symbolic role, representing a nation yet to be, developing national heroes, and giving a sense of pride in country by means of parades, reviews, and athletic competitions. The police may exert a profound influence simply because of the relations they publicly establish with other elements of government. Do they show themselves willing to work with a new national leadership? Do they work in harness with civilian bureaucracy? Police may also set an example by means of the techniques they employ to accomplish their objectives. In an underdeveloped country police are sometimes an island of modernity, eager to use the latest technical devices, organized on the basis of merit rather than status, and experimenting with functionally specific role playing. A local example of the utilization of these techniques may embolden others to innovate too. People in any country, whatever its stage of development, look over their shoulders for new ideas to use in solving their own problems, for the courage to do what they think is required, or simply for an example that will allow them to convince others of the sensibleness of their own plan. An underdeveloped country has fewer centers of innovation than a Western country and consequently the police may be a more persuasive example [44].

In Malaysia efforts have been made to institute changes in the image of the police. A police cadet corps program has been started to educate school children in civic consciousness, to develop an appreciation for the police, and to instill public assumption of responsibilities for crime prevention. They provide public information and education services in television and radio programs and press, and sponsor an annual "Police Week" in which open house at all police establishments is held in an attempt to enlighten and arouse public support and cooperation. A similar program has been adopted by Nigeria and Singapore.

If law enforcement, maintenance of the existing political structure, and education are considered possible functions, the latter is one that is peculiar to the police in the less developed countries [45]. The police can make significant contributions to this positive force, for they can furnish needed information, even of a technological nature, implement development policies, and encourage individual and group self-development. The police have played this part in Tanzania, where they have been used to implement the plans and philosophy expressed by Nyerere in the Arusha Declaration [46]. The police have performed similar functions in the social and economic development of the People's Republic of China in which they generally supervise, often with the help of local committees, lost and found departments, health and fire inspection, neighborhood work, and educational activities [47].

The police can also be extremely effective in crime prevention by providing on-the-spot adjustment of cases short of arrest, frequent and regular patrols in high crime areas, and advice to individuals and businesses on security measures; they can also act as counsel to young people who may be getting into trouble. Policewomen often play major roles in some of these activities. Preventive work of this kind is difficult, however, in countries in which countless police hours are consumed by the collection of license fees or taxes and traffic control. Emphasis on crime prevention and a better recognition of the social service elements of police work would, in the end, mean more effective police operations. The use of special police for juveniles, for example, has been found to be helpful in keeping youths out of trouble and in preventing abuse of the young. Such services, when and if available, are generally provided in urban areas: they are particularly needed in localities in which there are antisocial norms and values. Finally, developing countries have great opportunities for initiating wider public participation in police work. In the Soviet Union, for example, voluntary citizen police (People's Voluntary Militia) help to control crime, drunkenness, and disorderly conduct in factories, collective farms, and meeting places. Set up under local authority, they have their own officers and are independent of the control of the regular police, but they are answerable under the law to the Soviet and the courts.

The special duties of these units are the enforcement of public order, particularly on occasions of processions or meetings, and the prevention of hooliganism and drunkenness. The Voluntary Militia on public holidays, for example, marshal the crowds, man check-points, tour the streets, and visit bars and restaurants, admonishing drunken persons, and so on. Much of their work is preventive, such as surveying leisure facilities and promoting entertainment in neglected areas. While they possess powers of arrest, members of the Voluntary Militia seek to work by persuasion and the force of public opinion [48].

A United Nations Report has summarized some of the various possibilities open to less developed countries.

In some of the developing countries, there would seem to be an opportunity for some kind of social experimentation in law enforcement and the preservation of peace. In almost all these countries, police systems have been imported; the imports have included organizational structure, uniforms, training, mannerisms and traditions. In some of these countries, however, the systems have not firmly established themselves except perhaps in urban areas. Police characteristics of strict separatism, stern authoritarianism and legalized force may not therefore have impressed themselves in the mind of the people. Thus it might be possible to create a new type of law enforcement agency which has a new image. One might even go further and investigate the possibility of establishing a police force which was moulded around a core of professional officers who would be trained in criminal investigation and detection, but which was based on a concept of national service; citizens-at-large being asked to spend a few weeks each year serving such a force [49].

PRISON CONDITIONS IN DEVELOPING COUNTRIES

It has been estimated that the *daily* world prison population, political prisoners excluded, is between 1.5 and 2 million [50]. The *total annual* figures are much larger because of the large turnover in population. About 1.3 million, for example, are sent to prison for less than three to six months. Short-term prison sentences are particularly common in the developing countries. In Kenya 73% of the prison population in 1967 and 69% in Nigeria in 1965 were imprisoned for less than six months. In Ceylon in 1968 91% were in for less than a year and in Colombia in 1969 70% of the prison population served terms of less than a year. A fourth of the offenders in Uganda received sentences of a month or less. In recent years, in fact, a growing number of offenders have been given short-term sentences for failure to pay head taxes and for petty theft, common assault, and other crimes. Although some local jails are maintained in Uganda for suspects awaiting trial or convicted offenders serving very short sentences, government prisons represent the only real facilities for criminal detention [51]. In 1967 18,138 prisoners were admitted into the Uganda prison system. Persons awaiting trial are sent to the government prisons, and more than one-half of the number admitted into the system in 1967 fell into this category. The absence of alternative accommodations puts a severe strain on existing facilities and leads to overcrowding.

The use of imprisonment rests on the widely held belief that crime deterrence is achieved by severe punitive justice. In fact, many would solve criminality by even longer prison sentences or even greater use of the death penalty. When Kampala slum dwellers were asked what could be done to reduce crime, a common remark was "make the sentences long." This principle rests on cultural attitudes derived from a more traditional view of the offender held over from colonial rule. One writer has analyzed the views of Africans who favor severe imprisonment. They feel, he states, that they themselves live under circumstances of social deprivation and are thus understandably hostile to any measure that might seem to be "coddling" the prisoners.

In the eyes of many Africans—whether educated government officials or simple peasants out in the bush—persons in prison have been sent there because they committed some crime against society and therefore must be made to suffer and pay for it. It follows that prisoners must not be given advantages or pleasures which are not available to the population as a whole [52].

Yet prisons today are under attack everywhere because of the conditions in the system and because of their failure to rehabilitate offenders. There is a growing view that perhaps the only solution to this serious problem is the greater use of alternatives. In general, conditions appear to be much worse in the developing countries and few alternatives are available. Major reliance is put on prisons to deal with crime, yet few developing countries have any real system of parole (after care). Even in countries that support some probation system it is rarely used and supervision is usually lax. In Ghana, for example, probation as a method of treatment is confined almost exclusively to adults, but only one in several hundred convicted receives it [53]. In Uganda, which has had probation since 1947, the highest percentage of convicted persons placed on probation between 1960 and 1967 was 1.9 in 1964 and the lowest was 1.1 in 1967 (48.1% were fined and 4.4 received suspended sentences). In 1967 47,582 persons were convicted, but only 533 were put on probation. In India, where a national probation law was first enacted in 1958, the proportion of probationers is insignificant. In 1966, for example, a total of 374,862 persons was admitted to prison throughout India, but only 8044 were put on probation. Since a large proportion of prisoners in Uganda and India serve short sentences (in India 85% less than six months), there is ample room for the use of probation in this group alone. Fines could be more widely used and provisions made for their payment on an installment basis.

Most prisons in developing countries are merely caretaking or custodial institutions. They are overcrowded and completely devoid of rehabilitative programs. In Ghana's prisons, according to one study, "the criminal has largely been abandoned," and prisoners are "insufficiently occupied, insufficiently trained, and insufficiently educated to new habits of thought and conduct. The prisoner serves his time and departs, not noticeably better and perhaps the worse for the experience" [54]. The Laurel Report on the prison situation in the Philippines in 1969 stated that the living conditions in most prisons were "subhuman." This report describes in detail the conditions found in the Philippine National penitentiary, New Bilibid Prison, the largest prison in the world:

Cells are congested, unkempt and dingy. Toilet facilities are inadequate. . . . The committee discovered that the inmates of the provincial jail of a first-class province are allowed to go out of their cells for sunshine only once a week and for only one hour. Most inmates do not have uniforms and stay in their cells half-naked. At the Sablayan Penal Colony and Farm, there is no electricity to provide the inmates with light and other services. . . . In most cells of the New Bilibid Prison (9,000 persons) there are no beds for the prisoners. A majority of the inmates sleep on dirty and tattered mats laid on the cold concrete floor. Some even sleep in the corridors of the building. . . . The food is so meager and so ill-prepared that it could easily be mistaken for animal fare. Their food tasted like dishwater. Usually, there is only one vegetable viand cooked in a lot of broth and sometimes sprinkled with little pieces of inferior kind of meat. The prisoners eat this with a lot of boiled bad rice which has not been cleaned before cooking. . . . While in prison, the prisoners must also eat with their bare hands since eating utensils are not provided for them. At the new Bilibid Prison, a dining room has not been provided for the prisoners. The prisoners just squat any place they please and consume their fare unceremoniously. . . . Medical and dental services are poor and inadequate. In some jails, inmates have complained of the unavailability of aspirin. Psychiatric services are unheard of at the insular prisons. At the New Bilibid Prison, only 8 guidance counselors serve the needs of the more than 9,000 prisoners confined therein. . . .

The lack of discipline may be traced to the abhorrent atmosphere that the inmates find themselves in. Moreover, many prisoners resent the shabby treatment they receive from ill-trained prison guards and authorities. The lack of discipline is further aggravated by the inability of prison authorities to resolve the differences and rivalries among underworld gangs. . . . Sexual perversion is a perpetual problem in Philippine prisons. Sodomy in national as well as local prisons exists as an open secret even to prison authorities themselves [55].

López-Rey is probably the best authority on the subject of prison conditions in developing countries. He has had nearly 20 years of United Nations experience with them, and in a book published in 1970 he characterized prisons in various developing parts of the world [56].

As far as large closed prisons in Asia are concerned, most are overcrowded, and prison labour is seldom available and poorly if ever remunerated (p. 89).

Whether prison conditions in the Arab countries have improved since 1965 is difficult to ascertain, but up to that time they were seldom satisfactory (p. 91).

In Latin America, prison conditions vary from country to country but are generally unsatisfactory or really bad (p. 92).

For African countries prison data are frequently nonexistent, incomplete or out of date. . . . If (independence) has improved many aspects of national and individual life, it has not as yet made similar progress in the penitentiary field (p. 95).

In fact, customary criminal law in Africa views the use of prisons as a wasteful procedure. It was imported into the African scene as a punishment for crime and in traditional African societies was almost unknown.

The payment of compensation, or blood-money, by the offender to the offended was customary in many cases, even in the unlawful killing of a human being. The reason for this is partly to be found in the social policy of the African peoples, which centres around the land and its produce in the largely agricultural communities on the continent [57].

Some of López-Rey's comments on individual prison situations are revealing:

In Colombia, prison conditions are appalling, in spite of the fact that the directors of the Prison Administration have repeatedly drawn the attention of the Government to these conditions. The same may be said about Panama. The situation is better in Costa Rica, where the Government has been trying for years to replace the old Penitentiary and organize a Prison Service. In Guatemala, the Central Prison of Guatemala City and those in most of the other cities are still reminiscent of the prisons of more than a century ago. In Guatemala City Prison, I never found the traditional separation between persons awaiting trial and sentenced prisoners. The dormitories are poor and the Administration unable to procure either work or clothing. The central yard, fortunately large enough, brings back old scenes of prisoners left to their own devices to earn money for survival by selling "souvenirs," cooking or working for other prisoners, and repairing that which often seems to be beyond repair. Peru is one of the few countries in which, once in a while, prisoners collectively complain about lack of food. The colony of Sepa was still severely criticized in 1967 by prominent Peruvian professionals. The prisons of El Frontón, El Sexto, Lurigancho and the small prisons of Callao and Lima are actually run by the prisoners themselves. Lurigancho penitentiary, near Lima, visited by the writer in August, 1969, is a flagrant denial of penitentiary progress (pp. 93–94).

In Bolivia there is no Prison Administration proper, but a section in the Ministry of Justice and the Interior which has been trying for many years to improve the fragile structure of a prison organization which, as in many other countries, is frequently totally dislocated by political turmoil. The Panopticon of La Paz is little more than a prison where prisoners of every sort are kept with no attempt to apply any other treatment than that of custody. No prison labour is provided beyond giving facilities to some prisoners to work on their own. With few variations, the situation was the same until recently in the prisons of Oruro, Sucre, Potosi, Cochabamba, Santa Cruz de la Sierra, Trinidad and others. Prisons are usually run by the military or uniformed police. In Uruguay, which in the past played a leading role in prison reform, the general situation has deteriorated. Many years ago the construction of a large closed prison was decided on and started; it is still unfinished for lack of funds, and its musty cement structure has become a memorial to a mistaken prison policy (pp. 94–95).

The scarce data on Nigeria, Ghana, Dahomey, Togo and Senegal can only be regarded as reflecting generally unsatisfactory conditions (p. 95).

With respect to the Republic of South Africa (a country of 12,000,000 Africans, 1,000,000 Asians, and 3,000,000 Whites) according to the report for the period 1963–1966, as of June 30, 1965, there were 72,580 persons in custody, 60,477 of whom had been convicted. During the year ended 30 June, 1966, 339,143 sentenced prisoners and 204,773 unsentenced prisoners were admitted to prison, of whom 80,329 or about 39 percent were readmitted to prison as sentenced prisoners. Of the 339,143—male and female—only 1.8 percent are listed as white. The proportion of white in the general population is about 19 percent. Sentenced prisoners are classified as white, Bantu, Asiatic and coloured; by far the greatest proportion is Bantu followed by coloured and Asiatics. Of the above total, 91 percent were sentenced to periods of up to six months. Out of 281 prisoners sentenced to corporal punishment only (caning) 204 were Bantu, 52 white, 23 coloured and 2 Asiatic. While the proportions between sentenced white women and men were roughly 20 to one, those of Bantu and coloured was 6 to one, and that of Asiatics 45 to one. The report makes the point that, in order to avoid misapprehension, the category of prisoners apparently regarded as political detainees, with a single exception, are persons tried in open court, convicted and sentenced for offences against public security. Such persons fall under the respective group of ordinary sentenced prisoners, and on no occasion were more than 1,825 in custody, and on 30 June 1966 there were only 1,395. On the other hand, apart from referring to these persons as saboteurs and perpetrators of violence, no reference is made to the special legislation declaring them as such, or to relevant circumstances in which it is applied. No specific data are given about the different types of treatment applied to each of the four groups of prisoners, type of institution and personnel in charge. As for prison labour, nothing specific is said about remuneration, beyond the general assertion that the gratuity scales for internal employment have recently been considerably improved and extended. The whole prison system is run in accordance with the antidemocratic apartheid policy of the country (p. 96).

Obviously it would be unfair to leave the impression that all prisons in all developing countries are bad. Some systems are quite efficiently and well run, as in India, Brazil, Uganda, Kenya, and Tanzania [58]. The Uganda Prisons Service, by which approximately 17,000 prisoners were held in 1969, consist, for example, of 19 prisons and 11 prison farms, six of which contain 3000 to 7000 acres, organized by regions. Nine of the prisons house long-term first offenders and five, long-term recidivists. Twelve prisons serve as reception and classification centers from which inmates may be transferred to other institutions. In 1969 the staff numbered 190 senior officers, 3074 junior officers, and 166 technical personnel. Potential senior-officer staff take 24 months of training at the Prison Staff College and warders and wardresses are given six months of basic residential training.

A detailed study of the records of 863 offenders, aged 18 to 25, who were admitted in 1969 to the main prison at Murchison Bay near Kampala categorizes their offenses (see Table 36). Approximately one-third (36%) were confined for robbery and burglary and more for bicycle than

Table 36   Offenses of 863 Property Offenders, Aged 18
to 25 Admitted to the Main Uganda Prison, 1968

	Offense	No.	%
1.	Robbery, aggravated	94	10.9
2.	Robbery, other	45	5.2
3.	Burglary and housebreaking	141	16.3
4.	Shopbreaking	9	1.0
5.	Other breaking and entering	25	2.9
6.	Theft of motor vehicle	30	3.5
7.	Theft from motor vehicle (spare tires, accessories, etc.)	22	2.6
8.	Theft from motor vehicle (other property)	46	5.3
9.	Bicycle thefts	43	5.0
10.	Theft (by servants)	83	9.6
11.	Theft (all other kinds)	325	37.7
		863	100.0

auto theft. Unfortunately the Uganda prison system puts almost all its emphasis for reformation on vocational training and work experience. A recent United Nations report commented as follows on this system:

It has been found in many countries, again especially the highly industrialized ones with extensive and developed prison systems dating back many
years, that vocational training within the prison has a disappointingly low correlation with successful social readjustment and crime-free careers on the part
of the prisoners afterwards. This is quite likely to be another case of the situation varying from country to country. Uganda, as we already said, is primarily
an agricultural country, and vocational training emphasizing various farming
skills is therefore particularly appropriate. However, the Uganda authorities
in the long run will clearly be anxious to know exactly how much profit in
terms of less recidivism, as distinct from immediate economic benefit, the system
gains from this emphasis. Thus some record of which type of prisoners are given
vocational training and which are not will be kept, and also of which prisoners
who received vocational training have a successful post-prison career and who
find themselves in further criminal activity. In brief, the assumptions that fitting
a prisoner with a specific skill and the experience of regular work habits will
lead to his non-return to crime are ones which require testing extensively over
time [59].

It must be remembered, moreover, that the poor prison situations
are not necessarily or always due to wilful neglect or inefficiency, and the
limited resources usually available to operate prisons cannot be minimized. In the Ivory Coast, for example, in 1966 the total budget for the

entire penal system of two large prisons and 28 small ones, in which 4500 prisoners were confined, was 432,000 dollars and the daily maintenance allotment for each prisoner was 21 cents [60]. Limited financial resources, however, are not the only problems. In Tanzania, for example, large numbers of unconvicted prisoners are confined in prison because of lack of bail, the short-term prisoner's stay is too short for adequate study and treatment, the prisons lack not only money but adequately trained personnel, and there is no investigation department whose function would be to determine the root causes of criminal behavior [61]. Psychiatric facilities are either extremely inadequate or nonexistent, since there are few psychiatrists in the country. Many new African nations have no psychiatrists at all, and in Nigeria, the nation with the largest number of inhabitants, there were only 10 in 1966. Thus few African penal institutions can make use of psychiatric techniques, and few courts use psychiatric information and advice [62].

The prisons described here have been the usual closed institutions common to most countries. A number of open institutions, however, are well run and not overcrowded: Kundasale and Pallekele, organized as camps, and the prison farms of Anuradhpara and Batticoloa in Ceylon, the mobile camps for public works in India, Burewala in Pakistan, and the open institutions of Huay Pong and Aranyik in Thailand [63]. At the Sampurnanand Camp in India, where there are sometimes as many as 2000 prisoners, the inmates are employed in public works of various types. Living conditions here are far better than those of the majority of persons living in free society, and the inmates are paid the wages of free men. There is no exploitation, and educational and training programs are offered. The Reformatory Camps for young adult prisoners at Bulaware, Pakistan, constitute a remarkable institution organized in accordance with the Prisoners' Probational Act of 1926: first offenders are sent as "probationers" to farms, where they receive, free of charge, a piece of land and tools and sometimes a loan for the purchase of cattle. A system of cooperatives also facilitates the acquisition of most of the supplies and equipment needed for farming [64]. Inmates at the Model Prison in Lucknow, India, are allowed to work at various jobs in free society, including hawking various objects. They return at night and a deduction is made from their earnings for their keep. In most of the open and closed prisons in Latin America prisoners are allowed conjugal visits, a procedure now becoming more common, for example, in the United States [65].

Overcrowding

Overcrowding is a common, if not universal, problem in the developed countries. In developing countries it is likely to be severe, an obvious consequence of the marked increase in crime, the failure to build new institutions, particularly since independence, the number of prisoners awaiting trial, and the absence of the alternative programs found in developed countries. Some prisons are so overcrowded that they have become gigantic institutions. The largest penitentiary in the world, the new Bilibid Prison in Manila, for example, is twice the size of the largest in the United States, which itself, with its 4500 inmates, is far larger than any European prison. A study in Ghana concluded that although the Prisons Department appears to be making a reasonable effort to treat the prisoners humanely and, as far as possible, to apply measures directed toward rehabilitation, the appalling overcrowding frustrates both these objectives [66].

In Asia in 1970 overcrowding was prevalent in the prisons of New Delhi, for example, as in those of Bombay, Calcutta, Karachi, Colombo, and Bangkok [67]. Among Arab countries overcrowding was the general rule in 1965, even in the smaller prisons. It was common, for example, in Syria, as well as in prisons of the United Arab Republic. A similar situation applies to most of Latin America. López-Rey concluded that "although here and there (in Venezuela) improvements have been made, overcrowding, aggravated by the increasing number of detainees and prisoners sentenced for subversive activities, idleness and scarcity of staff and services were still the prevailing characteristics of the penal system at the end of 1967" [68].

In many former British and French colonial possessions Europeans and highly educated persons, or those who had held responsible positions, are still treated differently from the rank and file of the lower class prisoners. The former are usually given roomlike quarters rather than the barracks-type facilities of the other prisoners and are permitted extensive personal exemptions from prison labor, they are also given extra privileges, can take many personal possessions with them to prison, and are given better food. In the Ivory Coast such prisoners have usually been convicted of fraud, embezzlement, and involuntary manslaughter resulting from traffic accidents. This separation has grown out of the colonial problem of imprisoning their own people and the educated, upper-class background of many of their political prisoners. Nehru and hundreds of others who have ruled India, for example, are exprisoners, many of whom were confined for many years in prisons run by the British. This policy is defended today on the ground that educated persons of prominence could not survive under ordinary prison conditions and, in any event, the punishment would be severer for them.

Proportion of Prisoners Awaiting Trial

In nearly all developing countries persons awaiting trial are held in prison. This is often done in Europe, but rarely in the United States. Although the detention of offenders for long periods before trial is not peculiar to the less developed countries, the length of time in relation to the later sentence is peculiar to them. López-Rey has written that in his experience, based on repeated and often long visits to 16 Latin American countries,

the number of persons kept in prison awaiting trial, sometimes for very long periods, is usually higher than the number of convicted prisoners. When, during my visits, I raised the question of persons eventually sentenced to shorter periods than those spent in detention awaiting trial, the fact was admitted without exception [69].

In Colombia, for example, in 1964 only 6700 among 30,000 prisoners had been sentenced. Many had been awaiting trial for years, even a longer time than the possible length of the sentence if convicted. In Argentina in 1967 more than two-thirds of 19,903 prisoners were awaiting trial, the average felony case taking a year before the passing of sentence by the court of first instance. In India nearly half the prison population is awaiting trial. In Ceylon in 1965–1966 10,138 convicted prisoners and 23,500 unconvicted were awaiting sentencing or trial, most of them 6 to 18 months. In Thailand prisoners awaiting trial constitute about one-third, and in certain areas of the Philippines, 40%. In Iran in 1965 there were 8065 convicted prisoners and 10,645 awaiting trial, an appreciable number of whom had been waiting more than a year to be brought to court, some more than eight years [70]. These lengthy delays are usually the result of an overburdened, antiquated judicial system, inefficient procedures, and a far too heavy case load because of increasing crime in the urban areas. Moreover, bail is seldom used to release accused offenders pending trial. In developing countries this means that many persons plead guilty, and much of the prison administration's activities and resources are diverted from any assistance that can be given to the convicted prisoners.

To take the burden off the courts and to reduce the waiting time in prison developing countries might well consider an adaptation of the procedure in effect in several socialist countries of quasi-judicial institutions such as the comrade courts of the Soviet Union. These courts are public bodies elected by general meetings of workers, farmers, office employees, students, and neighbors at their places of work.

The comrade courts may apply any one or all of the following measures to a person who has been found guilty: ask the accused to apologize publicly to the collective or the victim; reprimand the comrade; impose a fine up to ten roubles; ask the manager of the collective to consider the accused's demotion; ask the accused to pay damages up to 50 roubles. The court acts not only in offences committed by members of the groups but also in matters of behavior which, although they do not constitute a breach of the law, are nevertheless clearly contrary to socialist morality and likely to develop into crime [71].

Prison Labor

Seldom do prisons of most developing countries provide employment for their inmates. When an inmate does work in prison, he earns almost no money for it. His idle time makes even worse the burden of serving his prison sentence. The absence of programs for prison work and failure to install machine shops and other equipment accounts in large part for this circumstance. The Laurel Report on prison conditions in the Philippines stated that most inmates of the closed penal institutions are virtually forced to spend their time doing nothing. In the New Bilibid Prison only one in eight prisoners is engaged in a governmental training program. This situation is, of course, different in the penal (agricultural) colonies in which almost every inmate is given a particular task [72]. One writer has described conditions in the main prisons of the Ivory Coast in Abidjan, which housed 900 prisoners in 1968.

Throughout my visit I was struck by the fact that the vast majority of the inmates seemed to be without anything to do. The European prisoners visit freely with each other back and forth in their rooms; and the African prisoners (most of whom are much younger—men in their late teens or early twenties) lie around in their rooms talking or playing at games such as checkers which they have improvised. Although the prisoners are awakened at six o'clock in the morning and the doors to their cells are locked by five in the afternoon, they are largely idle during the intervening hours. Aside from a small shed where wooden furniture is made, there are no workshops where the prisoners may be put to useful labor; and since the Prison Civile is located in the heart of Abidjan, there is no prison garden of any kind to occupy the prisoners and to allow them to grow their own food (which would, of course, help to defray the costs of operating the prison).

When I inquired why prisoners were not put to doing some kind of useful work outside the prison, such as clearing brush away from the highways, sweeping the streets, etc., I was told that in a society such as this, where the numbers of the unemployed roaming the streets in search of almost any kind of work are already so large, the government could not risk depriving people of even a few jobs by using convict labor. Prison details are occasionally seen on the outside, but they are only used for tending the areas around government buildings. The prisoners are strictly prevented from entering into economic competition with the rest of the population [73].

A trend in a number of developing countries, however, has been to use forced prison labor to produce agricultural and industrial products. This prison labor, particularly in open agricultural institutions that raise cotton, often brings in a financial return to the state well beyond the cost of maintaining the prison system. In Uganda one of the stated policies for the large prison farms, most of which produce cotton, is the production of revenue to the government; for example, in 1968–1969, in addition to food raised for institutional use, the prison system earned cash revenues of 2.3 million shillings, or about 330,000 dollars [74]. Prison labor can contribute little to the overall development of the country's technological skill or to criminal reform, and it is socially shortsighted as well. Whatever financial returns are achieved, they are counterbalanced by the production of more sophisticated criminals, fostered by the combined prison experiences of the inmates.

The Effects of Imprisonment

With the exception of Tanner's study of an East African prison, there are no studies of penal social systems in developing countries that would permit us to compare their social structures or the interaction of staff and inmates with studies that have been done in such countries as the United States [75]. Tanner constructed a typology of inmate adaptation to an African prison in terms of conformity, innovation, ritualism, withdrawal, rebellion, and manipulation [76]. Inmates did not suffer particularly from deprivation, since the living standards were generally above those of their own home. Even though the amount they could earn was small, they could buy things like tobacco. The limited supplies of goods was also eased by the relative simplicity of smuggling and the fact that even rubbish accumulation could satisfy some of their needs either for the status of possessing them or for exchange purposes. "Every search produced bottles, tins, rags, string, small articles of tin and wood manufactured within the prison, tinder sets and paper, with which a large part of the trading within the prison was carried on from day to day" [77].

Since most African prisoners are accustomed to extreme poverty, prison authorities have generally tended to regard the physical condition of their institutions as of high standard, compared with the outside. Even though the economic level of lower class prisoners in the developed countries is much higher, prison officials also often make much of the "greater opportunities" and the good living conditions of their prison facilities. This point of view ignores the African prisoner's entire life before he entered prison.

Life for many could not have been pleasant but the unpleasantness tended to be forgotten and the everyday affairs of life thought of as positive pleasures.

Everything that he had taken for granted before, that he could have a woman if he had the need and the money, have a drink, to be able to wander about on an evening, to speak when he felt like it—in fact to have a considerable amount of personal independence, all of which immediately disappeared with imprisonment. Even an illiterate, diseased, homeless vagrant had a large measure of this individuality. Every one of the prisoners outside had an identifiable role which differentiated him from the others, gave him some satisfactions and made him reasonably pleased with his life, if only in retrospect when he lost it by conviction and imprisonment [78].

Under colonial rule, Tanner claimed, East African prisoners experienced a great sense of unity in their opposition to European prison authority. Under African authority he found that the majority were more tractable, even though their lives were dominated by rules. Most accepted prison authority much as they would tribal or community authority. Prison authorities, however, tended to interpret this general obedience as "cooperation," based on their methods of operation. Despite their general conformity, however, some prisoners managed to gain advantages, whereas others were prepared to pit themselves against the system, being both defiant and irrational, in situations that did not justify a struggle, "with the result that they got increasingly heavy prison punishment which the authorities often recognized as virtually useless in deterring other similar offenses" [79].

There did not appear to be a code of convict behavior which defined the convict's relationship with authority. They did not take much action against those who were thought to be informers, or indeed against those who stole from their fellows. There was nothing in their code which prevented them from getting to know a warder. The only rule which appeared to be generally known and acted upon was the avoidance of quarrels between convicts—such friction was universally condemned. Most cells had quasi-formal arrangements for the settling of quarrels, the organization of duties and the enforcement of penalties for misbehavior such as committing homosexual acts in public or fouling the latrines. The convicts with the longer sentences were named judges and policemen, and gave out punishments such as walking on the knees twenty times around the cell, or carrying a bucket of water [80].

Contrary to conditions in many developed countries, homosexuality does not appear to be a major problem in East African prisons.

There was a very generalized dislike and loathing of homosexuality amongst almost all prisoners, even amongst those who had only become homosexuals during their imprisonment. Most of the prisoners were sufficiently near to their tribal origins to be bound by the concepts of customary law and no tribal system known in East Africa had a socially recognised place for the homosexual [81].

Like those in developed countries, each inmate interviewed stated that deprivation of liberty was the worst thing about prison life.

They were prevented from enjoying everything which they held to be good in life. Every convict interviewed expressed the opinion, both for himself and other convicts with whom he was associated, that no matter how poor the material conditions outside, no one would seek imprisonment for food and shelter. They stressed that the community life round their homes under any conditions provided satisfactions which prison could never replace [82].

As prisoners do everywhere, they felt isolated; their prison contacts were never without self-interest.

It is never sharing but the exchange of services for mutual advantage and protection. In sickness and health, a prisoner is alone and unlikely to receive or give help unless it is to someone's advantage to do so or because the authorities are potentially involved. On the one hand he may draw some strength from tribal identity and what he can create of clan and lineage groupings, while on the other hand he may be unable to develop these relationships, as would have been the case outside, by a full range of reciprocal goods and services [83].

The African prisoner may not in general suffer great social stigma, but he does suffer acutely from social isolation. One writer has described the inmates' feelings:

. . . clothed conspicuously different from his brethren at large in shorts and often barefoot, numbered instead of named, and exposed to the ridicule of his fellow men by being forced to do prison work traditionally taboo or normally relegated to women, is clearly conscious of his lot [84].

A major result of imprisonment in a developed country is the stigma that results from it, but there is little information on this subject in Africa other than the observations of nonAfricans. There appears to be a consensus that less stigma is attached to imprisonment when large numbers of people are arrested and imprisoned for transgressing minor statutes [85]. One study claims that those imprisoned in Uganda for poaching, violating liquor licenses, stock theft, and other laws of this nature do not see themselves as criminals. To the extent that this feeling is common among the people, Tanner claims that imprisonment may carry little social stigma [86]. A contrary view was found in a representative sample of urban Africans (70) in Lusaka and 50 in prison who were in almost complete agreement that imprisonment was a disgrace; "no African interviewed either inside or outside prison had any liking for the life, and the person sentenced to prison was always despised as a failure, as someone bringing disgrace and approbrium on his kith and kin" [87]. One exception was imprisonment for political offenses. Another study found that in a labor surplus employers may be more selective and the exinmate's bargaining position is irreparably damaged [88]. Tanner also noted that the better educated prisoners expressed greater concern over the affects of their imprisonment. One said he became fearful and angry when looking for a job because of the reactions of his friends: "I will find all my friends holding big responsible positions; hence they will take me for a spoilt man who can be good enough to dust their shoes" [89]. In Malaysia public fears, prejudices, and ignorance were also found to arouse hostility toward the exprisoner, factors that may not only contribute to recidivism but may also offer the offender justification for reverting to crime.

Alternatives to Prisons

The expenditure of billions of dollars in the construction of numerous and costly prisons has probably been the greatest mistake the more developed nations have made in crime-control practices in the last 150 years. The use of prisons as a method of crime control is under serious attack in the United States and Great Britain and even in Sweden, which was thought to have the best system in the world. The most serious charges are the irrefutable evidence of high rates of recidivism which range from 50 to 80% and the high costs of construction and maintenance in terms of the poor results achieved. In fact, the most hardened criminals appear to be "produced" by the prison system. Research has indicated that men in prison are trained in more sophisticated crimes, at state expense, that homosexuality is rampant, and that the prison environment itself has a degrading effect on them. Isolated from relatives, friends, and their communities, they lose their initiative and become embittered and filled with hatred for society. In most cases prison inmates are even denied elemental civil rights. Most of all, they are labeled "exconvicts," a stigma that interferes with job procurement and family life and often destroys their own self-respect. A man's term in prison is held against him much more than his conviction of a crime. The police and the courts tend to react negatively to a person with a prison record, and this treatment by the legal system and by the community often leads to a "first-time loser's" embarking on a secondary or a career deviance [90]. Ex-inmates commit increasingly serious crimes, and those who become gang leaders on release from prison often indoctrinate noncriminals into criminal ways [91].

Yet, curiously, those persons who are or have been in prison do not constitute all of our criminals, nor are they necessarily our worst. Of all crimes committed only a small percentage of offenders is arrested, and an even smaller percentage is prosecuted, convicted, and imprisoned. Many who go to prison have been sentenced because they could not afford good lawyers or because they lacked sufficient influence on the prosecutor or judge. Nearly all prison inmates everywhere come from the lower classes, and it is this group that commits most of the crimes for which arrests are made; that is, burglary, larceny, auto theft, and robbery. Only 5 to at most 20% of all crimes involve violence, and most of these crimes are committed by lower class persons *against other lower class persons*. Few prison inmates come from the middle and upper classes, yet there are extensive violations of the law by businessmen, politicians, and government employees. For occupational and white-collar crimes by businessmen and politicians apprehension is rare and penalties are slight and seldom include imprisonment. In fact, it is the middle and upper classes who define "the criminal," who have the power to designate certain acts as crimes, and who insist on the enforcement of the law for certain categories of the population. In this sense, then, certain groups of people are being unduly punished for certain types of crime, their penalties are more severe, and they are more likely to go to prison. Thus they might be termed "political prisoners."

From this point of view, then, it is understandable why and how the excessive and widespread use of prisons in developing countries undoubtedly contributes to and will continue to be a factor in their rising crime rates, particularly in the urban areas. A Malaysian writer concluded that in spite of the serious and inherent limitations in the capacity of the prison to rehabilitate its inmates imprisonment is still considered to be the main means of rehabilitation [92]. In Ghana rehabilitation is prevented by overcrowding and antiquated regulations: "motivation, no matter how humane, cannot stretch the prisons to twice their size, or produce the open camps and other facilities urgently required" [93]. In 1971 the Director of Prisons in Venezuela spoke about the penal system in his attempt to justify the introduction of a law that would release certain offenders from prison sentences and attempt treatment in a free environment. He stated that imprisonment has been a complete failure in the task of re-educating an antisocial person, a fact amply demonstrated by the statistics on recidivism. "The difficult artificial community formed by the penal population with its wide diversity in backgrounds neither betters nor corrects, in principle, anyone" [94]. Moreover, some developing countries add a sentence of corporal punishment in the form of caning or flogging. After a study of a number of long-term recidivists in what was then Northern Rhodesia (Zambia) it was concluded that these penalties had nothing constructive about them, neither deterred nor had a retributive effect, and were usually imposed in a haphazard manner with little regard for the person or the offense [95].

In an attempt to determine their attitudes toward criminal law, a study was made in 1966–1967 of 202 adult male Puerto Rican prisoners in comparison to a nonoffender group of 204 laborers, 69 prison guards, and 137 policemen of the same class. It was found that the prisoners displayed a more unfavorable attitude toward law, legal institutions, and officials than the laborers [96]. The attitude of the prison guards was more favorable than that of the laborers, and the attitude of the police officers was the most favorable. The same attitudinal gradient was found to exist in the administration of the same schedule of "law items" to similar samples in Ohio, Ontario, Quebec, Rome, Athens, West Pakistan, and South Korea. The study concluded that the gradient that exists between laborers in free society and inmates of prison results from a differential internalization of life experiences concerned with involvement and noninvolvement in delinquency and crime and prison experience.

It is logical that many of the more developed countries are seeking alternatives to imprisonment, and such programs have great implications for the developing countries in which penal facilities are greatly overburdened and in which alternatives such as probation and institutional treatment in the community would be much less costly. The wider use of probation offers one of the most logical alternatives to imprisonment, yet in less developed countries it is largely unavailable and in relation to prison expansion has not been adopted despite the fact that it is not only less costly but in the long run might prevent much recidivism; for example, "on the whole the use of probation has not expanded in Uganda, relative to the increase in the activities of the rest of the social defence system, despite an absolute overall increase, approximately doubling the caseload" [97]. Clifford has suggested that some imaginative planning might make it possible for developing countries to adapt prisons and penal systems to their existing social realities.

Well-respected loyalties and values can often be exploited in the training for penal reform and crime prevention, once one breaks away from the idea that the only approach is that which has been adopted by developed countries. In Africa, for instance, the importance of compensation being paid to the victims of offenses can be made the objective for certain types of prison labour or extramural work. Development schemes and a variety of cooperatives can be adapted to give creative interests to offenders who might otherwise be held unproductively behind high walls. A more adaptable form of probation might be devised by training traditional chiefs to supervise the young in accordance with an appropriate statute. New forms of adoption and foster care might possibly be conceived to bring traditional family life more forcefully into the struggle with juvenile crime. Ordinary schools might be adapted to cope with special behavior problems. . . . The scope for open camp prisons is immense in developing areas, and agricultural settlements may well serve the economy and avert much recidivism, if properly adapted to serve the needs of offenders [98].

Several community-based types of facilities offer possibilities. Probation hostels or living centers for probationers would enable offenders to work or attend school during the day rather than being confined in prison. They would return to the center at night or on weekends and remain under supervision of a correctional worker. Work release programs of various kinds offer other possibilities for reformation. This approach combines an institutional program with participation in free society during the day, a significant factor, since nearly all offenders sooner or later return to free society, most of them after less than five years. In work release programs they associate with noncriminals rather than with other offenders in prisons and jails. It is theorized that the noncriminals with whom he works may have a positive effect in changing his attitudes and his criminal self-conception and help to remove him from his former criminal associates. These programs generally provide for payment of regular wages, with deductions for food, clothing, travel, contributions to supporting dependents, and payment of obligations.

Other programs provide release from institutions to "halfway houses," some run by government and others by private agencies, in which a period of residential treatment, supervision, and assistance is provided while the offender works or attends school outside [99]. Still another program is the "community treatment center," a daytime institution; where offenders can live at home, perhaps have a job or go to school, and attend the center daily for intensive rehabilitation. Probation offers another practical solution, for it permits each convicted person to participate in society. Well-supervised probation appears to be far more effective than prison treatment in preventing further crime [100]. In addition, a probationer can support his family and can even make payments for any reparation or restitution the victim requires.

It is often argued by those in the less developed countries that their situations are different and their treatment methods therefore must be different. It is claimed that the use of work release and similar methods in societies which have extensive unemployment and poverty does not seem logical to the general population. Moreover, many believe that punitive measures must be even harsher and that the various alternatives to prison or capital punishment would deter neither the offender nor others who might be contemplating commission of a crime. This assumption, however, is not supported by research data in developing countries. At least, there is some evidence that even when prison conditions are severe crime has continued to increase. In those countries in which the death penalty and long prison sentences have been instituted for armed robbery there seems to have been no diminution. During 1971 when Nigeria publicly executed more than 40 persons for armed robbery, four of them at one time in Ibadan before thousands of spectators, Nigeria continued to have an extremely serious armed robbery problem in 1972.

Studies conducted in developed countries cast great doubt on the deterrent value of severe sentences, particularly imprisonment [101]. Deterrence depends primarily on an appraisal of one's chances of being apprehended, and in most developing countries this chance is not great. It also depends on whether the person is oriented in terms of plans for the future or whether he is present-oriented, a characteristic of most lower class persons. It also depends a great deal on age. Youths do not give it much consideration, particularly if they belong to groups or gangs. The threat of punishment seems to have a markedly low effect when the crime is an outgrowth of an emotional argument or a dispute which may result in homicide or serious assault. Deterrence is also minimal when the illegal behavior has widespread support. We shall have to wait until later to see if similar findings apply to less developed countries. It would be a serious mistake, in criminal-law administration programs, to assume that they do not.

NOTES AND REFERENCES

1. See Albert J. Reiss, Jr., *The Police and the Public* (Princeton: Princeton University Press, 1971); Michael P. Banton, *The Policeman in the Community* (London: Tavistock, 1964); David J. Bordua, Ed., *The Police: Six Sociological Essays* (New York: Wiley, 1967); Wayne R. LaFave, *Arrest: The Decision to Take a Suspect Into Custody* (Boston: Little, Brown, 1965); and Jerome Skolnick, *Justice Without Trial: Law Enforcement in Democratic Society* (New York: Wiley, 1966).

2. David H. Bayley, *The Police and Political Development in India* (Princeton: Princeton University Press, 1969). For a discussion of the history and organization in most of the countries of the world see James Cramer, *The World's Police* (London: Cassell, 1964).

3. Bayley, *The Police and Political Development in India*, p. 422. Reprinted by permission of Princeton University Press. For an account of the situation in Nigeria see T. N. Tamuno, *The Police in Modern Nigeria* (Ibadan: Ibadan University Press, 1970).

4. Christian P. Potholm, "The Multiple Roles of the Police as Seen in the African Context," *The Journal of Developing Areas*, **3**:141 (January 1969).

5. Bayley, *The Police and Political Development in India*, p. 240. Reprinted by permission of Princeton University Press.

6. Cyprian O. Okonkwo, *The Police and the Public in Nigeria* (Lagos: African Universities Press, 1966), p. v.

7. "How Good is Your Police/Public Relation," *The Nigeria Police Magazine*, December 1962, p. 27, as quoted in Okonkwo, p. 31. For the later study see Tamuno, *The Police in Modern Nigeria*, p. 260.

8. Potholm, "The Multiple Roles of the Police as Seen in the African Context," p. 145.

9. Potholm, "The Multiple Roles of the Police as Seen in the African Context," p. 151. A report on East Pakistan [now Bangladesh] pointed out that the disproportionately slow growth of the police force had been adding to crime, thus compounding the problems developing from industrialization, urbanization, and accelerated social change. See A. K. Nazmul Karin, "Crime in East Pakistan since 1947," *International Review of Criminal Policy*, 18:52 (October 1960).

10. "Off-Beat Jobs Sap Police Strength," *Indian Statesman*, March 10, 1960.

11. Chung-Hyun Ro, "Seoul," in Aprodicio A Laquian, Ed., *Rural Urban Migrants and Metropolitan Development* (Toronto: Intermet, Metropolitan Studies Series, 1970) p. 161.

12. These surveys were conducted for Bayley and were made of rural and urban samples from South India (Bangalore and rural Mysore) and the Kanpur area in the north.

13. Bayley, *The Police and Political Development in India*, p. 204.

14. Okonkwo, *The Police and the Public in Nigeria*, p. 7.

15. Tamuno, *The Police in Modern Nigeria*, p. 266.

16. Eric Paul Kibuka, "Sociological Aspects of Juvenile Delinquency in Kampala 1962 to 1969," Ph. D. dissertation, University of East Africa, 1972, p. 732.

17. Bayley, *The Police and Political Development in India*, p. 198. Reprinted by permission of Princeton University Press. See also R. E. S. Tanner, "Some Problems of East African Crime Statistics," in Tanner, *Three Studies in East African Criminology* (Uppsala: The Scandinavian Institute of African Studies, 1970), p. 9. See also Chapter 1.

18. Bayley, *The Police and Political Development in India*, p. 416. Reprinted by permission of Princeton University Press.

19. *Ibid.*, p. 178.

20. *Ibid.*, p. 191.

21. *Ibid.*, p. 219.

22. Okonkwo, *The Police and the Public in Nigeria*, pp. 63–74.

23. Bayley, *The Police and Political Development in India*, p. 414.

24. For a discussion of specific police programs directly related to community relations, see *The Police*, Special Task Force Report, the President's Commission on Law Enforcement and Administration of Justice (Washington: U. S. Government Printing Office, 1967), pp. 149–163 and pp. 221–228.

25. Potholm, "The Multiple Roles of the Police as Seen in the African Context," p. 152.

26. Bayley, *The Police and Political Development in India*, p. 419. Reprinted by permission of Princeton University Press.

27. Alejandro Melchor, "Urbanization in the Philippines," *Conference Papers*, Rehovot Conference on Urbanization and Development in Developing Countries, Rehovot Israel, 1971.

28. United Nations Social Defence Research Institute, *Social Defence in Uganda: A Survey for Research*, Publication No. 3, Rome, Italy, 1971. The preliminary report on which this was based was prepared by Eric P. Kibuka, Lecturer in Social Administration, Makerere University, Kampala.

29. *Uganda Argus*, Kampala, Uganda, June 13, 1969; Sutherland and Cressey, *Criminology*, p. 376.

30. *Social Defence in Uganda*, pp. 43–44.

31. *Social Defence in Uganda*, p. 42.

32. *Social Defence in Uganda*, p. 45.

33. This level of education approximates graduation from grade school in the United States.

34. Kibuka, "Sociological Aspects of Juvenile Delinquency in Kampala 1962 to 1969," 1972.

35. R. E. S. Tanner, "Some Problems of East African Crime Statistics," Makerere Institute of Social Research, Kampala, Uganda, 1964, mimeographed.

36. *Uganda Argus*, Kampala, December 7, 1968.

37. *Social Defence in Uganda*, p. 26.

38. This has long been one of the means of dealing with a thief in African villages.

39. Musa T. Mushanga, "Criminal Homicide in Western Uganda," M. A. thesis, Makerere University, Kampala, Uganda, 1970.

40. "Crime a Growing Problem for Africa: Robbery is Bringing Harsh Punishment," *The New York Times*, Tuesday, July 27, 1971, p. 2-C.

41. Victor D. Du Bois, *Crime and the Treatment of the Criminal in the Ivory Coast*, [VDB-1-'68] Fieldstaff Reports, *West African Series*, 11:No.1, 7–8 (1968).

42. *Paris-Match*, August 12, 1972, pp. 22–25.

43. Bayley, *The Police and Political Development in India*, p. 411.

44. *Ibid.*, pp. 25–26. See also Potholm, "The Multiple Roles of the Police as Seen in the African Context," who points out that the police in developing countries represent the regime by assisting in the integration of the country, as modernizing agents, as channels of upward mobility, and as means of rule adjudication or adjustment of laws to the particular situations (pp. 146–147).

45. Gill H. Boehringer, "Development in Criminology in Tanzania," East African Social Science Conference, Kampala, Uganda, 1969.

46. Potholm, "The Multiple Roles of the Police as Seen in the African Context," pp. 146–147. See also Julius Nyerere, *Freedom and Unity: Uhuru Na Umoja* (London: Oxford University Press, 1967), pp. 124–125.

47. Ezra F. Vogel, "Preserving Order in the Cities," in John Wilson Lewis, Ed., *The City in Communist China* (Stanford: Stanford University Press, 1971), p. 86.

48. Cramer, *The World's Police*, pp. 404–405. See also Harold J. Berman, *Justice in the USSR* (New York: Knopf and Random House, 1963), pp. 286–288, and John N. Hazard, Isaac Shapiro, and Peter B. Maggs, *The Soviet Legal System* (Dobbs Ferry, N. Y.: Oceania Publications, 1969), rev. ed., Chapter 2.

49. *Community Preventive Action*, Working Paper of the Secretariat, Third United Nations Congress on the Prevention of Crime and the Treatment of Offenders, Stockholm, Sweden, August 9–18, 1965, p. 19.

50. Manuel López-Rey, "Crime and the Penal System," *Australian and New Zealand Journal of Criminology*, 4:17 (March 1971), and *Crime: An Analytical Appraisal* (New York: Praeger and London: Routledge & Kegan Paul Ltd., 1970), p. 236.

51. In 1972 military prisons were used extensively for various types of detainee.

52. Victor D. Du Bois, *A Visit to an African Prison*, [VDB-2-'68] Fieldstaff Reports, Vol. XI, No. 2, 7, West Africa Series, 1968.

53. Robert B. Seidman and J. D. Abaka Eyison, "Ghana," in Alan Milner, Ed., *African Penal Systems* (London: Routledge & Kegan Paul Ltd. and New York: Praeger, 1969), p. 76.

54. *Ibid.*, p. 83.

55. *Laurel Report on Penal Reforms*, Report on the Philippine Penal Institutions and Penology, Senator Salvador H. Laurel, Chairman, Senate Committee on Justice, 1969, quoted from pp. 265–267. In one escape attempt in 1971, 14 inmates were killed and six were killed in another. In 1970 riots on death row, where more than 400 were confined, resulted in the deaths of scores of prisoners.

56. López-Rey, *Crime*, pp. 89–97. Although López-Rey also deals with developed countries, Conrad has emphasized them in his comparative study of correctional practices in the United States, the United Kingdom, France, the Netherlands, Scandinavia, and the USSR. See John P. Conrad, *Crime and Its Correction: An International Survey of Attitudes and Practices* (Berkeley: University of California Press, 1970).

57. T. O. Elias, "Traditional Forms of Public Participation in Social Defence," *International Review of Criminal Policy*, 27:18 (1969).

58. See, for example, Vidya Bhushan, *Prison Administration in India* (New Delhi: S. Chand, 1970): see also the detailed description of Uganda prisons in *Social Defence in Uganda*, pp. 53–76.

59. *Social Defence in Uganda*, pp. 72–73.

60. Du Bois, *A Visit to an African Prison*, p. 11.

61. M. R. Nyamka, "Various Aspects of the Prison System in Tanzania—Problems and Prospects," *Social Defence*, 4:29–39 (1968).

62. Alan Milner, "M'Naghten and the Witchdoctor: Psychiatry and Crime in Africa," *University of Pennsylvania Law Review*, 114:1134–1169 (1966). See also Alan Milner and Tolani Asuni, "Psychiatry and the Criminal Offender in Africa," in Milner, *African Penal Systems*, pp. 317–364.

63. López-Rey, *Crime*, pp. 89–90.

64. *Ibid.*

65. R. M. Marsh, "A Mexican Prison," *Judicature*, 5:325–326 (1971).

66. Seidman and Eyison, "Ghana," in Milner, *African Penal Systems*, p. 83.

67. López-Rey, *Crime*, p. 89.

68. *Ibid.*, p. 93.

69. *Ibid.*, p. 69.

70. *Ibid.*, p. 68.

71. United Nations, *Social Forces and the Prevention of Criminality*, working paper prepared by the Secretariat, United Nations, Third Congress on the Prevention of Crime and the Treatment of Offenders, Stockholm, Sweden, August 9–18, 1965, p. 11. See also Berman, *Justice in the USSR*, 1963, and Hazard, Shapiro, and Maggs, *The Soviet Legal System*, 1969.

72. *Laurel Report on Penal Reforms,* p. 266.

73. DuBois, *A Visit to an African Prison,* pp. 5–6.

74. *Social Defence in Uganda,* pp. 60–61. See also the comments on emphasis on vocational training in Uganda prisons in Chapter 8.

75. R. E. S. Tanner, *An East African Prison* (Uppsala, Sweden: The Scandinavian Institute of African Studies, 1970), and Tanner, "The East African Experience of Imprisonment," in Milner, *African Penal Systems,* p. 299.

76. Tanner, *An East African Prison,* pp. 142–147.

77. Tanner, "The East African Experience of Imprisonment," in Milner, *African Penal Systems,* p. 301.

78. Tanner, *An East African Prison,* p. 128.

79. Tanner, "The East African Experience of Imprisonment," in Milner, *African Penal Systems,* p. 311.

80. *Ibid.,* p. 306.

81. Tanner, *An East African Prison,* p. 349. Here Tanner did make exceptions in some Arab, Afro-Arab, and Somali communities.

82. *Ibid.,* p. 126.

83. Tanner, "The East African Experience of Imprisonment," in Milner, *African Penal Systems,* p. 314.

84. Christopher Harwich, *Red Dust: Memories of the Uganda Police, 1935–1955* (London: V. Stuart, 1961), p. 145.

85. James S. Read, "Kenya, Tanzania and Uganda," in Milner, *African Penal Systems,* p. 145.

86. Tanner ,"The East African Experience of Imprisonment," in Milner, *African Penal Systems.*

87. William Clifford, "The African View of Crime," *The British Journal of Criminology,* 4(5):483 (July 1964).

88. Tanner, "The East African Experience of Imprisonment," in Milner, *African Penal Systems.*

89. *Ibid.,* p. 300.

90. Edwin M. Lemert, *Human Deviance, Social Problems, and Social Control* (Englewood Cliffs, N. J.: Prentice Hall, 1967), pp. 40–60.

91. A subject in the Kampala study made the following comment about persons who steal: "They never accept that they are thieves when they are caught but only when they come back from prison do they feel they are thieves."

92. Ibrahim bin Haji Mohamed, "The Need for a Central Agency for Better Coordination against Agencies and to Promote Sound Policies for the Prevention of Crime and the Treatment of Offenders with Reference to Malaysia," Fourth United Nations Congress on the Prevention of Crime and the Treatment of Offenders, Kyoto, Japan, 1970.

93. Seidman and Eyison, "Ghana," in Milner, *African Penal Systems.* See also DuBois, "A Visit to an African Prison."

94. "La Suspension del Proceso y de la Pena en Venezuela," Ministerior de Justicia, Dirrecion de Prisiones, Caracas, Venezuela, 1971.

95. William Clifford, *Profiles in Crime* (Lusaka, Zambia: Government Printer, 1964).

96. Jaime Toro-Calder, Ceferina Cedeno, and Walter C. Reckless, " A Comparative Study of Puerto Rican Attitudes Toward the Legal System Dealing with Crime," *The Journal of Criminal Law, Criminology and Police Science*, 59:536–541 (1968).

97. *Social Defence in Uganda*, p. 89.

98. William Clifford, "Training for Crime Control in the Context of National Development," *International Review of Criminal Policy*, 24:14 (1966).

99. Arthur Pearl, "The Halfway House: The Focal Point of a Model Program for the Rehabilitation of Low Income Offenders," in Frank Riessman, Jerome Cohen, and Arthur Pearl, Eds., *Mental Health for the Poor* (New York: The Free Press, 1964), pp. 497–508.

100. See page 00. For a discussion of the subject of probation and other noninstitutional measures with particular reference to developing countries, see the reports on the subject published by the United Nations.

101. Franklin E. Zimring, *Perspectives on Deterrence*, A Monograph Series in Crime and Delinquency Issues published by the National Institute of Mental Health Center for Studies of Crime and Delinquency, United States Public Health Service Publication No. 2056, January 1971.

Chapter 9 The Prevention and Control of Crime in Developing Countries

In this comparative criminological study available data about crime in developing countries have been analyzed in terms of several important frames of reference, all of which are significant in any explanation of criminal behavior in the developed countries: urbanization, slums, differential association, and differential opportunity. Some conclusions have been reached about the applicability of these frames of reference to the less developed countries and the nature of crime. Before analyzing the significance of this problem in terms of programs of controlling and preventing crime in these countries, it is important to summarize some of the findings on which any program of criminal policy must be based.

Among the many general aspects of the developmental process, which encompasses the combined effects of urbanization and industrialization, migration and the resultant growth of slums, increased availability of consumer goods, and the extensive changes in normative standards of behavior, a sharp increase in property crime in nearly all the less developed countries is most prominent. The almost unanimous findings, despite some uncertainties surrounding statistical reports gathered from the developing countries, support the generalization that crime, particularly property crime, is rapidly increasing and becoming one of the major problems of the developmental process. The current crime rates of most of these countries are rising more rapidly than those of the developed countries. Although not increasing rapidly in absolute numbers, the rates of increase are more acute at this point of development in those very countries that have had previously rather low rates typical of most traditional societies.

Because of the increase in crime in developing countries, urgently needed developmental resources must be diverted to crime control. Additional manpower, transportation, special equipment, and buildings must be provided for police, courts, and prisons. In some instances street lighting is being improved, largely to guarantee more adequate security. Perhaps of even greater importance is the fear generated for the security of persons and property, a situation that had not been anticipated as a concomitant of independence.

Until now the rather sharp increases in crime in the less developed countries have been misleading because they are limited to that comparatively small proportion of the population in the cities where crime is concentrated. The dominant feature of the developing world is the accelerated rate of urbanization; characteristic village life is rapidly replaced by urban living patterns. Not only are the urban areas growing at a rate two to three times the rate of population growth, but population expansion in the developing countries gives them a greater potential for urbanization. Urbanization in the less developed countries today is proceeding much more rapidly than it did in the developed countries and the circumstances surrounding it differ distinctly; the tendency is to concentrate in large primate cities. Urbanization in the Third World represents, first of all, a generally high birth rate, a marked drop in the death rate, and an increasing and unprecedented expansion of Western education and culture into the most remote rural areas. The burgeoning rural populations force the young to seek alternate means of existence in urban areas, and the cities themselves draw many of them because of the fuller life they offer.

A series of factors combines to aggravate the crime problem in the developing countries. Vital resources for the drive toward sustained economic growth become concentrated in the primate cities, and once this process has been initiated investment naturally follows. The forces of modernization therefore control population movements and maximize the criminogenic effects of urbanization. In addition, the urban way of life in the developed countries characterizes the present situation in many primate cities of the developing world—heterogeneity, anonymity, rapid social change, competitiveness, emphasis on material goods, and individualism. Although small enclaves remain in which people carry on some of their traditional ways, they are constantly being exposed to the larger urban world. The heterogeneity and density of the city force people into slum neighborhoods with which they have little affinity or basis of understanding. The lack of intimate ties, plus the protective cover of impersonality and anonymity, radically reduces both internal and external control of criminal behavior. The city offers greater opportunities for theft and greater possibilities of collaboration with other offenders and with "fences" for the disposal of stolen goods. Urban areas generate the motivation, rationalization, skill, and low risk of detection.

The migrant is faced with the difficult choice of accepting the urban way of life or attempting to recreate some semblance of a traditional life style in an unfamiliar setting. Although the sense of community, self-importance, and belonging is often weakened or lost in migration, the impact of drastic changes in social environment can be mitigated by contact with settled relatives or friends in the urban area. As they, in turn, however, have become affected by the anonymity of the city, this help tends to decline. New social alignments based on urban criteria of status and importance emerge. Many migrants choose the alternative of a short-term commitment to the city and even return to their villages if and when their economic goals are fulfilled. For those who stay on there are many impediments. Work is hard to find and may involve a frustrating and fruitless search of many months, during which time all needs must be met with cash money. At the same time the migrant is exposed to contrasts in life style unparalleled in the village. Ultimately many of them are drawn into some type of criminal activity.

Since not all migrants nor all urbanites commit crimes, this study has attempted to isolate and understand the backgrounds of those who were more likely to commit them. The analyses proceeded on two levels, first, the factors on the individual level and, second, the factors that affect crime rates in different urban communities. It is only by understanding the problem of criminality on both levels that realistic suggestions for crime prevention and control can, hopefully, be formulated.

What clearly emerged as a dominant factor in the background of the Kampala offender, compared with the nonoffender, was the comparative absence of experiences and supportive agents that could prepare him for urban life. The offender more often had only village life as a frame of reference before arriving in Kampala. When he did make his way to the city, he seldom had relatives or friends to offer him food and shelter and to guide him in his adaptation to city life. Furthermore, even when the offender did have relatives there, he tended to avoid them and to a much greater extent found close friendships outside his own tribal group. The offender was somewhat of a paradox, for he did maintain his connections with his village kin and he often owned land there. The offender thus seemed to be a person who maintained his village identification but who failed to form social ties that would enable him to make a successful adjustment to this new style of urban living.

As in the developed countries, the slum is the main focus of crime in the developing countries. Crime is committed by its residents and most of it occurs within its confines. Not all slums have high crime rates, however. Factors such as physical conditions, socioeconomic status, or population stability do not distinguish between slum communities with high and low crime rates. The low crime rate community appears to have a much higher degree of unity, expressed by a higher incidence of visiting, participation in local organizations, restricted friendship patterns, and stability in family relationships. By cultural homogeneity and strong emphasis on tribal and kin ties members of the low crime community manage to evade the heterogeneity, impersonality, and anonymity that prevailed in areas of high crime. The predominance of primary bonds in a neighborhood reduced the propensity to steal from a neighbor and made the unnoticed entrance of a stranger less likely. Older persons demonstrated a critical capacity to maintain the unity of the population and helped to enforce compliance to community rules.

Modernization also has a great impact on criminal behavior in less developed countries, some forms being more, others less, common than in the rest of the world. Property crime, which makes up nearly all crime in any city in all countries, increases sharply because of a marked decline in informal social controls, greater opportunities for theft, and the rising prestige of material possessions, however small, as status symbols. Since even the simplest object, such as a used shirt, a light bulb, or a piece of iron pipe, represents a desirable increment in wealth, the potential market for stolen goods is much greater than in almost any developed country. Also the opportunities for theft are greater because of the difficulties of protecting property and the absence of security measures. Special markets, usually regarded as regular establishments, are often readily available in the cities for the disposal of stolen goods.

As a country develops robbery with violence and the threat of violence increases. In the developing countries armed attacks, which represent a growing problem in isolated nonurban areas, are made on homes, motor vehicles, and buses on the highways, and the spread of industrial, banking, and business enterprises requires the transportation of large sums of money, usually with few guards. The increase in robbery is due in part to the training acquired among growing prison populations, since more and more offenders are being taught sophisticated criminal techniques in their willingness to resort to force.

Auto theft in general occurs less frequently in developing countries because of the scarcity of automobiles and the inability of many persons to operate them. More frequent is the theft of parts and accessories for which there is a ready resale market, particularly when import restrictions are heavy. Those who do steal automobiles, however, usually have a fairly high level of sophistication, having learned how to elude alarm systems, trigger steering column locks, and evade private guards. Theft for the sole purpose of a short ride is much less common, as is vandalism by youth. As these countries become more highly developed, however, such offenses will undoubtedly increase. Also increasing in number and significance will be such offenses as check forgery, embezzlement, and the use of stolen credit cards.

Certain offenses, such as the use of children for illegal purposes, are more common in the developing countries. Theft by servants is also a common offense, since the availability of cheap manpower enables even persons of quite modest means to hire them. When the victim is a commercial employer, it is impossible to say whether employees steal more in the developed or the less developed countries. Other offenses that may be more frequent in the less developed countries are food adulteration, cattle theft, begging, certain political offenses, black marketeering in money, rioting over food shortages, village disputes, and political grievance protests. Most of them can be expected to show decreased rates with increased development, although the record of some more highly developed countries in the sphere of political crimes has not been good.

Many developing countries report much higher rates of violent crime, such as homicide and assault, than the developed. When the probable high degree of under-reporting in less developed countries is considered, the gap may be even greater. Violence is generally a subcultural phenomenon associated with specific cultural factors in its use to settle disputes, as, for example, the emphasis on "machismo" in Latin America or certain African tribal definitions. As in the developed countries, the most frequent offender tends to be a young male in his twenties. Again, as in developed countries, the evidence indicates that violent acts generally originate in disputes between relatives, friends, and acquaintances. Prostitution is probably less common in the developing countries largely because it is an urban phenomenon and they are still predominantly rural. In the cities, on the other hand, it is often greater because of the abnormal sex distribution in many of them and the scarcity of economic opportunities for unattached women, which leads them into some sort of temporary sexual relationship or prostitution. The modal characteristics of prostitutes in these countries vary by marital status and in the motivations for entering this occupation, although most of them are migrants from rural areas. The status of the prostitute in the cities probably carries less stigma and is more open and less organized than it is in the more developed countries.

Corruption in business and government appears to increase as a country becomes modernized, being most prevalent in the intense phases of industrialization. It is generally agreed that corruption of government officials is an acute problem in most countries of Asia, Latin America, and Africa and that many persons and their families have amassed large fortunes by holding political office. Common forms of crime by businessmen

in developing countries include the violation of income tax laws and import, export, and currency control regulations and embezzlement. An
elaborate system of kickbacks often accompanies every phase of governmental activity, including even small purchases by government agencies,
and graft is associated with the granting of licenses and privileges of all
types. The extensiveness of corruption grows out of nepotism, for the
transition from a traditional to a rapidly modernizing industrial society
has not yet resulted in the transfer of village loyalties to a serious dedica-
tion to an emerging nation. Corruption of officials in high places frequently comes from the industrial and commercial classes who seek special
privileges.

Numerous studies indicate the importance of companions and gang
membership in the promotion of criminal behavior in cities of developed
countries. Crime also appears to be transmitted and committed by groups
in developing countries, although these groups vary by organization, size,
and nature of their behavior. Gangs and other criminal groups furnish
an alternate source of support in place of family units which are often
severely disrupted by the effects of urbanization. In the Kampala study
the offenders reported closer friendships with persons who had been in
trouble with the police. Their attitudes and activities reflected their asso-
ciative patterns. They were essentially more isolated from experiences
that might negatively define criminal behavior, but at the same time had
greater contacts and activities that would be more likely to reinforce
these patterns.

IMPLICATIONS OF EXPERIENCES OF DEVELOPED COUNTRIES

Most Western European countries, as well as the United States and
Japan, have serious crime problems: even a highly affluent and socially
progressive country like Sweden has trouble of this nature. The picture
presented to the planners of developing countries who, hypothetically,
must expect more crime to accompany urbanization, an increase in productivity and per capita income, and literacy, is a discouraging one.
Because of the rapidity of urbanization, with sudden shifting from the
traditional to the modern, it is quite possible that crime and delinquency
may present more acute problems in the developing countries than in the
developed countries. They may even become greater. Yet this situation
may not, and need not, be so discouraging as it may seem. The high crime
rates of developed countries are products of almost no long-term planning in the area of crime control. The situation in most countries has
gradually become worse, and little in the past has been done to correct it,

mainly because of inadequate knowledge of the cause of crime or of measures, other than punitive ones, to deal with it.

Persons from developing countries often fail to realize that extensive and rapidly rising crime rates, general poverty, rural living, extensive migration of young males to the cities, and the growth of slums, all were characteristic of the developed countries 75 to 125 years ago. In England and France, for example, the failure of their economic and social systems in the nineteenth century to adjust rapidly to the great increase in city population was related to the increase in crime at that time. There had been much internal migration in the first half of the nineteenth century, towns were growing rapidly, and the people lived in a world of flux. Most criminals resided in certain slum areas, were under 20 years of age, and engaged in criminal activities either in casual groups or in organized youth gangs. In the early period of industrialization, up through the 1850's, older criminals made use of children in their crimes.

Indeed, if we are to look for a parallel in the field of crime with the England of the first 60 years of the nineteenth century, it is not to the England of the twentieth century that we should look, but to those countries that are today undergoing the experience of industrialisation and urbanisation. . . . The people of nineteenth-century England, like the people of many parts of Africa and Asia today, were not only building physical assets for their descendants. They were, slowly and painfully and at no small price, developing a new way of life. They were learning to live in an urban, industrialised society [1].

The rapid changes in urbanization and industrialization in England had great impact on the original residents of the towns and on the young migrants. The increase in urban population brought about changes that directly or indirectly affected everyone in the large cities. The young unmarried migrants who lived in lodging houses were particularly exposed to criminal and other deviant influences, but the social atmosphere of the large cities had potentialities for deviance for most youths. Since many of these people were poor, it was assumed by many that poverty made them criminals. A careful study of crime in nineteenth century England concluded, however, that the crime rate of that day, particularly in the urban areas, was not to an important extent a consequence of their poverty nor in the sense of the immediate pressures of need. "It was not usually poverty that governed the operations of the criminal class, and the adult honest poor did not, as a general rule, turn to crime, however straightened their circumstances" [2].

Perhaps it is because there has been a lack of consensus about what causes crime that the developed countries on the whole have not been successful in dealing with it. Many omissions and mistakes in crime control have been made over the last century or more. A lack of adequate criminological theory for effective planning has accounted for some of these problems, as it does today in those countries in similar stages of development. These errors have not only resulted in the growth of extensive and sophisticated criminal behavior patterns, which are transmitted to each new generation, but they have been extremely costly; for example, much effort and money has been wasted in the developed countries on their individualistic approaches of personal maladjustment that requires the use of expensive psychological and psychiatric treatment facilities. Although this approach has been shown to be invalid and the treatment largely unproductive, it continues to be proposed as a sound program by some in the field. On the other hand, only recently has the importance of slum living to crime and of the police in their relations to the public been more thoroughly recognized. The use of severe prison sentences to deal with crime is only now being seriously questioned in overall crime programs. Capital punishment, widely employed from time immemorial, has been almost completely discredited as an effective method of controlling crime.

William Clifford, a well-known United Nations expert who has worked in various attempts to control crime in a number of developing countries, has pointed out some of the basic fallacies underlying many current programs in crime control in developed countries:

> It is assumed, for example, that raising living standards, increasing income, eliminating unemployment, providing social welfare services, improving housing and offering medical or psychiatric services, where necessary, will reduce crime—or, at least, will prevent the commission of more crimes. As yet, however, there is little proof of this. Not only does the training for these services lack validation, the services themselves have not yet fully established their effectiveness in crime prevention. As an example, affluent societies seem to have more crime rather than less; the spread of education has been accompanied, as a rule, by an increase in delinquency. As for treatment doubts have been cast on the effectiveness of social work. However, none of this is really conclusive yet and these measures may be preventing more crime than is known. Nevertheless, such reports encourage a healthy skepticism about preventive or treatment measures popularly thought to be effective [3].

All effective social defense measures in the long run must be predicated on a valid theory of human behavior. Without it, one can hardly suggest what specific social defense measures should accomplish in the prevention and treatment of crime and delinquency. Extensive worldwide evidence now exists to support the position that criminal behavior involves the learning of norms in the same manner as noncriminal behavior is learned. Criminal norms are acquired primarily by group association and participation in deviant subcultures, such as those existing in the slums, in youth gangs, and in certain occupations. When criminal behavior becomes more developed, that is, moves from primary to secondary deviation, persons acquire more distinct social roles, self-conceptions, and rationalizations and participate in wider deviant subcultures. Within this theoretical framework we can understand why crime is much more likely to occur among young urban slum-resident males. Basically, crime is related to social and group factors, and this fact is extremely important and highly relevant in national development planning for the area of social defense.

These modern concepts, along with the previous failure to curb or prevent crime, and the adoption of some measures, such as improvements in police administration, better education, and better municipal administration, as in some Western European countries and the United States, should enable any kind of society to plan more effectively for crime control. Still, city growth has been left largely to chance, and the social consequences of migration, particularly on the young have not been entirely anticipated. Today developing countries should be able to foresee more adequately and to plan for the problems associated with migration and urbanization. The recognition that crime, for example, is primarily a problem of the young in all countries may make it possible for the developing countries to do a number of things. The United Nations has stated that crime prevention depends largely on the adoption of an adequate and comprehensive policy for a nation's youth. This is truer, they state, for countries in which more than half the population is in the young age range. The participation of youth can provide development planning and its implementation with the drive and dynamic quality that will more adequately ensure the success of the plan and is the greatest promise for crime prevention [4]. The young can be more effectively incorporated into decision-making bodies. In the United States and in Great Britain, for example, the voting age has recently been lowered to eighteen, and in the United States several states have lowered the age of responsibility to eighteen. Theoretically such approaches to youth will promote a greater interest in national development and engender wider compliance with the law. Some countries, such as Tanzania, have initiated national service programs for youths, and similar programs are integral parts of the government of the People's Republic of China.

PLANNING FOR CRIME CONTROL

The United Nations list of indicators of socioeconomic development throughout the world shows an association of this development with improved health, better working conditions, and broader educational facilities. Although this list does not include crime in its index of development, it might not be amiss to state, as does López-Rey, that crime is also a reasonable indicator of a good standard of living [5]. If a country were, for example, to claim to have no crime problem, it could well be assumed to have had little socioeconomic development. Norval Morris, who was at one time director of the United Nations Institute for Asia, which dealt with the prevention and treatment of crime, was frequently asked by relatively underdeveloped Asian countries with little crime and delinquency but with rising rates what they should do to stop this trend. His answer, although admittedly facetious, had much truth:

He urged them to ensure that their people remained ignorant, bigoted, and ill-educated; that on no account should they develop substantial industries; that communications systems should be primitive; and that their transportation systems should be such as to ensure that most of the citizens lived within their own small, isolated villages for their entire lives. He stressed the importance of making sure their educational systems did not promise a potential level of achievement for a·child beyond that which his father had already achieved. If it was once suggested that a child should be able to grow to the limit of his capacity rather than to the ceiling of his father's achievement, he pointed out, the seeds of the gravest disorder would be laid. He stressed the universal human experience that village societies are entirely capable of maintaining any discordance or human nonconformity within their own social frameworks and never need to call on centralized authority to solve their problems. He would take time to sketch, with a wealth of detail, the horrors of increased delinquency and crime that would flow from any serious attempt to industrialize, urbanize, or educate their communities. He would conclude with a peroration against the establishment of an international airline [6].

In a sense, therefore, developing countries face a dilemma. On the one hand, they must plan for development and, on the other, they must recognize that the price for such development will probably be a marked increase in crime. A partial solution, or mitigation, of the problem is to include criminal policy in overall developmental planning and to foresee crime control measures at least 5 to 10 years in advance. United Nations reports have pointed out that social defense planning, that is, the entire range of crime control, must be an essential part of planning for national development. The planner must know how "to deal effectively with the various aspects of development so as to achieve economic growth and higher levels of living, while at the same time preventing crime or containing it within limits acceptable to the society" [7]. Most developing countries, unfortunately, relegate crime control planning to a secondary place because of the widespread and erroneous belief that by improving general socioeconomic conditions crime will automatically be eliminated.

López-Rey has stated that the "wishful thinking of some governments has already led them to regard criminal policy as having no substantive character of its own and crime as a problem which will almost automatically be solved by socio-economic development or planning" [8]. He notes that this mistake has been made in the past by most of the developed countries and that they are still paying a heavy price for it. Even with successful socioeconomic development ordinary crime in these developing countries will not necessarily be reduced, and, in addition, development brings with it new types of crime.

It is understandable that because of the limited financial resources available to most less developed countries pressures are exceedingly great to develop industries, agriculture, education, housing, and health facilities. The position is often adopted that crime control measures can wait until the country is sufficiently prosperous to afford them. It may then be almost too late, and certainly costly, if the experiences in developed countries today are any indication of the trend. Their choice of priorities can be understood, however, since it has been repeatedly pointed out in numerous United Nations reports that crime can be controlled by greater economic and educational development, better housing, and improved health, nutrition, and child-care services. Although it is true that socio-economic development results in many significant improvements in the life of a society, such as increased life expectancy, better health and nutrition, and better educational opportunities, we cannot assume that this kind of improvement also leads to less crime. If a crime-control program is approached from a multiple factor point of view, with as many facets of government as possible involved, the proper emphasis on crime control can be missed. To propose to do everything is to confuse the issue and the result will be an ineffective program. On the other hand, in certain slums of large cities in which criminal peer groups have grown up and in which stolen goods can be easily disposed of, specific programs can be instituted to do something about particular situations, as in the case of better police, social defense manpower training, and improved court procedures [9].

Less developed countries must, of necessity, evaluate programs and look into the costs and benefits that may accrue from the adoption of various crime-control measures [10]. The use of valuable productive resources to deal with crime must be made on a realistic basis in relation to total expenditures in order to promote more effective development with less crime. One United Nations report concluded that a key problem in delinquency control is to ascertain patterns or systems of preventive action and to determine at what points the chances are the greatest that the intervention will be effective and beneficial; for example, it might be best to make the risk of arrest more certain by providing additional manpower, transportation, equipment and buildings for police, courts, and prisons. In other instances, additional street lighting might be more effective than an increase in the number of police officers [11].

More adequate planning of crime control may take two directions. A country can start by increasing its current expenditures and by making more effective use of its funds. It can adopt the wider perspectives of an economic and social planner and develop newer and more comprehensive schemes. In any country, developed or developing, social control measures operate chiefly to maintain some degree of containment. Police, courts, and prisons, are always handicapped in both, so that only the most crucial "criminality" can be acted on with those resources allocated to them. This is particularly true of the less developed countries. Planning in crime control therefore requires the application of the concepts of cost/benefit analyses and input-output ratios. These factors involve the quantification of data on crime and on criminal justice administration [12]. To determine cost/benefit analyses systems research has been applied in the more developed countries to various problems like the national economy and air traffic control and is now being proposed for the criminal justice systems of police, courts, and correction agencies.

The essence of this technique is to construct a mathematical description or model of the system in the light of which it is possible to conduct simulated experiments which may indicate how the real life system may be better organized and operated. This sort of experimentation by the manipulation of models is particularly appropriate in the criminal justice area, where intervention in the complex of actual operations is often impractical. Unfortunately at present much of the data required for a complete analysis is not available. But once the necessary information is obtained—and modern information technology makes this possible—it will be possible to estimate both the costs of present operations and the consequences and possible benefits of any proposed changes in the system [13].

It is unrealistic, however, to expect that development programs in general should be designed to serve solely the cause of crime and delinquency prevention. We cannot use the possibility of crime as a negative yardstick with which to evaluate the transformation of old social institutions and the creation of new ones. Development programs in industrialization and detribalization may be urgently needed for economic growth. A United Nations report states the following:

The process of development is thus liable to generate as many potentially criminogenic situations as it succeeds in eliminating. Crime may sometimes be accepted as a social cost, i.e., the price a country may have to pay for social change and economic growth; the problem is to minimize this cost, if it cannot be eliminated altogether [14].

Morris and Hawkins have this to say:

In this sense juvenile delinquency and crime are functional and not dysfunctional; they are, at the present level of our knowledge, costs that must be paid for other socially valuable development processes in the community [15].

CHANGES IN CRIMINAL LAW AND PROCEDURE

Greater knowledge is now available to less developed countries of programs that can increase the effectiveness of the criminal justice process. Many developing countries have inherited systems of criminal laws and procedures, as well as courts, police, and correctional systems, that fail to fit their current needs, and it is most unfortunate that the national programs of these countries seldom incorporate changes in the criminal justice system into their plans, López-Rey points out that the diversity of the population and the rapid socioeconomic changes raise questions about the adequacy of the criminal justice system. Since, he says, "this system embraces police, criminal law, criminal procedure, organization of courts, and institutional and non-institutional treatment of offenders, it should be regarded as one of the most important factors in the prevention of crime, and in the effectiveness of crime policies" [16]. Crime as a social problem cannot be reasonably reduced so long as the present criminal justice systems are not organized or reorganized in accordance with national development. This is as essential as socioeconomic planning.

By definition a criminal is a person who breaks the criminal law in which certain values whose violation precipitates a penal sanction are embodied. In most developing countries, and in many of the developed, the values that these laws have supposedly been designed to protect are seldom re-examined. In less developed countries the social order often changes so rapidly that they need to re-examine the criminal procedures as well. The penal codes which are usually abstract and largely unrelated to present and future social realities should be constantly re-examined and re-evaluated. Many of the legal codes were adopted long ago, often under colonial regimes. In India the penal code dates from 1860, for example, and revisions have been few. Although they have been amended here and there, the penal codes of Nigeria, Zambia, Malawi, Kenya, Uganda, and Tanzania are still based essentially on the Colonial Office Model Codes, the main source of which was the *Queensland Penal Codes of 1899,* and the Italian Penal Codes of 1889 which, in turn, were based largely on the Sardinian Code of 1859 and the *Penal Code of the State of New York of 1881* [17]. López-Rey wrote that he knew of no Latin American penal codes that had been based on an "appraisal of national reality," the main models having been Spain, Italy, Germany, and, indirectly, France. Most of the criminal codes on which the developing countries have based their own have had almost nothing in common with the social structure and other social conditions of the developing country; for example, beginning with the Indian Penal Code of 1860, the statutory limit for criminal responsibility is age 7 in India, yet according to Hindu tradition the age at which a child can be punished by the state is 14 and among Muslims only when he is old enough to reproduce. Consequently in India there are relatively few criminal cases brought against persons under 12.

Criminal code revisions remove certain acts from the criminal code, and criminal sanctions could be reserved for those on which there is more general consensus. Criminal codes should be reviewed to reassess their social significance. Most developing countries, for example, could follow current developments in the United States, Great Britain, and the Scandinavian countries to "decriminalize" certain offenses with respect to personal morality [18]. Recommendations have been made that criminal sanctions be removed from public drunkenness, gambling, the use of drugs, and certain sexual practices such as prostitution and homosexuality. Most of the offenses that regulate public morals seem to be out of tune with the society in the developed countries; in the developing they seem to be even more anachronistic. Many of them have found their way into African countries, for example, in colonial penal codes and in the rigid attitudes of the missionaries and their mid-Victorian personal morals which they imposed on the "natives." It has been argued that in areas in which criminal laws are obviously highly ineffective attempts to enforce them create disrespect for the police and divert police attention from the detection and prosecution of offenses such as burglary, about which there is more general consensus.

In a similar fashion the loose concept of "juvenile delinquency" in developing countries tends to cloud police work; even more, it confuses criminal statistics. If juvenile delinquency is to have any meaning, it should refer to offenses by juveniles which, if committed by an adult, would result in criminal prosecution [19]. Actually most developing countries have made more progress in this position than have developed countries like England, the United States, and Canada, which have a loose definition, as have many former British colonies. In most European and Latin American countries, as well as many in Africa, "delinquent" refers only to those who have committed a criminal offense. The 1960 United Nations Congress on the Prevention of Crime and the Treatment of Offenders recommended that the "scope of the problem of delinquency should not be inflated" and that the meaning of the term delinquency be restricted, as far as possible, "to violations of criminal law and that even for protection, specific offenses which would penalize small irregularities or maladjusted behavior of minors, but for which adults would not be prosecuted, should not be created" [20]. Other noncriminal juvenile acts would then be dealt with outside police and criminal administrative processes. There is, however, often a conflict between customary procedures and the use of formal judicial measures in dealing with juveniles. One study has pointed out that "the idea of taking suspected juveniles to court is foreign in practically all parts of Uganda and to many people it has a stigma attached to it, and a juvenile who has been to court even if not convicted will socially never be the same afterwards" [21].

Criminal code revisions could bring changes in penalties and thus, hopefully, reduce the penal severity of some and make other adjustments best suited to developing countries. They can also be contradictory. If, for example, a criminal code were to be revised in terms of realistic public opinion, the penalties might become even severer. In a representative sample of Africans in Lusaka, Zambia, it was commonly thought that offenders were treated too leniently. "Everyone thought that murderers should hang and that sentences should be longer" [22]. Moreover, adultery was regarded as a serious offense that should call for a heavy penalty not only for the man but for the woman as well [23]. Most felt that even the conditions of imprisonment should be made harsher. Such a punitive attitude is often expressed by the general public in the developed countries, but it is much more widely voiced in many developing countries.

The less developed countries are much more likely to use the death penalty, as shown in a group of replies to a survey conducted by the United Nations in 1969 [24]. Among the 22 countries that have abolished the death penalty, except for unusual circumstances in some, only eight are less developed countries and all are in Latin America—Argentina, Brazil, Colombia, Costa Rica, Ecuador, Panama, Uruguay, and Venezuela. Although many of the European countries have abolished the death penalty, and the United States has recently, (it has also been abolished in Iceland, Israel, and New Zealand), it still applies in all the countries of Africa and Asia. No country uses the death penalty more in proportion to its population than South Africa. In some less developed countries it is employed extensively, as in Iran, where during 1969–1972 the government executed more than 100 drug smugglers. In India, the land of Buddha and Gandhi, 319 were sentenced to death in 1960 and 67 were executed [25]. A comparison of those sentenced with those actually executed shows a marked decline since independence [26]. The United Nations has issued various studies of capital punishment, and in 1971 the General Assembly passed a resolution indicating "the desirability of abolishing this punishment in all countries" [27].

Nonpayment of fines can be transformed into a prison sentence in every country but the Soviet Union, and consequently this penalty has always benefited those with some financial means. In developing countries this procedure is particularly unrealistic, since the great majority of offenders are poor or unemployed. In Ceylon, for example, there has been a great increase in those sentenced to prison for default of fines—4765 in 1966–1967 and 7045 in 1967–1968. "The situation is similar in many developing countries, in spite of the improvement of material living conditions which has not as yet reduced the gap between the haves and the have-nots, and maintains discrimination in criminal justice" [28] It is doubtful, moreover, if it would solve, although it might help to solve, the nonpayment of fines. It might be done in part if an installment method of paying were devised or if the fines were calculated on a "day-fine" system according to the person's earnings. Low income and unemployment, however might still present problems.

A further difficulty is that fines and imprisonment are penalties collected by an impersonal state and thus do little to restore the damage or loss caused to the victim or the victim's family. Restitution to the victim or compensation to the victim has particular merit as a substitute for both fine and imprisonment in less developed countries [29]. This was the traditional method of settling offenses in most countries, and it still remains so in rural areas, particularly in African societies. In the present Ethiopian code, for example, restitution to the injured party is provided within the legal process [30]. One expert on African criminology has suggested not only the traditional penalties of compensation but other customary methods of extramural labor or fining the parents of juveniles [31]. Since these are the ways in which Africans have traditionally dealt with offenders, they would be understood, and provision is already made for them in the law. Provision might also be made in the future for a system of "extra-mural labor," as it is in effect in some African states, which would ensure that those without the means to pay the compensation could work on their own time to earn the needed money. This system not only has cultural foundations in the community but the added appeal of being an economic measure. In Tanzania a person sentenced to imprisonment for six months or less for the non-payment of a fine not exceeding 1000 shillings may be released for employment by a government department, or local authority, on public works which are not part of the prison labor program.

It would be a mistake to assume, however, that a great deal of traditional criminal law could be embodied in a modern criminal code. There are exceptions, as in the case of Tanzania; to prevent large-scale cattle stealing and killing among certain tribes President Nyerere adopted a policy in 1967 of rounding up sometimes as many as 4000 people at a time, the deportation of cattle thieves for resettlement outside their tribal areas, and efforts at permanent settlement of those tribes that are particularly given to cattle stealing. Although he stated his belief in criminal law and those procedures adopted from the British, he stated that an insufficient police force and the inadequacies of strict legal procedures made it imperative for him to invoke what he termed, as head of state, the traditional "law of the Chief." Likewise, Tanzania has a policy of rounding up prostitutes in urban areas and sending them back to their village homes. This probably has only a short-term effect, since many of them soon return to the cities. Boehringer has pointed to two negative unanticipated consequences. First, as a result of their being publicly labeled, they may become confirmed in the role, thus lessening the chances of their leaving it. Second, their return to the rural areas may induce others to take up this often exciting and lucrative change from a routine existence [32].

Circumstances have so drastically changed that the control of certain acts must now be vested in the state. Although people in some rural areas of Africa agree with the Ugandan migrant to Kampala who said that "it is good to steal from other people and other villages," neither a developing country as a whole nor the cities can function effectively by permitting thefts and robberies or assaults and murders. Milner has well expressed the situation in reference to the African legal system.

The demise of customary criminal law has largely meant the abandoning of those offences, procedures and sanctions which were evolved so as to be peculiarly sensitive to the local cultures. In the light of modern conditions, it is clearly right that many of them should have been abandoned: tribally oriented rules and practices which discriminate against non-members of the tribe, procedures which fail to meet international standards of fairness, and penalties which can be stigmatized as barbaric, have little place in the modern, forward-looking state. It must be remembered too that the cultures to which the customary laws were sensitive are rapidly being modified. The kinds of laws and procedures which are appropriate to resolving disputes in small, universalistic, face-to-face societies at a given economic level are not necessarily appropriate to the government of contemporary, internationally oriented nations [33].

Admittedly, much of the behavior defined as a crime, as well as the severity of the penalties attached to it, is determined by those who have the political and economic power to influence what acts are crimes and how they are to be enforced in the society. In developing societies, whether under a colonial rule or following independence, it can well be said that the greater the conflict of interests between the segments of a society the greater the probability that the power segments will formulate the criminal definition [34]. Moreover, the application or nonapplication of criminal law will vary a great deal, depending on whether the interests of those who are powerless conflict with those in power. This holds extreme significance for what and who is determined a criminal, for the severity of a penalty, and for the stereotyped conception of "the criminal." It has much bearing, too, on developing countries. Here corruption in government and business is seldom regarded as a criminal act; instead, "the criminal," as defined by law, usually turns out to be a young slum resident who is often a recent migrant. The criminality of those in high places who accept bribes, fail to pay taxes, or violate currency control regulations are generally ignored because being in power, they determine who is the criminal and what action should be taken. A Venezuelan criminologist has pointed out that the differential implementation of law according to social class is a central issue and should be studied with care, since "we know we live in a criminological reality characterized by crimes which enjoy total impunity on one side and crimes which are punished in the most arbitrary and severe form on the other side. Such legal disparity is conditioned in its greater part by the social class of the individual offender" [35]. In this sense, then, crime is sociopolitical, and probably little can be done without a change in the power structure or strenuous efforts being made to control such behavior and to equate it as criminal, as Nyerere did in Tanzania [36].

Power not only determines the definition of crime, it has much to do with the administration of justice. In Venezuela, for example, where usually more than 70% of the accused are awaiting trial, most of the prison population come from the lower economic classes. The offender experiences many delays before being brought to trial, the total time often exceeding the legal sentence imposed. Persons with sufficient power and money, on the other hand, can be released on bail until the court has decided how to dispose of their cases. Those who cannot pay bail remain in prison waiting for a sentence that may never come. In one court study in period 1965–1969, for example, two-thirds of the cases took more than three years to resolve, with the result that only 30.5% of the convicted eventually received prison sentences; 64% (mostly those with means) were never sentenced, due to stays in court proceedings. The differential attitude toward social class and crime means that in Venezuela there are two clearly defined types of crime and two ways of dealing with them; crimes committed by persons with economic means and those committed by persons with none. The first type receives no sanction at all, whereas the second is the object of the most extreme and arbitrary sanctions. A generalized belief that only the poor are criminal, whereas the rest of the population consists of "decent" people, has a real basis, since the public judges from those who go to prison. In addition, they are the persons who appear in the official statistics; for example, since crimes against the person actually represent felonious homicides and serious injuries committed in traffic accidents (not usually included in statistics as they are committed by persons with economic means), we are omitting 77.9% of all crimes against the persons committed from 1959 to 1968 in Venezuela. During this period, however, the number of deaths produced in traffic accidents was 2.5 times the number produced in other circumstances. Homicides committed in traffic are rarely sanctioned, since legal mechanisms come into play and also the argument that "there was no intention of killing or wounding such a person." On the other hand, crimes of violence committed by persons with no economic means and traditionally considered as rural offenses are severely punished. Discrimination between types of criminal as it exists in Venezuela becomes more noticeable in the treatment in the mass media, particularly the press. The press emphasizes the overt type of crime committed by the socioeconomic status of the offender [37].

López-Rey has pointed out that much of the data needed for an adequate revision of the penal codes of developing countries is not strictly legal [38]. A revised code must utilize demographic data: it must contain the population distribution by age, an estimate of the political, social, and economic structure of the country and its correlation with crime trends, a determination of the sources of wealth that need to be protected by the penal code, crime trends and projections, correlations between police, judicial, and correctional statistics, and statistics on recidivism.

CRIME STATISTICS AND POPULATION PROJECTIONS

No society can completely eliminate crime. All it can hope to do is to contain the amount of crime beyond which a country cannot operate efficiently or which causes undue concern among the people. Effective planning in crime control depends on reasonably accurate estimates of the extent and trend of the crime problem, the types of crime, and where it is concentrated. Unfortunately the criminal statistics of less developed countries are far from adequate, in some cases almost nonexistent. What is available indicates a general increase almost everywhere. This increase however, is based on minimal figures; with reasonably accurate statistics, crimes reported to the police would undoubtedly be much higher. López-Rey reports for example, that in the United Nations juvenile delinquency surveys conducted in developing and semideveloped countries he has found, often to the surprise of many authorities concerned, that the extent of "unknown crime," even though only tentatively estimated, is many times larger than the recorded crime [39]. Developing countries must establish reasonably efficient organizations to record criminal statistics and reporting must be made mandatory. The use of computers, moreover, makes possible much more rapid planning of reports, better detail, and more significant breakdowns of data.

Whenever increased measurements of crimes are foreseeable, it should be possible to anticipate and develop more effective crime prevention policies and programs. National planning demands some idea of the costs of crime so that the effects of its reduction can be calculated [40]. Much additional information is required to provide for expected criminal trends as well as types and patterns related to projected structural changes in the society. It is already possible to project, at least in broad terms, the amount and types of crime in a society five years hence by using certain assumptions of population growth, rate of urban growth, police strength, and so on. In fact, the developing countries can draw on the experiences of the developed countries to make such forecasts less speculative [41]. An interesting example of this kind of projection has been reported: a crime index is based on the ratio between the observed number of crimes each year and the number expected, assuming certain age-specific figures about the propensities to commit crimes and the actual age distribution for a given year [42].

Planning of criminal policy requires knowledge of population growth in developing countries, for the larger the population the greater the crime. Some degree of population stability, with a low net reproduction rate, has been achieved in some developed countries, whereas many developing countries have a high rate of increase that will affect the rise in crime. Such population projections are decisive in the formulation of many policies, but their role in relation to criminal policy up to the present has been modest. Although they have been used more often to project prison populations in order to ascertain the need for building new penal institutions, López-Rey points out that in the criminology of the future these projections must be used in other ways [43]. In particular, projections are needed of the proportion of male youth, since crime is closely associated with the younger age groups, and developing countries have and will continue to have large numbers of young people. One estimate, for example, is that in some African and Latin American countries the proportion of persons aged 15 to 24 in the population between 15 and 64 will be almost 38% by 1980 [44]. Another important projection for planning crime-control measures are trends in urban growth, both internally and by migration, and the potential rural reservoir for urban growth. If the United Nations estimates that the cities of Africa, for example, will increase six times in the next 30 years, we can estimate with some assurance that urban crime will increase in a similar proportion to the total population.

PREVENTING THE OCCURRENCE OF CRIME

Developed countries have had much experience that should be helpful in preventing crime in the first place. Measures of simple precaution, for example, the wider use of checks, and improved security in transporting company payrolls or large sums of currency to and from banks could prevent many crimes. Although forgery might be increased, the losses at the present time are far greater from theft of currency. Banks could be more widely used for the safety of cash funds, often kept hidden around the house, and as a safeguard for jewelry and other valuables which represent convertible wealth for rich and poor alike. Business firms need more alarm and other protective systems, and the homes of the poor need simple locks. Cities of most developing countries are also woefully deficient in street lighting.

Since widespread corruption appears to be an integral part of the development process, it is logical to suggest that all countries should provide national planning of strong measures to prevent it. An African political expert has suggested a steady but continuous effort in schools, colleges, and news media to develop negative attitudes toward corruption. This would not be the usual short, violent campaign that follows the exposure of flagrant cases of corruption but one that would continue for years [45]. Concerted efforts could be made to develop more resistance to corruptive acts among civil servants, since it is extremely difficult in a rapidly developing country to remove the opportunity. By means of educational procedures and disciplinary measures, along with increases in salaries and status, civil servants might become less vulnerable to corruption. Finally, existing and projected laws should be examined to eliminate those that tend unnecessarily to increase the opportunity for corruption. Corruption in Asia, according to Myrdal, might well be dealt with if the recommendations of the famous Santhanam Committee on corruption in India were to be followed. The report of this committee urged simpler and more precise rules and procedures for political administrative decisions that affect private persons and business enterprises and closer supervision, along with increased remuneration of low-paid civil servants to improve their sense of status and security. The main theme of their proposals was that discretionary powers should be decreased as much as possible, that agencies of vigilance, such as special police departments, be strengthened, and that the penal code and other laws and procedures should be changed to permit speedier and more effective punishment of corrupt officials. In addition, it recommended that measures be taken against private persons who corrupt public servants, that income tax reports and assessments be made public, and that the practice of declaring public documents confidential be limited. Since this committee recognized that ministers and legislators must remain above suspicion, it also proposed codes of conduct for such categories of politicians and special procedures for complaints against them. It further proposed that business concerns not be allowed to contribute to political parties and that those who make *bona fide* complaints be fully protected. On the other hand, it recommended that newspapers be prosecuted if accusations are made without supporting evidence [46]. These measures might be adapted with profit by more developed countries as well. There is another element in the prevention of corruption in developing countries: "To keep the public services pure and free from corruption it is also essential that leaders and particularly ministers do not make undue show of their economic opulence" [47]. If these leaders live in luxurious mansions, have expensive limousines, send their children to expensive schools, and indulge in extravagant living, it will tend to corrupt the civil service who will say, "Why not me?" and be tempted to try to get rich by any means including corruption [48].

CURBING THE RATE OF URBANIZATION

Christiansen has predicted, on the basis of various data, that countries in which the process of industrialization and urbanization is continuing, as it is in most if not all countries of the world, must expect further increases in crime and delinquency [49]. In most developing countries, completely uncontrolled migration to the cities, even to the primate cities, has resulted in a disruption of planned development, overurbanization, and the inability to meet the needs of these "festering" urban areas. Rather than being a "necessary" aid to economic growth, this rapid growth appears, at this point in history at least, to have decreased the general welfare of a large proportion of the people living there [50]. Hypothetically, therefore, by slowing down the rate of urbanization it should be possible to slow down the rate of crime growth. It should also correct some of the problems associated with overurbanization. Planned migration is far from simple, however, and to be really effective some kind of pass system as well as other controls over population movements that would be unpalatable and difficult, if not impossible, to enforce in most countries, would be essential. These measures would probably divert needed police from other duties. In some socialist countries such as Poland and the USSR regulation of population movements has been attempted, largely by an internal passport system and the regulation of employment, housing, and access to urban services. South Africa controls the residence and movement of the non-European population by a pass system whose violation is followed by severe penalties. These systems have meant heavy investment in governmental machinery and elaborate means of control and communication that might well be beyond the capacities of most developing nations [51]. It is virtually impossible to visualize enforced housing control in developing countries in which urban housing is often simply makeshift huts and shacks.

Since developing countries have one or at most a few major cities in which their developmental programs are concentrated, the best alternatives to continued population concentration may be a program of small-scale and cottage industries in rural areas, the development of new cities, and the decentralization of new industrial, commercial, and governmental programs to rural areas. Others advocate concentrated decentralization to, or the development of, cities of 100,000 or more on the grounds that such decentralization is more viable in attracting migrants [52]. Employment provided by these programs, if carried out on a large scale, would help to keep rural people, particularly the young, from moving to the larger urban areas. In Abidjan and elsewhere these programs have been tried, and Du Bois presents an account of the Ivory Coast's effort in this respect.

The Ivoirien government is aware of the dangers which such centralization presents: an impetus to an uncontrolled influx from the rural areas; overcrowded housing conditions; a growing number of unemployed roaming the streets; an overtaxing of such public facilities as schools, hospitals, the transportation system, etc.; and a rise in the incidence of juvenile delinquency and crime. In order to offset this overcentralization, the government has in recent years undertaken steps to encourage the establishment of business and industry in other parts of the country by extending credit facilities and generous tax advantages to firms willing to establish themselves there. At the same time, it has taken imaginative and energetic steps to deal with the problem of the rural exodus by improving the living conditions of the people in the interior.

In order to make the upcountry areas more attractive to potential investors, the government has undertaken a vigorous program to improve the road system throughout the country. The government has also obtained support for the construction of a huge $100 million hydroelectric project on the Bandama River, which will be the basis for opening the entire center of the country to industrialization. In January, 1968 the government will begin work on the new port of San Pedro in the southwestern part of the country.

The government thus hopes to create thousands of new jobs in various parts of the country away from Abidjan and, at the same time, to make living conditions in the rural areas more pleasant, salubrious, and remunerative for the people who live there. These developments should help both to relieve the pressure on the capital and to spur development in the more remote and less favored areas [53].

So great is the potential volume of migration from the rural areas that the larger cities can be expected to increase in spite of all efforts to decentralize. Since the youth of developing countries find the large or primate city particularly attractive, decentralization would probably not drastically reduce migration even if there were better opportunities for employment elsewhere. Moreover, improvements in agricultural production and the mechanization of agricultural procedures will not only drive even more people to the cities but will require the cities to provide greater services and transport and marketing facilities, all of which will further increase the urban population [54]. Although crime probably would be reduced if the size of the urban concentrations were controlled by decentralization, such plans must be carefully examined in terms of benefits and costs; for example, what are the productivity costs in large versus smaller urban centers, the cost of community facilities and services in relation to city size, and the cost of transporting materials and products? In general, the large city would fare much better in these respects.

Special considerations are essential in planning for the migration of young males with some education. Whereas the developed countries must concentrate on school dropouts or on vocational training projects for skilled jobs, the developing countries are struggling with programs that cannot provide more than a primary education for only a percentage of the eligible children and can offer little vocational training. Rural youth are becoming more and more dissatisfied with the limited opportunities to use the education they have managed to obtain, for this education has raised their expectations dramatically. Even with a few years of primary schooling, farm work no longer appears to be acceptable to many of the young, and this marginality is particularly acute for those who cannot obtain a higher education, either because they do not qualify, because they lack financial help for books or supplies, or because there simply are not enough secondary schools. Similar situations are faced by those with secondary educations who cannot find suitable jobs in a country in which the economy is developing too slowly. These unemployed rural youths, emancipated from traditional ties, become potential sources of trouble when they drift to the cities [55]. In other words, as one United Nations publication indicates, some of the advantages of the increased educational opportunities at all levels in all developing countries have been offset by unemployment rates and related problems faced by the young [56].

It is essential that less developed countries recognize the relation of educational planning to urban drift and criminality. Improved national planning could reduce urban youth migration and the large-scale unemployment of educated young people in the cities. There is a need to plan educational systems that will relate more effectively to training programs in general and to vocational opportunities. Malaysia, for example, has an extensive program for youth training as well as vocational centers and community programs to keep the rural youth from migrating. Another basic approach would be an effective nationwide effort to educate people in the values of broad cultural and social enrichment and in a fuller participation in the nation's progress as well as in earning a livelihood. In this approach to education for education's sake one has a different approach than that allowed by the narrow view of manpower surveys, wherein estimates are made of the needs of the society in terms of so many doctors, lawyers, engineers, and teachers. A developing country should provide its people with a healthy discontent for existing conditions and encourage progress and action for improvement [57]. According to Adame Curle, it is the lack of education that hampers economic development despite the enormous amounts of technical and financial help given to developing countries. The expansion of educational facilities may, in itself, be unsuccessful in dealing with the criminal behavior of youth; there is need for more specific education in the traditional values of a less developing country, in problems of social relationships, and in the understanding of national objectives. Unfortunately the educational system of many developing countries is complicated by the retention of a formalized Western school system which largely ignores the problems of acculturation and does little to prepare the child for a changing world [58].

Several less developed countries, such as Mali, Zaïre, Malagasy Republic, and Tanzania, have established youth service brigades to absorb the large numbers of unemployed youths and to provide the channels through which surplus labor can be directed to a variety of public works and rural settlement projects. Others, such as the Ivory Coast, Chad, and Gabon, have made military service compulsory and use the conscripts for works of national importance [59]. Such programs are, of course, short-term and, if unemployment programs are not available on their discharge, may make youths even more discontented.

PLANNED MIGRANT COMMUNITIES AND RECEPTION CENTERS

Migrants might be able to avoid a "slum way of life" if they could be guided to certain areas especially planned for them. This kind of planning has been followed in some countries where cheap land in less

crowded parts of a city has been acquired for the construction of shacks
or houses, often by self-help, according to an established plan. Abrams
argues that a "planned slum" is better than an unplanned one if it consists of separate shelters individually owned. Without programs that
acknowledge the inevitability of the slums, costly, permanent, and unim-
provable slum formations can only be the end products [60].

In these planned communities persons with common backgrounds
can live in closer association, the transition from village life can be made,
and the strains of urban living lessened. Some existing social controls can
be maintained, and the deviant influences of existing slums can be minimized to some extent. New community organizational structures could be
developed in a manner as orderly as possible and deviant influences as
effectively controlled as possible, without which physical improvements
are wasted. Laquian points out that "planned slums" will not work if
they are conceived *only* in terms of physical structures, like "rational
street layouts, sub-standard housing, fire hydrants, schools, medical centers, drainage facilities, water and electric services" [61]. If they lack the
human component of community organization, neighborhood activities,
local identity, and other social aspects that help to differentiate a disor-
ganized slum from a viable community, the places will only become
worse. "A program of urban community development, therefore, should
be planned hand in hand with the development of an 'organized slum' "
[62]. If these programs are to be satisfactory, however, some sort of governmental agency must be created to coordinate all activities related to
slums and squatter settlements [63]. This and other measures for assisting
slum dwellers in housing and amenities are not easy.

Because of the patronage relationship of urban planning to politics in many
developing countries, and particularly because of the dominance of landowning
interests in politics, the prospects of decisive action in favour of the community
as a whole on any significant scale are generally bleak [64].

One serious problem, however, faced by governments in their attempts to provide services to squatters is their illegal status. Since the
legal system in most developing countries has not kept pace with the
rapid rate of urbanization, slum and squatter dwellers are denied basic
urban services simply because they have no status under the law. A
United Nations report has concluded that there is a need to redefine the
legal system and to analyze it anew in terms of the prevailing conditions
[65]. The traditional legal concepts of private ownership of vacant land
formulated under conditions of low levels of urbanization have been
rendered obsolete by current crowded urban conditions, yet these statutes
and codes remain on the books and must be observed by the government
administrators.

Some of the developing countries have attempted to regulate migration and to help the new arrivals by opening planned reception centers. In the Cameroon, for example, the rural migrant, unprepared for the complexities of urban life which may eventually lead him into trouble, may be introduced to certain of its social and economic aspects and receive training in a particular skill. The migrant can then be "placed" in a certain job and in a specific community when he is thought to be ready to go on his own. Commenting on this approach, a United Nations report stated that although its rationality is obvious the expense of a fully operational program would be tremendous. "Furthermore, in many cities, the problem is not so much the directing of rural-urban migrants to reception centers as it is dealing with people already living in slum conditions in the city" [66].

Another United Nations publication has stressed the importance of preparing young migrants for city experiences beforehand to prevent a later development of criminal patterns. Since, in any case, many young people will migrate to the cities, they can become familiar with the social experiences they will meet there, the nature of criminality in the urban areas, and the resources that may or may not be available to them in the urban environment [67]. Tanzania has an extensive program to help unemployed urban youth to return to the rural areas and work in special programs.

In those countries that make up the "Maghreb," Algeria, Morocco, and Tunisia, particularly Tunisia, urbanization is deeply rooted in the history of the country, and the movement of people from the rural to urban areas, long a tradition, has resulted in a system of movement in stages: from a nomadic to seminomadic life, then to living in settled areas in the countryside, then onto the city's outskirts, and finally from these suburban areas into the very heart of the city [68]. In these suburban areas and in the central "Medina" new arrivals tend to group according to "familial, tribal or provincial affinities." In Tunisian cities there are often certain houses for people of a village who are given food and shelter and helped in their orientation to city ways. "There is one for the people of Gavès, another for those of Djerid, and still another for those from Bja or from Kairouan" [69]. Through such means as this some of the disturbing and criminogenic forces associated with urbanization and industrialization are kept under some form of control.

REDUCING CRIMINALITY IN SLUM AREAS

Explanations of crime in terms of urbanization, industrialization, and population growth are useful for overall planning, but they are far too general and broad in scope for those who must deal with the immediate crime situation. A far more productive program pinpoints the attack on the slum way of life, a program that planners might also operationalize more effectively. As has been pointed out in some detail, urban slums are the main locus of ordinary crime in developing countries, as indeed they are elsewhere. Here criminality appears to be a product of a way of life that exists in most slum areas, although fortunately not in all. In view of the rapid increases in slum populations it is extremely important that plans for crime control be concentrated in those areas. Most of the slums in the large cities of the developing countries contain not a hundred or even a few thousand people; often hundreds of thousands live there and are increasing rapidly. In these growing areas it is extremely difficult for police and other outsiders to control theft, the sale of stolen property, violence, prostitution, and illicit drug or alcohol traffic without the reasonable support of large groups of local citizens. The control of crime and delinquency must involve the ordinary citizen, particularly those who live in the slums themselves [70]. All too often it is the slum dweller who must bear the main burden of criminality in the slum. Reliance cannot be placed exclusively on governmental agencies and personnel or on legal procedures as implemented by the police, the courts, and the prison system. The efforts of outsiders such as police officers may be ignored or even ridiculed by the community residents. Worst of all is the feeling of apathy about what they can do to improve local conditions or to control crime. An intensive study, for example, of slum dwellers in Puerto Rico, both those in shacks and rehousing projects, found that despite the many serious community problems recognized by the people few cooperative efforts were made to alleviate them [71]. The apathy of many Lima slum dwellers was revealed in interviews with a sample of 239 persons, of whom 38% stated that they had lost interest in their surroundings, 60% had lost belief in the value of education as a means of achieving success, 38% had lost confidence in the police, and 32% thought a person in difficult financial circumstances had a right to steal [72]. More than half the men in the high-crime area of Kisenyi in Kampala were generally apathetic, and when they were asked about what they thought people could do to improve things in the local community said "nothing can be done." Only one-third of the low-crime rate area residents took such a pessimistic view (see Table 37). These feelings of apathy and fatalism in slum areas have often led to a generalized suspicion of the world beyond their slums, including "government" and politicians, welfare groups, and the educated, philanthropically inclined élite. Slum dwellers are also more tolerant of deviant behavior, even though they are often the victims of it, for they have become ambivalent toward quasi-criminal activities committed against the "outside" world [73].

Table 37   Responses to the Question, "What Do People Think They Can Do to Improve Things Around this Area?" Kisenyi and Namuwongo

	Kisenyi		Namuwongo	
	No.	%	No.	%
1. Nothing	129	57.6	94	37.5
2. Discussions and attempts to encourage cooperation	6	2.7	16	6.4
3. Lend money to friends to set up small businesses	7	3.1	3	1.2
4. Build better houses and schools; clean up	35	15.6	64	25.5
5. Report crimes and avoid fighting	8	3.6	5	2.0
6. Work hard at jobs	12	5.4	24	9.6
7. Rely on city council, authorities, or government	25	11.2	34	13.5
8. Other	2	.9	11	4.4
Total	224	100.0	251	100.0
Don't know or no response	37	14.8	51	18.0

For these reasons the local slum community can become the focal point in dealing with crime and other deviant behavior. Slum dwellers need to develop a better understanding of what crime means to their communities; they need to eliminate those influences around them that are conducive to the growth of these patterns, to reduce the use of violence in settling disputes, and to help others to understand the role of the police and other agencies of social control. A major United Nations report has stressed this approach of urban community development as the principal instrument for dealing with social change and has pointed out the functions that such community groups in slum areas could perform.

1. Identification with and participation in a small, cohesive group could provide a framework of incentive, social control, and protection from exploitation, for the unaccompanied young adult in-migrant who might otherwise be swept into a pattern of conflicting social values.

2. For a community to take stock of the opportunities it offers and needs would be a sound first step towards preventive-action.

3. Supervised probation might be provided through a suitable lay resident in the delinquent's own milieu [74].

In addition to helping with the control of crime and delinquency, slum people can do a great many other things for themselves; for example, they can make minor repairs and maintain their own housing in better condition, whether publicly or privately owned, perhaps with community-owned tools [75]. They can improve sanitation, get rid of rats, establish credit unions and cooperative stores, promote cooperative ownership of recreational equipment and library materials, and cooperate with teachers in increasing motivation for learning. Some self-help efforts in job training have also been conducted by local slum communities.

Some slums are so heterogeneous and local social control so limited that it is necessary to help the residents to organize into self-help development councils if they are to be successful in treating problems like sanitation and health or crime and delinquency. One United Nations report pointed out that well-organized participation by slum residents is a vital element in their social development and that since the slum community is seldom recognized as a political entity, with its own legal identity, a unified community association should be formed to represent the slum community in its various contacts [76]. Another report stated that so far experience in developing countries, in which problems of urbanization are serious, has shown that "there is considerable scope for developing a number of self-help activities at the neighborhood level and for identifying and training local leaders who can organize groups for local action" [77]. For some time programs of rural community development have been widely used in developing countries in various parts of the world, particularly in Venezuela, Colombia, the Philippines, India, Pakistan, and Zambia [78]. There have also been many programs to control crime and delinquency in developed countries like the United States, the best known of which are the Chicago Area Projects and those of Saul Alinsky's Industrial Area Foundations, like Chicago's Woodlawn project.

To engage local slum communities in crime control programs effective local community relations must be created where little or none now exists. Potential indigenous leaders must be found and allowed to assume direct responsibility for initiating changes. There will always be slum residents who are dissatisfied with local crime and other conditions and who want to make changes. Improvement in a slum area depends to a great extent on the motivation and interest of such leadership. In the Barrio Magsaysay community development project in Manila the first step was a leadership survey.

A leadership survey serves not only to identify the leaders but also enables the community development team to get a profile of their characteristics. From this knowledge of the leaders, possible patterns of cooperation and possible types of projects that may become successful may be drawn up. Knowing the leaders also facilitates entry into the community [79].

The following is an example of the way in which such a community self-help program may work to deal with crime:

About eight hundred families of squatters from shacks in various pockets of Delhi were re-grouped in one slum colony as part of a rehabilitative measure. These people were from low-income groups and came from a variety of social groups with diverse customs, taboos, traditions and social institutions. Anti-social activities such as traffic in women for prostitution and illicit distilling of liquor were carried out by some people on an individual and group basis. The Department of Urban Community Development of the city government had previously organized a citizens' development council, and meetings were held to plan strategy. The illicit distilling of liquor and traffic in women were most common among members of a criminal tribe, the Sansis, which consisted of about forty-eight families. This group had its own spy system, as well as close alliances with some officials, and was thus able to operate with virtual impunity. The action group of the citizens' development council encouraged the residents themselves to inform the police of the most opportune times to carry out the raids. Further, the group sponsored or encouraged secret meetings of residents at which participants took oaths to boycott liquor brewed in the area. The two-fold drive of police raids and resident-sponsored activities eliminated the illicit manufacture of liquor. The traffic in women for prostitution was somewhat more difficult to eliminate as it was controlled by a smaller but more dangerous group. In spite of many warnings given by members of the action group and the citizens' development council, the traffic continued unabated. At last a public clash occurred between the anti-social group and the citizens' group which lasted nearly an hour, the members of the antisocial group were overpowered and handed over to the police for eventual trial. Thus the group was broken up [80].

The work of organizing slums could be carried out by a municipal department of community services. We can visualize large cities in developing countries being broken down into units of approximately 5000 persons or into smaller units in which there would be some degree of local leadership, initiative, and organization. A hundred units of 5000 would constitute 500,000 persons with whose local leaders the city government could work, 200 units thus containing a million persons. Djakarta, the capital of Indonesia, provides a good illustration of the potentialities of this form of urban community development for crime control [81]. This city of five million has been divided for some 30 years into *kelusahans,* or wards, of about 200,000 persons. A ward is subdivided into approximately 10 *rukun wargas,* or citizen groups, of 20,000 persons, each ward then subdivided into *rukun tetanggas,* or neighborhoods, of about 500 each. The head of the ward is appointed by the government, whereas the heads of the other two groups are elected by the citizens of the area.

The programs offer numerous civic activities; one in particular stresses maintaining cleanliness. The work of all three groups is coordinated by the Department of Social Welfare and the Department of Home Affairs, which operate at the national and civic levels. In 1969 Tanzania set up local ward development committees which were granted the power to impose "traditional sanctions" against persons who either fail or refuse to take part in designated self-help schemes. The People's Republic of China, as well as most of the other socialist countries, such as Yugoslavia, have similar decentralized urban controls and responsibilities.

In most Chinese cities, for example, particularly in Shanghai, Peking, and Tientsin, there are local self-government or residents' committees at the "neighborhood" level (about 50,000 people), the "lane level" (1000 to 3000 people), and the level of "groups" (one to several hundred) who may be the inhabitants of a single apartment house. Besides dealing with illegal activities in their areas, residents' committees manage some or all of the following:

Welfare—preferably finding or creating minor employment for the unemployed and needy rather than dispensing funds; health and sanitation—organizing "antipest" campaigns, inspecting and installing toilet facilities, disposing of manure, and organizing neighborhood sweeping and cleaning details on a rotation basis; mediation—resolving disputes among neighbors and married couples; cooperative services—organizing nurseries, kindergartens, playgrounds, clothing repair teams, and mess halls; minor administrative tasks—assisting in rationing administration and the collection of rents and utilities payments. Of course basic-level Party and state organs guide and encourage the committees in these tasks on the grounds that healthy, harmonious neighborhood life reduces labor absenteeism and raises popular morale, that service activities free more hands for "productive labor," and even that nurseries, playgrounds, and other group activities provide education in the "superiority of collective life." Whatever the Party attitude might be, however, the residents and their representatives do participate in some of the decisions and nearly all of the management on such neighborhood projects [82].

Some programs of self-help are already in existence in slum areas of developing countries and these groups can be effectively used in crime-control programs. They are usually tribal, village, ethnic, religious, regional, or caste groups but in some cases are based simply on geographic proximity. Although they do carry out some self-help programs, many of their activities could be more systematic and they could take on additional functions. Studies have consistently pointed out that slum and squatter community residents are often organized to handle certain communal activities with the aid of external government agencies. It is important that any crime-control program identify these groups and use them and the techniques of social control they have evolved. A United Nations report regarding these groups states the following:

Tribal associations have had many social and economic successes in aiding their members to cope with urban life. One function has been to ease emergency economic pressures in individual cases; another has been to provide the social cohesion the migrant urgently needs in a new and complex environment. Both of these considerations are closely related to the prevention of crime, since the failure to find solutions to urgent socio-economic problems may precipitate criminal acts. The contributions of tribal association to an orderly process of urbanization deserve study with a view to the possible strong support of them by government as one phase of social policy [83].

Most of these self-help groups have been formed by people who have migrated to the cities and have settled in neighborhoods in which they have some connection, relatives, friends, or simply other people from their home communities. One writer has stated that shantytowns or squatter settlements in Latin American cities can be viewed in two ways :"(1) that they are slums, blighted areas, belts of misery, incubators for disease, crime, social disorganization and personality disorder; and (2) that as semi-rural enclaves they make available new possibilities for urban social reconstruction on the basis of neighborhood communities, regional and kinship ties, mutual-aid associations, and small-group political activity" [84]. Many residents of the slum *barriados* of Peru maintain some of their close village ties and form organizations to cooperate in self-help improvements in urban areas [85]. The people of *Kampongs* in urban areas of Indonesia also keep up some rural community ties despite their crowded living conditions, ties that have implications for crime-control measures [86]. In India Mohalla committees in the slums of some cities date from Mogul times as part of a system called "Mir Mohalla" in which a certain person was designated "chief of the locality" for an urban neighborhood. These organizations have been carried over into present-day India under different names and with different functions, but with a variety of self-help programs [87]. Tribal and village mutual-aid groups are common in West African cities [88]. In Freetown, Sierre Leone, a system of tribal headmanship and voluntary association, reported by Banton, has considerable influence on the lives of tribal people settled in various parts of the city. They might be, he says, utilized more systematically as a means of organizing self-help for the newcomer [89]. The headmen in Freetown participate in crime control by furnishing bail and helping with the administration of estates of deceased persons and other matters [90].

THE APPLICATION OF CRIMINOLOGICAL RESEARCH TO CRIME CONTROL

Attempts to apply scientific criminological knowledge to the solution of criminal behavior will probably encounter the same problems in the less developed countries as they have encountered in the developed. Szabo has discussed the resistance of administrators and the reasons underlying their resistance in the area of criminal justice [91]. Administrators of police, prison, and probation services, particularly the civil service bureaucracy, tend to maintain the *status quo*. As agents of the government they conform to traditional practices and often have relatively little latitude in which to operate. Many of them have been trained in schools of law, by the military branches, or in schools of prison or public administration in which their training has not been conducive to the acceptance of the latest findings in the field of criminological research. The attitudes of the public on crime and the criminal are emotional and often vehemently expressed, and government officials and legislators may be unwilling to take the risk of damaging their political futures by attempting to change crime-control policies.

If current criminological knowledge were to be effectively applied to reduce the total cost of crime, there would probably be four levels of operation [92]. The first would be directed at preventing crimes, the identification of the causes of crime, and the rehabilitation of offenders. At the second level interest would be directed toward better methods of controlling crime, including the apprehension and conviction of criminals. At the third level would be the reduction of operational costs of the criminal justice system by improving its performance and effectiveness, the relation of the system to the community, and improvements in selecting and training personnel. At the fourth level would be the development of a center for the study and measurement of crime and the careful evaluation of existing programs. Morris and Hawkins have stressed the need for evaluative research in criminology, particularly the relative deterrent effects of different sanctions and correctional practices [93].

It is particularly important in developing countries to have good research programs and to collect good statistical data to evaluate the ongoing programs. A United Nations report, primarily with reference to developing countries, emphasizes the importance of criminological research.

The treatment of rehabilitation of offenders implies inquiries into the rates of reconviction of different types of offenders subjected to the different forms of treatment, experiments with new or modified methods of penal or rehabilitative treatment for diverse offender groups (including juveniles) and interdisciplinary investigations of past and present methods. There should be attempts to understand and explain the phenomenon of *general* deterrence (the preventive effect of a penal system—or a particular aspect of it—on criminality in the population at large) and *special* deterrence (the inhibitive effect of a measure on an individual); analyzing the result of the attempts to reduce recidivism and trying new approaches, examining the functioning of different kinds of correctional systems with specific reference to the roles played by different types of personnel, seeking the best location and most appropriate design of the several institutions; studying the effects of long-term and short-term imprisonment; probing the dynamics of the prison as a social control system; studying and perhaps experimenting with the development of the "inmate culture"; investigating the use of community resources in rehabilitating offenders; experimenting with and evaluating the integration of prisoners and their work into broader schemes of national development; comparing different combinations of institutional and extra-institutional measures, etc. [94].

Basic research in the area of crime is lacking in most of the developing countries at present. What is available is often only routine official statistics, often of only limited value. Research on the nature of offenders and crime-producing forces is needed. Research personnel need training in the design of studies, construction of questionnaires and interview schedules, reliable techniques for sampling studies of the population, preparation of the data for analysis, and the application of the proper statistical techniques. Even if good personnel were available, the absence of proper records might handicap this kind of research.

It has been estimated that probably not more than 1500 persons in the entire world are engaged in criminological research for more than part-time [95]. Among these criminologists who devote at least half their time to research 80% or more are associated with universities. Qualified and experienced research personnel are scarce, particularly in less developed countries, partly because they are being used in other fields. Few universities have professionally trained criminologists. Not only are there few persons trained in criminology but the numbers with general social science backgrounds are limited, as are library resources. The same is true in the government; those in the area of crime control have had little professional training in the broad area of criminology. Despite limited resources, the United Nations has tried to remedy this situation. The services of experts in what is called "social defense" have been provided to several countries, some on a short-term basis, others for a year or two. For a number of years the United Nations has conducted regional meetings in this area, and every five years they hold an international congress on the prevention of crime and the treatment of offenders (Geneva, 1955; London, 1960; Stockholm, 1965; and Kyoto, 1970; Toronto, 1975), to which most of the developing countries send representatives [96]. In addition, a United Nations Asia and Far East Institute for the Prevention of Crime and the Treatment of Offenders has been conducted at Fuchu, and this institute is now supported by Japan [97]. A United Nations Social Defence Section is maintained in New York, and the United Nations Social Defence Research Institute in Rome is primarily interested in problems of developing countries. An increasing number of graduate students and faculty members are securing graduate training in criminology at various universities abroad.

Institutes or centers devoted to criminological research in less developed countries are growing, but their number is not great. Nearly all research done by some 86 institutes or organizations dealing with crime in Latin America is devoted to criminal law and procedure [98]. A number of fairly significant criminological research studies are now being carried out at the Criminological Research and Teaching Institute of La Plata in Buenos Aires Province, the Latin American Institute of Criminology in Sao Paulo, the Institute of Criminology, University of Colombia, and the Institute of Penal and Criminological Sciences of the Central University of Venezuela. Since 1968 the Venezuela Institute has issued a series of monographs and translations such as Edwin H. Sutherland's *White-Collar Crime*. The work of the Institute and the Research Division of the Bureau of Crime Prevention in the Ministry of Justice have made Venezuela one of the most promising places for the future development of criminological research in Latin America. The works of Rosa del Olmo, Juan Manuel Mayorca, and Elio Gomez Grillo have been particularly significant. A sociological approach is beginning to be emphasized in Latin America [99].

For many years the Tata Institute of Social Sciences near Bombay, India, has run a well-developed training and research program in crime and corrections under the direction of J. J. Panakal. The first Indonesian Institute of Criminology was set up as far back as 1948 at the University of Indonesia through the initiative of a Dutch professor of criminal law. It now has an interdisciplinary faculty from various departments and sections on forensic medicine, criminalistics, criminal law, and criminology. Unfortunately, financial resources are limited despite a serous crime problem in Indonesia. A similar institute was established more recently in Sumatra at the University of DiPonegoro. The University of Louvanium in Kinshasa has a Research Institute in Criminology and Social Pathology, founded by Professor Guy Houchon but now being administered by Africans. Makerere University in Uganda has had an African criminologist on its staff since 1971. Abidjan Institute of Criminology at the University of Abidjan was established in 1971 in cooperation with the International Centre for Comparative Criminology at the University of Montreal, which was organized in 1969 primarily for a teaching program in criminology. Under their auspices the First West African Conference in Comparative Criminology was held in Abidjan in 1972 [100]. In 1972 an Institute of Criminology at the University of Lagos was being formed. All of these programs should help in the future to further the inclusion of more studies of crime in developing countries in comparative criminology.

NOTES AND REFERENCES

1. J. J. Tobias, *Crime and Industrial Society in the 19th Century* (London: B. T. Batsford, Ltd., 1967), pp. 49–50. Reprinted by permission of Schocken Books. Inc.
2. *Ibid.*, p. 244.
3. William Clifford, "Training for Crime Control in the Context of National Development," *International Review of Criminal Policy*, 24:9 (1966).
4. United Nations, "The Prevention of Delinquency in the Context of National Development," United Nations Publication ST/SOA/SG/CG.2/WP.1, Geneva, 1968.
5. Manuel López-Rey, *Crime: An Analytical Appraisal* (New York: Praeger and London: Routledge & Kegan Paul Ltd., 1970), p. 189.
6. Norval Morris and Gordon Hawkins, *The Honest Politician's Guide to Crime Control* (Chicago: University of Chicago Press, 1969), p. 49.
7. Provisional Draft of the Final Report of the Fourth United Nations Congress on the Prevention of Crime and the Treatment of Offenders, Kyoto, Japan, 1970, p. 10.
8. López-Rey, *Crime*, pp. 187–188, and "Crime Problems and the United Nations Congresses on the Prevention of Crime and the Treatment of Offenders," *Kriminologisches Aktualitat*, Mainz, Federal Republic of Germany, 1968, p. 9.
9. See, for example, Franco Ferracuti and Maria Cristina Giannini, *Manpower and Training in the Field of Social Defence: A Commentary and Bibliography* (Rome: United Nations Social Defence Research Institute, Publication No. 2, 1970).
10. See, for example, articles that deal with the evaluation of methods used in juvenile delinquency prevention programs in less developed countries, particularly Africa, Latin America, and the Arab countries in Vol. 21 of the *International Review of Criminal Policy*. See also Carol H. Weiss, *Evaluation Research: Methods for Assessing Program Effectiveness* (Englewood Cliffs, N.J.: Prentice-Hall, 1972).
11. United Nations, "The Prevention of Delinquency in the Context of National Development," p. 24.
12. Leslie T. Wilkins and Thomas Gitenoff, "Trends and Projections in Social Control Systems," *Annals of the American Academy of Political and Social Science*, 381:125–136 (January 1969).
13. Morris and Hawkins, *The Honest Politician's Guide to Crime Control*, p. 240. See also Alfred Blumstein, "Systems Analysis and the Criminal Justice System," *Annals of the American Academy of Political and Social Science*, 371:104–126 (May, 1967).
14. "The Prevention of Delinquency in the Context of National Development," pp. 9–10.

15. Morris and Hawkins, *The Honest Politician's Guide to Crime Control*, p. 50.

16. López-Rey, "Crime Problems and the United Nations Congresses on the Prevention of Crime and the Treatment of Offenders," pp. 12–13.

17. See López-Rey, "Crime and the Penal System," p. 11.

18. Morris and Hawkins, *The Honest Politician's Guide to Crime Control*, and Herbert Packer, *The Limits of the Criminal Sanction* (Stanford: Stanford University Press, 1968).

19. Thorsten Sellin and Marvin Wolfgang, *The Measurement of Delinquency* (New York: Wiley, 1964) use this definition of juvenile delinquency.

20. *Second United Nations Congress on the Prevention of Crime and the Treatment of Offenders* (London: United Nations Publication 1960, Sales No. 61.3).

21. Eric P. Kibuka, "Juvenile Delinquency in Uganda Urban Areas with Special Reference to Kampala and Mbale," mimeo, University College of Swansea, 1964, p. 41.

22. William Clifford, "The African View of Crime," *The British Journal of Criminology*, 4:484 (July 1964).

23. *Ibid.*, p. 482.

24. United Nations Economic and Social Council, "Capital Punishment," United Nations No. E/4947, February 23, 1971 and "Nations Holding to Death Penalty," *The New York Times*, April 3, 1972, p. 8-C.

25. C. L. Maheshwari, "Death Penalty in India," *The Journal of Correctional Work*, Lucknow, India, No. 12, October 1965, p. 82.

26. *Ibid.*

27. "Nations Holding to Death Penalty," *New York Times*, April 3, 1972. See also Clarence H. Patrick, "The Status of Capital Punishment: A World Perspective," *Journal of Criminal Law, Criminology and Police Science*, 56:398–404 (December 1965).

28. López-Rey, "Crime and the Penal System," p. 17.

29. Stephen Schafer, *The Victim and His Criminal: A Study in Functional Responsibility* (New York: Random House, 1968).

30. Steven Lowenstein, "Ethiopia," in Alan Milner, *African Penal Systems* (London: Routledge & Kegan Paul, 1969), p. 45.

31. William Clifford, "Zambia," in Milner, *African Penal Systems*, p. 255.

32. G. H. Boehringer, "Aspects of Penal Policy in Africa, with Special Reference to Tanzania," *Journal of African Law*, 15:183–184 (Summer, 1971).

33. Alan Milner, "Introduction," in Alan Milner, Ed., *African Penal Systems*, (London: Routledge & Kegan Paul Ltd., and New York: Praeger, 1969), pp. 6–7.

34. Richard Quinney, *The Social Reality of Crime* (Boston: Little Brown, 1970), p. 17.

35. Rosa del Olmo, "Sentencing Practices in Caracas, Venezuela's Penal Courts," paper presented at annual meeting of the Society for the Study of Social Problems, Denver, Colorado, August 1971.

36. William Edgett Smith, *We Must Run While They Walk: A Portrait of Africa's Julius Nyerere* (New York: Random House, 1972).

37. Communication from Rosa Del Olmo, Head, Research Division, Bureau of Crime Prevention, Ministry of Justice and Professor of Social Problems, University of Venezuela, Caracas, Venezuela.

38. Manuel López-Rey, "Aspects et Problèmes de la Codification Pénale à L'Heure Actuelle," *Revue de Science Criminelle et de Droit Pénal Comparé,* **20**:1–49 (1965).

39. López-Rey, *Crime,* p. 23.

40. J. P. Martin, "The Cost of Crime: Some Research Problems," *International Review of Criminal Policy,* **23**:57–63 (1965).

41. "Social Defence Policies in Relation to Development Planning," p. 22.

42. Gösta Carlsson, "Response, Inertia and Cycles," *Acta Sociologica,* **2**:139 (1968).

43. López-Rey, *Crime,* p. 182.

44. *Ibid.,* p. 219.

45. M. McMullan, "Corruption in the Public Services of British Colonies and Ex-Colonies in West Africa," in Arnold J. Heidenheimer, *Political Corruption* (New York: Holt, Rinehart & Winston, 1970), p. 330.

46. Gunnar Myrdal, "Corruption: Its Causes and Effects," in Heidenheimer, *Political Corruption,* p. 543.

47. Abraham Kiapi, "Legal Control of Official Corruption in East Africa," University Social Sciences Council Conference, Makerere University, Kampala, December 31, 1968, p. 25 (mimeographed).

48. *Ibid.*

49. Karl Christiansen, "Industrialization and Urbanization in Relation to Crime and Delinquency," *International Review of Criminal Policy,* **18**: (October 1960).

50. William McCord, *The Springtime of Freedom: The Evolution of Developing Societies* (New York: Oxford University Press, 1965), Chapter 2.

51. United Nations, *Improvements of Slums and Uncontrolled Settlements,* a report of the Interregional Seminar on the Improvement of Slums and Uncontrolled Settlements, Medellin, Colombia, February 15–March 1, 1970 (New York: United Nations, 1971), p. 165.

52. Lloyd Rodwin, *Nations and Cities: A Comparison of Strategies for Urban Growth* (Boston: Houghton Mifflin, 1970).

53. Victor D. Du Bois, *Social Aspects of the Urbanization Process in Abidjan,* West Africa Series, Vol. X, 1967, p. 8.

54. Robert Heilbroner, *The Great Ascent* (New York: Harper and Row, 1963).

55. Report of the United Nations Interregional Seminar on Development Policies and Planning in Relation to Urbanization, Pittsburgh, Pa., October 24–November 4, 1966 (ST/TAO/SERC/97), p. 7.

56. *Policy Issues Concerning the Future Evolution of Community Development,* United Nations Working Paper No. 2, WGRCD/XV/ May 14, 1968, p. 24.

57. Adame Curle, *Educational Strategy for Developing Societies* (London: Tavistock, 1963). See also William Clifford, "Unemployed Youth in Congo (Leopoldville)" United Nations Technical Assistance Board, Leopoldville, Social Affairs Section, March 1966.

58. Evelyn Pierre, J. P. Flamand, and H. Collomb, "La Délinquance Juvénile à Dakar," *International Review of Criminal Policy,* No. 20, 27–34 (December 1962).

59. William Clifford. "The Evaluation of Methods Used for the Prevention of Juvenile Delinquency in Africa South of the Sahara," *International Review of Criminal Policy,* **21**:22 (1963).

60. Charles Abrams, *Man's Struggle for Shelter in an Urbanizing World* (Cambridge: Massachusetts Institute of Technology Press, 1964), p. 252.

61. Aprodicio A. Laquian, *Slums are for People* (Honolulu: East-West Center Press, 1971), pp. 201–202, by permission of The University Press of Hawaii.

62. *Ibid.*

63. Aprodicio A. Laquian, *The City in Nation-Building: Politics and Administration in Metropolitan Manila* (Manila: School of Public Administration, 1966).

64. D. J. Dwyer, "Absorption Problems of In-Migrants in Metropolitan Cities of Developing Countries," Rehovot Conference on Urbanization and Development in Developing Countries, Rehovot, Israel, August 16–24, 1971, p. 3.

65. *Improvement of Slums and Uncontrolled Settlements*, p. 162.

66. *Ibid.*, pp. 165–166. Voluntary organization can help in urban areas of many countries.

67. "Quelques Considérations sur la Prévention de la Délinquance Juvénile dans Les Pays Africains Subissant des Changements Sociaux Rapides," *International Review of Criminal Policy*, **16**:45 (October 1960).

68. Abdelwahab Bouhdiba, *Criminalité et Changements Sociaux en Tunisie* (Université de Tunis: Les Mémoires du Cérès, 1965), pp. 96–100.

69. *Ibid.*, p. 98.

70. Juan Manuel Mayorca, "La Prevención A Priori Del Delito," en *Prevención Del Delito* (Caracas: Ministry of Justice, 1971), p. 169.

71. Lloyd Rogler, "Slum Neighborhoods in Latin America," *Journal of Inter-American Studies*, **9**:507–528 (1967).

72. H. Rotondo, J. Mariategui, B. Bambaren Vigil, B. Garcia Pacheco, and P. Aliaga, "Estudios de Psiquiatria Social en Areas Urbanos y Rurales," *Actos Bero-Espanoles de Psiquiatria y Neurologia*, **20**:198–210 (1961). See also David Garcia Estrada, "Tepito," *Criminalia*, **32**:375–383 (1966).

73. See, for accounts in the developed countries, Gerald D. Suttles, *The Social Order of the Slum* (Chicago: University of Chicago Press, 1968).

74. Report of the Secretary-General, *Community Development in Urban Areas* (New York: United Nations, 1961), pp. 12–13. See also Milton S. Rosner, "Community Development and the Delinquent," *Human Problems in Central Africa*, **38**:1–10 (December 1965).

75. *Improvement of Slums and Uncontrolled Settlements*. See also Marshall B. Clinard, *Slums and Community Development: Experiments in Self-Help* (New York: The Free Press, 1966 and 1970) and Francis Violich and Juan B. Astica, *Community Development and the Urban Planning Process in Latin America* (Los Angeles: Latin American Center, University of California Los Angeles, 1967).

76. *Improvements of Slums and Uncontrolled Settlements*, pp. 1, 12.

77. *Policy Issues Concerning the Future Evolution of Community Development*, Working Group on Rural Community Development, Administrative Committee on Co-ordination, Geneva, July 10–15, 1968 (ACC/WGRCD/WV/Working Paper No. 2).

78. Clinard, *Slums and Community Development*, 1970; Talton F. Ray, *The Politics of the Barrios of Venezuela* (Berkeley, University of California Press, 1969); Carolos A. Mendoza and Sheila Olmos de Manzo, *El Desarrollo de la Communidad* (Caracas: Fondo Editorial Comun, 1971); Carola Ravell, Ramon Pinango, and Giovanna Gonzalez, *El Desarrollo de la Comunidad Como Tecnica de Induccion del Cambio Social* (Caracas: Fondo Editorial Comun, 1969); and Laquian, *Slums are*

for People, 1969. For a discussion of the Chicago Area Projects and Saul Alinsky's Industrial Area Foundations see Clinard, *Slums and Community Development,* pp. 121–124.

79. Laquian, *Slums Are for People,* p. 109. Reprinted by permission of The University Press of Hawaii.

80. Clinard, *Slums and Community Development,* p. 239. See also Clinard, "The Organization of Urban Community Development Services in the Prevention of Crime and Juvenile Delinquency, with Particular Reference to Underdeveloped Countries," *International Review of Criminal Policy,* 20:31–36 (1962).

81. Willem F. Wertheim, *Indonesian Society in Transition: A Study of Social Change* (The Hague, Netherlands: N. V. Vitgeverij W. Van Hoeve, 1956).

82. James R. Townsend, *Political Participation in Communist China* (Berkeley: University of California Press, 1967), pp. 163–164. Originally published by the University of California Press; reprinted by permission of The Regents of the University of California. See also Ezra F. Vogel, "Preserving Order in the Cities," and Janet Weitzner Salaff, "Urban Residential Communities in the Wake of the Cultural Revolution," in John Wilson Lewis, Ed., *The City in Communist China* (Stanford: Stanford University Press, 1971), pp. 75–96 and pp. 289–324.

83. "The Maintenance of the Extended Family System or Alternatives to It," *Prevention of Types of Criminality Resulting from Social Changes and Accompanying Economic Development in Less Developed Countries,* A/Conf. 17/4, p. 12.

84. Richard M. Morse, "Recent Research on Latin American Urbanization: A Selective Survey with Commentary," *Latin American Research Review,* 1:41 (1965).

85. José Matos Mar, "The Barriados of Lima: An Example of Integration into Urban Life," in Philip M. Hauser, Ed., *Urbanization in Latin America* (New York: International Documents Service of Columbia University Press, 1961), pp. 170–190.

86. Ann Ruth Willner, "Social Change in Javanese Town-Village Life," *Economic Development and Cultural Change,* 6:234 (April 1958).

87. Clinard, *Slums and Community Development,* p. 193.

88. The Secretary-General of the United Nations, *Community Development in Urban Areas* (New York: United Nations, 1961), p. 9. See also Kenneth Little, "The Role of Voluntary Associations in West African Urbanization," *American Anthropologist,* 59:579–596 (August, 1959).

89. Michael Banton, *West African City: A Study of Tribal Life in Freetown* (London: Oxford University Press, 1957), p. xv. See also Banton, "Social Alignment and Identity in a West African City," in Hilda Kuper, Ed., *Urbanization and Migration in West Africa* (Berkeley: University of California Press, 1965), pp. 131–174.

90. Banton, *West African City,* 1957.

91. Denis Szabo, "Applied Criminology and Government Policy: Future Perspectives and Conditions of Collaboration," *Issues in Criminology,* 6:55–84 (Winter, 1971).

92. See the crime control program of Alfred Blumstein, quoted in Szabo, "Applied Criminology and Government Policy," pp. 76–77. See also M. S. Sabnis, "Research Utilization and Policy Formulation in Social Defence," *Social Defence* (India), 6:9–22 (1970).

93. Morris and Hawkins, *The Honest Politician's Guide to Crime Control,* p. 253.

94. *Organization of Research for Policy Development in Social Defense,* p. 19.

95. Szabo, "Applied Criminology and Government Policy," p. 62.

96. Benedict Alper and Jerry F. Boren, *Crime: International Agenda* (Lexington, Massachusetts: Heath, 1972). International concern and collaboration in the treatment and prevention of crime has had a long and varied history, beginning with the first conference in 1843 in Florence. Between 1846 and 1970 more than 80 major international conferences on this subject have been held.

97. See Norval Morris, "United Nations Activities in the Field of the Prevention of Crime and the Treatment of Offenders," *International Review of Criminal Policy*, 22:57–64 (1964).

98. Franco Ferracuti and Roberto Bergalli, "Criminological Research Trends in Latin America," Excerpt from Publication No. 1, United Nations Social Defence Research Institute, Rome, Italy, 1970.

99. Roberto Bergalli, *Criminologia en America Latina* (Buenos Aires: Ediciones Pannedille, 1972), p. 44.

100. *Premier Collogue de Criminologie Comparée d'Afrique Occidentale*, Institut de Criminologie d'Abidjan, Abidjan, June 1972.

Appendix A   Test Scores and Levels of Significance

	Table	Test	Score	Significance
Number of moves in migration[a]	13	χ^2	1.07	NS
Urban experience before arrival in Kampala[a]	14	χ^2	15.48	.001
Aid on arrival in Kampala[a]	15	χ^2	16.47	.001
Contact with relatives in Kampala[a]	16	χ^2	40.88	.001
Diversity in tribal friendships		F	8.78	.01
Contact with relatives in home village[a]	17	χ^2	12.14	.001
Ownership of land in village[a]	18	χ^2	3.35	NS
Intent to return home permanently[a]	19	χ^2	.06	NS
Friends in trouble with the police[a]		F	11.93	.001
Relatives in trouble with the police[a]		F	0.92	NS
Steal from strangers or other villages[a]		F	1.01	NS
Attitudes toward theft[a]		F	27.75	.001
Personal deviance[a]		F	18.73	.001
Illegal beer brewing		F	.08	NS
Urban activities, recreational[a]		F	28.81	.001
Urban activities, deviant[a]		F	1.52	NS
Occupation[a]	22	χ^2	16.92	.001
Education		F	19.60	.001
Material aspirations[a]	23	χ^2	2.2	NS
Educational aspirations (self)[a]		F	10.87	.001
Educational aspirations (sons)[a]		F	19.30	.001
Educational aspirations (self), high education[a]		χ^2	14.97	.001
Educational aspirations (self), medium education[a]		χ^2	6.23	NS
Educational aspirations (self), low education[a]		χ^2	21.05	.001
Educational aspirations (sons), high education[a]		χ^2	.49	NS
Educational aspirations (sons), medium education[a]		χ^2	6.82	NS
Educational aspirations (sons), low education[a]		χ^2	21.82	.001

(Continued)

	Table	Test	Score	Signifi-cance
Need for illegitimate means[a]		F	20.20	.001
Lack of opportunity[a]		F	3.03	NS
Need for illegitimate means (25 and under)[b]	24	F	11.94	.001
Need for illegitimate means (over 25)[b]	24	F	60.50	.000
Lack of opportunity (25 and under)[b]	24	F	7.33	.01
Lack of opportunity (over 25)[b]	24	F	22.10	.001
Standards of health and cleanliness in area[b]		F	3.74	NS
Diversity in tribal friendships (25 and under)[b]		F	2.77	NS
Diversity in tribal friendships (over 25)[b]		F	25.52	.001
Contact with relatives in Kampala (25 and under)[b]		χ^2	.07	NS
Contact with relatives in Kampala (over 25)[b]		χ^2	1.01	NS
Mobility in Kampala (25 and under)[b]		F	9.53	.01
Mobility in Kampala (over 25)[b]		F	14.36	.001
Length of residence in local community (25 and under)[b]		F	1.44	NS
Length of residence in local community (over 25)[b]		F	.34	NS
Whether would move to another local community (25 and under)[b]		χ^2	4.66	NS
Whether would move to another local community (over 25)[b]		χ^2	.89	NS
Number of homes in local area where visit (25 and under)[b]		F	6.49	.01
Number of homes in local area where visit (over 25)		F	17.14	.001
Willingness to give economic aid to neighbors (25 and under)		F	3.91	NS
Willingness to give economic aid to neighbors (over 25)[b]		F	.68	NS
Stability of relations between men and women in area (25 and under)[b]		F	43.34	.000
Stability of relations between men and women in area (over 25)[b]		F	83.83	.000
Exclusivity of friendship in local community (25 and under)[b]		F	.96	NS
Exclusivity of friendship in local community (over 25)[b]		F	.91	NS
Participation in community organizations (25 and under)[b]		F	5.80	NS
Participation in community organizations (over 25)[b]		F	11.19	.001
Religious services attendance (25 and under)[b]		F	20.82	.001
Religious services attendance (over 25)[b]		F	32.43	.000

(*Continued*)

	Table Test	Score	Signifi-cance
Education (25 and under)[b]	F	4.37	NS
Education (over 25)[b]	F	18.67	.001
Occupations (25 and under)[b]	F	2.65	NS
Occupations (over 25)[b]	F	.78	NS
Home ownership (25 and under)[b]	χ^2	3.25	NS
Home ownership (over 25)[b]	χ^2	14.06	.001
Participation in urban organizations (25 and under)[b]	F	.60	NS
Participation in urban organization (over 25)[b]	F	1.18	NS
Civic participation (25 and under)[b]	F	.72	NS
Civic participation (over 25)[b]	F	.00	NS

[a] Offenders versus nonoffenders.

[b] High crime community (Kisenyi) versus low crime community (Namuwongo).

Appendix B Rotated Factors of Differential Opportunity

Loading		Factor 1. Need for Illegal Means
.626	1.	Some of the most respectable persons earn money illegally.
.692	2.	There are grown up people in your area who help young boys earn money illegally.
.491	3.	It is hard to earn much money without doing something illegal.
.561	4.	Honest jobs do not pay well.
.663	5.	For a guy who wants to earn plenty of money illegally there are contacts in your area.

Loading		Factor 2. Lack of Opportunity
.791	1.	You will never have the same possibilities to succeed as males from other areas.
.530	2.	Your parents cannot give you the chances that most young people have.

[a] Both the quartimax and varimax methods of rotation were used, and the factor structure was the same for both methods with only a few points difference in the loadings.

Name Index

Rao, Kamala, 75
Rao, S. Venugopal, 70, 74, 211
Ravell, Carola, 293
Ravenholt, Albert, 73
Ray, Talton F., 293
Raymaekers, Paul, 212, 213
Razeh, Adnon-el, 170
Read, James S., 252
Reckless, Walter C., 29, 253
Rein, Martin, 188
Reiss, Albert J., Jr., 33, 104, 204, 211, 248
Rho, Young-Hee, 128
Rhodes, A. Lewis, 204, 211
Riby-Williams, James, 104
Riessman, Frank, 253
Ro, Chung-Hyun, 104, 249
Rodwin, Lloyd, 128, 292
Rogler, Lloyd H., 129, 156, 161, 166, 170, 293
Rosenquist, C. M., 211
Rosner, Milton S., 293
Rotondo, H., 168, 293
Rouch, J., 70
Ruiz de Chavez, Leticia, 32
Russett, Bruce, 14

Sabnis, M. S., 294
Safa, Helen, 166
St. Clair, David, 75
Salaff, Janet Weitzner, 294
Schafer, Stephen, 291
Schaff, Alvin H., 103
Schmandt, Henry J., 166
Schnore, Leo F., 102
Scotton, Carol Meyers, 128
Seidman, Robert B., 31, 251, 252
Shah, Jyotsna H., 76
Shapiro, Isaac, 250, 251
Shaw, Clifford R., 99, 167, 211
Sheth, Hansa, 70, 71, 130, 168, 189, 190, 199
Shoham, Nahum, 170
Shoham, Shlomo, 170
Short, James F., Jr., 178, 184, 204, 209–210, 211, 214
Simmel, Georg, 104
Simpkins, Edgar, 72
Simpson, George, 189
Singh, Debi, 41
Singh, Inder Jeet, 213

Singh, Sampat P., 29
Sjoberg, Gideon, 78, 85
Skolnick, Jerome, 248
Smith, David Horton, 9
Smith, William Edgett, 291
Sofer, C., 129
Solvay, S. A., 28
Solzbacker, Regina, 107, 169
Southall, Aidan W., 32, 71, 97, 107, 112, 129, 144
Sovani, N. V., 102
Spaulding, John, 189
Spergel, Irving, 190
Srivastava, Shankar Sahai, 167, 168, 213
Steffian, John, 165
Stokes, Charles J., 165
Straus, Jacqueline H., 73, 74
Straus, Murray A., 73, 74
Stren, Richard E., 171
Strodtbeck, Fred L., 178, 184, 209–210, 211
Stryker, Sheldon, 168
Stycos, J. M., 29
Suliveres, Isabel, 103, 166
Sutherland, Edwin H., 103, 131, 177, 189, 193, 208, 211, 214, 250, 289
Suttles, Gerald D., 156, 166, 293
Szabo, Denis, 84, 287, 294

Taft, Donald R., 191
Tamuno, T. N., 248, 249
Tanner, R. E. S., 33, 71, 95, 107, 208, 214, 241–244, 249, 250
Teune, Henry, 29
Thomas, Elizabeth Marshall, 71
Tiger, Lionel, 105
Tobias, J. J., 29, 290
Toby, Jackson, 32, 177
Tooth, G., 17, 105, 130
Toro-Calder, Jaime, 31, 59–60, 103, 130, 168, 253
Townsend, James R., 294
Trueblood, F. M., 128
Tschoungui, S. P., 32, 131
Turner, John F. C., 137–138, 165
Turner, Roy, 101

Ugandizaga, Elsa, 171
Uriba, Pedro Nel Rueda, 73

Subject Index

Abidjan, confidence games in, 38–39
  criminological research, 289–290
  juvenile delinquency, 83, 196
  markets for stolen property, 38
  population growth, 80
  prison labor, 239
  prostitution, 63, 65–66
Accra, juvenile delinquency, 83, 196, 199–200
  population growth, 80
  prostitution, 64, 197–198
Addis Ababa, population growth, 80
Adultery, 268
Africa, age of urban population, 85
  armed forces, 217
  armed robbery in nonurban areas, 40
  capital punishment, 268
  corruption, 51–52, 258–259
  and crime statistics, 26
  criminal law and prisons, 233–234
  detention laws, 49
  homicide, 57–58, 60–61
  incidence of crime, 82
  increase in crime, 12
  juvenile delinquency, 12
  nepotism, 185
  police, 217, 218–219
  population growth, 77
  poverty, 173
  prostitution, 63–66, 119
  rate of urbanization, 80, 91
  school dropouts, 181
  slums, 132
  urban ethnic heterogeneity, 119
  urban life and religion, 161
  urban population growth, 7
  voluntary organizations, 160
Age and urban crime, 84–85
Agra, prostitution, 68

Alcoholism, 83
Alexandria, juvenile delinquency, 82–83
Algeria, corruption, 52
  increase in crime, 12–13, 172
  juvenile delinquency, 82
  proportion of police to population, 219
  urbanization, 280
Anomie, and abjudication, 185
  defined, 176
  as model, 176–177
Arab countries, increase in crime, 12–13
  migrants, 115
Argentina, capital punishment, 268
  corruption, 52
  juvenile delinquency, 12, 198
  prostitution, 64
  test of differential opportunity theory, 178
  violent crime, 59
  see also Buenos Aires; Cordoba
Armed forces, 217
Arrests, methods of recording, 106–107
  multiple, 98–101, 196–197
  ratio of to crimes, 12
  single offender, 98–100
Arusha Declaration, 229
Asia, armed robbery in nonurban areas, 40
  capital punishment, 268
  corruption, 51–52, 258–259
  homicide, 57–58, 59
  increase in crime, 12
  poverty, 173
  prostitution, 63
  slums, 132
  urbanization, 80
Aspirations, economic, 181–183
Assault, 17–18, 195, 258
Athens, inmates' attitudes toward criminal law, 246
"Atimia," defined, 10

prisoners awaiting trial, 238
prison sentences, 231
rural community development, 283
urban migration, 108
see also Bogota
Colombo, juvenile delinquency, 196
prison overcrowding, 238
Colonialism and police, 216–218
Communication, and cultural background,
150
decline of in urban areas, 89
in developing countries, 8–9
language barriers, 111
Communication integration, and crime rates,
164
defined, 156
and friendships, 160
and home ownership, 163
and individual relationships, 158–160
and participation in organizations, 160–
162
and stability of population, 157
Community organization, and poverty, 173
and social control of crime, 149–150
Comparative criminology, goal of, 1–2
and developed societies, 1
studies in, 3–4
Comparative sociology, revival of, 2–3, 28,
29
Comrade courts, 239–240
Confidence games, 38–39
Congo, see Zaïre
Cordoba (Argentina), and functional integration, 162
juvenile delinquency, 190, 200–201
Corruption, 69, 209
in business and government, 258–259
as crime, 53–54, 271
effects of, 56–57
and government contracts, 53
prevention of, 274–275
and tax collections, 53
Costa Rico, capital punishment, 268
prison conditions, 234
Counterfeiting, 16
Credit cards, misuse of, 69, 258
Crime, and the business cycle, 189
deterrence, 248
in developed countries, 172
and learning theory, 193–195, 261–262
measurement of in slums, 143–144
and poverty, 172–176
prevention, 274–275
proportion cleared by arrest, 25, 98–99
and slums, 116–117, 139–142

and students, 181
see also Corruption; Homicide; Theft; etc.
Crime control, and crime statistics, 272
and criminological research, 287–290
fallacies of, 261
in history, 295
modern concepts of, 262
and overall developmental planning, 263–
266
resources needed, 254–255
in slums, 283–286
Crime statistics, 11
as basic minimum figure, 28
comparisons across national borders, 31
and crime control, 272–274
and juvenile delinquency, 267–268
methods of reporting crime, 26
and police facilities, 25
and population distribution, 27
reported crimes, 22
Criminal justice systems, need for change,
266–272
Criminal tribes, 194–195
Criminal Tribes Act, 194
Criminological research, and crime control,
287–290
Crop destruction, 62
Cuba, and education, 30
Cultural integration, and contact with
relatives, 155–156
and criminal behavior rates, 153–156
defined, 153
and tribal diversity, 155
and tribal homogeneity, 154–155
Cyprus, violent crime, 60
Czechoslovakia, homicide, 57–58

Dacca, slums, 132
Dacoity, 16, 40–42
Dahomey, prison conditions, 234
Dakar, juvenile delinquency, 84, 196, 197
population growth, 80
property crime, 17
slum population, 133
Dancing, 209–210
Death penalty, see Capital punishment
Decriminalization, 267
Delhi, beggar population, 48
community self-help programs, 284
food adulteration, 46
heterogeneity of, 86–87
police duties, 218–219
prison overcrowding, 238
Denmark, homicide, 59
urbanization, 82